INTROD

In 1933, King George V
still recovering from the after:
Nazi Party leader Adolf Hitle
Germany, and Japan announced that it would leave the League
of Nations. The Loch Ness Monster was seen for the first time
and the newly released film, *King Kong,* was thrilling audiences at the picture palaces.

Meanwhile, in Hoxton – a deprived area of East London –
in October of that year, two bouncing baby twin boys entered
the world and began a journey that would lead to them becoming the bogeymen of post-war Britain, forever etched into the
British collective consciousness.

As youngsters growing up on the rough, tough streets of
London's East End, Ronald and Reginald Kray were nothing
out of the ordinary – but their innate toughness and exceptional fistic skills saw them quickly rise to a position of dominance
among their peers. By the time they were 16, Ron and Reg were
notorious in their local area of Bethnal Green; they led a gang
of young tearaways, intent on spreading their influence into the
wider East End of London.

Over time, their reputation for violence spread and they began to see that the fear they were able to generate created opportunities to make money. Criminality was clearly the means
by which they could bring their natural talents to bear, make a
name for themselves, and prosper. By the early 1950s, the Kray
twins and their gang – which later came to be known as *The
Firm* – were on the rise in London's underworld. Numerous
criminal gangs operated in London during the 1950s and '60s,
some equally as powerful and dangerous as the Krays and some
even more so. It could be said that, as criminals, the Kray twins
were unremarkable, but they possessed something that made
them unique – a desire for publicity and a love of the limelight.

Once their criminal activities began to achieve a modicum of financial success, the twins started moving in circles inhabited by the rich and famous. Stars of stage and screen, celebrities, aristocrats, sports stars, and even politicians – all seeking a fashionable flirtation with the malevolent – were drawn to the dangerous duo like moths to a flame. Mixing and mingling with the glitterati of London's glamorous West End clubland turned the twins, by association, into celebrities themselves, becoming as much a part of the 1960s London scene as any famous personality of the day.

In 1969, the twins were jailed for life but, rather than disappearing from the public gaze, interest in the twin cockney crims began to snowball – beginning in 1972 with the publication of the bestselling book, *The Profession of Violence*. The story of the Krays, as penned by the author John Pearson, caught the imagination of a large section of the British public and prompted a tidal wave of books, articles, television documentaries, and two major feature films. Both twins are now dead, and to those who were around during their heyday in the '50s and '60s, the Krays are now just a distant memory, but their story lives on – thanks in no small part to the 1990 film *The Krays*, starring Martin and Gary Kemp and, more recently, in 2015, *Legend* starring Tom Hardy.

Most people in Britain have, at least, heard of the Kray twins, and opinions on them are many and various. But whether you love them, love to hate them, or perhaps something in between, their story – the latter part of which was set against the backdrop of the 1960s, the decade that saw Britain change from monochrome to glorious Technicolor – has it all: love, intrigue, glamour, violence, horror, tragedy and, not least, thanks to Ronnie Kray, a scandal that came close to causing the destruction of the British political system.

Since the 1972 publication of John Pearson's book, *The Profession of Violence* – which was for many years, and to

THE KRAYS

A CRIME AND A PLACE

THE ULTIMATE KRAYS HISTORY & TOUR GUIDE

By Andy James

Copyright © Andy James 2024

All rights reserved. No part of this book may be reproduced or transmitted in any form or by any means without the prior written permission of the author, nor be otherwise circulated in any form of binding or cover other than that in which it is published and without a similar condition being imposed on the subsequent purchaser.

Every effort has been made to fulfil requirements with regard to reproducing copyright material. The author will be happy to rectify any oversights at the earliest opportunity.

To my son Dan, for all your help, and to Carole, for your patience and encouragement.

THE KRAYS' MANOR

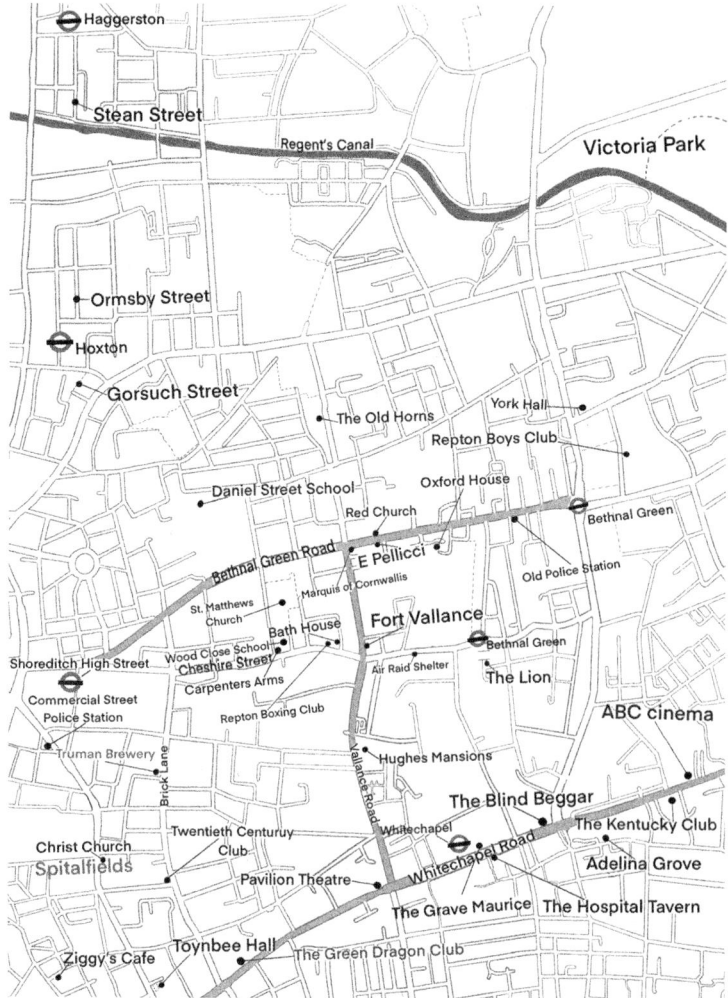

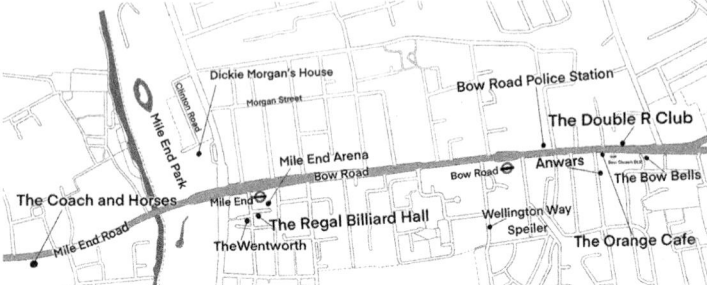

Dickie Morgan's House
Clinton Road
Morgan Street
Mile End Park
Bow Road Police Station
The Double R Club
Mile End Arena
Bow Road
Anwars
Bow Road
Bow Church Rd
The Bow Bells
The Coach and Horses
Mile End
Mile End Road
The Regal Billiard Hall
TheWentworth
Wellington Way
Speiler
The Orange Cafe

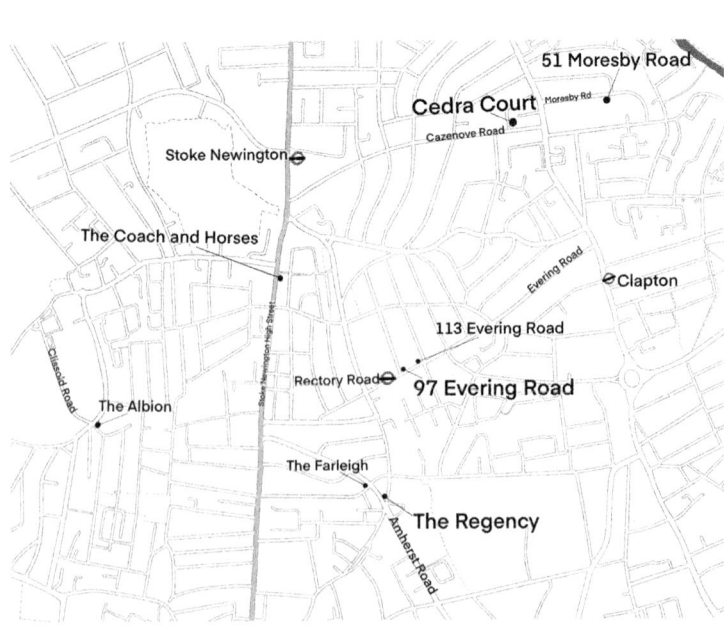

51 Moresby Road
Cedra Court
Moresby Rd
Cazenove Road
Stoke Newington
The Coach and Horses
Evering Road
Clapton
113 Evering Road
Rectory Road
97 Evering Road
Cilesdd Road
The Albion
The Farleigh
Amherst Road
The Regency
Stoke Newington High Street

some extent still is, the seminal work on the Krays – a great deal more information has come to light. Many books have followed in which friends, associates, family members, and the twins themselves have committed their recollections to print. Journalists covering the Krays' story as it happened, and Nipper Read – the policeman responsible for nicking the Krays – have done the same. Writers of true crime and makers of television documentaries – digging deep and uncovering new information – have added to this body of knowledge, which is now considerable and covers almost every conceivable aspect of the life and times of the Brothers Kray.

Much of the Krays' story, as we now know it, is based on indisputable facts, but a great deal is gleaned from – sometimes conflicting and biased – anecdotal accounts. With such a wealth of material from so many different sources and perspectives available to read and watch, it was, until recently, a little difficult for anyone with more than a passing interest to navigate the sea of information and gain a good understanding of the story in full – complete with all the tales, facts, incidents, and events in the order and context in which they happened. Then, in 2015, John Bennett's excellently researched book, *Krayology*, came along, in which he presents the full story with dates, places, and events in sequence; it dispels a few myths and reveals a treasure trove of new information drawn from historical archives. In 2019, the doyen of London criminal history, James Morton, published his book, *Krays: The Final Word*, which reveals yet more new information, examines and adds to the old, and could be described as the conclusive account of the Krays' story.

So what is there left to be said? Why write another book?

This book is intended to take the reader on a historical guided tour through the world of the Kray twins, stopping off at places of interest along the way. Some of the tour follows a well-trodden path, but many less well-known byways are explored, producing a few surprises en route – even for the most avid reader of Kray books. Locations, sites, and buildings that feature in the story of the Krays are the focus and are listed as they appear in the narrative. With the help of historical trade directories and other archive material, the exact whereabouts of some of the important but previously overlooked locations are revealed and, along with the more familiar landmarks, an explanation of their relevance – what happened there and when – is given. Some of the buildings have now gone but many, often having undergone a change of use, still stand. For example, *The Orange Cafe* on Bow Road, where the twins whiled away their days on the run from army conscription in 1952, is long gone, but the building remains and is now *The CityStay Hotel*. Some of the pubs used by the Krays are still trading, the most well-known of which is *The Blind Beggar* on Whitechapel Road, where Ronnie Kray shot and killed George Cornell in March 1966, but there are others to be discovered too.

There are two ways in which this book can be used: simply go straight to the listed location for a little historical background and an explanation of what happened there, or read the full story of the Krays which, along with the more well-known facts and events listed in chronological order, includes some less-written-about happenings that will undoubtedly be of interest to Kray aficionados.

In these high-tech days in which we live, most of us carry smartphones, and it is very easy to access a picture of almost every location as it is now – and, in some cases, as it was in the time of the Krays. For this reason, and the fact that the inclusion of numerous pictures and photographs would simply make the book too big, just a few – which would be slightly more difficult to track down on the internet – are to be found within these pages.

Locations

The East End

The story of the Krays begins and ends in the East End of London – an area of the capital that, in the first half of the 20th century, possessed a unique cultural identity shaped by shared hardship and the diverse range of residents from all corners of Europe and beyond who, from the 17th century onwards, came and settled there. With Jewish, Irish, German, and Romany Gypsy blood running through their veins – and a strong sense of belonging to the East End and all its 'ways' – the Kray twins were truly products of their environment.

London's East End is the historic heart of wider East London. Its boundaries are neither clear-cut nor official, but the Aldgate Pump,[1] just a short distance east of the City of London financial district, is often regarded as its beginning. With Shoreditch, Hoxton, Haggerston, and Hackney to the north and the River Thames to the south, the East End, by and large, stretches east as far as the River Lea, taking in the districts of Whitechapel, Bethnal Green, Stepney, Mile End, and Bow. Other areas such as Poplar, Limehouse, and Stratford may or may not be included depending on the opinion of whoever is doing the talking.

Rapid urban growth in the 18th and 19th centuries swallowed up pre-existing villages and hamlets east of the Tower of London and created the East End as a distinct entity – and the hub of small manufacturing industries processing materials arriving at London's docks. Concentrated in the East End, and well away from the more affluent West London, many of

---

1   Dating from the late 1700s and standing at the junction where Aldgate meets Fenchurch Street and Leadenhall Street (EC3A 2AD), this is a historic landmark; a water pump that has come to symbolise the start of the East End of London.

the early industries were unpleasant, smelly, and dangerous. Slaughterhouses, lime kilns, fish farms, breweries; lead smelting, leather tanning, and gunpowder production to name but a few of the many trades taking place well away from the noses of well-to-do West Londoners. The ever-expanding industry in the East End and its close proximity to the docks attracted more and more people from near and far to settle in the area, creating a melting pot of cultures and nationalities.

French Protestant Huguenots, fleeing persecution in their home country in the late 17th century, formed the first major wave of immigration into the East End. Bringing with them silk weaving skills, they settled and worked in the Spitalfields area. After the Protestant German King George I ascended to the British throne in 1714, he was followed by a wave of German immigrants, many of whom settled in the Aldgate area. Built in 1762, *St George's Lutheran Church* on Alie Street is the last remaining physical evidence of this major wave of immigration into East London. Large numbers of indigenous rural poor, having left the land in search of a better life, were joined in the mid-19th century by thousands of Irish fleeing the potato famine and looking for work at the docks or with any of the small industries. Romany Gypsy horse traders added to the mix, and ships' crews from Africa, India, and China formed permanent settlements around the docks. The latter half of the 19th century saw probably the biggest influx of immigrants to the East End as thousands of Ashkenazi (European) Jews arrived, escaping from the pogroms (persecution) in Russia and Eastern Europe. From then onwards, Jewish customs, traditions, trades, and skills played a large part in shaping the character of the East End.

The huge increase in the population of the East End during the 19th century was not matched by the provision of housing, resulting in overcrowded and unsanitary living conditions. Quickly built, poorly planned housing created a warren of dark, dirty streets and alleyways where thieves, robbers, and scally-wags of all persuasions could easily hide from the police – who had little effect in controlling the high level of criminality. Jack the Ripper – known among the inhabitants of the East End at the time as *Leather Apron* – stalked the narrow, dimly lit thoroughfares of Whitechapel in 1888 and was responsible for the gruesome murders of at least five women.

Many of the more successful inhabitants of the area were eventually able to move away, leaving only the very poorest behind, and by the late 1800s, the East End had become synonymous with poverty, squalor, disease, crime, and violence. Little was to change throughout the late 19th and early 20th centuries, and the East End developed a cultural identity all of its own. The interwoven tapestry of diverse ethnic and cultural influences, coupled with a sense of isolation from the rest of the capital, resulted in East Enders coming to regard themselves as members of a separate, self-contained race apart, with its own traditions and rules. Strong family loyalties and a sense of community was the East End's way, but so too was an acceptance that there was little chance of a better life by any means other than criminality of one kind or another.

This was the world that the Kray twins, in 1933, were born into: a rough, tough world with no frills, where low-level violence was a part of everyday life, and where skills with the fist would determine a young man's position in the social hierarchy.

The Kray twins' reign as Kings of the East End slowly developed during the 1950s and reached its zenith in the 1960s, a time when the East End – and, to some extent, the country as a whole – was on the cusp of a social and physical sea change that would sweep away the old cockney East End and bring in the new modern multi-cultural East End we know today. Immigration was again gathering pace, this time largely from Bangladesh and other parts of the declining British Empire. Most of the old Victorian terraced streets that had survived

Hitler's bombs were in the process of being torn down as part of a huge slum clearance programme and being replaced by high-rise blocks which, in some cases, created vertical slums instead of horizontal ones and have since been demolished. Radical urban development in the 1960s cleared away the buildings of the old East End, but disappearing along with them was a unique community and culture that had evolved over generations. It could be said that the Kray twins were representative of a culture in its final throes; the last generation of a world long gone and products of an environment that now exists only in memory.

Brian McConnell, crime reporter for the *Daily Mirror*, wrote the first book about the Krays. *The Rise and Fall of the Brothers Kray* was published in 1969, immediately after the twins' trial and sentencing to life imprisonment. In his book, McConnell gives an account of his investigative trips to the Krays' homeland in the East End of the 1960s and his impressions of those who dwelt there. McConnell describes the East End as the "*outside privy of the conurbation*" and waxes lyrical about the *cockney* being a member of a "*race apart;*" insular and clannish with innate characteristics that include the "*inbred violence of the Saxon.*" McConnell saves his best example of sweeping generalisations and negative stereotyping for the old people who, he says, at the offer of a drink, "*will spring to their feet and perform cockney ritual dances like Knees up Mother Brown.*"[2] Such narrow views and opinions, laced with cheap platitudes, are a long way from acceptable in today's more enlightened world but are perhaps, to some extent, reflective of how the East End was seen at the time by *some* outsiders.

---

2   McConnell, Brian. *The Rise and Fall of the Brothers Kray*. London: David Bruce & Watson, 1969.

"Up and down the City Road, in and out The Eagle, that's the way the money goes – Pop! goes the weasel."

This verse from the famous nursery rhyme refers to *The Eagle* pub in Hoxton (*'appy oxton'*) where, after spending all available money on drink, a visit to the pawnbroker for a loan secured against the 'weasel' (weasel and stoat – cockney rhyming slang for coat) was once standard practice.

The Eagle

2 Shepherdess Walk, London N1 7LB

Nearest TFL station: Old Street underground.

Built in 1901, the pub – now in the heart of *hipster* land – is still trading, serving a range of craft ales, cocktails, and trendy food from a seasonal menu; a far cry from the rough East End boozer it once was. Echoes of the past remain, as many of the original fixtures and fittings have been preserved, but the cool, relaxed ambience bears no resemblance to the pub of the past when Hoxton was among the most deprived areas of the East End, known for its violence and poverty. *The Eagle* is the perfect place to begin a tour of the Kray twins' world because, from the early 1900s onwards, it was a favourite watering hole of the Kray twins' paternal grandfather, 'Mad' Jimmy Kray, and later – during the 1920s and '30s – their father Charles. Even by the standards of the day, *The Eagle* was known as a rough pub; it was home base to the notorious Hoxton *Whizz Mob*, a gang of thieves, pickpockets, and con men who preyed on anyone but who specialised in working the racetracks and football crowds. No Saturday evening at *The Eagle* would be complete without a punch-up or two, as many a drink-fuelled argument would be settled with fists outside *on the cobbles.*

Unlike today, and until relatively recently, London's East End was very much a no-go area for those looking for a pleasant evening out. Groups of young men, in particular, from other parts of London would be regarded with suspicion and not necessarily made welcome. During the Kray twins' time, outsiders simply didn't go to the East End with its dilapidated, dull grey streets, bomb sites, and lingering whiff of danger.

Now considered a part of trendy Shoreditch, Hoxton is at the heart of the recently gentrified East End and the epicentre of so-called *hipster* culture. Vintage clothes markets, indie coffee shops, and quirky bars, restaurants, and street-food stalls abound. Former factories and warehouses adorned with street art (graffiti) now provide cool co-working spaces for digital marketing and media companies or *urban-chic* living spaces with a price tag of over half a million pounds for the smallest studio apartment (a bedsit). Although Hoxton has now become fashionable and vibrant, attracting new businesses into the area, the recent changes are not necessarily welcomed by everyone. Much of Hoxton, like other *gentrified* parts of the East End, remains a deprived area with many residents struggling to make ends meet. New businesses attracted to the district are not catering to the needs of local people, and soaring property prices have pushed up rents and placed pressure on social housing.

James William (Jimmy) Kray – the twins' paternal grandfather, affectionately known to Ronnie and Reggie as "Farvie" – was born on the 4th of April 1884 in Bethnal Green. The family moved to 40 St John's Terrace (renamed Gorsuch Street after 1909) in Hoxton, where Jimmy lived with his mother, father, sister Betsy, and three other children from his mother's previous marriage.[3] The name *Kray* is Austrian, or possibly German, but local people believed that the Krays were Romany Gypsy folk descended from horse dealers who had settled in the area.

Jimmy found work as an electrical apprentice at a cable makers company and, at the tender age of 17, he married his sweetheart – Louisa Eliza Turner – at *St Anne's Church*, Hoxton[4] in 1901. Life soon became a struggle for Jimmy Kray; he lost his job at the cable makers and with a wife, small child, and another one on the way, he was forced – like so many others – to take whatever back-breaking, poorly paid work he could get.

Life was harsh for the majority of East End families in the late 19th and early 20th centuries. Most lived from hand to mouth in just one room, and the loss of paid work or sickness could lead to homelessness and destitution within a matter of weeks, leaving families with no options other than the workhouse. Once inside the walls of these dreadful Victorian institutions, families were separated and condemned to a life of misery and toil, from which it was difficult to escape. But Jimmy wasn't going to let that happen; after a time, he found his way to the street markets of the East End where he became a costermon-

---

3   Bennet, John. *Krayology*. London: Mango Books, 2015.

4   Built in 1870 and situated at Hemsworth Street, Whitmore Estate, London N1 5LF, the Victorian Gothic church survived the bombing of the East End during World War II and still stands today, serving the local community.

ger, selling flowers from a hand cart. Using his newly discovered talents as a salesman and wheeler-dealer, Jimmy was able to scrape together a half-decent living to support his ever-growing family. James, born in 1901, was followed by John George in 1902, Albert Charles in 1904, Charles David (the Kray twins' father) in 1907, Alfred in 1909, William George in 1911, Dorothy in 1919 and, finally, Charlotte in 1921.[5]

Following the outbreak of the First World War in July of 1914, Jimmy took the King's shilling and joined the King's Royal Rifle Corps (KRRC) on 14 September 1914. After a short period of training he was shipped to France where, in the spring of 1915, Jimmy's regiment took part in the *Second Battle of Ypres*, which cost the lives of 59,000 British and Canadian soldiers and was the first occasion that the Germans used poison gas as a weapon. Much of the battle was an unimaginable, savage, desperate life-or-death struggle fought at close quarters. Jimmy Kray was wounded in the chest during the fighting and, after receiving treatment, he was awarded the Silver War Badge, honourably discharged, and shipped back to England in 1916.

Jimmy returned home to join Louisa and the children, living together in a single room. Once again, providing for his family became Jimmy's priority and he returned to trading in the markets, this time as a 'Wardrobe Dealer' or 'Hawker,' going door to door and buying second-hand clothes that would be sold from a stall in *Brick Lane Market*; a profession he would continue for the rest of his life.

Hardworking and moderately successful in business, Jimmy Kray continued to provide for his family, but there was another side to him – he was a notorious brawler. Small in stature but having fought Germans to the death, hand to hand, during

---

5   Bennet, John. *Krayology*. London: Mango Books, 2015.

the war, he had no fear of a punch-up with anyone. Drinking and fighting in the pubs around Hoxton – and gaining a reputation as a ferocious battler – enabled Jimmy to use his pugilistic prowess to supplement his income. There was money to be made by taking part in that most sacred of East End traditions: bare-knuckle fighting for cash. Anyone going toe to toe with Jimmy would likely be fighting on the defensive, as Jimmy would come at them like a whirlwind, never taking a backward step; a style that gained him the nickname 'Mad' Jimmy Kray.[6] Nowadays, Jimmy's heavy drinking – and his violent behaviour following the horrors of trench warfare that he experienced during the First World War – would raise questions about post-traumatic stress disorder.

In 1920, Jimmy, Louisa and family moved to number 26 Gorsuch Street, just a few doors along from his childhood home at number 40. The Kray twins' paternal grandparents would remain there until Jimmy died from a heart condition, aged 65, in 1949, when the twins were 16. Louisa, the twins' grandmother, died a year later in 1950.

Fighting man 'Mad' Jimmy Kray was certainly an influence on the young Kray twins' lives, but perhaps the greatest influence in shaping their future came from their maternal grandfather, Jimmy 'The Southpaw Cannonball' Lee, so-called because of the knockout left-hand punch he delivered with regularity during his days as a fighting man. James 'Jimmy' Charles Lee was born eight years before their paternal grandfather Jimmy Kray, in Bethnal Green in 1876. His mother's family were Irish and his father's were of Jewish and Romany Gypsy descent.[7] Like Jimmy Kray, Jimmy Lee was a renowned East End fight-

---

6   McNeil, Paul. timedetectives.blog 6 Feb 2022.
7   Pearson, John. *The Profession of Violence*. London: Weidenfeld & Nicolson, 1972.

ing man, but unlike Jimmy Kray, he was a lifelong teetotaller, having seen his father Jimmy 'Crutcha' Lee spend the last 17 years of his life interned in *Long Grove Asylum* suffering from a mental condition that Jimmy believed was caused by heavy drinking. From an early age, Ronnie and Reggie would listen, wide-eyed, to tales told by both grandfathers of boxers, bare-knuckle fighters, and villains of the old East End. Both nature and nurture would ensure that the twins were endowed with a natural fighting ability and imbued with a sense that not only was violence acceptable - it was the means by which status and approval were gained.

Jimmy Lee married Mary Ann Houghton – whose family were of German and Irish heritage – on 17 January 1898 at *Saint Paul Old Ford Church*[8] in Bow. Jimmy made his living driving a wagon pulled by a pair of Shire horses, but the work – although regular – was poorly paid and barely provided enough to keep a permanent roof over the heads of his growing family. As was all too common at that time – especially in the East End of London – Jimmy and Mary Anne's first child, a boy, died shortly after birth. Joseph, a second son, was born in 1899, followed by their first daughter Rose in 1907, Violet (the twins' mother) in 1909, May in 1911, and finally John in 1914. Paying regular rent was something Jimmy chose not to do, or was unable to do, and the family moved from one address to another, sometimes staying only a few weeks in each place.

On more than one occasion, when the property owner arrived to collect the overdue rent, Jimmy would take exception to the landlord's attitude and give him a beating. Negotiation

---

8   Built in 1878 and situated at Church Street, St Stephen's Rd, Bow, London E3 5JL, the recently restored Victorian Gothic church, unlike so many others, survived the London Blitz and still stands today, serving the local community.

and compromise were unknown concepts to Jimmy Lee, so the family were left, once again, having to find somewhere to live at short notice. Eventually, by 1914 – the year of the birth of their last child, John – Jimmy and family managed to achieve settled status at a home in London Street, Bethnal Green, a road that runs alongside the railway arches carrying the train line into Liverpool Street station. London Street is now called Dunbridge Street, the name having been changed in 1938.[9]

Rose, the eldest girl, was dark-haired, quick-tempered, and feisty, with a streak of devilment. She resorted to the fist at the slightest provocation and was, so the story goes, a match for any man in a fight. In later years, Rose was adored by the twins and became their favourite aunt. Violet (the twins' mother) – nicknamed 'Doodle' by the family – was a cheerful blonde-haired little girl who sang a lot and who happily spent time lost in her own dream world. May, the youngest, was very similar to Violet in both looks and temperament. Pretty blonde May caught the attention of the local boys, who called her 'Dinah' and who would often serenade her with the popular song of the day, *"Dinah, is there anyone finer?"*

Jimmy was a little too old for front-line service in the trenches during the First World War, as conscription for married men wasn't introduced until the summer of 1916 when Jimmy was 40 – the upper age limit for conscripts. Instead, according to Reggie in his book *East End Stories*,[10] Jimmy Lee served for a period with a branch of the army called the Royal Flying Corps (which, in 1918, became the RAF), operating the new fighting aeroplanes.

Although, as a teetotaller, Jimmy was never involved in

---

9   Bennett, John. *Krayology*. London: Mango Books, 2015.

10   Kray, Reggie and Gerrard, Peter. *Reggie Kray's East End Stories*. London: Sphere, 2010.

the popular East End pastime of pub brawling, he was very much a fighting man. Not only would he resort to the fist when he was upset – which happened often enough – but he would also actively seek out and take on any opponent, gloves on or bare-knuckle, for money or just pride, no matter their size or reputation. The outcome was generally the same; it was only a matter of time before the South Paw Cannonball's left-hand punch left his opponent beaten and unconscious. Many years before the Lee and Kray families became joined by marriage, the twins' two grandfathers met as bare-knuckle fighters on several occasions. Jimmy Lee would always claim: *"Mad Jimmy Kray never got the better of me – not once."*[11]

Jimmy Lee was a remarkable character and a man of many talents, who would try his hand at anything to make a living and provide for his family. Not only was he an accomplished pugilist with a knockout punch – which, during his younger days, enabled him to supplement his income – but he also possessed an extraordinary talent for performance. Jimmy entertained audiences at theatres and music halls in the East End and beyond. His performance included song and dance routines, poetry recitals, and the playing of a variety of musical instruments. Jimmy's talents didn't end there; he also performed astonishing feats of acrobatic skill and daring that would leave audiences gasping in amazement. Jimmy was known for an act that involved placing the end of a white-hot poker on his tongue – incredibly without harming himself – but perhaps his most famous trick was balancing on bottles placed on the steps of a ladder, and then climbing the ladder… on his hands.

Jimmy Lee's many talents did not, however, include a flair for business. He would regularly try his hand at various mon-

---

11   Lee, Joe and Smith, Rita with Gerrard, Peter. *Inside the Kray Family.* London: Carlton Books, 2008.

ey-making schemes but his skill at balancing on bottles did not carry over to balancing the books. Jimmy saved his money, grew his haulage business, and eventually ran 22 horses – before going bankrupt. Having been left a little money after his father's death, Jimmy decided to open a fish and chip shop, but within five or six weeks the shop and the money were gone. Another venture – selling fruit and vegetables from a handcart, for a period – ended with a court appearance for non-payment of money owed on his weighing scales. There was always regular work in the markets of the East End to fall back on, however, and Jimmy saw out his working life as a market porter.

Jimmy 'Cannonball' Lee was a constant presence in the lives of the young Kray twins, and – like their paternal grandfather, Jimmy Kray – he would fill their impressionable young minds with stories about the fighting men of the East End. Jimmy knew them all, and most of them – boxers and villains alike – were personal friends of the Southpaw Cannonball, dropping by regularly for a cup of tea and a chat. Although Jimmy Lee took pride in staying on the right side of the law and tended to keep the villains he knew at arm's length, the twins would regularly overhear talk of fighting and violence.

Throughout his long life, Jimmy remained fit and active, regularly cycling the 80-plus miles to Southend and back just for the fun of it, a practice he kept up well into his seventies. After the demolition of the terraced houses in Vallance Road and Dunbridge Street in 1969, Jimmy and Mary Ann were moved to a maisonette in nearby Cheshire Street. Jimmy died on his birthday in 1971, aged 94, and Mary Anne – the twins' grandmother – died shortly afterwards in 1972, aged 91.

Prior to his retirement from the stage in the 1930s, Jimmy appeared on the bill at various theatres and music halls in the East End, and occasionally further afield. Jimmy's last performance was at the *Portsmouth Empire Palace Theatre* when he was in his fifties. According to Jimmy's eldest son Joe, at different times, his father appeared on the same bill as Marie Lloyd, Old Mother Riley, and even Charlie Chaplin before he became a Hollywood star.[12]

One of several East End theatres and music halls in which Jimmy Lee is reputed to have performed in the early 20th century is *The Pavilion Theatre*, close to his Dunbridge Street home on Whitechapel Road.

The Pavilion Theatre

191-193 Whitechapel Road, London E1 1DN.

Nearest TFL station: Whitechapel underground.

Heading east along Whitechapel Road – on the left, just before the junction with Vallance Road – there is a plot of land that has remained vacant since 1962. This was the site of the 3,000-seat *Pavilion Theatre*. Built in 1858, the theatre catered for the East End's large Jewish community and staged mainly Jewish productions in the Yiddish language. The theatre closed in 1934 and the building stood empty and unused until 1940, when it was severely damaged by Hitler's bombs. The building was demolished in 1962 and, to this day, the plot remains empty.

Jimmy 'Cannonball' Lee – the Kray twins' grandfather – is reputed to have performed at the theatre but, whether this is true or not, the ruined building certainly featured in the lives of the young Kray twins. During the 1940s, the youngsters and their friends would sneak into

---

12   Ibid.

the derelict theatre and spend many a happy hour exploring and playing in the cavernous, eerie interior.

Charles David Kray, the twins' father, was born on 10
March 1907 and, from a young age, worked alongside his father in the 'wardrobe dealing' business. When he reached his
teens, he began working on his own account, and by 20 he was
making a good living for himself. Like his father, Charles, was
silver-tongued, charming, and astute, with a natural flair for
business – but, unlike his father, he was not a fighting man. He
was certainly a drinking man, however; he fraternised with all
the fighters and villains in the pubs of the East End, but he was
clever enough to avoid unnecessary trouble, choosing instead
to channel his energy into making money.

Possessing the good looks of the Kray family, the charm of
the natural salesman, and a pocketful of cash, Charles had the
pick of the girls in the East End. He chose pretty 17-year-old
Violet Lee from Bethnal Green. Jimmy Lee, Violet's father,
was far from happy with his daughter's choice of beau and demanded that she put an end to the relationship. Snobbery was
fit and well at this time, even in the East End, and although only
half a mile apart, Bethnal Green people believed they were *a
cut above*, tending to look down their noses at the inhabitants of
Hoxton. The Kray family were known to the Lees and Jimmy
considered them to be a rough 'flash' lot. Violet, however, had
no intention of ending her relationship with Charles Kray – so,
after agreeing to her father's demand, she continued the liaison
in secret.

Accompanied only by Charles' best man, Harry Hopwood,
Violet and Charles were married at Kingsland Road registry
office on 6 March 1926 and, by the autumn, Violet was pregnant. Jimmy Lee was furious and vowed to have nothing more
to do with his daughter. Initially, the newlyweds moved in with

Charles' Aunt Betsy at 40 Gorsuch Street, later moving to number 26 to live with Charles' parents.

On 9 July 1927, Violet gave birth to a son, Charles James. After hearing of the birth of a grandchild, Jimmy Lee's attitude towards his daughter began to mellow and, married or not, he wanted her back home – where, as far as he was concerned, she belonged. Eventually, around Christmas time, he decided on a rescue mission and, accompanied by his eldest son Joe, marched over to Hoxton to bring his *Violi* home. Arriving at the house in Gorsuch Street, Jimmy and Joe could hear the sounds of a party going on. After banging on the door, it was answered by a stranger who asked, and was told, what they wanted. From inside the house, Jimmy Kray was heard shouting, *"Who is it?"* and the stranger replied, *"It's Jimmy Lee and he wants a word with his girl."* Jimmy Kray shouted back, *"Tell the old bastard to fuck off!"* Jimmy was incandescent with rage, and had it not been for the intervention of his son Joe persuading his father to calm down, Jimmy would probably have smashed the door down and caused some serious damage to persons within.[13] Outraged and angry, but also deeply hurt, Jimmy walked away. Some time would pass and the twins would be born before Jimmy would grudgingly accept his daughter's choice of husband and enable her and her new family to rejoin the Lee family fold.

In December 1929, Violet gave birth to a baby girl. The baby died in her mother's arms just a short time after entering the world. It has recently come to light – through the publication of the 2001 book, *Inside the Kray Family* by Joe Lee and Rita Smith with Peter Gerrard – that husband Charles may well have been responsible for the baby's death. Charles was away

13   Lee, Joe and Smith, Rita with Gerrard, Peter. *Inside the Kray Family*. London: Carlton Books, 2001.

much of the time working *on the knocker* – buying second-hand clothes to sell on the family stall in Brick Lane – but on his return, he would drink heavily and become violent towards his wife. After one such incident towards the end of Violet's pregnancy, she began to lose blood and, knowing that something was wrong, begged Charles to stay and look after her – but he took no heed and left her alone to deal with the premature birth of a baby girl. The baby, also named Violet, died shortly afterwards. Violet, understandably, fell into a deep depression after losing the baby but, as was the way at the time, for better or worse, she carried on and stayed with Charles.

Gorsuch Street

Nearest TFL station: Hoxton overground.

Lying between Hackney Road and Kingsland Road in Hoxton is a small thoroughfare that, until recently, was known as Gorsuch Street, home to several generations of the Kray family. Originally called St John's Terrace until the name was changed in 1909, the tiny street of Victorian terraced cottages no longer exists either in form or name. Nothing is left of the street as it once was; the houses were bombed out of existence during the Second World War or demolished shortly afterwards, and the street name was recently deleted from the map. The Royal Mail terminated the postcode (E2 8HA) in April 2018, and the stretch of road that was once Gorsuch Street now forms part of Gorsuch Place.

As a child Jimmy Kray – the twins' paternal grandfather – lived at number 40 Gorsuch Street with his parents and left after getting married in 1901. Jimmy Kray, his wife Louisa and their family returned to live at number

26 Gorsuch Street in the 1920s, and Charles Kray – the twins' father – was living here with his parents when he met and married Violet Lee, the twins' mother. Betsy Kray – Jimmy's blood sister – was living in the childhood home at number 40 with her husband George Cook when nephew Charles and his new bride Violet moved in after getting married in 1926. Shortly afterwards, Charles and Violet moved in with Charles' parents Jimmy and Louisa at number 26 and it was here, in July 1927, that Charlie Kray – the twins' elder brother – was born. Harry Hopwood, Charles Kray's friend and best man at his wedding, lived at number 28 Gorsuch Street with his family. Harry Hopwood would feature in later episodes of the Krays' story and remain a close friend of the Kray family – until he gave evidence against the twins at their trial in 1969.

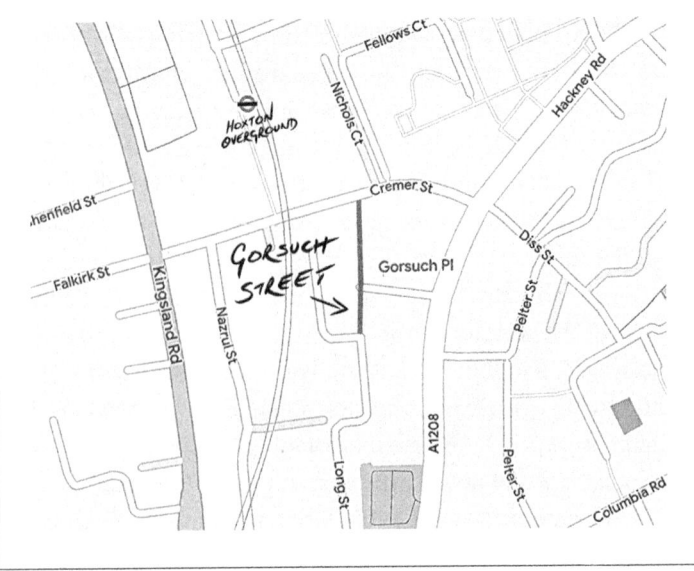

Although Violet had no contact with her father at this time, she kept in touch with the rest of her family and, by the early 1930s, she had become weary of living amongst the Kray family at Gorsuch Street. Her eldest brother Joe, his wife Cissy, and their two young children Connie and Joe had recently moved into a new home in a large building at 68 Stean Street, Haggerston. Joe and family took the two basement rooms and one on the ground floor. Another ground-floor room was occupied by a docker and his family, and Joe's mother and father-in-law – the Whittingtons – lived in the two rooms on the first floor. Two rooms at the top of the house were vacant, and Violet asked Joe if he would 'put a word in'– which, of course, he did. In 1932, Violet, Charles, and their five-year-old son Charlie moved in. Joe Lee's son Joe Jr. was just a year older than Charlie, and both boys attended nearby *Laburnum Street Primary School*, just a short walk – crossing the Regent's Canal – from their front door in Stean Street.

Laburnum Street Primary School

Laburnum Street, London E2 8BA

Nearest TFL station: Haggerston overground.

Built in 1908, the three-storey redbrick building survived the bombing during World War II – but, following an unsatisfactory OFSTED report, it was demolished in 2005 to make way for *The Bridge Academy*, which now occupies the site.

Charlie Kray, the twins' elder brother, attended the school between 1932 and 1938 from the age of 5 to 11. Charlie's cousin Joe Lee also attended the school.

October 1933 is remembered by Charlie as a time when Grandma Lee, Aunt Rose, and Aunt May would visit Stean Street more often than usual. One day, while they were there, Charlie and Joe were given a few pennies to spend and told to go out and play until they were called. Eventually, around 8pm, the boys were told that they could come back in. Charlie was told to go up to his mum's bedroom and, on entering, Violet – holding what appeared to be two little dolls, one in each arm – said, *"Say hello to your brothers; this one's Reggie and this one's Ronnie."*

"Where did they come from?" asked Charlie.

"I bought them," his mother replied.

"But Mum," said Charlie, *"why did you buy two?"*

It was Tuesday 24 October 1933 and the Kray twins had arrived.[14]

Life continued at Stean Street and Violet, overjoyed by the arrival of her beautiful identical twin boys, found some happiness at last. Filled with pride, she would push them – scrubbed clean and dressed in matching baby clothes – through the streets of Hoxton in their new pram. Twins, after all, were special, and Violet delighted in the attention local ladies gave them, stopping her and cooing over her beautiful twin babies. Her sisters Rose and May were around much more, eager to take turns taking the twins out in their pram and soaking up some of the reflected admiration. Meanwhile, young Charlie took a bit of a back seat, though he continued to enjoy life; he became passionate about sport and spent most of his spare time running. Charlie also participated and excelled in athletics, football, and boxing, a discipline in which he showed particular promise.

---

14   Kray, Charlie with McGibbon, Robin. *Me and My Brothers*. London: Grafton, 2008.

Stean Street

Haggerston, London E8 4EL

Nearest TFL station: Haggerston overground.

Stretching between Dunston Road – which runs along the bank of the Regent's Canal – and the coincidentally named Lee Street at the northern end, Stean Street has been completely redeveloped. Nothing remains of the thoroughfare as it was in the 1930s, except perhaps for a short stretch of wall running between the *Momentum Gym* and *JC Motors*.

In 1932, the Kray twins' parents – Violet and Charles – and their five-year-old son Charlie left Gorsuch Street and moved into two rooms on the top floor of a building at number 68 Stean Street. Ronnie and Reggie Kray were born here on 24 October 1933, and this was home to the Kray family until they moved to the house in Vallance Road, Bethnal Green in 1938.

One day in 1936, when the twins were three years old, little Reggie became sick and feverish and, by the evening, Ronnie too was ill. Both became progressively worse – particularly Ronnie, who began to develop breathing difficulties. Seeing her twin boys in such distress, Violet began to suspect the worst, believing they had contracted that most feared of all childhood diseases of the day: the dreaded and potentially fatal *diphtheria*.

She was right: both boys were taken and put into isolation wards at separate hospitals. Reggie was taken to the *North*

Eastern Fever Hospital[15] in Tottenham and Ronnie, whose condition appeared to be more serious, was taken to *Homerton Eastern Fever Hospital*[16] in Hackney.

Separated from their mother – and from each other, for the first time – Violet was only able to gaze in anguish at her beloved twins through windows at the ends of the wards. Within a short time Reggie began to recover and, after a few weeks, he returned to Stean Street, healthy, happy, and back to his usual young self. Ronnie, on the other hand, was making little progress towards recovery. After weeks of watching her little boy suffering from a distance, Violet decided on a course of action that was much against the wishes and advice of the doctors: she removed Ronnie from the hospital and took him home.

Years later, Violet told John Pearson – the twins' biographer – how she *"understood her Ronnie better than all them doctors,"* and how, despite being told of the danger, she decided to take Ronnie home, believing that what he needed most was to be reunited with his mother and twin brother. She may well have been right; after a period of nursing him day and night, little Ronnie did indeed recover.[17]

Ronnie was now over his illness but something had changed;

---

15 St Ann's Rd, London N15 3TH. In 1948, following the creation of the new National Health Service, the *North Eastern Fever Hospital* became a general hospital and was renamed *St Ann's Hospital*. Most of the buildings that had been erected in 1901 still survive today.

16 Situated at Homerton Row, London E9 6SR and opened in 1870, the isolation hospital administered treatment for patients with infectious diseases for over a century, eventually closing in 1982. Shortly afterwards, most of the old buildings were demolished to make way for the new *Homerton Hospital*, which now occupies the site.

17 Pearson, John. *The Profession of Violence*. London: Weidenfeld & Nicolson, 1972.

he had become more introverted and needy towards his mother, slower and quieter than Reggie, and quick to break into a tantrum. Some of the changes in Ronnie's behaviour were likely the result of the long separation from his mother at a young age, but diphtheria – an all too common disease among children until 1940, when mass vaccination was introduced – is known, in some cases, to cause lasting damage to the nervous system. This may well be, therefore, the origin of the mental illness that plagued Ronnie for the rest of his life.

Charles' drunken – and sometimes violent and abusive – behaviour towards his wife continued, quickly becoming an unwelcome part of the weekend routine for those living at Stean Street. Violet's brother Joe, who lived downstairs, would hear the commotion and intervene, sometimes having to give Charles *'a couple of right-handers'* to calm him down. Eventually, Joe's in-laws, the Whittingtons, having had enough of this all too regular occurrence, asked Charles, Violet and family to leave.[18] Charles' drink-fuelled violence towards his wife would continue, on occasion, for some time to come – until one day, when the twins were around 15, it came to an abrupt and dramatic end. Ronnie gave his father a 'right-hander' and said to him, *" If you ever touch our mother again I will fucking kill you."* Charles never again laid a finger on Violet.[19]

After leaving Stean Street late in 1937, Violet and Charles, their ten-year-old son Charlie, and the four-year-old twins moved into cramped, run-down accommodations at various addresses in the Hoxton area. Then, in the late summer of 1938, they found and moved into a permanent home in Bethnal Green. Jimmy Lee – helped very much by the birth of his twin

---

18   Lee, Joe and Smith, Rita with Gerrard, Peter. *Inside the Kray Family.* London: Carlton Books, 2001.

19   Peat, Kim. *Secrets of the Krays.* BritBox: ITN productions, 2021.

grandsons – had, by this time, softened his attitude towards his daughter, and when 178 Vallance Road, just around the corner from her parents' home, became available, Violet, Charles, and the family moved in. Hardly the last word in luxury but despite being damp, infested with mice, and the whole house shaking every time a steam train heading into Liverpool Street station passed along the nearby railway viaduct, the family's new home was theirs and theirs alone – a step-up from their previous cramped and inadequate living spaces.

During the war years, as further houses on Vallance Road became vacant, the rest of Violet's extended family gradually moved into the row of seven workers cottages, with three rooms upstairs, two rooms and a kitchen at the back on the ground floor, no bathroom, and a toilet in the small yard at the rear of the house. Next to arrive was Violet's younger brother John and his wife Maud, who moved into 172. Shortly afterwards, her sister Rose Wiltshire, who was married and separated, moved into 176 with her son Billy, and finally, youngest sister May Filler, her husband Albert, and their little daughter Rita moved into 174. With four siblings and their families now occupying adjacent houses and their parents Mary-Ann and Jimmy living at the end of the row – just around the corner on Dunbridge Street – this particular part of Vallance Road came to be known by the locals as *Lee Street*.

178 Vallance Road

Bethnal Green, London E2 6HR

Nearest TFL station: Bethnal Green overground.

178 Vallance Road is probably the most important location in the Krays' story and a *must-see* on any tour of the Krays' stomping grounds. Sadly, the row of seven

Victorian workers cottages that were built around 1860 – of which 178 was one – are now gone, having been demolished in 1969 and replaced by a row of modern houses. *Fort Vallance*, as the house would later become known, was home to the twins from the age of five in 1938 until 1968, when the Kray family were moved – shortly before the twins' arrest – to a modern council flat in Bunhill Row, Shoreditch. Throughout their criminal careers, and despite periods staying at a number of different locations, Vallance Road was always home base for the twins – and the centre of the Krays' activities.

Despite the so-called slum clearance programme of the 1960s, when most of Bethnal Green's Victorian houses were swept away, a few examples of houses of the same era and style as those on Vallance Road survive here and there. Albert Cottages and Victoria Cottages on nearby Deal Street are two such examples.

The early 1960s-built flats directly across the road from the Krays' house would have been familiar to the twins. Footage of Reggie cleaning his car outside the family home with the flats in the background – taken on a cine camera by the twins' uncle, Albert Filler – exists and can be viewed on YouTube.

Surprisingly, some of the original paving slabs outside the houses on Vallance Road are still in situ, and there is a fire hydrant cover that – according to the twins' cousin, Rita – is the same as it ever was and marks the spot where her mother, the twins' aunt, May, who lived at 174, would place a chair and sit outside on warm evenings.[20]

20   Lee, Joe and Smith, Rita with Gerrard, Peter. *Inside the Kray Family*. London: Carlton Books, 2001.

September 1938 was also the beginning of the school year, and time for the twins – who would be five years of age in October – to begin their education. Elder brother Charlie began his secondary education in 1938 at *Scawfell Street School*, whereas the twins began their schooldays at *Wood Close School*, just a five-minute walk from their new home in Vallance Road. Reggie remembered this early period at *Wood Close* fondly, recalling polished parquet floors, singing songs accompanied by an echoing piano, and the compulsory hour of rest after lunch when the children would be encouraged to sleep for an hour on camp beds lined up in the school hall – or outside on warm summer days.[21]

With the prospect of war looming on the horizon, children were issued with gas masks, and air-raid drills became part of the school's daily routine. Reggie also remembered another significant event in his young life – his first fight. According to Reggie, it was with a *bully* who was bigger and older than himself called George Tappin. Reggie was enjoying the scrap until he was floored by a well-delivered punch. Undaunted, little Reggie was happy to continue until, when warned that a teacher was approaching, Reggie, his opponent, and the group of children who were watching ran off in all directions.

Brother Charlie, on seeing Reggie's black eye, announced that it was about time the twins learned some boxing skills. So, at six years old, the twins – helped by Charlie and encouraged by their two fighting grandfathers – gradually began to learn the skills that would eventually lead to their success as professional boxers.[22]

---

21   Kray, Reggie and Gerrard, Peter. *Reggie Kray's East End Stories.* London: Sphere, 2010.

22   Ibid.

Wood Close School

33 Wood Close, Bethnal Green, London E2 6DT

Nearest TFL station: Bethnal Green overground.

Built in 1900 as a primary school for children between the ages of 5 and 11, the Kray twins began their schooldays here in September 1938. World War II saw the closure of schools in Inner London, and Violet and the twins were evacuated to Suffolk in the late summer of 1940. Around a year later, after the worst of the London Blitz was over, Violet and the twins returned to London; the school reopened and the twins continued at *Wood Close* until the summer of 1945, when they were 11.

Just a short walk along Cheshire Street from the site of the Krays' Vallance Road Home, the school – now called *William Davis Primary School* – still stands. The exterior is largely unchanged.

This early part of the twins' education – as infants at *Wood Close School* – was cut short when, in September 1939, the gathering storm clouds heralding war with Germany finally broke and war was declared. Schools in Inner London and other large cities were closed in anticipation of large-scale bombing raids, and children were evacuated en masse to the safety of more rural areas. *Operation Pied Piper* began in 1939 and hundreds of thousands of school-age children – and mothers with children below school age – were evacuated to the country and billeted with host families.

Violet resisted the first wave of evacuation but, as the Blitz began in the summer of 1940, she and the children joined the voluntary mass exodus. Violet, the six-year-old twins, and thirteen-year-old Charlie left the East End and moved to Suffolk – along with Violet's sister May and her three-year-old daughter Rita. Interestingly, the standard procedure for evacuation was that only children below school age could be accompanied by their mother, but somehow Violet managed to side-step this rule, and the family took up temporary residence in the home of Dr Arthur Style and his wife Clare at *East House* in the small market town of Hadleigh in Suffolk. In an interview appearing in the *Daily Mirror* on the 5th of March 1969 – the day after both twins were found guilty of murder – Clare Style remembers her wartime lodgers:

"My first thought was: what horrible little boys. And so they were. They were full of rough and tumble and quite unlike my own children. I recall vividly how shocked I was that they could not read. I spent long periods teaching them to read. When they showed some mastery, I insisted they learn the Lord's Prayer."

Ronnie and Reggie found themselves in a new and exciting world in which they were free to roam and explore. A far cry from the harsh, grimy streets of the East End, the Suffolk countryside – with its winding lanes, green fields, woods, and streams – provided a magical playground for the twins and was the beginning of a love affair with the countryside that would last for the rest of their lives.

East House

George St, Hadleigh, Ipswich, IP7 5BE

The large 18th-century house – later described by

Ronnie Kray as a *"mansion"*– was, in 1940/41, home to the Style family and, for around a year, refuge for Violet Kray, the twins, and Charlie, evacuated to Suffolk to escape the London Blitz.

Violet missed the East End and Charlie looked forward to going home, but the twins loved their new and wondrous countryside environment.

East House was given a Grade II listing in 1950 and, in 1963, Arthur and Clare Style sold the house. The historic building was used as a community centre for some years, but by 2006 it had fallen into disrepair and was left empty, becoming progressively more derelict over the next decade. In 2017, work began to restore *East House* to its former glory and today it is, once again, a magnificent private residence.

Mindful of the disruption to children's lives at this time, the government was keen to minimise the interruption and damage to their education. Evacuated children were, as far as possible – even if only on a part-time basis – to be accommodated in local schools, and so the twins attended *Bridge Street Boys School* in Hadleigh.

Bridge Street Boys School

3-5 Bridge Street, Hadleigh, Suffolk IP7 6BY

Aged seven, Ronnie and Reggie Kray began attending the school on 25 November 1940. Accounts suggest that during their school years in the East End, the twins' behaviour was nothing out of the ordinary and presented no serious problems. Perhaps the standards of expected behaviour in Hadleigh were different, because the school register held at Hadleigh Archives reveals that the twins were expelled. By 20 December 1940, both twins had "left" the school and were receiving private tuition with Mrs Style at *East House* where they lodged.

Bridge Street Boys School was opened in 1853 and remained a school for well over a century until its closure in 1968. After the school was closed, the building was used as a concert hall for several decades and is currently *The Old School,* a venue for music and cultural events.

While the twins were making friends, bloodying a few noses, and revelling in the fresh air and boundless freedom of the Suffolk countryside, Charlie was missing the East End – but he found the locals friendly and made the most of his time there. He found work in a fish and chip shop and, later, as a tea boy in a factory making coir matting.[23]

Charlie's Chip Shop

Charlie Kray accompanied Violet and the twins to Hadleigh during 1940/41 to escape the worst of the London Blitz. While there, he found work in a fish and chip shop.

---

23 *Cooke and Sons* matting factory, located less than ten minutes' walk from *East House* on Duke Street, was the town's biggest employer. The building – a former 19th-century silk mill – was demolished in 1995 and a modern housing development called *Silk Mill Close* now occupies the site. (Hadleigh Archives).

There were two fish and chip shops in Hadleigh at this time; one called *Sissons* at number 65 High Street and another, opened in 1938, called *Lenny's* at 12 Angel Street.[24] Happily, and rather surprisingly, both shops are still in existence and trading. *Sissons* is now called *The Tudor Fish and Chip Shop* and *Lenny's* still trades under the same name.

Exactly which of the two shops (both are just a few minutes' walk from *East House*) employed young Charlie Kray during the war is not known, so two portions of delicious fish and chips – one at each – is highly recommended.

Charlie settled into life in the country and the twins were having a whale of a time, but their mother Violet was ill at ease. Although her sister May and her little daughter Rita were living nearby, Violet missed the rest of her family, her own home, and the familiarity of the East End. Her husband Charles – the twins' father – would turn up and stay from time to time, and while there he would make use of the local hostelries, especially *The Cock Inn,*[25] just a few yards along the street from *East House*. Charles' heavy drinking, frowned upon by some of the locals, was a source of some embarrassment for Violet and no doubt added to her disquietude and longing to get back to the East End.

After a year or so in Hadleigh, the worst of the London Blitz was over and, although intermittent bombing raids continued, Violet decided to return to the East End. Violet's brother John

---

24   Hadleigh Archives.

25   Still open and trading today at 89 George Street, Hadleigh, Suffolk IP7 5BP.

drove to Suffolk in his truck, collected the family, and brought them back to Bethnal Green. Schools reopened and the twins, now aged eight, returned to *Wood Close School* to continue their education. Cousin Rita had, by now, reached school age and was also attending *Wood Close*. Ronnie and Reggie – protective towards the little girl – would each hold one of her hands and escort her to and from school every day, guarding her from the rough and boisterous behaviour of the older boys. Rita adored her identical twin cousins and thought of them as two versions of the same person, calling them the "two ones," a name that stuck and would be used by the family for years to come.[26]

Charlie Kray had begun his secondary education at *Scawfell Street School* in Hoxton back in September 1938 when the twins began attending *Wood Close*, but his time there was cut short. After the family returned to London, following a year away in Suffolk, Charlie had reached school-leaving age.

Scawfell Street School

Scawfell Street, London E2 8LS

Nearest TFL station: Hoxton overground.

Charlie began attending *Scawfell Street* in September 1938 at age 11, where he excelled at sports and was picked for the school football team. Charlie's secondary education, however, was interrupted by World War II. Summer 1940 saw a second wave of the evacuation of children from London and other cities to the safety of

---

26   Lee, Joe and Smith, Rita with Gerrard, Peter. *Inside the Kray Family.* London: Carlton Books, 2001.

the countryside, and Charlie accompanied Violet and the twins to Suffolk. The family returned to London around a year later. It is unlikely that Charlie, then having reached the school leaving age of 14, returned to his bomb-damaged school for any length of time, if at all.

Scawfell Street School was demolished in the early 1960s to make way for *Haggerston School*, built in phases between 1964 and 1967 and opening in 1966 when the main building was completed.

After the Blitz ended in the summer of 1941, Londoners were able to resume some kind of normal life, but sporadic air raids continued and – once again – intensified between January and May 1944, a period known as the *Baby Blitz*. Then, towards the end of the war, in June 1944, in retaliation for the Allied bombing of Germany and prompted by the Normandy landings, Hitler deployed his newly developed terror weapons and launched V1 flying bombs – and, later, V2 rocket attacks – on London. March 1945 saw the last V2 fall on London and the end of a period that claimed the lives of over 40,000 civilians, with thousands more injured.

When the air-raid warning sounded, East Enders would hurry to their nearest air-raid shelter – which, for the Kray/Lee family, was situated under the nearby railway arches on Dunbridge Street.

Air Raid Shelter

Dunbridge Street, London E2

Nearest TFL station: Bethnal Green overground.

Located approximately midway between Vallance Road and Bethnal Green overground station are railway arches numbers 86 and 87, which were used as public air-raid shelters during the war. By the summer of 1941, the worst of the London bombing was over, though occasional air raids continued. Following their return from being evacuated to Suffolk in the summer of 1941, the Kray family – along with other families in the immediate area – took shelter here.[27]

---

27 Minutes of the Civil Defence Committee L/BGM/A/18.Tower Hamlets
    Local History Library & Archives.

> Although the shelter would have provided some protection from blasts and splinters, it is most unlikely that it would have withstood a direct hit.

Reggie and Ronnie – protected by the innocence of childhood and unable to fully understand the real danger that they and those around them were in – found excitement and thrills listening to the *'crump!'* of exploding bombs, and peeking out of the shelter to watch the searchlights and pyrotechnic tracer fire from the anti-aircraft guns piercing the night sky. Adults, however – crammed together in the gloom of the railway arches, with makeshift sleeping arrangements and primitive toilet facilities – found the experience less enjoyable.

Granddad Jimmy Lee took it upon himself to keep spirits up and do what he could to relieve the anxiety of his captive audience. Assuming his role as a veteran entertainer, and having made a portable stage for himself from wooden pallets, he would organise competitions, lead sing-songs, and recite poetry of his own creation – including his showpiece, *"Hitler, we'll have none of you."*

During World War II, the East End of London suffered the worst of Hitler's bombs, which killed and injured thousands, reduced large areas to rubble, and turned the docklands into an inferno. When the air-raid sirens sounded on 3 March 1943, people living close to Bethnal Green underground station made their way down the steps to the safety of the platforms below. A salvo of rockets was discharged from a battery in nearby *Victoria Park*, and the shattering noise made by the rockets was mistaken for the sound of exploding bombs. The sense of urgency increased, and someone lost their footing on the steps and fell – causing a crush in which173 people lost their lives. It was the worst loss of civilian lives in a single event in the whole of the war.[28]

Just five weeks before the end of the war in Europe (the war against Japan continuing until September 1945), another tragic event occurred in Bethnal Green, this time close to the twins' home. One morning in the spring of 1945, nearby apartment blocks were struck by a German V2 rocket, resulting in massive destruction and a terrible loss of life. When the rocket struck, Reggie and Ronnie were still in bed and the shock wave from the blast threw them from their beds, smashed every window in the terrace, and caused damage to the roofs. Running downstairs to join their parents and Charlie already standing outside the house – the young twins saw a mountainous cloud of dust rising into the sky from what had been, until a few moments previously, *Hughes Mansions*. Some of the dead and injured were known to the Kray family.

Hughes Mansions and the Dewdrop Inn

Nearest TFL station: Bethnal Green overground.

Neither of these two locations could be described as places of importance in the Krays' story, but both are very close to other Kray landmarks, and are certainly worthy of note – and perhaps a slight detour to take a look.

---

28   A commemorative plaque can be seen above the Roman Road entrance to the station, and there is a memorial sculpture called the *Stairway to Heaven* – which was completed in 2017 – in nearby Bethnal Green Gardens.

Hughes Mansions, Vallance Rd, London E1 5BJ

Just a few hundred yards from the site of the twins' home – along Vallance Road, in the direction of Whitechapel, on the left-hand side of the road – is an apartment block with an easily visible sign above the first-floor windows that reads:

HUGHES MANSIONS, ERECTED AD 1928 BY THE STEPNEY BOROUGH COUNCIL.

On Tuesday 27 March 1945 at 7.21am, the last German V2 rocket to reach London fell on *Hughes Mansions* – a group of three residential apartment blocks – killing 134 people and injuring many others. When the rocket struck, the central block was completely destroyed and very little of the block immediately to the east was left standing. Although having sustained severe damage to the rear, the western block still stands today and faces directly onto Vallance Road. Commemorating Britain's second-worst V2 rocket attack, a modest memorial plaque can be seen in the garden area of the estate close to the eastern block, which was rebuilt soon after the war. Only the V2 rocket that landed on a busy *Woolworths* department store in New Cross, South London on 25 November 1944 – killing 168 people – claimed more lives.

The Dewdrop Inn, 71 Vallance Rd, London E1 5BS

Immediately across the road from *Hughes Mansions*, on the corner of Buxton Street, is a building with a blue plaque on the wall that was clearly once a pub. *Earl Grey's Castle* opened in 1901 and is said to have been a meeting place for Russian communists – including Lenin and Trotsky – planning revolution while staying in London. In 1926 the pub was bought by Quaker and philanthropist Mary Hughes, to whom the blue plaque is dedicated. Renaming it *The Dewdrop Inn* (do drop in), she converted the pub into a place of rest, refuge, and non-alcoholic refreshment for the homeless, running it until her death in 1941.

The building, never reopening as a pub, was converted for residential use and, more recently, was made into a luxury dwelling. In 2017, the *Daily Mirror* announced that the *"Kray twins' local East End boozer"* was up for sale.[29] The former pub at 71 Vallance Road, which closed seven years before the twins were born, is sometimes mistaken for a *Krays pub*. The point of interest with this particular building – now an exclusive art gallery called *Dewdrop* – is that contrary to a fairly popular belief, the building, although interesting in itself, has nothing whatsoever to do with the Krays… not a sausage.

Death and tragedy were parts of everyday life in the East End during the war but, despite all this, childhood for the twins was – for the most part – a time of fun and adventure. Bomb sites and ruined buildings provided an exciting adventure playground to explore and organise stone-throwing battles with their enemies. Having gained a reputation as good fighters, other boys were keen to tag along and the twins soon gathered a following, becoming gang leaders at an early age. Inside their home – as far as their mother Violet was concerned – the twins were little angels, but outside on the streets of Bethnal Green, things were different. Ronnie and Reggie fought with local kids all the time, and their reputation was such that the *Terrible*

---

29   www.mirror.co.uk>uk-news 14 Oct 2017.

Twins, as they came to be known, were blamed every time a child was hurt or something was broken, whether they were responsible or not.[30]

Despite loving a good scrap, Reggie was fairly easy-going by nature, but Ronnie was touchy and quick to take offence at the slightest perceived liberty taken by other boys. This, in turn, led to more fights in which Reggie would of course backup his brother and join in – the beginning of a pattern of behaviour that would continue into adulthood.

Knowing there would always be a good dinner of potatoes and stew waiting for them when they came home, the twins would clean themselves up after a scrap and prepare to plead innocence in case word of their antics had reached Violet. *"It wasn't our fault,"* they would claim and, of course, Violet – who refused to see any wrong in her lovely boys – would believe them. Violet's home cooking, which the twins so loved, was occasionally supplemented with that most traditional of London fare: the cockney staple, pie and mash.

Ron and Reg would be sent along to collect the grub from *G. Kelly* in Bethnal Green Road and, while there, the mischievous twins took delight in unscrewing the tops of vinegar bottles so that customers would unwittingly pour the lot onto their dinner.[31]

---

30   Pearson, John. *The Profession of Violence.* London: Weidenfeld & Nicolson, 1972.

31   *East London Advertiser*, online, 9th March 2015.

G Kelly

414 Bethnal Green Road, London E2 ODJ

Nearest TFL station: Bethnal Green underground.

Since the mid-Victorian era, eel and pie shops – selling minced beef pies and mashed potato, with a gravy made from eel cooking liquor and parsley, known simply as *liquor* – have provided working-class Londoners with cheap, nourishing meals. Hot stewed or cold jellied eels, once plentiful and cheap, were (and still are) sold alongside.

In 1915, Samuel Robert Kelly opened an eel and pie shop on Bethnal Green Road, close to Paradise Row, and ran it with his wife Matilda.

In 1925, friend of Charlie Chaplin, George Alex Stephens, composed the famous song about an Ashkenazi Jewish girl called Nellie Moss who sits alongside Joe "*on Mother Kelly's doorstep, down Paradise Row.*"

Samuel and Matilda had four children and, in 1939, their son George Kelly opened an eel and pie shop on Roman Road in Bow, later taking over *L S Harris Stewed Eel Shop* at 414 Bethnal Green Road.

Other Kelly family members opened eel and pie shops and, further along Bethnal Green Road at number 284, is *S & R Kelly*, certainly in existence when the twins were young and happily still trading today.

G Kelly – at 526 Roman Road – is still open and trading but sadly, the shop at 414 Bethnal Green Road, thought to be the one most used by the Kray family, closed and never reopened after lockdown.

During the war years, when the twins were aged between 7 and 12, they saw very little of their father; not only was he working away much of the time, but he was also on the run from the authorities. Having received his call-up papers in 1940 to join the army and fight for his country, Charles chose not to go. He was, of course, the sole breadwinner for his family. He had never taken orders from a superior and he had no intention of letting Hitler change that. Evading conscription was common practice in the East End, and Charles was far from alone in his choice. East Enders had long seen themselves as separate from mainstream society – underprivileged, ignored, or looked down on by the rest of the country. True or not, a sense of patriotic duty was not exactly burning in the hearts of every cockney – *"Why should I go and fight for them? What have they ever done for me?"*

Throughout the war years and afterwards – until 1953, when an amnesty was granted – Charles was effectively a fugitive and, as such, times spent at home were few and far between. On the occasions when Charles did put in an appearance, he was taking a risk should the police call – and they did, frequently, until the end of the war. When the police came knocking or simply barged in, Charles would skip over the wall in the backyard and have it *'away on his toes'*, or hide next door in sister-in-law Rose's house. Or, if there wasn't time to get out, he would hide in cupboards, under the sink, or under the stairs. Hot-tempered Aunt Rose would let her feelings be known when the police came calling, turning the air blue with a torrent of verbal abuse and four-letter words.

During this time, the twins, understandably, ceased to see the police as trusted figures of authority who were kind and there to keep everyone safe; instead, they developed a hatred for police that would stay with them for the rest of their lives.

Charles was not the only fugitive from military conscription frequenting the Lee households on Vallance Road. Aunt

Rose – who was divorced from her husband William Wiltshire – had, according to Reggie, *"a couple of blokes hiding out in her house for ages."*[32] Also, the twins' cousin, Joe Lee – after joining the navy and then, against his wishes, being transferred to the army – decided to go *'on the trot'* and spent time hiding in the homes of his aunts, uncles, and grandparents. Harry Hopwood, Charles Senior's close friend, was another draft dodger using Vallance Road as an occasional hiding place. Little surprise that *Lee Street* also became known among the locals as *Deserters Corner*.

When not working away or putting in the odd appearance at Vallance Road, Charles – in order to avoid the attention of the police – stayed for a time in South London at the home of his friend Bob Rolfe. While staying south of the river in Camberwell, Charles would of course patronise the local pubs, and it is likely that it was during this period that he came to know the notorious and legendary London villain, Frankie Fraser.

During an interview by Fred Dinenage for a TV documentary in 2010, Frankie recalls meeting the very young Kray twins:

"When I was 19, I'd just come out of Chelmsford Prison and I used to drink with their father. It was during the war and sometimes, when the pubs used to shut at three o'clock in the afternoon, we would go to a club – or sometimes I'd go home with their dad and have a meal. They were nine years of age; they used to call me Uncle Frank. Years later, we had a good laugh about it."[33]

---

32   Kray, Reggie and Gerrard, Peter. *Reggie Kray's East End Stories*. London: Sphere, 2010.

33   *The Krays by Fred Dinenage*. Woodcut Media, 2010.

Frankie Fraser was a leading figure in London's underworld from the 1940s to the 1960s, during which time he worked with gang boss Billy Hill and later with the Richardson brothers. His reputation for extreme violence gained him the moniker 'Mad Frankie Fraser'. During the period he spent as a member of the Richardson Gang, tensions developed between the Richardsons and the Krays – and, for a while, Frank and the twins found themselves on opposing sides. Just as matters were about to come to a head, however, Frank and the other leading members of the South London firm were arrested and imprisoned, so the predicted gang war never took place. In later life, Frank became an author, ran London gangland tours, and made regular appearances on TV. Frank died in 2014 aged 90 years, 40 of which had been spent behind bars.

Charles used another bolt-hole in which to lay low during the war. Elsie, a relative on Violet's side of the family, was married to a farmer and living near the small market town of Tring in Hertfordshire. Charles would go there on occasion and stay for a while when the police were hot on his tail – and, on at least one occasion, he was joined by Violet and the twins, who were excited to be staying in the country for a second time. Ronnie and Reggie were in their element once again, roaming and exploring the meadows, poppy fields, and rolling countryside of the Chiltern Hills, and stealing apples from the orchards of the nearby *Rothschild Estate*.

Rose Wiltshire, née Lee – the twins' aunt – loved her sister's twin boys and lavished them with affection. Even when she was short of money, she would make sure the twins received a present or a treat every week without fail. Naturally, the twins loved their Aunt Rose and she was a great influence on their young lives. Rose understood Ronnie and could see that he was *different,* troubled perhaps, and that he needed just that little bit more love and attention. Rose could be moody and, like her father, she had a very short fuse, resorting to violence at the drop of a hat. Fists would fly at the slightest provocation and, whether her anger was directed at a man or a woman, Rose would always come out on top, gaining her the reputation in the local area as someone not to be messed with. Perhaps Rose saw something of herself in Ronnie.

Rose's son, Billy Wiltshire, had clearly inherited something of his mother's temperament and, as a youngster, was a rascal of the highest order. Billy was five years older than the twins so, naturally, Ronnie and Reggie looked up to their older cousin Billy. They would follow him wherever he went, sometimes joining in his fights and taking on much older, much bigger boys. Billy found great amusement in the playing of cruel tricks on his young cousins. Leaving the twins crying after pushing them into the dark, spider-infested space under the stairs at their grandparents' house – and then nailing the door shut – was hilarious as far as Billy was concerned. Making the boys climb inside a barrel and then rolling it along the cobbles, crashing into anything that happened to get in the way, was the source of even more fun. During a game of war in the rubble of one of the bombsites, Billy threw a brick grenade and scored a direct hit on young Reggie's head, resulting in streaming blood, a trip to the hospital, and six stitches.

When Billy Wiltshire saw the twins with rolled towels under their arms, heading in the direction of the public bath house on Cheshire Street, he saw an opportunity to play one of his favourite tricks. Waiting until one of the twins was undressed and soaking in the bath, Billy would climb over the cubicle wall, jump down, and push the unlucky twin's head underwater. After holding it there for way too long, he would eventually let go, leaving the poor lad gasping, coughing, and spluttering. But that was only half the fun to be had – so it was up and over into the next cubicle to do the same to the other twin.

The Bath House

Cheshire Street, London E2 6JD

Nearest TFL station: Bethnal Green overground.

Built in 1898, the elegant red brick and white stone, Grade II listed building is a former public bath and wash-house for washing both bodies and clothes. Situated close to the Krays' Vallance Road home, the bathhouse was used regularly by the Kray twins.

During the 19th and early 20th centuries, such amenities were essential, as the majority of houses in the area had no internal bathrooms. Towards the end of the 1960s, most of the Victorian terraces were demolished or condemned, and the residents rehoused in modern apartments with bathrooms. Washing machines became more common in the home and coin-operated laundrettes appeared on every high street, resulting in the closure of the old public bath and wash houses.

Formerly the washhouse, the single-storey part of the building is today home to the famous *Repton Boxing Club*. The two-storey bath house has been converted into luxury apartments, but the outside of the building remains much the same as it was. The words *Men's Baths* and *Women's Baths*, ornately carved in stone alongside scrolls and cherubs, can be seen above the two separate entrances at the front of the building.

As young boxers, Ronnie and Reggie trained at the *Repton Club* but not here at this site. *Repton Boxing Club* was located at 16 Victoria Park Square, Bethnal Green, and did not move here to its current location until 1971 – two years after the twins were sentenced to life imprisonment.

Footage of the interior of the washhouse exists and provides a fascinating glimpse into the past. Just search YouTube for 'British Pathe, London Wash House, 1970-1979'.

Charlie Kray took up boxing again when the family returned from Suffolk to the East End. Granddad Lee, keen to help his grandson with his boxing, fixed up a punch bag in one of the upstairs bedrooms of the Kray family house, and the young twins watched with fascination as their older brother skilfully hammered away at the bag. Eager to learn, Ronnie and Reggie began accompanying Charlie on early morning runs, copying his shadow-boxing and footwork as they ran. Charlie could see that the twins were full of enthusiasm and serious about their boxing, so he created a little gym in the upstairs room of the house, adding a speedball, skipping ropes, and weights to the punch bag already there. Soon, the twins were inviting their friends around to train and spar, and before long, the little boxing gym at the Krays' house became *the* place to be for dozens of aspiring young boxers – especially as Violet would keep them all well supplied with sandwiches and lemonade.

Boxing was immensely popular among East End boys and was seen as one of the few ways – apart from criminality – that a young man could make something of himself and escape from a life of drudgery and back-breaking work that barely paid enough to make ends meet. Some of the boys who spent time at the twins' house in this period did indeed go on to have successful boxing careers, but there was one boy who proved to be an exception to the rule and went on to achieve great success in the world of show business. Later remembered by Ronnie as a *"great little fella,"* singer, songwriter, actor, and all-round entertainer Kenny Lynch, OBE, became a household name in the 1960s and '70s.[34]

In 1944, the penultimate year of the war, Charlie – who was 18 and who had previously joined the Naval Cadets at Hackney Wick for the excellent boxing training facilities – decided to sign on for the Royal Navy, before he was called up by the army. Cousin Joe Lee joined at the same time and the pair were shipped off together to do their basic training. After training, Joe was drafted to Devonport in Plymouth to join a ship, but Charlie was kept behind to join the navy's boxing team. Charlie achieved great success as a welterweight, boxing in the inter-service championships, but his time in the navy was cut short and he was discharged on medical grounds. Boxing twice a week against the army and the RAF may well have been the cause of Charlie's chronic migraines, but whatever the cause, before the end of the war, Charlie was back in Bethnal Green.

The dream of becoming world champion boxers dominated the young twins' lives and, with the help and encouragement of their older brother Charlie, they were developing skills and working hard towards achieving their ambition. They continued training and sparring with their friends in the home gym, and they were now spending a couple of evenings a week at a youth club held in the crypt of *Spitalfields Church*. Later described by Reggie *as "a rough little club with a good atmosphere where everyone mixed in together,"* this club provided various activities including table tennis and snooker, but – most importantly, as far as the twins were concerned – it offered boxing training. In his book, *The Profession of Violence*, author John Pearson refers to the twins' first boxing club as the *Midgets Club* in Whitechapel, but it was in fact the *Vallance*

---

34   Kray, Reg and Ron with Dinenage, Fred. *Our Story*. London: Pan Books, 1988.

Club in the crypt of *Spitalfields Church*, run by a very small gentleman called Mr Davis.[35]

Christ Church Spitalfields

Commercial St, London E1 6LY

Nearest TFL station: Aldgate East underground.

Believing that the "*Godless masses*" of the East End and other outlying areas of the capital were straying from the righteous path of Anglican Christianity, the government of the day sanctioned the building of several new churches, each with a spire high enough to dominate and outshine any foreign or non-conformist places of worship. Designed by architect Nicholas Hawksmoor in the English Baroque style, the church was consecrated in July 1729. By the 1950s, the magnificent 18th-century church had fallen into disrepair and the near-derelict building was earmarked for demolition. Due to the efforts of the *Hawksmoor Committee*, however, the building was saved and a gradual, ongoing period of restoration began, ending in 2004 when the Grade I listed church was finally fully restored to its original splendour.

As youngsters, Ronnie and Reggie Kray joined a youth club held in the church crypt called the *Vallance Club*. Among the activities available to the children – and most importantly to the twins – was boxing training,

---

35   Kray, Reggie and Gerrard, Peter. *Reggie Kray's East End Stories.* London: Sphere, 2010.

provided by a man named Bill Gates.[36]

In 2015, the church crypt – once the location of the Kray twins' first boxing club – was fully refurbished and now houses the *Cafe in the Crypt*, and space for meetings, functions, and community events.

By 1944, when the twins were approaching 11 years of age, Charlie could see that they were ready to take the next step towards more serious competitive boxing, so he took them along to his old club, the *Robert Browning Club* in South London. Becoming members of the club meant that the twins would soon be facing opponents in official amateur boxing matches. Acceptance into the club, therefore, was dependent on the twins being able to demonstrate a good level of skill and ability, so they were required to audition by sparring for a few rounds with one of the club's more experienced members. Charlie Simms, the club's resident trainer, was duly impressed by both twins and signed them up immediately.

Within a short time, the twins were enjoying success on the junior amateur circuit. Reggie fought with skill and natural talent in a disciplined technical boxing style, but Ronnie achieved equal success through sheer aggression, constantly going forward and slugging in the style of a street fighter.

36   Ibid.

The Robert Browning Boxing Club

Trafalgar St, London SE17 2TP

**Nearest TFL station:
Elephant and Castle underground.**

In 1944, Charlie Kray took his ten-year-old twin brothers along to the club where he'd begun his amateur boxing career – the *Robert Browning Club*, based at the *Nelson School* in South London. After demonstrating a good deal of natural talent and ability, the twins were accepted into the club and soon began competitive boxing as juniors.

Built in the early 1900s, the school – originally called *Sandford Row School* – later became the *Nelson School* and then, in the 1960s, the name changed again to *Walworth Secondary School*. Today the school is called *South Bank University Academy*.

September 1945 saw the Japanese surrender and, at last, World War II was finally over. That same month, Ronnie and Reggie – just a few weeks before their 12th birthdays – began their secondary education at *Daniel Street School* in Bethnal Green. In general, both twins took well to their time in education, settling into school life without any major problems. Although neither was regularly top of the class, they were a long way from the bottom. Boxing continued to be the main focus of the twins' lives and, after starting at *Daniel Street*, they were quick to join the school boxing club run by the games teacher, Mr Bell. Interviewed at the end of the 1960s by the twins' biographer, John Pearson, William Evans – the twins'

principal teacher – had only good things to say about his former pupils. He described them as *"salt of the earth"* characters; tough fighters but cooperative and *"never the slightest
trouble."*[37]

Daniel Street School

Gosset Street, Bethnal Green, London E2 6NW

**Nearest TFL station:
Shoreditch High Street overground.**

Built in 1900, *Daniel Street School* was a secondary
school attended by pupils between the ages of 11 and 16.
Ronnie and Reggie Kray spent just over three years of
their lives here, beginning in September 1945 when they
were 11 years of age. Ronnie's school leaving certificate shows that he was eligible to leave on 17 December
1948, when the twins were 15[38]

In 1959, the school changed its name to *Daneford
School* and, in 1997, it became *Bethnal Green High
School*. Shortly afterwards, the name changed again to
Bethnal Green Technology College and then in, January
2012, changed yet again to *Bethnal Green Academy*. In
February 2015, the school hit the headlines when students Shamima Begum and two friends left the UK and
travelled to Syria to join the Islamic State. After an investigation by counter-extremism officers – and to be rid

---

37   Pearson, John. *The Profession of Violence*. London: Weidenfeld &
      Nicolson, 1972.

38   www.dailymail.co.uk By Jemma Carr for Mailonline 18 Mar 2021.

of the negative associations – the school was renamed *Green Spring Academy Shoreditch* in 2015, changing yet again in 2018 to *Mulberry Academy Shoreditch*.

Moving ever onwards and upwards in the world of amateur boxing, the twins were clocking up an impressive record of junior titles. Charlie's collection of boxing trophies – displayed on the mantelpiece at Vallance Road – was gradually being added to with the twins' own silverware. When the twins had to fight each other in the final of the 1946 Hackney School Championships, the fighting twins from Bethnal Green were given column inches in the local newspapers. This was the second year running that the twins had faced each other in the final, Ronnie having been given the decision on the previous occasion. This time, in a close-fought contest with the judges having difficulty awarding the correct points to the correct identical twin, Ronnie was once again declared the winner.

After learning the ropes and beginning their amateur boxing careers at the *Robert Browning Club*, the twins moved their training base closer to home, joining the *Webbe Club* in Bethnal Green where they came under the care of ex-professional fighter and trainer of young amateur boxers, Harry 'Kid' Berry.

Oxford House &
The Webbe Boxing Club

Derbyshire Street, Bethnal Green, London E2 6HG

Nearest TFL station: Bethnal Green underground.

Established in 1884 in a former school and moving to the current purpose-built, redbrick, four-storey building in 1892, *Oxford House* was one of the first *University Settlement Houses*, where students and graduates from Oxford and other universities could stay and work voluntarily to help the poor of London's East End. An important part of the work undertaken was the establishment and running of clubs and societies to promote recreation and education for underprivileged members of the community. One such club founded by *Oxford House* in 1888 was the *Webbe Institute*, a boxing club named after the late Oxford cricketer and philanthropist, Herbert Webbe. Originally based in premises at 95-97 Cheshire Street, on the corner of Hereford Street, the *Webbe Institute* relocated to *Oxford House* after the outbreak of war in 1939, where it occupied a downstairs hall until its closure in 1948.

During the mid-1940s, the young amateur boxers Ron and Reg Kray trained at the *Webbe Institute* based in *Oxford House* under the guidance of their trainer, Harry 'Kid' Berry.

Today, Grade II listed *Oxford House* is a charity-funded community hub and arts space with a Victorian chapel and cafe.

Following the closure of the *Webbe Institute* at *Oxford House*, *The Webbe Boys Club* was re-established at the original Cheshire Street location and remained open until the mid-1950s. The Victorian building – with its steps leading to an arched doorway on the corner of Hereford Street – still exists, having now been converted into residences.

Harry Berry, the twins' trainer, made his living as a hawker; buying second-hand clothes and selling them from a stall in *Brick Lane Market*. Jimmy Kray – the twins' paternal grandfather – along with his sons, also ran a stall in the same market. The East End's premiere *hawking* families – the Berrys and the Krays – therefore, were well known to each other. During school holidays and sometimes at weekends, the twins would help out on the Kray family stall, using the opportunity to sharpen their footwork by dodging and weaving among the crowds in the bustling market.

Harry Berry's eldest son, Ted, was five years older than the twins and was well on his way to becoming one of Britain's most promising fighters. Tragically, however, Ted's career came to an abrupt end in 1949 when he suffered a detached retina and lost his sight in one eye. Harry Berry's younger son, Checker – who would also go on to box professionally for a short time – was closer to the twins' age and would remain a friend of both for years to come. Both of the Berry brothers, Ted in particular, would feature in a dramatic and shocking episode later in the Kray twins' story.

In 1946, the 12-year-old twins were involved in an incident that would lead to their first-ever court appearance – and reinforce their already ingrained hatred of the police.[39] One summer's day, the twins and their friend Alfie Miller took the train to Chingford to enjoy a day in – what was then – unspoilt countryside. Armed with sandwiches, cake, a bottle of water, and Reggie's Diana .177 air rifle, the three lads spent the day larking about in the woods and fields, climbing trees, searching streams for fish, and taking pot-shots at suitable targets with Reggie's airgun. Around 4pm, the tired and dishevelled lads, having run out of food, decided to take the train back to Liverpool Street. Aboard the train, the fun and games continued as the boys wrestled each other, bounced on the seats, and

---

39   Kray, Reg and Ron with Dinenage, Fred. *Our Story*. London: Pan Books, 1988.

laughed heartily when Alfie was lifted up by the twins and dumped in the overhead luggage rack. Yet more fun was to be had when Reggie decided to take a few shots with the airgun, out of the window of the speeding train.

When the train arrived at Liverpool Street station, the three boys – not realising they'd done anything seriously wrong – were collared by two burly, plain-clothes railway policemen. Tired, scruffy, and now frightened, the boys were made to give a statement, told that they would probably be sent to *borstal*, and then taken home in a police car. Violet was informed that the boys would have to appear in court in four weeks' time, charged with dangerously discharging a firearm in a public place. Then, with the threat of the twins' detention in *borstal* hanging over their heads like the Sword of Damocles, there began a month of anxiety for the family.

Finally, the day arrived, and the twins – accompanied by Violet and Aunt Rose – made their first-ever court appearance at *Toynbee Juvenile Court*. Fortunately for the twins, and much to the relief of their tearful mother and aunt, the boys were given a good stern telling-off, bound over to keep the peace, and allowed to leave.

Toynbee Hall

28 Commercial St, London E1 6LS

Nearest TFL station: Aldgate East underground.

Situated between Aldgate and Spitalfields, and named after the *Oxford University* historian and social reformer Alfred Toynbee, the building – designed in the Tudor/ Gothic style of an Oxbridge college – was built and opened in 1884.

Closely associated with *Oxford University* and funded by charitable donations, this – the first of several London *University Settlement Houses* – was created to allow students from Oxford, Cambridge, and other universities to stay for a period, witness first-hand the poverty and deprivation in London's East End, and develop practical solutions to the problems associated with hardship.

One of the many services designed at *Toynbee Hall* to improve the lives of local people was the creation of a juvenile court held in *Toynbee Studios*; a newly added building that opened in 1938. With the purpose of providing a more informal and less intimidating environment than a police court, tribunals involving children were held in the studios' wood-panelled music room.

The 12-year-old Kray twins made their first-ever court appearance here, charged with discharging a firearm (air rifle) in a public place.

Today, *Toynbee Hall* is a charitable institution, staffed by volunteers and providing a range of services, programmes, and activities aimed at helping members of the community. The largely unchanged music room, which once doubled as a juvenile court, is on the first floor of the studios building and is today used mainly as a lecture hall. Arrangements can be made in advance to tour the interior of *Toynbee Hall* and see the music room.

In 1947, when the twins were 13, they met in the ring for a third time in the final of the London Schools competition at *York Hall* in Bethnal Green. Ignoring their elder brother's advice to "*take it easy and put on a good show*," the twins tore into each other and fought like demons for three furious rounds. This time the judges were unanimous and it was Reggie's arm that was raised at the end of the fight. Afterwards, in the dressing room, their mum Violet – who had been ringside and was horrified to have seen her lovely boys attack each other with such ferocity – made the bruised and bloodied twins promise that they would never fight each other ever again.[40] They never did fight each other again in an *official* boxing competition, but knocking the daylights out of each other would continue on a regular basis throughout their lives as free men.

One particular brotherly scrap has become the stuff of legend after being dramatised in the 1990 feature film *The Krays*, starring Martin and Gary Kemp. Some accounts say it happened when the twins were just ten years old, but in his book, *East End Stories*, Reggie suggests it happened sometime *after* fighting in the final of the schools competition, when they were at least 13. Give or take a few years, the young Kray twins and a group of pals visited a travelling fair set up on a cleared bombsite in Turin Street, just off Bethnal Green Road. The main attraction for the twins was Alf Stewart's boxing booth, where the crowd were entertained by local men who fancied their chances in the ring against one of Alf Stewart's resident fighters. Cash prizes were awarded to likely lads who could stay on their feet and survive for three rounds, but far more failed than succeeded. The job of the resident fighter was to make the chancer look good and to entertain the crowd for a couple of rounds before sending him to the canvas with a just-hard-enough body punch.

During a lull in proceedings, when there was no one brave enough or drunk enough to climb into the ring, Alf Stewart announced: *"Right, now for something different. If any of you lot want to settle a difference or have a bit of fun, get up in this*

---

40   Kray, Charlie with McGibbon, Robin. *Me and My Brothers*. London: Grafton, 1988.

ring, fight it out, and I'll see you all right."[41]

Without saying a word to each other, Ron and Reg put their hands up and climbed into the ring. Accompanied by the whoops and cheers of the crowd, the twins steamed into each other with their usual savagery and gave a consummate performance of skilled brutality. Declaring the contest a draw, Alf Stewart gave the twins seven shillings and sixpence each and told them that they were welcome to come and give a repeat performance anytime they liked.[42]

By 1948, the *Webbe Boxing Club* at *Oxford House* had closed and the twins joined *Repton Boys Club*, where they would continue to train under the watchful eye of Harry Berry and enjoy more success and local fame. Both twins added to their tally of junior titles and Reggie made it as far as the Great Britain Schoolboy Championship semi-final at *Wembley Arena* – but, on the day, he failed to make the weight and had to miss the fight. Ronnie and Reggie remained members of the Repton amateur boxing club for the rest of their amateur careers and continued a close association with the club after turning professional in 1951.

---

41   Kray, Reggie and Gerrard, Peter. Reggie Kray's *East End Stories*. London: Sphere, 2010.

42   From the early 1900s onwards, the Stewarts – a family of boxers – ran boxing booths in travelling fairs throughout the country. Alf Stewart, aka Spider, achieved fame as a professional boxer and then through his fairground booths. After Alf's death in 1948, his daughters, *The Fighting Stewart Girls*, continued the family business.

Repton Boys Club

University House, 16 Victoria Park Square, Bethnal Green, London E2 9PE

Nearest TFL station: Bethnal Green underground.

Now converted into apartments, the Grade II listed building with an adjoining redbrick Gothic revival-style chapel was completed in 1888 and used as a clubhouse by the *University Settlement House* initiative.

Established and funded by the Repton public school in Derbyshire in 1884 to cater for '*a lower class of boys*' in London's East End, *Repton Boys Club* was brought under the umbrella of *Oxford House* in 1895. After occupying premises at several different locations in the Bethnal Green area, the club was given a more permanent home at *University House* in the 1920s. It is here that the Kray twins trained and honed their boxing skills from 1948 to 1951, when they turned professional.

After *Repton School* withdrew its support in 1971, the club moved briefly to *Bethnal Green Working Men's Club* at 42-46 Pollard Row, E2 6NB, and then to its current location in the former washhouse next to The Bath House on Cheshire Street.

The *Repton Club* has been called Britain's oldest boxing club, and it is certainly among the most famous, having produced many champions and an Olympic gold medallist (Audley Harrison). Numerous TV programmes, music videos, and films feature scenes shot in the retro-style boxing gym on Cheshire Street; one of the most notable of which is Guy Ritchie's 1998 film, *Lock, Stock and Two Smoking Barrels.*

By 1948, Britain was beginning to emerge from the shadow of darkness cast by six years of war; blackout curtains were gone, restrictions were relaxed, and the crushing weight of fear and national anxiety was lifted. Although rationing, austerity, and hard times would continue for some time to come, overall, Britain was breathing a sigh of relief and looking towards a better future.

During the war years – and for a couple of years afterwards – the streets of the East End were relatively trouble-free, but now teenagers were roaming the streets again, looking for excitement. Ronnie and Reggie – now aged 14 – had, until this time, completely dedicated themselves to their boxing and had lived their lives accordingly. Early to bed, regular meals, early to rise, and pounding the pavement every morning in all kinds of weather.

Soon, their brother Charlie noticed that the twins were beginning to stay out later in the evenings, were secretive about their whereabouts, and sometimes neglected their early morning runs. Fighting in the street was nothing new to the twins, but it was beginning to become a far more serious business. From the moment they entered the world, the twins possessed a kind of telepathic connection, where each knew what the other was thinking. Now, as teenagers, they discovered that they could use this power to their advantage and fight as a single coordinated unit. This – along with the punch of a sledge-hammer that each possessed through years of boxing training – made them unbeatable in a gang fight, even when they were outnumbered.

Until now, the twins had found that their fists alone were enough to settle any dispute, but the ante was being seriously upped on the streets and the Queensbury rules needed to be put to one side. Soon learning that the only rule on the streets was to win – and by whatever means necessary – the twins had no problem accepting that fists, boots, head butting, or whatever else could be used against them – they must do it first and do it harder. The twins' pursuit of power, status, and excitement was leading steadily towards an inevitable raising of the stakes, and it wouldn't be long before weapons would enter the arena… along with the risk of far more serious consequences.

Ron and Reg worshipped their mum throughout their lives and, as children, they knew she was a soft touch and that they could get away with anything. During the twins' formative years, their father Charles was not around enough to impose any kind of discipline, and on the odd occasions when he tried, Violet would berate him. Charles did take an interest in his sons' boxing and was encouraging, but he was not – and never had been – a respected authority figure in the twins' lives. Charles was powerless to change the direction in which the twins were clearly heading and now, as teenagers, the die was well and truly cast.

Violet always received adequate housekeeping money, and young Charlie, Ronnie, and Reggie had always been well-fed and clothed, enjoying a better standard of living than most of the other children in the area. Charles certainly provided for his family in a material sense, but he was not a *family man,* preferring instead to spend the time – when he wasn't away working – drinking in his favourite East End pubs. Arriving back in London after a few days out of town *on the knocker,* Charles – often accompanied by his younger brother, the twins' uncle, Alf – would make straight for his hostelry of choice, *The Crown and Anchor* near Liverpool Street station.

The Crown and Anchor (The 99 Pub)

Moorgate, London, EC2M 6XQ

Nearest TFL Station: Moorgate underground.

Situated at 171 Moorgate, close to Liverpool Street station and the adjacent Broad Street station (demolished in 1986), *The Crown and Anchor* was nicknamed the '99' – so-called because, prior to a change in road boundaries and numbers, the pub's address was 99 Finsbury Pavement.

This was a favourite pub of the twins' father Charles. After a trip to the provinces to ply his trade as a *wardrobe dealer* (buying second-hand clothes and jewellery to sell on), the '99' pub would be his first stop on arriving back in London. Charles spent much of his spare time in the pub and, in the early 1950s, he would be joined – on occasion – by Charlie and the twins, who spent short periods working with their father *on the knocker*.

Now demolished, the pub stood close to the junction with Ropemaker Street. The newly built *Moorgate Hall* now occupies the site.

Charles Kray's drinking was not confined to *the 99* pub; he would visit several other pubs in the East End and, when on home turf, he could often be found in *The Marquis of Cornwallis* on Bethnal Green Road, just a few minutes' walk from home at 178 Vallance Road.

The Marquis of Cornwallis

304 Bethnal Green Road, London E2 0AG

Nearest TFL station:
Bethnal Green underground/overground.

Built in 1835 and situated on the corner of Bethnal Green Road and Vallance Road, the pub was Charles Kray's local; he would spend a lot of time here, often in the company of his younger brother, the twins' uncle, Alf.

The pub is not known as a regular *Krays pub* but, considering its close proximity to their Vallance Road home and the fact that their father drank here, it's a safe bet that the twins visited the pub occasionally.

Happily, the pub still exists. In 1919, Tower Hamlets Council granted protection to *The Marquis of Cornwallis* and 34 other pubs in East London, preventing them from demolition and redevelopment in the foreseeable future.

The pub has recently undergone some refurbishment, but the basic layout is much as it ever was and it retains its identity as a traditional East End boozer.

Charlie – now in his early twenties – was earning a living with his father in the second-hand clothes business, and after continuing to do well as an amateur boxer, he had for some time been thinking about turning professional. This he did, winning a points victory over his first opponent Jack Allen in a four-round welterweight contest on 22 November 1948 at *Leyton Baths*. Charlie would go on to have a total of 18 professional fights between 1948 and 1951, winning 11 and losing 6, with 1 draw.[43]

On Christmas Day 1948, Charlie married his sweetheart, Dorothy (Dolly) Moore. As was the accepted way in the East End at the time, sons and daughters would marry and share a parental home for a while until they were able to find a home of their own. So, after dismantling the home gym in the upstairs back bedroom at Vallance Road, Charlie and his new bride moved in.

Also in December 1948 the twins left school; now it was time for them to consider how they were going to earn a living.

---

43   BoxRec boxrec.com

Uncle Joe Lee, who worked at *Billingsgate Fish Market*, told the twins that he might be able to put a word in and find each of them a job – if they were interested. They were, and they started work at *Farren and Barrow Ltd*, fish sellers, on Saturday 8 January 1949.[44] Farren and Barrow ran several stalls within *Billingsgate Market*, as well as two shops at 5 and 127 Lower Thames Street.[45] Ronnie was put to work in the haddock market as an *empty boy*, collecting and stacking empty fish boxes, and Reggie was sent to the shop on Thames Street to learn the business of selling fish to customers.

Both twins enjoyed the busy market atmosphere with its hustle, bustle, and cacophony of shouts from the porters as they pushed barrows laden with boxes of mackerel, haddock, herring, cod, and skate, or – wearing special leather hats – carried the boxes stacked high on their heads, a practice known as 'nutting' the fish. Initially, the twins found the work interesting and exciting, but it wasn't long before the novelty wore off; less than four months after starting, they both left on 30 April 1949.

Old Billingsgate

16 Lower Thames Street, London EC3R 6DX

Nearest TFL station: Monument underground.

Old Billingsgate is the name now given to the Victorian building that was originally the world's largest fish market, *Billingsgate Fish Market*. Built in 1875 to replace an earlier market building, the magnificent

---

44   Bennet, John. *Krayology*. London: Mango Books, 2015.

45   Kelly's Post Office Directory of London, 1950.

Grade II listed building still stands today and is used as an events venue. Notice the two fish-shaped weathervanes on the roofs of the east and west towers facing the Thames.

Shortly after leaving school in December 1948, the 15-year-old Kray twins began working at *Billingsgate*, but soon lost interest in the work and left in April 1949.

In 1982, the fish market relocated to Canary Wharf and is now situated at Trafalgar Way, Poplar, London E14 5ST.

17 June 1949 saw the Kray family travel to Cambridgeshire for their annual fruit-picking holiday. Even Charles Senior took time out from work to join Violet and the twins for what was the highlight of the year. Many East End families couldn't afford a fortnight's 'bucket and spade' holiday at Margate or Southend-on-Sea so, as had been the tradition for generations, there was a mass exodus to the orchards and fields of rural southern England to enjoy the country air for a few weeks in the summer and earn a little money at the same time.

Families were accommodated in military-style wooden huts with plywood partitions for privacy. On this, the second occasion that the family visited the farm near Wisbech in Cambridgeshire, they arrived to find that there were no bunks left for the twins – or for their friend Pat Butler, who had come along this time. Bill Shippey, the farmer, had no hesitation in telling the family that the boys were welcome to stay with him and his wife Mavis in the farmhouse.[46] Terrors on the streets

---

46 *Park House*, 160 Gorefield Road, Leverington, Wisbech PE13 5BE. Built in 1720, *Park House* is a Grade II listed, early Georgian, private residence in the Cambridgeshire fenlands, and it is here that the Kray

of Bethnal Green the twins may have been, but otherwise they were generally respectful, thoughtful, and polite towards most older people. Bill Shippey and Mavis were impressed by the boys' behaviour, and so began a long-term friendship that would continue into the prison years.[47]

Ambitions and aspirations in the world of work were not the driving force in the young twins' lives – far more important was their boxing and their status in the local area as street fighters – but they needed to earn a few quid, so after returning to the East End in the autumn of 1949, they began a succession of short-lived, casual labouring jobs. Charles, their father, did nothing to encourage the twins to seek advancement in the world of legitimate employment, telling them instead that getting up at the crack of dawn and working for a *guv'nr* was a mug's game.

Sometimes, the work they found provided the opportunity to supplement their wages by stealing and selling goods. While working in the packing department at *Joyce's Lingerie* in Old Street, Reggie made more money than he was paid by stealing and selling ladies' underwear – and, while working at a perfume factory, the size of the product made it easy to conceal a few bottles in his clothes. Stacking crates of beer at *Truman's Brewery* on Brick Lane provided a change of scenery but the work, as usual, was boring and tedious. Getting through the day was made a little easier for both twins as they helped themselves to much more than the daily allowance of two pints of light or brown ale, consequently spending the day in a mild stupor.[48]

---

twins stayed with the Shippey family for several weeks in the summer of 1949 while fruit picking in the nearby fields.

47 Gorefield in the Past Facebook group. Kray, Reggie and Gerrard, Peter. *Reggie Kray's East End Stories*. London: Sphere, 2010.

48 Ibid.

Truman's Brewery

Brick Lane, London E1 6RU

Nearest TFL station: Shoreditch High Street overground.

The Black Eagle Brewery on Brick Lane was originally founded in the 1660s. Joseph Truman took control of the brewery in the 1680s and, over the next 200 years, *Truman's Brewery* expanded – eventually, in 1873, becoming the largest brewery in the world. In the 20th century, following the rise of large consolidated British brewing companies, *Truman's* failed to successfully compete and the brewery closed in 1989.

In 1949, the 16-year-old Kray twins began a series of transient jobs which lasted for just a few weeks. One such job was stacking crates at *Truman's Brewery*.

Most of the buildings on Brick Lane between Woodseer Street and Buxton Street – now home to a variety of businesses – were part of the brewery complex. The large building known as the *Boiler House* – built in the 1830s, and to which the iconic *TRUMAN* chimney was added in 1930 – is currently a venue for exhibitions, parties, and cultural events.

Eventually, unable to stand the tedium of menial jobs for more than a few weeks at a time, the need to earn some money drove the twins to their last resort: they joined their father and brother Charlie *on the knocker*. Neither of the twins possessed *the gift of the gab*, so going door to door and persuading householders to part with old clothes and jewellery was not something they were good at or enjoyed. Even so, they stuck it out on an occasional basis until, in 1952, they were called up for their National Service in the army. Meanwhile, their reputation for violence was growing, and an increase in the use of weapons in teenage gang fights was a trend that the twins embraced wholeheartedly. Ronnie in particular was obsessed with weapons and began collecting an array of knives, razors, coshes, bayonets, swords, and even a couple of handguns, which he would hide in a box under his bed at Vallance Road.

In 1947, the twins' uncle, John (Violet's younger brother) and his wife Maude had opened *Lee's Cafe* at 119 Cheshire Street,[49] opposite the twins' Vallance Road home. Now, the 16-year-old twins, having no full-time employment and spending only odd days working with their father, took to hanging around the cafe during the day.

Another regular at the cafe – sometimes accompanied by his villainous friend, Tommy Venables (father of the twins 'friend, Shaun Venables) – was Bobby Ramsey. Having first met Ramsey through boxing, the 16-year-old twins soon fell under the influence of the older boxer and villain. Ramsey, who no doubt saw potential in the young twins, was a hard man who – among his other misdeeds – was associated with London's top villain and gang boss, Billy Hill. Always eager to hear stories of fighting and violence from anyone, the twins were transfixed by Ramsey's tales of beatings and cuttings dished out by one or received by another.

From this time onwards, Bobby Ramsey remained closely involved with the twins, sometimes playing a bit part in their story, while at other times taking centre stage. Mesmerising the young twins was one thing, but Ramsey's charm was such that, a few years hence, he even managed to attract the interest of

---

49   Bennet, John. *Krayology*. London: Mango Books, 2015.

the twins' pretty young cousin Rita, who accompanied him on a few dates – but who lost interest when she discovered more about his lifestyle. In later life, Ramsey – who died in 2004, aged 82 – was involved in the security business and worked as a film extra/actor, making brief appearances in various television and film productions including *The Sweeney*, *The New Avengers*, *Quadrophenia*, and two *Carry On* films.

Apart from the occasional day spent working with their father and brother, much of the twins' time was taken up by the most important pursuit for many 16-year-old boys: hanging around with their friends and discussing the latest gossip in the world of fighting. *Petticoat Lane Market* was a regular rendezvous on Sunday mornings and, one such time – while congregating with their friends outside *Ziggy's Cafe* in Cobb Street – the twins saw the man who topped the list of the who's who of fighting men. Moving through the parting crowd towards *Ziggy's*, and cutting an impressive dash in his beautifully tailored American gangster-style clothes, was the legendary Jewish East End gangster, Jack Spot – with two of his senior lieutenants, Moishe Blueboy and Little Hymie Rosen, in tow.

Some years later, the twins would come to know Jack Spot well and, although not directly instrumental in his demise, they would be quick to step into his shoes and crown themselves Kings of the East End Underworld.

Ziggy's Cafe

4 Cobb Street, Spitalfields, London E1 7LB

Nearest TFL station: Aldgate East underground.

Ziggy's Cafe – close to the site of *Petticoat Lane Market* – was, in the late 1940s and early 50s, a hangout of choice for the young Kray twins and their friends. *Ziggy's* was also an occasional meeting place for the CEO of East End villainy at this time: Jack Spot and his associates. Ziggy, the cafe owner, was a friend of Jack Spot and, like Spot, he was Jewish and tough – ever ready with his trusty truncheon to deal with troublemakers.

Happily, the building at number 4 Cobb Street still stands, and the premises that were once *Ziggy's Cafe* are currently a Fancy Goods shop, which has been closed and empty for some time.

Word of the twins' exploits was spreading, and the level of violence they were using was steadily ramping up. Finding themselves barred from many of the cinemas and dance halls in their immediate vicinity, the twins and their ever-growing gang of followers were beginning to seek fun – and meet the challenge of other gangs – beyond the borders of Bethnal Green.

One of many incidents leading to a lack of places to go in Bethnal Green took place at the twins' local cinema. After the manager of the *Rex Cinema*[50] in Bethnal Green Road told the twins and their friends, *"I don't want you lot in here causing trouble,"* Ronnie hit the man on the chin and sent him to the floor.[51] Fighting with other teenagers who are looking for trouble is one thing, but attacking a man just doing his job is another. It appears, at this point in their lives, the twins felt justified in attacking anyone who incurred their displeasure – and no one, no matter who or what they were, was off limits.

---

50   281-285 Bethnal Green Road, London E2 6AH. Originally opened as *Smart's Picture House* in 1913, the cinema was remodelled in the Art Deco style and opened as the *Rex Cinema* in 1938. In December of 1949 the cinema was taken over; it was renamed *The Essoldo* and remained open until 1964. The building was demolished in 2020 and the site currently remains empty, awaiting redevelopment.

51   Kray, Reggie and Gerrard, Peter. *Reggie Kray's East End Stories*. London: Sphere, 2010.

Hackney Empire, situated a mile and a half away from the twins' home turf in Bethnal Green, became a favourite haunt for the twins and their gang, both to watch the show and to look out for rival youth gangs. One night, while sitting in the gods (cheap seats), Reggie noticed a young gang leader who had apparently been broadcasting his intention to get his hands on one of the twins. After seeing the youth in question leave his seat and head for the toilets, Reggie followed him and smashed the youth in the face with a length of bicycle chain, causing severe injuries to his nose and mouth. Satisfied with his work, and knowing that the incident would serve to enhance his reputation, Reggie left his victim moaning and bleeding heavily on the toilet floor.[52]

Hackney Empire

291 Mare Street, London E8 1EJ

Nearest TFL station: Hackney Central overground.

Built and opened in 1901 as a music hall, *Hackney Empire* staged variety shows featuring the greatest show business names of the day. Among the stars topping the bill at various times during the first half of the 20th century were Marie Lloyd, Stan Laurel, Charlie Chaplin, W C Fields, and George Formby.

In 1949, the 16-year-old Kray twins and their friends took to frequenting *Hackney Empire* to watch the show and, at the same time, look for trouble with other gangs. On at least one occasion, the violence was extreme and

---

52   Ibid.

left one youth badly injured after Reggie Kray smashed him in the face with a piece of bicycle chain.

Hackney Empire was bought by ABC in the mid-1950s and used as a television studio for several years. In 1963, the theatre became a bingo hall and a venue for 1960s-style *all-in wrestling*. In 1984, *Hackney Empire* became a theatre once again, staging shows featuring the new brand of *alternative comedy*. Today, the beautifully restored and refurbished Victorian/Edwardian theatre is an iconic venue for comedy, music, opera, theatrical productions, television awards, and pantomimes.

Around this time, when they were 16, the twins began frequenting *The Royal*, a cavernous dance hall in Tottenham where gangs from different areas of North and East London gathered, creating an atmosphere of simmering tension that would inevitably lead to violence erupting at the drop of a hat. Billy Webb, who – along with his brother Ron – led the dominant gang of Tottenham boys at *The Royal* – remembers the twins accompanied by around 20 friends, sitting poker-faced and glaring, waiting for the opportunity to do what they did best…and what they enjoyed the most.

Billy and the Tottenham boys – who referred to Ronnie Kray as 'boot nose'– realised their top-tier position was under threat and that it was just a matter of time before there would be a showdown. Eventually, the cold war looked like it was about to turn hot when word came through that the Krays were coming over on Saturday to take revenge on one of the Tottenham boys for insulting a girl. The boy in question had asked the girl to dance and when she refused he said, *"What are you, a fucking Princess?"* Unbeknown to him, the girl was Rita, the twins' cousin. Preparations were made and Billy Webb and his boys were 'tooled up' and ready, but on this occasion, it seems that both sides decided that discretion was the better part of valour and it was agreed that an apology would end the matter. Peace was restored after the Tottenham boy was made to stand in front of an audience and humiliatingly beg Rita for her forgiveness.[53] This fragile détente between the two gangs held for a while, but there would be plenty more violence and bloodshed at *The Royal* over the next year or two.

The Tottenham Royal

417 High Road, Tottenham, London N17 6RD

Nearest TFL station: Bruce Grove overground.

Originally opened in 1910, the building was initially a roller skating rink, changing a year later to an ice-skating venue called *The Canadian Rink*. In 1925, it was converted to a dance hall and renamed *The Tottenham Palais*. Later, it was acquired by the Mecca Leisure Group and became *The Tottenham Royal*.

The Kray twins and their gang began spending time at *The Royal* in late 1949, when they were 16, and could be found there fairly regularly until they turned their attention elsewhere around 1953. *The Royal* was a gathering place for gangs of youths from different areas of London, and the main attraction for the twins was the prospect of a fight – and the opportunity to enhance and spread their reputation for violence.

During the early post-war years when the twins were

---

53   Webb, Billy. *Running With the Krays*. Edinburgh: Mainstream Publishing, 1993.

regulars, big dance bands led by Ted Heath, Joe Loss, and Victor Silvester played at *The Royal*. Later, as the 1950s wore on, *The Royal* ushered in the new music era, hosting bands playing rock and roll. During the 1960s, the music was provided by resident local band *The Dave Clark Five*, plus many guest artists who would go on to become '60s legends – including *The Animals, Manfred Mann, The Troggs*, and *The Who*. The 1970s saw *The Royal* host regular disco, soul, and reggae nights and, from the 1980s onwards, the building underwent several transformations and new identities including *The Mayfair Suite, The Temple, The United Nations Club*, and *The Zone*. In 2004, the building was demolished and replaced by a row of shops with residential apartments above.

The dawn of the 1950s saw the BBC broadcast its first election results programme; Labour won the election and Clement Attlee began a second term as Britain's Prime Minister. Britain sent 4,000 troops to Korea where the Cold War was developing a hotspot, and Albert Pierrepoint – Britain's chief hangman and jovial landlord of the *Help the Poor Struggler* pub in Oldham, executed one of his regular customers found guilty of murder.

The disturbing increase in the use of weapons in teenage gang fights, and the Kray twins' willingness to use them, was leading Ron and Reg down a path that ran perilously close to a meeting with Mr Pierrepoint – in his professional capacity.

On the evening of Sunday 12 March 1950, the twins and their gang visited *Barrie's Dance Hall* in Mare Street, Hackney. There was no trouble inside the dance hall that night, but around 11 pm, as Roy Harvey – a clerk from Dalston – and a group of friends, which included Wally Birch and Dennis Siegenberg,[54] left the premises to make their way home, they became aware that they were being followed by a large group of youths about 30-strong. Suddenly, Harvey and his friends were set-upon by the larger group. Harvey's companions managed to escape and run away, but Harvey was punched to the ground, kicked, and viciously beaten with a variety of weapons, including chains and a cosh. After the frenzied attack, a young woman present tried to help Harvey as he lay badly injured on the pavement in a pool of blood. Next to him, were two abandoned lavatory chains with handles and a length of bicycle chain.

Harvey was taken to hospital by ambulance where he was found to have severe injuries consistent with the use of heavy objects and a chain. Witnesses to the attack told the police that the Kray twins were involved, and they were arrested along with 18-year-old Thomas Organ and 17-year-old Patrick Aucott. Charged with causing GBH, the twins were at first held in police custody and then taken to appear at *North London Magistrates Court* where they were placed on remand and sent to *Wormwood Scrubs*.

---

54   In 1967 in Newcastle, Dennis Siegenberg was convicted of the murder of Angus Sibbet in a case known as the '*one-armed bandit murder*,' serving 12 years in prison.

Barrie's Dance Hall

372 & 374 Mare Street, London, E8 1HR

Nearest TFL station: Hackney Central overground.

Barrie's was a school of dance, which – in the 1950s – doubled as an evening meeting place, featuring music, for young people.

In March 1950, the 16-year-old Kray twins were involved in a vicious attack outside the dance hall on a youth by the name of Roy Harvey. Harvey suffered serious injuries resulting from the use of chains and other heavy objects used as weapons.

The ground floor of the building that was once *Barrie's Dance Hall* is now the *Nationwide Building Society*, and the upper floor area is a martial arts studio (now closed).

Harvey was reluctant to give evidence in court but, after some persuasion by the police, he agreed to take the stand. Following several appearances at the magistrates court, during which it came to light that Harvey had been threatened and the young woman witness warned that her face would be slashed with a razor if she gave evidence, the twins were sent for trial by jury at the *Central Criminal Court*. Local newspaper reports of the committal proceedings quote the magistrate as saying,*" This boy has been beaten by beasts."*

North London Magistrates Court

82 Stoke Newington Road, London N16 7XB

Nearest TFL station: Dalston Kingsland overground.

Between 1889 and 1965, the purpose-built redbrick and white stone late Victorian building was a magistrates court. The Kray twins made several appearances here in March and April 1950, charged with GBH following the attack on Roy Harvey outside *Barrie's Dance Hall*. The twins were remanded in custody and the case was sent to be heard at the *Old Bailey*.

After the closure of the magistrates court in 1965, the building lay empty for years. During the late 1990s, an organised squatters group occupied the building for a period to provide shelter for refugees. Now, following a recent conversion to residential apartments, the building is called *St John's Court*.

During the trial at the *Old Bailey* in early May, the twins admitted throwing a few punches but denied using any weapons. As the trial progressed, witness statements were withdrawn, identification of the accused became *uncertain*, and the extent of the twins' involvement remained unsubstantiated. After hearing the evidence, or lack of it, the judge dismissed the case and the twins were acquitted. It appears that even as 16-year-olds, the Kray twins were powerful and feared enough to influence the outcome of a trial.

During the course of the trial, Father Hetherington – the vicar at *St James the Great Church* in Bethnal Green – spoke up for the twins as a character witness, telling the court, perhaps naively, that this recent behaviour was out of character, doubtless a *one-off*, and that they were essentially good, kind boys who, he believed, would see the error of their ways and never again stray from the straight and narrow. Ron and Reg liked Father Hetherington and, as youngsters and members of the church youth club, they were polite, respectful, and always willing to help out at jumble sales and other church activities. It seems that, on this occasion, this *other side* to the twins' characters had earned them some money in the bank.

Apart from being bound over to keep the peace following an incident with an air rifle in 1946, the 16-year-old Kray twins had no serious criminal records. Towards the end of 1950, less than six months after their acquittal from a charge of GBH, another brush with the law left the twins with the first serious blot on their copybook.

One day, in the early autumn of 1950, Ronnie Kray and a group of friends were gathered in the street, outside a cafe in Bethnal Green, when they were approached by a policeman. Accounts vary as to exactly what happened next but, following an exchange of words, Constable Donald Baynton either grabbed Ronnie's arm, poked him in the stomach, or pushed him hard in the back. Whatever the provocation, Ronnie proceeded to punch the policeman in the face.

Most accounts say that the incident took place outside *Pellicci's* cafe on Bethnal Green Road, but Ronnie's close friend Laurie O'Leary stated, with assurance, that it happened outside *Hookers* cafe on the corner of Mape Street.[55] In 1950, there were three cafes in fairly close proximity on Bethnal Green Road. *E Pellicci* at number 332 (still trading

---

55   TV documentary, *Reggie Kray: The Final Word*. Blue Post Production, Mission Television, Murder My Darlings, Warner Vision International, 2001.

today), another *E Pellicci* run by a different family member, two doors along at number 338 (now *Cafe 338*), and *Hookers Refreshment Bar* at number 382 (now 380, *Rani Jewels*), on the corner of what was then Mape Street. Following the enlargement of *Weavers Fields Park* in the 1960s, the north end of Mape Street became Derbyshire Street.

E Pellicci

332 Bethnal Green Road, London, E2 OAG

Nearest TFL station: Bethnal Green underground.

The wonderful Anglo-Italian cafe, with its delightful, original, Grade II listed Art Deco interior, has been run by the Pellicci family since 1900. Today, it is a must-see (and a must-eat) destination for anyone with an interest in the Krays.

Ron and Reg were regulars at the cafe from childhood until the time of their arrest, and many-a-morning they could be found here enjoying breakfast, often in the company of their associates. During the Krays' time, the cafe was run by Nevio Pellicci and his wife Maria. *Pellicci's* became so popular that a second cafe was opened two doors along at number 338, which was run by Nevio's brother Terry until its closure in the 1980s. Number 338 is still an eatery, now called *Cafe 338*.

Pellicci's cafe has been used as a location for numerous television productions and several feature films – most notably the 2015 Krays biopic *Legend* starring Tom Hardy.

Following the assault on PC Baynton, Ronnie was arrested; he was taken to *Bethnal Green Police Station*, pushed into a cell, and given a beating by a number of police officers. Later, he was charged with assaulting a police officer and released on bail. When Reggie discovered what had happened to his brother he went looking for Baynton, found him, delivered several more punches to his face, and ran off. Later that evening, an inspector arrived at Vallance Road accompanied by PC Baynton, who looked the worse for wear. Eventually, after some arguing, it was agreed that if Reggie gave himself up and nothing more was said about police brutality towards 16-year-old Ronnie, Reggie would be treated well by the police and they would do all they could to ensure leniency by the court.

Reggie duly handed himself in and both twins appeared at *Old Street Magistrates Court* on 1 November charged with assaulting a police officer. Leniency was indeed granted; the twins were given two years' probation and allowed to go.

Bethnal Green Police Station

458 Bethnal Green Road, London E2 OEA

Nearest TFL station: Bethnal Green underground.

Replacing an earlier Victorian police station, the building on Bethnal Green Road – which was completed in 1911 – was, until the early 1990s, *Bethnal Green Police Station*.

Following an assault on PC Donald Baynton in October 1950, Ronnie Kray was arrested, taken to the police station, placed in a cell and, allegedly, given a punitive slap or two. The twins would find themselves at this police station on several occasions in the future, the next time being in 1952 after they were arrested for desertion from the army during their compulsory National Service days.

In 1931, author George Orwell had an overnight stay in the cells. Orwell spent a period of time immersing himself in the seamier side of East End life to draw inspiration for his writing, and deliberately set out to be arrested for drunkenness. In his famous dystopian novel *1984*, it is said that his description of the cells at the *Ministry of Love* was inspired by his night in the cells at *Bethnal Green Police Station*.

The former police station building on Bethnal Green Road – next to *The Shakespeare* pub, on the corner of Ainsley Street – is now a hostel offering budget accommodation for female travellers called *Hostelle*. Bethnal Green's current police station is situated a short distance away at 12 Victoria Park Square.

Continuing to assert themselves and wanting to meet the challenge of other gangs in areas beyond Bethnal Green, the twins and their crew would prepare for an evening out – where trouble was likely – by selecting a weapon from the Vallance Road armoury, stashed in a box under Ronnie's bed.

As Reggie Kray later said, *"We spilt a lot of blood in those days but the sight of it never had the slightest effect on us."*[56]

Sometimes, Reg Kray's weapon of choice was a sword that he would conceal down a trouser leg. His only problem with carrying (or using) the potentially lethal implement was that it was difficult to sit down on the bus that took them to their

---

56   Kray, Reggie and Gerrard, Peter. *Reggie Kray's East End Stories.* London: Sphere, 2010.

chosen venue. Other times, when trouble wasn't necessarily expected, the twins would venture out without being *tooled up*, confident in their ability to deal with any problems using their fists alone. One such incident occurred when the twins were 17, and has since become fabled in the Kray twins' story, probably also providing the inspiration for a memorable and shocking fight scene in the 2015 Krays biopic *Legend*.

Late one evening, Ronnie and the twins' friend Pat Butler were enjoying a drink in *The Coach and Horses* pub on the Mile End Road when, just before last orders, they were joined by Reggie. Ronnie told Reggie that he was just in time as he'd been receiving threatening looks from a nine-strong local gang gathered at the other end of the bar. Trouble was inevitable and, knowing that Pat Butler was not a fighter, the twins told him to make himself scarce.

Without having to discuss in detail what they were going to do next, the telepathically linked twins ran out of the door, giving the impression that they were scared. Four members of the local gang followed but lost the twins as they ran, ducked into an alleyway, and then doubled back and re-entered the pub by the other door. Now with the odds improved in the twins' favour, Ronnie and Reggie set about the remaining five members of the gang, tearing into them ferociously and leaving them with nowhere to go but the floor. Thinking they'd lost the twins to the London streets, the remaining four youths went back to the pub and met the same fate as their friends.

This was by no means the only time that the twins prevailed against superior numbers, but the *Coach and Horses* incident elevated the twins' reputation in the East End to almost mythical heights.

The Coach and Horses

380 Mile End Road, London E1 4RQ

Nearest TFL station: Stepney Green underground.

From a position standing outside *Queen Mary University People's Palace* at 327 Mile End Road, if you look directly across Mile End Road you will see the site of the former *Coach and Horses* pub. It was demolished in the 1960s to make way for the large modern housing estate that now takes up the south side of this part of Mile

End Road. Happily, *The Bancroft Arms* – still displaying its original *Truman's* signage and just a few yards from where *The Coach and Horses* once stood – survived the large-scale demolition project and is still trading today.

Not to be confused with *The Coach and Horses* in Stoke Newington – which features later on in the Krays' story – this pub was, in 1951, the scene of the legendary pub brawl where Ron and Reg took on a nine-strong local gang and emerged victorious, with a much-enhanced reputation as unbeatable street fighters.

Having decided to take their boxing to the next level, the twins turned professional in 1951 under the management of Jack Jordan, who also managed their brother Charlie. Harry 'Kid' Berry continued as the twins' trainer, but as licensed professional boxers, they moved on from the Repton amateur club and began training and sparring with other professionals at *Jack Solomons Gym*[57] in Soho and *Bill Klein's Gym* in nearby Fitzrovia, both of which they had visited previously when their brother Charlie had taken them there to meet some of the well-known professionals of the day, who were happy to spar a few rounds with the keen young amateurs.

---

57   41 Great Windmill Street, Soho, London W1D 7NB. Retaining the name of the famous boxing promoter, the former boxing gym is now *Jack Solomons Club*, an exclusive speakeasy-style cocktail club.

Bill Klein's Olympic Gym

46 Fitzroy Street, London W1T 5BR

Nearest TFL station: Warren Street underground.

Born in Bochum, Germany on 26 October 1866, trapeze artist, wrestler, weightlifter, and boxer William Hugo Klein settled in London around the turn of the last century, where he ran gyms in various parts of the city. Professor Bill Klein opened his last gym in 1930, in the basement of 46 Fitzroy Street, and kept it running until his death – aged 90 – in 1957. Klein's gym was a no-frills establishment with an aroma of liniment oil and sweat, but with an atmosphere that appealed to many fighters – including the Kray twins, who trained here both as amateurs and professionals.[58]

Now a private residence, stone steps lead down to the basement of the Grade II listed Georgian building where Klein's gym was located.

Ronnie and Reggie, aged 17, made their debut as professional boxers on the same bill at the famous East End boxing venue, the *Mile End Arena* on 31 July 1951. Ronnie, fighting at welterweight, stopped his opponent Bernie Long in the second round of a scheduled six-round contest, and Reggie, boxing at lightweight, easily outpointed Bobby Manito over six rounds.

58   Daley, Alex. *Fighting Men of London*. Durrington: Pitch Publishing, 2014.

Mile End Arena

Maplin Street, London E3 4SX

Nearest TFL station: Mile End underground.

Mile End Arena was a ramshackle, open-air site – described by some as a 'bear pit'– with only a hut for the boxers to change and no showers, not even a tap. To prevent their boxing boots from getting dirty, fighters were carried piggyback through the crowd to the ring. With walls of crumbling, whitewashed brickwork and rickety corrugated iron, the arena could hold up to 2,000 spectators, some of whom simply climbed the walls to get in and watch the fights taking place in a ring with a canopy above, which sometimes needed to be held up with a broom when it rained. Basic and near derelict the arena may have been, but the atmosphere there was apparently second to no other venue and is remembered fondly by fighters and spectators alike. Ronnie and Reggie Kray boxed here in their first professional fights on 31 July 1951.

Having first opened for boxing in April 1933, the arena held its last show in September 1953; it had to close due to the introduction of a heavy tax on live entertainment, which put many small-time promoters out of business. Boxing matches were held during the summer only; during the winter, the site became a fairground, which of course included the obligatory boxing booth.[59]

Directly behind Mile End tube station is *Coopers*

---

59 www.boxingnewsonline.net

> *Court,* a student halls of residence complex and it is here that the East End's most iconic boxing arena was located.

Both twins were showing promise – especially Reggie, whose ring-craft demonstrated that he had the potential to go on to bigger things. After Reggie's six professional fights and Ronnie's five, the twins were making a mark in the boxing world and gradually progressing towards a higher position in the rankings. Reggie, employing his talented, stylish, disciplined approach, had won all six of his fights on points. Ronnie had won four, all inside the distance; indicative of his powerful, aggressive, slugging style. Ronnie's only loss was due to a disqualification in the second round of his last fight.

One sure sign of a boxer's upward trajectory in the 1950s was an appearance at one of London's two most prestigious boxing venues: *Harringay Arena* or *The Royal Albert Hall*. All three Kray brothers – Ronnie, Reggie, and Charlie – were on the bill at *The Royal Albert Hall* on 12 December 1951.

First up was Ron, who started well and had his opponent, Bill Sliney, down for a count of eight in the first round – but, after an accidental clash of heads, Ron's left eye began to close and he found it difficult to see. Bill Sliney boxed cleverly, taking advantage of Ron's blind side, and won a narrow points victory after six hard-fought rounds.

Next up was Reg, who displayed all the talent and skill of the gifted boxer he was, winning a decisive points victory against Bobby Manito – the same opponent he'd beaten in his first professional fight five months earlier.

The last of the three brothers to fight was Charlie, who hadn't fought for almost a year but who took the fight to get some extra money for Christmas. Vicious body punches sent Charlie to his knees three times before he was eventually stopped in the third round by the unbeaten and very talented Lew Lazar from Aldgate.

Afterwards, in the dressing room, all three brothers were in good spirits, laughing and joking as Jack Jordan arrived to give the three warriors their well-earned pay. Knowing that this was to be Charlie's last fight, Jack handed Charlie his full £25 purse without taking his manager's cut.

As it turned out, this was to be the last time that any of the three brothers would fight in the ring as licensed professionals. Looming on the horizon was an altogether different kind of fight in which the twins would take on their biggest opponent yet – the British Army.[60]

In February 1952, at age 56, King George VI died of lung cancer and the 25-year-old Princess Elizabeth became Britain's new Queen. Later in the year, Prime Minister Winston Churchill announced that the United Kingdom had an atomic bomb. Bill and Ben the *Flower Pot Men*, and Harry Corbett's glove puppet *Sooty*, appeared on TV for the first time, watched by a mere 14 per cent of the population who were lucky enough to own a television set. London smog, an almost ever-present feature of life in the capital, took a turn for the worse in December and produced the worst *pea-souper* yet experienced, claiming an estimated 4,000 lives. On Wednesday 21 May 1952, London crime boss Billy Hill masterminded Britain's largest post-war robbery. The Eastcastle Street Robbery netted Billy and his gang £287,000 – around 8.5 million in today's money.

Meanwhile, back at Vallance Road, Ronnie and Reggie – having turned 18 in October of the previous year – awaited the arrival of their call-up papers, summoning them to report for

---

60   Fry, Colin and Kray, Charlie. *Doing the Business*. London: John Blake Publishing, 2011.

their compulsory National Service in the armed forces.

Following the Second World War and continuing until 1960, Britain required all healthy young men between 17 and 21 years of age to serve Queen and country in the armed forces for a period of two years. Between 1949 and 1960, most young men received their call-up papers shortly after their 18th birthday. Small numbers were conscripted into the RAF, fewer still into the Royal Navy; by far the majority of young men served their time in the British Army.

February 1952 saw the expected arrival of two brown envelopes at Vallance Road, instructing the twins to report to the *Tower of London* to join the Royal Fusiliers (City of London Regiment). Ron and Reg were certainly not interested in joining the army and wearing a "*bloody stupid uniform*" but, on condition that they could pursue their boxing and become physical training instructors, they decided to give it a try.

On 20 March 1952, wearing their best blue suits, the twins arrived at the *Tower* to begin what was about to be a two-year-long personal battle with the British Army. Acceptance of authority – especially uniformed authority – was an alien concept to Ron and Reg. Rules imposed by outsiders were not applicable in the twins' world, where those who gained their admiration and respect generally did so by breaking rules rather than following them. This, along with the fact that their father had been on the trot from the army throughout most of their childhood, meant that knuckling down to two years of army discipline was never really on the cards.

Waterloo Barracks

The Tower of London, London EC3N 4AB

Nearest TFL station: Tower Hill underground.

Waterloo Barracks is a large, imposing, neo-Gothic-style building within the walls of the *Tower of London*, which was – until 1960 – home to the Royal Fusiliers (London Regiment). Built in 1845 by the then Constable of the Tower, the Duke of Wellington, the barracks could accommodate up to 1,000 soldiers. In 1960, the London Regiment left *Waterloo Barracks* and, in 1968, the London Regiment amalgamated with the Royal Northumberland Fusiliers, the Royal Warwickshire Fusiliers, and the Lancashire Fusiliers to form the Royal Regiment of Fusiliers. *Waterloo Barracks* – now known simply as the *Waterloo Block* – currently houses the Crown Jewels. The adjacent building, formerly the officers' quarters, is now *The Fusilier Museum* and remains the administrative headquarters of the regiment.

Ronnie and Reggie Kray first arrived here on Thursday 20 March 1952 to begin their compulsory National Service, but what was supposed to be two years of army life turned into a period of multiple desertions, recaptures, lock-ups, and eventual dishonourable discharge in November 1953.

After reporting for duty at the *Tower*, the twins – along with the other recruits – were herded together, shouted at by NCOs, issued with kit, and marched to their accommodation. Next came the shouted lecture on how fortunate they were to be accepted into the ranks of the esteemed and historic regiment. After listening to a corporal expounding loudly on the rules of conduct, regulations, and the maintenance of kit, the twins decided they weren't going to put up with all this army nonsense. Glancing at each other, and with no words necessary, Ron and Reg began to walk away.

"And where might you be going?" asked the corporal.

"We don't like it here; we're off home to see our mum," was the reply, as the twins continued to walk towards the door.

Outraged at the audacity of the two young upstarts, the corporal grabbed Ronnie by the arm. True to form, a well-aimed punch connected with the corporal's jaw and sent him sprawling. Nonchalantly, the twins strolled unchallenged out of the *Tower*'s main gate and were home at Vallance Road in time for tea.

After spending the evening at *The Tottenham Royal*, the twins were woken the next morning by the expected arrival of the police at Vallance Road, at which point they were arrested and taken to *Bethnal Green Police Station*. Within a short time, soldiers arrived, handcuffed the twins, and escorted them back to the *Tower* where they were placed in *Waterloo Barracks* cells, under the clock tower.

The twins were fortunate to receive only one week of incarceration in the cells. Striking a corporal is a serious offence that would normally warrant a more severe punishment, but as it happened on their very first day in the army – and as it could not be determined exactly which twin had delivered the blow – the commanding officer decided to exercise leniency.

Confusing and confounding authority figures as to which of the then identical twins had actually done the deed *("No sir, not me sir!")* was a ploy the twins had used to their advantage in the past, and would do so again in the future. This was to be the first of numerous escape and recapture events and, after this – the first of their jaunts – the twins were joined in the punishment cells by another East End bad lad, Dickie Morgan.

Hailing from Mile End and conscripted into the Fusiliers after serving a sentence in *Portland Borstal*, Morgan was a serial thief who'd spent most of his life to date thieving, dodging the police, and doing time in approved schools and borstals. His total disregard for authority – coupled with a wicked sense of humour – appealed to the twins, and he would remain one of their closest friends and associates throughout their criminal careers.

Conditions for prisoners in the punishment cells were harsh, but sleeping on bare boards and eating the minimum rations of poor food didn't bother the twins much at all. In fact, they treated the experience as a bit of a lark and an opportunity to exercise their toughness. After a week, they were released to begin some serious soldiering but, predictably, this was not to be; they took advantage of the relaxed security and escaped again, this time taking Dickie Morgan with them.

Dickie Morgan lived with his family at 32 Clinton Road, close to Mile End tube station, and this – the first of many visits to Dickie Morgan's house throughout their time on the run from the army – proved to be an eye-opening experience for Ron and Reg. Despite the fact that the twins' close family were fighters and wheeler-dealers, they were essentially law-abiding. The Morgan family, on the other hand, were dyed-in-the-wool criminals. Dickie's father was just beginning a prison sentence for his part in a warehouse robbery, and two of Dickie's brothers were likewise serving time at Her Majesty's pleasure.

Dickie's mother welcomed the twins into her home and busied herself cooking bacon and eggs for two more brothers, the three deserters, and the constant traffic of local criminals dropping in and passing through. Chez Morgan was, for the twins, a fascinating and inspiring place where they were entertained by stories of audacious criminal capers and given a glimpse into an exciting world of anarchy and adventure.

Dickie Morgan's House

32 Clinton Road, Bow, London, E3 4QY

Nearest TFL station: Mile End underground.

Clinton Road is located just off Grove Road on the north side of Mile End Road. Most of the terraced houses from number 37 to 96 still exist but, sadly, Dickie Morgan's house has gone; it would have occupied a spot in what is now *Mile End Park*.

32 Clinton Road was the home of the twins' close friend Dickie Morgan and was visited frequently by Ron and Reg Kray during their time on the run from the army in 1952.

Very close by is the aptly named Morgan Street, where Ronnie would later, in 1956, be arrested following an attack on Terrence Martin.

Unable to stay too long – as the army would have, by now, contacted the local constabulary and given them the escapees' addresses – the twins and Dickie Morgan snatched a few hours' sleep at Clinton Road and were up and off over the garden wall before dawn.

Throughout the summer of 1952, an absurd cat-and-mouse game of escape and recapture played out. Long periods on the run – followed by stiffer sentences and ever stronger, unheeded warnings by the commanding officer – became routine. Occasionally, there were very brief periods where it looked as though the twins might settle down and tow the army line. They even made it as far as the .303 rifle range at Purfleet, where both Ron and Reg demonstrated an exceptional lack of ability to shoot straight.[61] But such periods were short-lived anomalies and it was just a matter of time before the twins would be off *on the trot* once again.

As they were on the run from the army during frequent periods in 1952, the twins needed to survive without any fixed accommodation or income. They were unable to stay in one place for any length of time as they knew it wouldn't be long before the police came knocking. Most days were spent drinking endless cups of tea in cafes, where they felt safe, and evenings at various dance halls and other haunts – including a seedy snooker club on Eric Street called *The Regal*. Nights were spent at a variety of locations where friends and acquaintances in the criminal world could provide a safe place for them to grab a few hours' sleep.

Wally's Cafe in Hackney was a regular bolt-hole. Wally – the owner, and sympathetic to their plight – would often provide the twins with a meal and, on at least one occasion, let them stay in the cafe overnight to sleep. Wally welcomed the criminal fraternity to his cafe and was himself a dabbler in the dishonest. Following a dispute over a consignment of stolen whiskey the previous year (1951), Wally had taken a beating from the prominent London hardman, Buller Ward.[62]

In the early 1950s, *Wally's Cafe* was a popular hang-out for local criminals, including the notorious Nash brothers from Islington, Ronnie Diamond and his Diamond Gang, and the highly respected guv'nr of the manor, Tommy *Scarface* Smithson. Handsome, dapper, and dangerous, with a fearsome reputation, Smithson was an imposing figure with a majestic

61   Pearson, John. *The Profession of Violence*. London: Weidenfeld and Nicolson, 1972.

62   Ward, Henry and Weeks, David. *Bullets, Blood and Broken Bodies*. New Breed Publishing, 2008.

presence that impressed the young Kray twins. These older, well-established criminal characters – and Smithson in particular – were, in the twins' eyes, fine examples of what a man should aspire to be. It was important to them, therefore, to be known in these circles and to forge friendships that could be useful in the future.

Wally's Cafe

13 Well Street, London E9 7QX

Nearest TFL station: London Fields overground.

Located close to London Fields and Hackney bus garage, *The Regal Cafe* – known to its patrons as Wally's – was a daytime haunt for local criminals. For the Kray twins, who in 1952 were on the run from the army, it was a safe place to spend time, scrounge a meal, and build relationships with more senior members of the criminal fraternity.

Hackney bus garage closed in 1981, and the site at 27 Well Street is now a Lidl supermarket. A little further west along Well Street – at number 13, on the corner of Weston Walk – is the site of *Wally's Cafe*, now *Perfect Fried Chicken*. Wally's is often described as being '*right next*' to the bus garage. Immediately behind the building on Weston Walk is the entrance to an army cadet base, occupying an area that once formed part of the bus garage complex.

Security at the Royal Fusiliers' *Tower of London* base could not be described as *tight*, so the twins found little difficulty in escaping whenever they chose. On more than one occasion they simply donned their civilian clothes, mingled with the *Tower*'s civilian visitors, and walked – unchallenged – out of the main gate. Equally, it was not difficult for friends and relatives to visit the twins at any time, even when they were under punishment and confined in the guardroom. Charles – the twins' father – was himself a fugitive from army conscription and had been since the beginning of the war. Even so, claiming that he was one of the twins' uncles, he had no difficulty in paying them a visit. Less than a year later, World War II deserters would be granted amnesty as part of the new Queen's coronation celebrations.

On the trot once again, with eyes out for somewhere to lie low, the twins heard that Billy Webb – their rival from *The Tottenham Royal* – was also on the run from the army and in a similar position to themselves. Billy was sought out as a possible ally whom they could trust and who might prove useful to them. After meeting up at a cafe in Tottenham High Road, Billy Webb agreed to let the twins stay with him at a flat he was renting in Finsbury Park. After a time – realising that three young men of conscription age without obvious employment, who were staying in a flat together, were likely to arouse suspicion among the locals – they decided to move on before someone reported them to the police. On the run once again with no fixed abode, the three young men continued to seek out and use a variety of refuges where they could get their heads down for the night – sometimes sneaking into Billy's parents' house or Vallance Road after dark for a fresh change of clothes and a few hours' precious sleep.

Pat Butler, veteran of the *Coach and Horses* incident and a mutual friend of both Billy Webb and the twins, was serving time in *Borstal*. When he heard that his friends were on the run together, he decided to escape and join them. Dickie Morgan regularly put in an appearance too, and the group of five fugitives would spend time roaming the streets of London together. Sometimes, all five would stay at Dickie Morgan's house at Clinton Road – where Dickie's mother welcomed them, happy to let them come and go as they pleased.

Another regular sanctuary used by the twins and their friends was the 24-hour-opening *Lyons Corner House* on Coventry Street in the West End. Once the regular daytime clientele were tucked up in bed, the *Corner House* – with restaurants and cafeterias on several floors – became a night-time haunt and meeting place for all manner of dubious characters and social outcasts. Criminals, prostitutes, homosexuals (still illegal in the 1950s), fugitives from justice, and young men on the run from National Service would congregate and mingle in this comfortable, nocturnal netherworld.

Sometimes, the twins and their fellow deserters would stay up for three days and nights without a wink of sleep, drinking tea, taking Black Bombers (amphetamine pills), and chewing the tape from inside Benzedrine inhalers to stay awake and suppress their appetite. Runaway boys were among the night-time clientele at the *Corner House*, and Ronnie's obvious interest in them was the first indication of his homosexuality – which was noticed by others. While chatting to one of the *Corner House*'s regular flamboyant homosexual characters known as the *Duchess*, the twins' friend Billy Webb heard something about Ronnie that came as a surprise: *"It takes one to know one,"* said the Duchess, *"and that's definitely a queen."*[63]

---

63   Webb, Billy. *Running with the Krays*. Edinburgh: Mainstream Publishing, 1993.

Lyons Corner House

13 Coventry Street, London W1D 7AB

Nearest TFL station: Piccadilly Circus underground.

First appearing in London in 1909 – and operated by the market-dominant food and hospitality company, J. Lyons and Co. – *Lyons Corner Houses* were huge catering establishments, decorated in the Art Deco style with ground-floor food halls and restaurants of different styles on four or five floors.

Founded in 1884 by the Jewish immigrant families Salmon and Gluckstein – along with a relative by marriage, Joseph Lyons – the Lyons brand was a household name in Britain throughout most of the 20th century. The corner houses were the flagships of the company and remained a London institution until the last one, at Marble Arch, closed in 1977. During the 1950s, there were four of these establishments in London: three corner houses situated at Tottenham Court Road, The Strand, and Coventry Street, and one *Maison Lyons* at Marble Arch – which was much the same as the corner houses but which operated under a different management structure. The Coventry Street *Corner House* at the junction of Rupert Street – between Piccadilly Circus and Leicester Square – was, for a time in the 1950s, open 24 hours a day.

Ronnie and Reggie, along with their friends, spent many-a-night in the Coventry Street *Corner House* during 1952, when they were on the run from the army.

The Coventry Street *Corner House* closed in 1970, and the ground floor of the building – which is now occupied by *Bubba Gump Shrimp Co.* – was the food hall and entrance. Also at street level, opening in 1954, was Britain's first ever hamburger joint; the Wimpy Bar opened and operated under licence by the Lyons company.

Tommy Smithson, with whom the twins had become friendly, would often join them in the *Corner House*. A Liverpool-born ex-merchant seaman, compulsive gambler, tough fighting man, and villain of the highest order, Smithson – whom they had first met at *Wally's Cafe* – was greatly admired by the twins. Very much an independent operator and not part of an established firm, Smithson's complete lack of fear and non-caring attitude frequently brought him into conflict with other gangsters. Smithson had opened a *spieler* (illegal gambling club) in nearby Archer Street – just a two-minute walk from the *Corner House* – and would sometimes offer the twins the use of the place to grab some sleep and bed down on the chairs or the snooker table during the day when the club was closed. Illegal gambling joints like this one in the West End brought in big money, and control of this very lucrative business was, at the time, largely in the hands of the Billy Hill and Jack Spot criminal organisation – but Smithson paid no heed whatsoever to the rules set by others. He was clearly treading on toes and it was only a matter of time before matters would come to a dramatic head.

In 1953, already in the bad books, Smithson fought with – and cut – Freddie 'Slip' Sullivan in *French Henry's*, a Soho club run by Billy Hill's mistress, Gypsy. Sullivan had a brother – Sonny – in the Jack Spot/Billy Hill gang and, as was the underworld's way, retribution was due. Word reached Smithson a week later that a peace offering was on the table and that there was no reason why the situation couldn't be sorted out amicably. Consequently, Smithson was lured to a meeting with Hill and Spot behind the Black Cat cigarette factory[64] in Mornington Crescent, Camden Town, where he surprisingly handed over the gun he was carrying when asked to do so by Billy Hill. This was the signal to attack, and Smithson was sub-jected to a ferocious beating by Hill, Spot, and several cohorts in which he was hit with an iron bar, razor slashed all over his face and body, and given Billy Hill's trade mark 'V' cut on both cheeks. Smithson was then thrown over a wall in *Regent's Park* and left to bleed to death. Amazingly, after losing five pints of blood, he survived – though 47 stitches had to be put into his face alone.

Billy Hill paid Smithson £500 for taking his punishment like a man and honouring the underworld code of silence, which should have been the end of the matter. However, rather than skulking away, Smithson – with his wounds barely healed – began opening more spielers in Soho. This time, Spot and Hill employed a different tactic and used their paid-off contacts in the police to close the clubs down. Left with little choice, Smithson went back to Hackney – but not before giving Jack Spot a severe beating with a pipe wrench.[65]

Smithson's is a story of living and dying by the sword, and he met his end on 25 June 1956 when he was shot in the neck by Maltese gangsters. Tommy Smithson – who had earned him-self the nicknames *Scarface* and *Mr Loser* – was found dying

---

64 Built in an Egyptian/Art Deco style, the *Carreras Cigarette Factory* produced Black Cat and other brands of cigarettes until its closure in 1960. The building in Mornington Crescent, Camden (NW1 2JE) was converted into an office block and, in 1996, was restored to its former glory, complete with black cat statues guarding the main entrance.

65 Ward, Henry and Weeks, David. *Bullets, Blood and Broken Bodies*. New Breed Publishing, 2008.

outside a Kilburn brothel at number 88 Carlton Vale, near the junction with Cambridge Road. Bizarrely, his last words to the people who found him are said to have been: *"Good morning, I'm dying."*[66]

Always on the lookout for a means of making some money, while on the run in 1952, an opportunity arose for the twins through another regular at the *Corner House*. Ex-professional boxer Johnny Hudson from Covent Garden was in the unlicensed boxing business and would frequently put on shows, mostly outside London. Ronnie recalls:

"I remember boxing in an unlicensed show at Bexley in Kent. I was matched against a farmer and he started to butt me in the face. So I kneed him in the groin. The crowd wanted to lynch me but I won the fight and collected my fiver."[67]

In October 1952, Ron and Reg were arrested and returned to the *Tower*. It must have been, by now, clear to the Fusiliers that there was little hope of the twins ever settling down and soldiering, but still the absurd game continued. The troublesome twosome were sent to *Colchester Military Detention Barracks* to serve a punitive month in the glasshouse. The four weeks of incarceration, during which they were subjected to the harshest of military regimes, was a punishment designed to teach wayward recruits a lesson and make them see the error of their ways – but rather than breaking the twins' spirits and bringing them to heel, the experience simply galvanised their determination to continue their fight, leaving the army with no choice but to throw them out.

---

66   kilburnandwillesdenhistory.blogspot.com

67   Kray, Reg and Ron with Dinenage, Fred. *Our Story*. London: Pan Books, 1989.

In December 1952, the twins were released from Colchester and returned to the *Tower* but, predictably, within a matter of days, they escaped yet again. After remaining at large for a couple of weeks, their luck ran out when they were spotted in *The Orange Cafe* in Bow by PC Roy Fisher who, having been involved in a previous arrest, recognised the twins immediately. Ron and Reg appealed to the policeman to let them go until after they'd spent Christmas with their family – when they would, of course, hand themselves in – but PC Fisher was having none of it. Unsurprisingly, the twins then resorted to their usual method of dealing with such situations and delivered a punch or two to the policeman's head before running off into the darkness of the early evening, making good their escape.

Punching soldiers and running from the army was one thing, but assaulting a police officer was a far more serious business that would bring about not only punishment from the army, but also a likely appearance in a civilian court. Rounding up army deserters was probably not the highest of priorities for the police, but now – after an assault on one of their own – the ante was significantly upped.

Following the assault on PC Fisher, it would have been wise for the twins to keep from showing their faces in the Mile End area but, regardless of the risks, they continued to hang around in Mile End, spending time at *The Regal* billiard hall in Eric Street, staying at Dickie Morgan's house, and drinking tea with their friends in *The Orange Cafe* on Bow road. Ron and Reg were eventually arrested on 19 January 1953.

The Orange Cafe

94b Bow Road, London E3 3AA

Nearest TFL stations: Bow Road underground and Bow Church DLR.

Located just a minute's walk from Bow Road tube station and directly across the road from the site of *The Double R Club*, the building that once housed *The Orange Cafe* is now the *CityStay Hotel*.

During their time on the run from the army in 1952, the Kray twins and their friends used the cafe as a regular daytime hang-out. Just before Christmas 1952, PC Fisher attempted to arrest the twins for desertion outside the cafe but was punched several times before the twins ran off and escaped.

The *CityStay Hotel* made the headlines in September 2018 after it was discovered that the two Russian 'Novichok' poisoners stayed at the hotel prior to travelling to Salisbury and carrying out the poison attack on Sergei Skripal and his daughter Yulia.

Appearing at Thames Magistrates Court on 26 February 1953, charged – for the second time – with assaulting a police officer in the execution of his duty, the twins claimed they had merely pushed the policeman while trying to escape. The magistrate gave the twins a month each in *Wormwood Scrubs*. Having spent the best part of a year on the run or in army detention, *Wormwood Scrubs* was no great hardship for the twins and the month passed without incident. Still only 19, they found that their reputation for violence afforded them some respect from the older, more experienced criminals from whom there was much to be learned. With useful contacts made and future possibilities revealed to them, their month in the *Scrubs* was an important learning curve and a stepping stone on their road towards their planned criminal future.

Wormwood Scrubs

160 Du Cane Road, London W12 OAN

Construction of the famous prison – which still operates today – was completed in 1891, and the road on which it stands is named after the prison's designer, Sir Edmund Frederick Du Cane. Much of the open area surrounding the prison was scrubland, hence the name *scrubs*, and *wormwood* (Artemisia absinthium) is a weed that once grew there in profusion. In the past, wormwood was used to treat a variety of maladies – including sexual dysfunction – and it is still used today as a vital ingredient in the once-banned French tipple, absinthe.

Ron and Reg Kray were first sent to the *Scrubs* on remand after assaulting PC Baynton in 1950, and then again in early 1953 for a month's sentence following an assault on PC Fisher, who attempted to arrest them for desertion from the army.

By now, it must surely have been abundantly clear to the army that there was no hope whatsoever of turning the Kray twins into disciplined soldiers, and the sooner they could be rid of them, the better. However, there was a necessary process of detention, trial, and punishment that had to occur before they could be dishonourably discharged.

Following their release from *Wormwood Scrubs* in the early spring of 1953, the twins were taken to *Howe Barracks*[68] near Canterbury to be detained, awaiting a court-martial.

Shortly after arriving at *Howe Barracks* – where they were reunited once again with their pal Dickie Morgan – the twins, now more rebellious than ever and even more determined to ensure their early release from the army, planned a bold escape. On Friday 3 April 1953, Ron, Reg, Dickie Morgan, and their new-found friend – the delinquent regular soldier Ted Bryant – overpowered their guards and were off *on the trot* once again.

The twins' father Charles and his friend Harry Hopwood were waiting in a vehicle outside the barracks, ready to take the twins and their friends straight to London – but the run-aways took off in the wrong direction and failed to make the rendezvous. After fighting with a posse of pursuing soldiers, jumping over walls, and wading through a river, they came across a clapped-out lorry that they were able to get started – but it wasn't long and they hadn't got far before the lorry broke down. Continuing on foot – and jumping into hedges whenever they saw the headlights of an approaching vehicle – the band of renegades made it as far as Eltham, just ten miles shy of London, before being arrested by the police. The incident made the newspapers and on Saturday 4 April 1953, *The Daily News* (London) ran the story *'Four Escape Guardroom'* on page one.

It would be another month before their court-martial hearing, and as the twins had no intention of quietly biding their time, the shenanigans continued with ever-increasing creativity. Smashing up their cells, overpowering and tying up their

---

68 *Howe Barracks*, Littlebourne Road, Canterbury, Kent CT1.Built in the 1930s and closed in February 2015, very little evidence of the former barracks remains. Some of the land is taken up by new housing and an 11-acre public park called *Legacy Park*.

guards, ripping up uniforms, setting fire to bedding, punching NCOs, and rooftop protests were just some of the disruptive and outrageous antics dreamed up and perpetrated to make their captors' lives hell. One day, having had quite enough of this nonsense from the four young hooligans, the Colour Sergeant arrived to take charge of the situation. In full dress uniform – complete with medals and red sash, having come straight from parade – he entered the guardroom and began to give the motley crew a shouted dressing-down – but barely half a dozen words into his *"This behaviour will not be tolerated"* speech, the latrine bucket was thrown over him.[69]

At last, on 11 May 1953, the court-martial took place and the twins' time battling with the army was almost at an end. Pleading guilty to all charges, Ron, Reg, and Dickie Morgan were sentenced to nine months' detention at *Shepton Mallet Army Prison* in Somerset, after which they were to be dishonourably discharged. Ted Bryant, their friend and regular soldier, was given one year. Once again, their story made the newspapers, and on Tuesday 12 May 1953, the *Daily Herald* covered the proceedings at the court-martial hearing under the page three headline: '*Inseparable Twins.*'

Detaining the twins in the *Howe Barracks* guardhouse while awaiting their transfer to *Shepton Mallet* was understandably deemed to pose a risk of escape, so – unusually – the twins were held in Canterbury civilian prison[70] for 14 days before their army escort arrived to take them to *The Mallet.*

---

69   Pearson, John. *The Profession of Violence*. London: Weidenfeld and Nicolson, 1972.

70   Following the prison's closure in March 2013, it was bought by *Canterbury Christ Church University* and the site now forms part of the university campus. The original prison entrance can be seen from Longport (A257), Canterbury CT1 1PJ.

During their time at *Shepton Mallet*, knowing that any serious misdemeanours would simply prolong their time there, the twins – for the most part – conformed with the rules and settled down to do their time. The army prison routine, with hard physical training and team games, proved no great hardship; in fact, it enabled the twins to regain their previously lost level of peak physical fitness.

Surrounded by the cream of the country's up-and-coming young criminals, friendships and contacts were made that the twins thought may prove useful in the future. Two characters who would play important parts in the twins' story, as yet to unfold, were serving time at *Shepton Mallet* at the same time as the twins. These were Johnny Nash – one of seven brothers constituting the notorious Nash family from Islington – and Charlie Richardson, with whom the twins apparently got on well. Good relations were not to last, however, as in the future, Charlie Richardson and his South London gang would become the Krays' arch nemeses and most bitter rivals.

Shepton Mallet Prison

Frithfield Lane, Shepton Mallet, Somerset BA4 5LU

Prior to its closure in 2013, Shepton Mallet was Britain's oldest operating prison. Originally opening in 1625, the prison was expanded and added-to during the 18th and 19th centuries, and remained a functioning prison until its closure in 1930. During the Second World War, the prison was reopened as a military prison used initially by the British Army and later by American forces.

After the war, the prison continued as a military glasshouse, and it was during this time, in 1953, that the Kray twins were interned here for six months before being dishonourably discharged from the army.

Returned to civilian use in 1966, the prison under-went several changes in its function and category of in-mates before its decommissioning and final closure in March 2013. Shepton Mallet Prison has been used as a location for various television and film productions – no-tably the 1967 film The Dirty Dozen and, more recently, the 2020 ITV drama *Des*, based on the arrest and trial of the serial killer Dennis Nilsen, starring David Tennant. Today, the former prison is open to the public as a histor-ical tourist destination.

After serving six months of their nine-month sentence, the twins were released and dishonourably discharged from the army on 13 November 1953, one year and eight months after their initial conscription.

Following their release from *Shepton Mallet* army prison in the autumn of 1953, the twins went home to Vallance Road, and – now with a clear vision of where their future lay – began the next phase of their lives. At just 20 years old, the twins were fully aware of how they could use their natural talents to make money, but they knew that to advance their criminal careers, they needed to make contact with – and learn from – London's top-tier criminals. The place to do it was *The Vienna Rooms* in Crawford Place, just off the Edgware Road in London's West End. Frequented by businessmen, prostitutes, and criminals, *The Vienna Rooms* was a second-floor restaurant and gathering place of choice for London's villains to meet, renew acquaint-ances, and talk business.

The Vienna Rooms

19 Crawford Place, London W1H 4LG

Nearest TFL station: Edgware Road underground.

Now aged 20, Ron and Reg Kray – on their quest to ingratiate themselves with London's top criminals and learn who was who and how they operated – began turning up at The Vienna Rooms, a second-floor restaurant and adopted meeting place for London's villains, in the autumn of 1953, shortly after their discharge from the army.

The original building that housed the Vienna Restaurant is now demolished and, today, a block of modern flats occupies the site. Across the road is another modern apartment building located between Cato Street and Molyneux Street. Crawford Place Police Station stood here in 1953 but was not, at the time, a fully functioning police station, having been closed in, or shortly after, 1933.[71]

Centre of attention at *The Vienna Rooms* were the two men at the top of London's criminal ladder, Jack Spot and Billy Hill – who were, at this time, working in partnership. Jack Spot, real name Jacob Comer, was born in 1912 – the son of Jewish immigrants – and grew up in the East End, where he established himself as a feared street fighter and gang leader from an early age. Some say that the name *Spot* came about due to a large mole on his left cheek, but Spot always maintained that it was because of his reputation for being 'on the spot' whenever Jews

---

71   hansard.parliament.uk Police Stations.

were in trouble.

Spot allegedly took part in the infamous *Battle of Cable Street* in 1936, leading his gang of Jewish toughs into battle with Oswald Mosley's fascist *Blackshirts* and the police. With no hesitation in resorting to extreme violence, and frequently using a razor to slice open his victims' faces, Jack Spot ensured he was the one paid to look after the security of local businesses. By 1953, Jack Spot had loosened his control over the protection rackets in the East End and had turned his attention west. After teaming up with Billy Hill in 1949, the two – together with their followers – banished all other gangs and established complete control of Soho's illegal gambling clubs and the very lucrative protection business. Jack Spot also involved himself in that most traditional of gangster pursuits – protecting on-course betting pitches and taking a big slice of the bookies' profits at the racetracks.

Fieldgate Mansions

Myrdle Street, London E1 1HA

Nearest TFL station: Whitechapel underground.

Just a short walk from Whitechapel underground station, close to the London Hospital, Fieldgate Mansions – Jack Spot's childhood home – still stands. Built around 1905, the substantial complex of tenement dwellings formed part of a mainly Jewish residential area. Scheduled for demolition in 1972, community action forced the council to abandon their plans, and the flats – which were refurbished in the 1980s – now provide mainly social housing.

Big, powerfully built, and beautifully dressed in the style of a screen gangster, Jack Spot had great presence and clearly commanded the respect of his followers – but it was stately, sharply dressed Billy Hill, with his quietly assured manner, who impressed the twins the most. Billy Hill was not a big man, but his lack of size was more than made up for by his supremely sharp criminal mind – and his lack of hesitation in using a knife when necessary.

Born in St Pancras in 1911, Billy Hill grew up in an established criminal family and embarked on his criminal career at an early age. Beginning as a burglar and committing his first stabbing at the age of 14, Billy Hill graduated – in the 1930s – to smash-and-grab raids, targeting jewellers and furriers. During the war, Hill and his gang took advantage of rationing and the scarcity of foodstuffs, petrol, and luxury items and made a pretty penny stealing and supplying goods on the black market. After the war, Billy Hill became involved in protection rackets, smuggling, and the masterminding and project managing of large-scale robberies. In the spring of 1952, the year before the twins began turning up at *The Vienna Rooms*, Billy and his gang successfully pulled off Britain's biggest post-war robbery – holding up a post office van and escaping with 18 mailbags stuffed with cash. The Eastcastle Street Robbery netted Billy and his boys £287,000 in used notes; around 8.5 million in today's money.

London's two top criminal bosses certainly made an impression on the twins, and both Hill and Spot soon became aware that the two young lads from Bethnal Green – who would sit quietly and listen attentively to their stories and those of their acolytes – were something special and not to be ignored. Having worked successfully in partnership since 1949, the relationship between Hill and Spot was, by 1953, beginning to develop cracks – and each knew that keeping the twins onside could prove useful in the future.

Billy Hill's Flat

4 Windsor Court, Moscow Road, Bayswater, London W2 4SN

Nearest TFL station: Bayswater underground.

The imposing 1920s redbrick apartment building situated between Salem Road and Moscow Place was home to London's top criminal gang boss and mentor to the Kray twins, Billy Hill. Hill moved into flat number 4 on the ground floor in 1961 and continued to live at – and conduct business from – the address until his death in 1984, aged 72.

In 1953, when Ron and Reg Kray first began associating with Billy Hill, he was living in an apartment above a warehouse that he owned at 51 Whitechapel Road. Now demolished, a Tesco Express occupies the site of Billy Hill's former home.

During the period the twins spent time at *The Vienna Rooms,* they made many friends and useful contacts – some of whom would remain close for many years to come. Ex-boxer Bobby Ramsey was already known to the twins from their boxing days and was a regular at *The Vienna Rooms*, now working as a bodyguard for Jack Spot. Always smartly dressed and the driver of a big American car, Ramsey had previously worked with Billy Hill when, in 1947, Hill opened a gambling club in Johannesburg, South Africa. Inevitably, this new venture brought Hill – assisted by Ramsey – into conflict with local gangsters and the resulting fracas left the top Jo'burg villain, Arnold Neville, needing a hundred stitches. After being arrested, Hill managed to skip bail and return to London, but Ramsey was locked up for 11 months and then deported.[72]

Another of the villains frequenting *The Vienna Rooms* with whom the twins became friendly was Jack Spot's right-hand man, Moisha Blueboy, real name Morris Goldstein. Moisha – sometimes known as *Blueball* – had been with Jack Spot since their childhood days in the East End and would remain loyal to the last. This was surprising, really, as Jack Spot had beaten Moisha up twice – and, on one occasion, drugged and molested his new girlfriend.[73] Ex-professional wrestler Moisha Blueboy was a conman and expert crooked card player, and it was through Moisha and his card skills that the twins came to meet the man who would, in the future, open many-a-door and help them out of many-a-sticky situation – Geoff Allen.

One evening, while the twins were in the company of Jack Spot and Moisha at *The Vienna Rooms*, a man named Jack Pokla approached Moisha and said, *"I've found a mug from the country who has plenty of money."*

Moisha told Pokla, *"Bring him here to The Vienna Rooms for a meal and we'll get him involved in a card game."*

Jack Pokla left and returned shortly afterwards with Geoff Allen in tow. Described by Reggie as *"a good-looking, well-dressed man in country tweeds, a pleasant sort with twinkling blue eyes,"* Geoff Allen was the kind of character who clearly sought to ingratiate himself with gangsters.

Allen's wealth had come from fraudulent dealings and bogus insurance claims within the property market, and he knew that conducting business outside the law was better done with

---

72   Clarkson, Wensley. *Billy Hill: Godfather of London*. London: John Blake Publishing, 2009.

73   Clarkson, Wensley. *Hit 'Em Hard: Jack Spot,King of the Underworld*. London: HarperCollins, 2002.

a few tasty gangsters onside. Within a short time, a carload of chaps – including Moisha and the twins – were following Geoff Allen's car on a 37-mile journey to his cottage in the village of Smith's Green in Essex.[74] Moisha and Geoff Allen played cards well into the small hours before calling it a day, by which time Allen had lost around £1,100. Smiling and jovial despite his loss, Allen explained to the group that he needed to wait until 10am when the banks opened to collect the money, and that he would meet them an hour afterwards at *The White Hart* hotel,[75] a few miles away in the village of Great Dunmow.

Promised a share of the winnings, the twins enjoyed a hearty breakfast at the hotel and eagerly awaited Allen's arrival, but excitement turned to concern as 11am came and went. One of the group had Allen's phone number, so Moisha called to find out the reason for the delay. *"I knew I was being conned,"* was Allen's reply, *"and if you come near this cottage you'll find me waiting with a shotgun."*

Surprisingly, it was left at that; the twins saw the funny side and the group drove back to London with nothing to show for their little jaunt. Sometime later, Reggie – impressed by Allen – travelled back to his cottage at Smith's Green and was invited in for coffee. Whether or not he collected any money, Reggie was happy with the outcome of the meeting, and this was the beginning of a firm friendship that would last until the twins' arrest in 1968.

---

74   Kray, Reg. *Born Fighter*. Century, 1990.

75   *The White Hart*, High Street, Great Dunmow, Essex CM6 1FS. Also known as *The Dunmow Inn*, the pub was situated on the high street of the village of Great Dunmow, close to *Stansted Airport* and 3.7 miles from the village of Smith's Green (CM6 1GH). Now demolished, retail units – including *William Hill* bookmakers – occupy the site on which the pub once stood.

Back in the East End, Ron and Reg were continuing to assert themselves, building on their reputation for violence and accumulating an ever-growing gang of useful followers and hangers-on. Their brother Charlie – in an effort to keep his younger brothers on the straight and narrow and steer them away from a life of villainy – encouraged the twins to resume their boxing careers, but Ronnie had lost interest altogether. On the other hand, Reggie did reapply for his boxing licence, and – despite his criminal record – it was granted. Surprisingly, PC Fisher – the policeman the twins had assaulted in 1952 – spoke to the board of control on Reggie's behalf, explaining that he was at fault during the attempted arrest and that Reggie only threw a punch due to provocation. Reggie began training again briefly, but it came to nothing as there were far easier – and more interesting – ways of making money.

Contacts in the docklands enabled the twins to acquire duty-free watches and other items that could be sold on for a nice profit; various scams and cons were plotted to relieve the gullible of their cash; and even the occasional foray into good honest stealing formed a part of their income.

Accompanied by friends Dickie Morgan, Dickie Mountain, and Ron Bennett, the twins began stealing lorries laden with goods of various kinds that could be sold on for a nice few quid. Lucrative as it was, however, stealing from legitimate businesses carried a high risk of a court appearance so, after a time, the twins chose to follow the advice of their mentor Billy Hill and *"only steal from thieves."* Taking money from those operating outside – or on the fringes of – the law was free of the risk of police involvement, and so began the business that would eventually form the cornerstone of their future career: extortion. It was only the criminal fraternity at this stage, but it was extortion nonetheless. Intimidating thieves into parting with their ill-gotten gains for a paltry sum, taking the gear outright, or simply demanding a large cut of the profits was work for which they were well suited.

Tony Mella, another regular at *The Vienna Rooms*, would sometimes accompany the twins when intimidation was required; the fearsome threesome would tour the East End and other parts of London in Mella's Sunbeam-Talbot car, frightening money out of petty criminals, buyers of stolen gear, and anyone involved in nefarious business.[76]

Italian-born Tony Mella was a former heavyweight boxer and much-feared street fighter. Cast in the same mould as Tommy Smithson, Mella was an independent operator and man of violence who, like Smithson, had a face that bore the scars of many an altercation. However, unlike Smithson, Mella was regarded by some as a bully. Mella would later establish himself in Soho, and by the early '60s he was running a string of clip-joints where punters would pay extortionate prices for watered-down beer and the prospect of a sexual encounter. No sexual encounter, however, would be forthcoming, and punters would leave with nothing except empty pockets – and possibly a black eye if they touched one of the girls or dared to complain.

Mella was not noted for his pragmatism, and his brash, cocky, and often arrogant style frequently brought him into conflict with other gangsters. Mella's head was scarred by a heavy glass jug that had been wielded by Billy Hill; his face was scarred by the flick knives of Frankie Fraser and Bert 'Battles' Rossi; and his back by razors after an attack by Maltese gangsters, who found him in his bed one night and cut him to ribbons. Even his buttocks were scarred, in this case by a bayonet in the hands of dwarf wrestler Royston Smith, aka *Fuzzyball Kaye*, who slashed a noughts and crosses grid on his

---

76 Webb, Billy. *Running with the Krays*. Edinburgh: Mainstream Publishing, 1993.

arse. Mella recruited his friend Big Alf Melvin as a bodyguard, promising him a share in the business – but Mella did not fulfil his promise and treated Alf as a mere minion, often belittling him in front of other employees.

Melvin's simmering resentment came to a head in Mella's *Bus Stop Club*[77] on Dean Street, Soho on the evening of Monday 28 January 1963. Alf Melvin produced a small calibre Browning pistol and shot Tony Mella three times in the back. The 39-year-old Mella staggered outside, collapsed in the street, and died. Afterwards, Alf Melvin remained at his desk in the club, placed the barrel of the gun under his chin, and blew his brains out.

Throughout 1953 and into the summer of 1954, Ron and Reg continued to use *The Vienna Rooms* in the West End as a base. Now, having soaked up a good deal of knowledge and inspiration from the characters they met there, it was time to look for a base of their own on home turf. *Ziggy's Cafe* was a handy meeting place in the East End, but the run-down *Regal* billiard hall was where the twins' friends knew they could usually be found – and it was fast becoming their hang-out and rallying point of choice. Situated on Eric Street – just behind Mile End underground station and just a stone's throw from the recently closed *Mile End Arena*, where the twins had made their professional boxing debut in 1951 – *The Regal* was the gathering place for all manner of shady and unsavoury characters. Petty criminals, National Service dodgers, and an assortment of local toughs and tearaways ensured that fighting and violence were always on the menu at *The Regal*.

Having first used *The Regal* as a hang-out during their days

---

77   *The Bus Stop Club*, 48 Dean Street, Soho, London W1D 5BF. The three-storey building that was once *The Bus Stop Club* is now *Rosa's Thai Restaurant.*

on the run from the army, Ron and Reg were in their element there, comfortable in the company of their own kind and secure in the knowledge that when it came to a fight, they were the rulers of the roost. Trouble and violence had long blighted the billiard hall and Samuel Martin, the owner, was powerless to do anything about it.

Suddenly, the violence escalated; the twins seemed to have no part in it but there was fighting and damage to the tables, fixtures, and fittings almost every evening. Samuel Martin appeared to have reached the end of his tether, and was despairingly talking of closing the place down and calling it a day, when the twins stepped forward with a proposition. This was the first example of the successful business format that they would use from then onwards for the rest of their career. They would 'look after' the billiard hall for him and make sure there was no more trouble. They would keep the takings from the snooker tables and refreshment bar and pay him £5 per week. Unsurprisingly, the violence stopped on the day that the twins' offer was accepted and, shortly afterwards, they became the legal tenants. Money was borrowed from their brother Charlie and, with the help of friends, the twins set about decorating, refurbishing, and generally smartening the place up. Within a short time, *The Regal* began to turn a nice profit. In late 1954, at just 21 years of age, the twins were in business and making money as *The Regal* became more and more popular.

The Regal Billiard Hall

Eric Street, Bow, London E3 4SW

Nearest TFL station: Mile End underground.

Opened in 1910 and closed in June 1940 due to the imminent threat – and thereafter reality – of German bombs falling on London, the 702-seater *Forrest's Electrodrome Cinema* never again opened its doors. After the war, the building underwent several changes of use until its opening as a 14-table snooker hall in 1952. Acquired by the Kray twins in 1954 and remaining in their hands until 1960, The Regal billiard hall was their first club, marking the beginning of their rise to power and infamy.

Coopers Court Sanctuary retirement apartments now occupy the spot where the long-demolished former cinema building, housing The Regal billiard hall, once stood.

The twins' reputation as unbeatable fighters was, by now, well-established in the East End, but there were still a few young men who fancied their chances and were prepared to offer a challenge. The result was almost a foregone conclusion – the challenger or challengers were left battered, bloody, and beaten. It was around this time that Reggie perfected his famous *cigarette punch.* Offering a cigarette with his right hand, Reggie would pick the moment when his victim's mouth was slightly open, their jaw relaxed, and then deliver a vicious left hook, almost invariably resulting in a broken jaw. Reggie spent hours practising the move on a punch bag and would be disappointed if the punch didn't allow him to add to his tally of broken jaws.

Ron and Reg Kray were abnormally tough; possessing a physical strength well beyond what would be considered normal for their size. Ronnie was five feet ten inches in height, with Reggie around an inch shorter. Ronnie tipped the scales at 12.5 stone and Reggie at 11. Their teenage boxing training had taught them how to use their fists with devastating effect, and their natural aggression meant that they usually struck first. In all their many fights – often against bigger men and sometimes greatly outnumbered – they never came off second best and were never seriously hurt. In mass brawls, they seemed to demonstrate a kind of telepathy that they'd possessed since childhood, each knowing what the other was doing and enabling them to fight as one invincible unit. Last but not least, they had no fear whatsoever and thoroughly enjoyed the violence; they loved it, it defined them, and often, they would do it just for fun. The more jaws broken, the more faces slashed, and the more people around to see it, the better. This was the key to their success and they knew it. Respect generated by fear gave them the power to manipulate others and, consequently, a world of possibilities opened up to them.

Although the twins' reputation was spreading, word of the full extent of their ability to conduct violence had not reached the ears of a local Maltese gang – either that or they simply didn't pay much heed. Either way, they turned up at *The Regal* one night looking to extort protection money from the twins.

Late one evening, after closing time, the twins were alone in *The Regal* – counting the takings and stacking the chairs – when they sensed trouble. In walked the Maltese gang, casually but menacingly looking around, stroking the new green baize on the tables and examining the cues with feigned interest. The word 'protection' was barely out of the leader's mouth before Ronnie reached behind the bar for a cutlass and Reggie for a knife. *"Protection from what?"* shouted Ronnie as he swung the blade at the gang leader. Realising they had bitten off more than they could chew, the gang fled in terror. Ronnie, waving the cutlass, chased them outside, and as they piled into their car trying desperately to escape, Ronnie furiously set about the vehicle with his weapon. Windows were smashed and scything blows delivered to the bodywork as the car pulled away. Unsurprisingly, that was the last they saw or heard of the Maltese gang.

Ron and Reg were the main attraction at *The Regal*; they were always surrounded by friends, followers, and any number of young tearaways looking for fun and excitement. Trusted friends of old formed the inner circle, among whom were Pat Butler, Johnny Squibb, Harry Abrahams, Eddie Alford, Shaun Venables, and army pal Dickie Morgan and his brother Chunky. Later on they made other close friends, including Curly King, Pat Connolly, Leslie Burman, and Colin 'The Duke' Osborne, so-called because of his more middle-class upbringing and genteel manner. Ex-heavyweight boxer and friend of the Kray family, Tommy 'The Bear' Brown – real name Tommy Welch – was generally around, and would look out for the interests of the young twins. This group of trusted friends and acolytes – a few of whom would remain with the twins until the end – was the beginning, and the earliest version of the gang that would later become known as *The Firm.* Over the years, some of the early gang would drift away, as girlfriends came on the scene and hanging around with the Krays became less of a *lark* and more of a serious business.

The Regal became the hang-out of choice for local villains, thieves, con men, and criminals of all persuasions. Safe from the ears and eyes of the straight world, criminal business could be discussed and arranged. Thieves could leave the tools of their trade on the premises, weapons were stored, and – for their cut in the proceeds – the twins would allow the cavernous *Regal* to be used as a *slaughter* – safe storage for stolen goods. Far better for local thieves to work with the Krays and pay them a share of the profits from a successful haul rather than having them find out for themselves and turn up demanding the lion's share.

Along with the takings from the club, sharing in the spoils of criminal enterprise provided a nice income for the twins. Revenue was further supplemented by utilising the forecourt area of *The Regal* as a used car lot. This particular venture had the effect of turning all other used car businesses in the area into rivals, and for the privilege of trouble-free trading in competition with the twins, there were payments to be made. If payment was not forthcoming, the used car dealers would be reminded of the vulnerability of their stock via a can of paint stripper and a lump hammer. Targeting used car dealerships marked the beginning of an expansion of the twins' extortion activities to include legitimate businesses.

The Wentworth Arms

Eric Street, Bow, London E3 4SR

Nearest TFL station: Mile End underground.

The Regal billiard hall was a hive of activity most of the time, busy and noisy with chatter and laughter. Ron and Reg were the centre of attention and sometimes, when they needed a bit of peace and quiet to talk to someone without distractions or interruptions, they would pop across the road to the local pub for a drink and a chat.

Directly across the road from the former Regal billiard hall stands *The Wentworth Arms*. Built and opened in 1871, the pub remains open today and retains all the charm and character of a traditional East End boozer.

Friendly and welcoming, with only superficial changes since it was frequented by the Kray twins and their
friends in the 1950s, *The Wentworth Arms* is a must-visit
on any tour of the Krays' East End.

Reggie had a natural flair for business, possibly inherited
from his father, and would rarely miss an opportunity to make
money. Ronnie, however, was more interested in the power and
notoriety and loved to be the centre of attention. Organising
and directing his band of faithful followers was Ronnie's area
of expertise, and sometimes at the billiard hall, he would make
his favourite announcement: *"Well we've decided on a little
row with so-and-so tonight. Who's for and who's against?"*

It was around this time that someone – probably Curly King
– dubbed Ronnie *The Colonel*, a title by which he'd be known
ever after. Each would select their favourite weapon and the
group would pile into old, battered cars and head off, with the
twins in the lead.[78] Once the fighting started, it was clear how
much the twins enjoyed the violence. Punching, kicking, slashing, and smashing with ferocity – there was no holding back,
always going to the limit. Both twins were natural leaders, respected and liked by their friends and followers, but all were
aware that no matter how friendly the twins could often be,
it was wise to tread a little carefully around them – especially Ronnie, who was prone to moods and could sometimes be
unpredictable.

In the rough, tough world of the East End in the '50s and
'60s, a young man's interests were best served by aligning
himself with the toughest and most powerful group around –

---

78   Pearson, John. *The Profession of Violence*. London: Weidenfeld and
      Nicolson, 1972.

so, for many, joining and making themselves available to the Krays was a wise and prudent move. Alone, most would find it difficult to rise above the lowest levels of the pecking order, and could be vulnerable to bullying and exploitation by bigger, tougher individuals or groups. Yes, they would sacrifice some freedom, but it was a small price to pay for the benefits of excitement spiced with a little danger, fun, laughs, and a new-found status. Swaggering into a crowded pub or club as part of the Kray entourage and hearing the conversation suddenly stop must have made a young man feel like a 'somebody.' Not to mention seeing the way to the bar being quickly made clear, and men looking at the floor to avoid eye contact while their girlfriends cast coy, furtive smiles. Little wonder that Ron and Reg attracted so many friends, followers, and hangers-on.

Reggie enjoyed a game of snooker but Ronnie preferred to sit in his favourite chair in the dimly lit, smoke-filled billiard hall, enjoying the mastery of all he beheld and watching the door to see who came and went. Ronnie surrounded himself with a group of good-looking younger men who appeared to vie for his attention. He used this loyal group of dedicated followers as a means of gathering intelligence and keeping abreast of everything and anything that was happening on their manor. The young men would be told to go and hang around in this pub or that club and would be rewarded with gifts, cash, and favours in exchange for information about rival gangs, various individuals, and the general *goings-on* in the East End.

Ronnie liked boys and made no attempt to hide his sexual preferences, which – considering society's attitude towards homosexuality in the '50s and '60s – was a bold choice. Ronnie's homosexuality was largely accepted or simply ignored by his friends and followers; no one had a problem with it or, if they did, it would certainly never be voiced. Brother Charlie, however, was not so accepting of it and was clearly shocked when Ronnie came out and told him. Neither was his father, who had little else to say other than, *"Disgusting!"*

By 1954, the relationship between London's two top criminal bosses – Billy Hill and Jack Spot – was on the rocks. Since the early post-war years, the two men had worked in tandem and gained control of the very profitable illegal gambling and protection business in London's booming West End, but the partnership was now in tatters. Billy Hill, knowing that he no longer needed Spot, was slowly but surely edging Spotty out of the picture and moving towards claiming the title of *King of London's Underworld* for himself alone. Many of Spot's men had decamped and gone over to join Billy Hill, where the prospects were better and the pickings richer.

In March 1954, Billy Hill left the country and travelled to Tangier in Morocco to embark on a Mediterranean boat trip – with a little intrigue and smuggling thrown in – and did not return to England until late summer of that year. Spot saw Hill's absence from London as an opportunity to make a comeback, but Hill was a shrewd and manipulative operator and had made arrangements for his interests to be looked after while he was away. Always one step ahead, Billy Hill had – for some time – been building a relationship with powerful Italian gangsters who operated from a social club in Clerkenwell.

Jack Spot saw that his power and influence were evaporating, but so too was his income – and his frustration only increased when he discovered that Billy Hill had masterminded yet another successful robbery. On 21 September 1954, Billy Hill's gang escaped with £45,000 in gold bullion from a security van outside the Holborn offices of the Dutch airline KLM.

It was spring 1955. Jack Spot was keen to hang onto what was left of his much-diminished empire and assert his control over his one remaining stronghold – the racetracks. In the days before, during, and immediately after the Second World War, the racecourses were where the country's top criminal gangs made their biggest killing. Until 1961, the racetracks were the only place where gambling was allowed, and whoever gained control of the prime bookmakers' pitches took a cut of every bet; in return, they made sure that the bookmaker could operate free from *trouble*. Fighting and violence bedevilled many a race meeting in the 1920s and '30s as vicious gangs fought for control of the betting – the most notorious of which were London's Sabini gang, led by Darby Sabini, and the Birmingham boys, led by Billy Kimber. After the war, Jack Spot and his gang – with the help of Billy Hill – became the dominant force at the racetracks.

The Epsom Spring meeting was imminent, and although by 1955 crime had, to a large extent, outgrown the racetracks, the Spring Meeting in late April remained a traditional day out and gathering place for London's top villains. The actions and attitudes of the *faces* attending the annual outing gave a barometer reading of the current climate within the criminal fraternity, and Jack Spot needed to raise his profile to show that he was still in the game.

Having known the Kray twins for a couple of years and recognising trouble where he saw it, Jack Spot had, until now, been careful to keep the boys from Bethnal Green at arm's length. But things had changed. Realising that he needed some younger, tougher allies, he swallowed his pride and went to see the twins at *The Regal*. Unbeknown to Spot, the twins were close to Billy Hill and regarded him as the example to be followed, but they received him politely and listened to his proposition. Spot wanted to take the twins to Epsom and give them a bookmaker's pitch to mind – all they had to do was keep an eye on their percentage. Ronnie later said, *"We never liked Spotty, never thought much of him,"* but they agreed to take him up on his offer, thinking it might be *interesting*.[79]

Completely unfazed by the gathering of London's most dangerous gangsters, the twins – suitably tooled up and accompanied by Shaun Venables and a few other friends – turned up in their van and proceeded to demonstrate complete disregard for what could easily become a dangerous situation. The twins' show of cocky indifference did not go unnoticed. Billy Hill was not present – he and his lover Gypsy Riley had boarded the new liner *Southern Cross* on her maiden voyage to Australia on 29 March – but his new friends and allies, the Italians, were there in force.

Simmering tensions in both camps could lead to the knives and razors coming out at any time, but the twins laughed loudly and joked with their friends, ignoring the racing, and at one point Ronnie stretched out on the grass and closed his eyes (probably pretending) to take a nap. One of the Italians knew the twins well enough to warn them of the danger they had put themselves in, but afterwards, Ron turned to his brother and said, "*The way these old men worry, Reg, fair makes you sick.*"[80] To those watching the twins, the message was clear: "*We're the up-and-coming firm and we don't give a fuck for anyone.*" Having made their intended statement through their demonstration of contempt for the old guard, Ron and Reg collected their cut and were driven off in their van.

According to the twins' biographer, John Pearson, not long after their show of insolent disrespect at the racecourse, some of the Italian gang – along with Billy Hill's right-hand man, Frankie Fraser – issued a challenge to the twins: to fight it out

---

79   Pearson, John. *The Profession of Violence*. London: Weidenfeld and Nicolson, 1972.

80   Ibid.

in an Islington pub. The exact truth of this part of the story is up for some debate, but it must be remembered that John Pearson is the only, purely objective, and unbiased chronicler to have been close to the twins during their time as free men.

Garry Bushell, in his book *Two Faced,* claims that the pub in question was *The Queen's Arms*. Expert on all things London underworld, James Morton, in his book *Krays: The Final Word*, points out that Frankie Fraser was away at this time receiving treatment in a psychiatric hospital. Fraser was serving a three-year sentence during which he had been sent to *Broadmoor* and was not released until late 1955.[81] Exactly who was involved, where it happened, or even if it happened at all, is unclear, but as James Morton says, *"Print the Legend."*

So, the legend goes: This prospect of a battle with London's established gangster elite was just what the twins were waiting for, so they filled their van with several of their best fighting men and set off from *The Regal*, armed to the teeth. Although nominally Spot allies this was no longer part of the Spot/Hill conflict, this was the twins' opportunity for glory – to smash the opposition and rule London. On reaching the pub, they found it empty, and after waiting until closing time, it became clear that the enemy wasn't going to show. Disappointed and deflated, there was nothing left to do except get back in the van and drive away. For some time afterwards the twins issued threats, challenges, and insults, but nothing came back – not a word.

---

81   Prison Years. madfrankiefraser.co.uk

The Queen's Arms, Islington

In the spring of 1955, the Kray twins – accompanied by a number of their best fighting men – travelled to *The Queen's Arms* in Islington for a pre-arranged fight with a posse of gangsters allied with Billy Hill. Ron, Reg, and their boys waited until closing time for the opposition to show up, but they didn't and the fight never happened.

Accounts vary and there is some doubt that the fight that never happened was even arranged in the first place. There is even more doubt about the location of the fight that may or may not have been planned and never took place.

There were, in 1955, two pubs called *The Queen's Arms* in Islington: one at 29a Penton Street (now a private hire venue called *The Chapel Bar*) and one at 19 Caledonian Road, still a pub, now called *Millers*.

Whether or not this pub – which *might* have a 50 per cent chance of being the *probable* location where absolutely nothing happened – is a worthwhile stop-off on a tour of Krays' London is debatable, but it's a nice friendly place to relax with a pint.

Billy Hill's trip to Australia had been cut short by the Australian authorities – who refused to allow him into the country – and he arrived back in England on 10 June 1955. It is possible that Billy Hill returned just in time to hear about the proposed battle and put a stop to it, thus explaining the no-show at *The Queen's Arms*. The last thing that Billy Hill needed was a full-scale war with bloodshed in a public place and the inevitable involvement of the police. Also, he was well aware of the potential power of the up-and-coming twins and the need to keep good relations for the future. Spot, too, was beginning to find the twins a bit too hot to handle, and no doubt realised that watching his back was not their main priority – watching his slow decline, more like, and waiting to take over what was left of his business interests. Jack Spot took the twins to the races several more times, but was careful not to pass on knowledge of the workings of his West End rackets, and gradually distanced himself from the boys from Bethnal Green.

The Kray twins were to play no further part in the Spot/Hill feud, but it continued and, on a summer's day in 1955, an incident occurred that would mark the beginning of Jack Spot's final steep decline into obscurity. Billy Hill's new right-hand man and prominent member of the Clerkenwell-based Italian gang, Albert Dimes, had been spreading the word that Jack Spot was finished and that he should surrender control of his bookies' pitches at the racetracks before they were taken from him. This bad-mouthing had reached Spot's ears and he was becoming increasingly frustrated, bitter, and consumed by rage.

Then, on the morning of Thursday 11 August 1955, by chance, Spot saw Albert Dimes – the focus of his complete and utter hatred – on a street corner in Soho. There, in front of dozens of shoppers and regular folk going about their business, a terrible fight ensued, which began in the street and continued as the two men fell through the door into the *Continental Fruit Stores* on the corner of Frith Street and Old Compton Street. Women screamed as a knife was produced and the two combatants quickly became drenched in blood. Spot seemed to be gaining the upper hand until Sophie Hyams, wife of the shop's proprietor, picked up the heavy pan from the weighing scales and brought it down on Spot's head, splitting his scalp. Eventually, after desperately fighting like wild animals in a life-and-death struggle, the two men became exhausted and Dimes pulled himself away, stumbled outside, and was helped into a taxi. Spot, bleeding profusely from his head and body, staggered into a nearby barber's shop, slumped into the chair and said, *"Fix me up,"* before passing out.

Such an incidence of extreme violence in a public place quickly alerted the police, and the two men who had been seriously injured and hospitalised were charged with GBH. At the subsequent trial at the *Old Bailey*, both were acquitted; Dimes because Sophie Hyams, wife of the proprietor of the *Continental Fruit Stores*, said Spot was the aggressor, and Spot because two dubious witnesses said it was Dimes who initiated the attack. Following the trial and acquittal of both men, the newspapers dubbed the '*Battle of Frith Street*' as '*The Fight That Never Was.*'

Continental Fruit Stores

34 Old Compton Street, Soho, London W1D 4T

Nearest TFL station: Leicester Square underground.

Here on the corner of Frith Street and Old Compton Street in busy, bustling Soho, a vicious fight between rival gangsters Jack Spot and Albert Dimes took place in front of dozens of onlookers on the morning of Thursday 11 August 1955. The infamous 'Battle of Frith Street' began on the pavement outside the *Continental Fruit Stores* (now *Balans* restaurant) and continued to a bloody conclusion inside the shop. Neither man could be described as the winner and both were taken to hospital suffering from serious knife wounds. Spot and Dimes were each charged with GBH but were both acquitted at the subsequent *Old Bailey* trial.

Six years later, after gambling was legalised in 1961, Albert Dimes opened a betting shop on Frith Street, op-

---

posite *Ronnie Scott's* at number 21 (now a restaurant called *Little Italy*).

Meanwhile, back in the East End, it was business as usual for the twins. Operating from their base at *The Regal* billiard hall, Reggie continued to channel his energy into making money. Violence was never far away but, for Reggie, it was *generally* purposeful and conducted towards that end. Ronnie, on the other hand, loved violence for the sake of it; he loved the notoriety that came with it and was beginning to style himself as a screen gangster.

In early 1956, an opportunity arose for Ronnie to realise an ambition and use a gun to shoot someone for the first time. Local car dealer Johnny Hutton was one of a growing number of business people paying the Krays to look after their security. During an argument with a disgruntled customer who claimed that the car he'd been sold was faulty, the customer, a dock worker, threatened to return with friends – and that there would be trouble. Hutton then spoke to Ronnie Kray, who became angry that someone had the audacity to make threats against a business that was under the protection of the Krays. Whether or not the dock worker knew the situation, he calmed down, returned to the dealership, and apologised to Hutton for his aggressive attitude. It was agreed by both parties that the problem could be resolved amicably. Ronnie Kray – who'd been waiting outside for the dock worker to return – however, wasn't interested in apologies. He stormed in and shot the docker in the leg. Reggie was furious and called his brother a "*fucking idiot*," knowing that shooting a member of the public would inevitably involve the police – and, sure enough, it did.

Before the police caught up with Ronnie, a plan was hatched to confuse and create doubt as to which of the identical twins was accused of the deed – a ploy they had used to good effect on many occasions in the past, and would again in the future. Ronnie was taken into hiding and Reggie was arrested. After appearing at an identity parade, Reggie was pointed out as the attacker by the injured man, but Reggie was able to produce identification and evidence that he was elsewhere at the time of the shooting. Next, the services of renowned East End fixer Tommy 'Red Face' Plumley were called upon and the docker was convinced that the matter need go no further. Now disabled, the docker accepted a *sweetener* of £3,000, enough for him to open a sweet shop. The money, of course, came out of Johnny Hutton's pocket.

John Hutton Motors Ltd.

601 Commercial Road, Stepney, London E1 0NE

Nearest TFL station: Limehouse DLR.

In the mid-1950s, situated on the corner of Commercial Road and White Horse Road, was a car sales showroom owned by Johnny Hutton. Hutton's was among the first legitimate businesses to be targeted by the Krays for protection money. Following a dispute with a customer – during which threats were made – Hutton contacted the twins and Ronnie Kray used the opportunity to realise an ambition of his: using a gun to fire at a live target for the first time. After shooting the dissatisfied customer in the leg, a combination of threats, bribery, and deliberate confusion over the identity of the twin responsible ensured that Ronnie escaped prosecution.

Nisa Local supermarket now occupies the site where Ronnie Kray shot and injured a member of the public.

In spring 1956, over in the West End, Jack Spot was all but finished. After hearing about an ill-thought-through plan by Spot to have him shot, Billy Hill ordered retribution and his number one enforcer – Frankie Fraser, now out of prison – went to work with his flick knife, cutting the faces of those involved in the plot and, in so doing, cutting any ties to Spot that his few remaining followers may have had. Bobby Ramsey, Spot's personal bodyguard, was ambushed outside *The Vienna Rooms*, his face slashed.

Jack Spot's last remaining spieler in Dean Street, Soho was gone and his interests at the racetracks were now firmly in the hands of Albert Dimes and the Italians. Without any significant back up or income, Spot was alone, vulnerable, and broke, with barely enough money to pay the rent on his flat in *Hyde Park Mansions*. Worse still, Spot feared not just for his own safety but also that of his pretty Irish wife Rita and his two young daughters. In desperation, Spot went to the police and asked for their protection, but after going to *Paddington Green Police Station* and speaking to a young detective sergeant by the name of Leonard 'Nipper' Read, he was told there was nothing they could do without hard evidence.

Billy Hill's team had a mole living in *Hyde Park Mansions*, just across the landing from Spot's abode; bookie Nathan Mercado was keeping Hill's gang informed of Spot's movements. Finally, at around 9.30pm on Wednesday 2 May 1956, the expected attack came: Spot and his wife Rita were set-upon by a gang of men outside their home at *Hyde Park Mansions*. Rita suffered only bruising, but Spot – who bravely tried to protect his wife and defend himself – was beaten with heavy objects, slashed with blades, and kicked mercilessly as he lay unconscious on the ground. Spot could easily have been killed but he refused to cooperate with the police investigation. Rita, on the other hand, named names and agreed to give evidence in court. Spot didn't stand in her way. Ultimately, Frankie Fraser,

Bobby Warren, Billy Blythe, Ginger Dennis, and Bert 'Battles' Rossi stood trial for the attack on Spot and were given prison sentences ranging from four to seven years.

Hyde Park Mansions

Cabbell Street, Marylebone, London NW1 5AZ

Nearest TFL station: Edgware Road underground.

This imposing Edwardian apartment building close to Edgware Road underground station was, during the 1950s, home to top London gang boss Jack Comer, better known as Jack Spot. It is also the scene of a vicious attack on Spot by a group of villains, which included the notorious gangster Frankie Fraser. Spot and his wife Margarita – or 'Rita'– were returning home on the evening of 2 May 1956 and, as they approached the street entrance to their flat at number 12, they were set upon by a number of men. Rita sustained only minor injuries but Spot was badly beaten with heavy objects and slashed with bladed instruments. Spot was taken to *St Mary's Hospital*, Paddington. The subsequent trial, in which Rita gave evidence against her husband's attackers, made the national news.

Footage exists of Jack Spot's wife Rita, her sister, and her daughter, leaving Hyde Park Mansions under police escort during the trial. It can be viewed at: britishpathe. com (Rita Comer has Police Escort).

Encouraged by his wife Rita – and with little other choice – Jack Spot turned his back on crime and tried to make a legitimate living, but his high-profile criminal background made regular employment hard to find. Eventually, Spot's marriage broke down and Rita took their two daughters and moved to America. Spot found work looking after a furniture store off Gloucester Road in Kensington, West London, and moved into the flat above. After living out the rest of his life in relative obscurity, Jack Spot Comer died in 1996 aged 83.

Interviewed shortly before his death for the 1994 Martin Short TV production, *Gangsters*, Jack Spot reflected on his life in the London underworld.[82]

Summer 1956 was mostly wet, grey, and cool in London, but life for the Brothers Kray was anything but dull. The Watney Street Gang were a band of young toughs from London's Docklands area who had grown up together, worked together at the docks, drank in the same pubs, and enjoyed a good brawl on a Saturday night. For generations, the *Watney Streeters* had been the traditional enemies of the Bethnal Green boys, but the latest version of the gang was no real match for the Krays and their team, who dubbed them 'weekend gangsters.'

Some of the Watney Street Gang were involved in small-time rackets in and around the docks, and one of their number – a young man by the name of Charlie Martin – had devised a scam involving a number of post office drivers. Parcels would be relabelled and sent to addresses where Martin would collect them. Ronnie Kray, via his information network, heard about Martin's little scam and demanded a share of the profits. Charlie Martin agreed but failed to comply and the payments were not forthcoming. Predictably, Ronnie became angry and Charlie Martin's name went into Ronnie's *in-tray* of persons to be dealt with. This was the first of a series of events that would

---

82   YouTube: Jack "Spot" Comer.

eventually bring serious consequences for Ronnie Kray.

Bobby Ramsey – Jack Spot's former bodyguard and long-time friend of the twins – had teamed up with Billy 'The Fox' Jones and taken over a drinking club called the *Stragglers*, just off Cambridge Circus in London's West End. Billy Jones, who worked at the docks and was involved in the allocation of labour there, also knew the twins well. Popular with rough and rowdy dockers, whom Billy Jones had initially encouraged to drink there, the *Stragglers* was the perfect place for after-pub-hours drinking – but drunken, foul-mouthed behaviour and regular fights were keeping the desired clientele, the West End set, well away. This was bad for business, so Bobby Ramsey suggested calling in the twins and offering them an informal partnership in the club. Ron and Reg jumped at the opportunity; it was just what they were looking for, a foothold in the West End's club-land. In no time at all, the twins put a stop to the bad behaviour and the *Stragglers* began to turn a nice profit. Reggie's *cigarette punch* ensured that any trouble was swiftly dealt with and nipped in the bud.[83]

Stragglers

17 Moor Street, London W1D 5AP

Nearest TFL station: Covent Garden underground.

In early 1956, Billy Jones and Bobby Ramsey opened a drinking club on Moor Street – just off Cambridge Circus in London's West End – and called it Stragglers.

---

83   Pearson, John. *The Profession of Violence*. London: Weidenfeld and Nicolson, 1972.

Drunken behaviour and fighting blighted the club, until the young Kray twins were brought in and given a share in the business. Ron and Reg soon put a stop to the trouble and the club began to make money – but success was short-lived. In the autumn of 1956, Ron Kray, Billy Jones, and Bobby Ramsey were found guilty of GBH and sent to prison. Shortly afterwards, the police closed the club down.

The Z Hotel on Moor Street, next to The Cambridge pub, now occupies the site of the Kray twins' first brief venture into London's West End clubland.

Trouble was no longer a problem within the club, but there was trouble afoot of a different kind. *Stragglers* partner Billy Jones had an altercation with Charlie Martin at the docks over the allocation and distribution of labour. The argument soon led to blows and, in the ensuing fight, Charlie Martin – the character who had welched on the redirected parcels deal with Ronnie Kray – beat up Billy Jones. Business partner Bobby Ramsey was not the kind of individual to let something like this go, so he drove down to Limehouse and beat up Charlie Martin. This was by no means the end of the matter, and the tit-for-tat violence continued.

Two nights later, Bobby Ramsey was attacked outside *The Artichoke* pub[84] in Stepney by Charlie Martin and a full complement of Watney Streeters; he was beaten unconscious and hit over the head with an iron bar. Ramsey recovered, but the

---

84   This pub on Jubilee Street was demolished shortly after the event as part of the development of the *Sidney Estate*. A replacement pub was built at 91 Stepney Way during the early '60s, but it closed in 2001 and has stood empty and become increasingly derelict ever since.

ante had been seriously upped and it was now time for the twins to get involved. Bobby Ramsey and Billy Jones were both widely known to be friends of the twins and, as such, this was effrontery of the highest order.

As far as the twins were concerned, their name and reputation were directly threatened. Ronnie Kray already had the hump with Charlie Martin over the parcel scam and now, after this, he wanted to shoot Martin. Having persuaded Ronnie that murder was probably not the best option, Reg helped formulate plans to inflict the most severe of punishment beatings on Martin and his Watney Street pals. It was decided that the attack would be carried out on the evening of Tuesday 28 August 1956.

Choosing a Tuesday night to strike – rather than a Saturday, when the Watney Street Gang would be out in full force – suggests that a full-scale battle was not the plan, more like a surgical strike against Charlie Martin and his immediate crew. Intelligence reports revealed that Martin and friends would likely be gathered in *The Britannia* pub in Chapman Street, Shadwell. Fearless as they were, the twins were not going to venture into enemy territory with only Ramsey and Jones for backup. Any number of loyal troops could have been mustered, but on this occasion they chose Ronnie Diamond and his Diamond Gang to help.[85]

Several cars left *The Regal* at around 9.30pm and arrived at *The Britannia* at 9.45 pm. Ronnie was first to enter the pub, but Charlie Martin and the Watney Streeters weren't there. It is possible that the gang somehow became aware of what was about to happen, and scarpered, sharpish through a back door – or perhaps, on the other hand, they were never there in the first place. What is certain is that Charlie Martin's brother Terry was

---

85   Morton, James. *Krays: The Final Word.* London: Mirror Books, 2019.

present, enjoying a game of cards with three friends. Ronnie was closely followed into the pub by Ramsey, who thought he recognised Terrence Martin as one of his attackers.

"I want you," said Ramsey.

"Come outside or we'll kill you 'ere," said Ron.

Martin was bundled through the door and struck on the back of the head with a bayonet. Outside the pub, he was viciously attacked with fists, boots, and various weapons by a group of men including Ron, Reg, Billy Jones, and Ramsey, who stabbed Martin with the bayonet under his right arm and in the shoulder. Once it was deemed that they'd done enough, several cars sped away from the scene. Martin, seriously injured, was helped back into the pub by two of his friends and then taken to the *London Hospital*.[86]

The Britannia

44 Morris Street, Shadwell, London E1 2NP

Nearest TFL station: Shadwell overground.

In the summer of 1956, the Kray twins and a number of their associates – including Bobby Ramsey – went to the pub looking for Watney Street Gang member Charlie Martin and his friends. Only Charlie Martin's brother Terrence was to be found when the Krays arrived, so he was bundled outside and subjected to a horrific beating with heavy objects and stabbed with a bayonet by Bobby Ramsey.

Established in 1891 and situated on the corner of

---

86   Bennett, John. *Krayology*. London: Mango Books, 2015.

Morris Street and Chapman Street, the pub remained open for well over a hundred years until it closed its doors in 2005. Afterwards, the building was converted into a fast food outlet called *Perfect Fried Chicken*, but the original pub sign remained in place and could be seen on the corner of the building above the door. Recently, the premises changed hands (or identity) and the occupying business is now the *Grill Hut*. Tragically, *The Britannia* pub sign was removed leaving only a bare wall, consigning a fascinating piece of social history to a skip.

Martin was seriously injured and, from his hospital bed, told the police who his attackers were – ultimately, this led to Ronnie Kray receiving a three-year prison sentence for GBH.

Shortly after the attack, while patrolling the streets in search of Charlie Martin and the rest of the Watney Street Gang, Ramsey's Buick – with Ronnie in the passenger seat – was stopped by police in Morgan Street, Mile End. Seeing that both men had blood on their clothing, the police searched the car and found a bayonet, a machete, and a crowbar. After searching Ronnie, he was found to be carrying a *Young America* revolver in his jacket pocket. Ronnie and Ramsey were arrested and taken to *Leman Street Police Station*.[87]

---

87   It was at *Leman Street Police Station*, under the command of Inspector Frederick Abberline, that the investigation into the Jack the Ripper murders was based in 1888. A new police station was built in 1891 and remained open until the late 1960s, when it was demolished and replaced by the current police station which opened in 1970 at 74 Leman St.

Ronnie was questioned about the gun, and it was found that four of the six chambers of the revolver contained live rounds. The bullets had been filed down, and the sergeant at *Leman Street* could not be sure if the intention was to turn the rounds into devastating and banned *dumdum* bullets, or simply make them fit into the chamber. Some accounts say that Reggie and Billy Jones were arrested at the same time and others that they went voluntarily to the police station. If this is the case, then it's more than a little surprising that Reggie didn't bother to change his bloodstained clothes first. When asked to account for the blood on his jacket and tie, Reggie said it was probably there due to closely watching boxers during sparring sessions. Ron and Reg Kray, Ramsey, and Jones were all charged with causing grievous bodily harm to Terrence Martin and were remanded in custody. Ron was also charged with the possession of a gun without authorisation and certification.

Martin was in a bad way and was kept in hospital for eight days, suffering from multiple lacerations and abrasions to his head and body – including a four-and-a-half-inch deep stab wound in his upper back.[88] Now, work needed to be done to ensure Terrence Martin wasn't going to talk. Persuading witnesses that it was not in their best interest to give evidence against them was familiar work for the Krays. The East End's traditional wall of silence and a little extra encouragement from their very own Mr Fixit – 'Red Face' Tommy Plumley – would no doubt produce the desired result. But, for once, it did not; Terry Martin was not willing to be fixed and became the chief witness for the prosecution.

All four of the accused were sent for trial at the *Old Bailey*, charged with grievous bodily harm. Police forensics back in 1956 were not what they are today, and blood found on the

---

88   Bennett, John. *Krayology*. London: Mango Books, 2015.

clothing of all four defendants, in Ramsey's car, and on the machete, crowbar, and bayonet could not be conclusively identified as Martin's. The clever defence council managed to create so much uncertainty over the individual identities of the twins – and whether or not one or both of them had been at the scene of the assault – that the judge had no choice but to accept that the bloodstains found on Reggie's jacket may well have come from sparring boxers.

On Friday 4 November, Reg Kray – who had pleaded not guilty to the charges – was acquitted. Ronnie, Ramsey, and Jones were not so lucky and, on 5 November, all three were found guilty as charged. Ramsey was sentenced to seven years imprisonment; Ronnie and Jones were given three years each. After passing the sentence, the judge – Sir Gerald Dodson – reflected on the premeditated nature of the brutal assault and how it was mere luck that Martin had not been killed. *"You plunged what otherwise is a respectable part of the East End into an abyss of brutality."*[89]

Unlucky for Ronnie Kray? Some might think so but, on the other hand, a sentence of only three years could be seen as extremely lucky. Only two years previously, the twins had committed a brutal assault on a man in a drinking club in Tottenham Court Road. The victim, who Reggie described as an 'African,' was beaten repeatedly over the head with a wooden truncheon until it broke, and a knife was plunged twice into his side. Afterwards, word reached the twins that the man was dead and both were worried they'd be hanged for murder. Luckily for the twins, the man survived, and witness intimidation ensured that they escaped a charge of attempted murder.[90] It's difficult to un-

---

89   *East London Advertiser*, 9 November 1956/ Bennett, John. Krayology. London: Mango Books, 2015.

90   Kray, Reg. *Born Fighter*. London: Century, 1990.

derstand how such a close call didn't cause the twins to think twice and, at least, reduce the level of violence to which they were prepared to go. Clearly, it did not.

Terrence Martin's savage beating with a crowbar, machete, and bayonet could so easily have resulted in his death. Also, had Charlie Martin and his friends been found and had Ronnie chosen to use the loaded revolver he was carrying, the result could have been catastrophic. Should someone lose their life in such a situation, it would be very difficult – in a court of law – to argue that there was no intention to kill when beating someone about the head with an iron bar, stabbing them repeatedly with a bladed instrument, or shooting them with a gun. In 1956, death by hanging was the penalty for premeditated murder and Ronnie Kray had, once again, come dangerously close to meeting Mr Harry Allen, who – after the retirement of Albert Pierrepoint a year earlier – was now Britain's appointed executioner.

Ronnie began his three-year sentence at *Wandsworth*, a category B prison, a notch below maximum security but nevertheless with a relatively harsh regime. Conditions were not a problem for Ronnie and he seemed to be settling in nicely – helped by the fact that he was surrounded by like-minded criminals, many of whom were from his home turf. During his time in *Wandsworth*, Ron met and became friendly with Frank Mitchell, a big powerful man who had a gentle, childlike manner towards those he trusted – but who was violent and dangerous towards authority figures and those he didn't. Mitchell was immensely strong, and prison warders were wary and careful about how they treated him. Ronnie very much admired this and would try to cheer Frank up when he was feeling low, often sending him presents of food and tobacco. Ronnie told Frank that he and his brother would look after him and make sure he was alright when he was released.

The twins' mother, Violet, worried terribly that separation

from his twin would be a problem for Ronnie, but Reggie visited regularly and neither twin seemed unduly concerned about being parted for a while. On the surface, Ronnie appeared to be doing fine, but to his friend from childhood – Laurie O'Leary, who knew him better than most – discernible signs of paranoia were beginning to show.

HMP Wandsworth

Heathfield Road, London, SW18 3HU

Nearest station: Wandsworth Common (Southern Railways).

On 5 November 1956, Ronnie Kray was found guilty of GBH and given a three-year prison sentence. Ronnie began his sentence at *Wandsworth Prison*, where he was among friends and given respect due to his standing within the criminal fraternity. While in *Wandsworth*, Ronnie met and befriended Frank Mitchell, a man notorious within the prison system.

Following a conviction for demanding money with menaces in 1959, Reggie also spent several months in *Wandsworth* where he too came to know Frank Mitchell.

Built in 1851, the Victorian prison is one of the largest prisons in the UK and holds around 1500 category B male prisoners.

Between 1878 and 1961, 135 inmates were hanged at *Wandsworth Prison*.

It was spring 1957, and with The Colonel away in prison, gang wars – and violence for the sake of it – were no longer top of the agenda. Reggie, therefore, was able to turn his full attention to the pursuit of new business opportunities. Reggie, still only 23, had for some time been toying with the idea of opening a new East End club – and, after hearing of available premises in a suitable location, it stirred him into taking the idea more seriously. Enquiries were made and a meeting arranged with the property owner at his office in Mayfair. Reggie explained that he was interested in renting the empty house at 145 Bow Road with a view to turning it into a licensed drinking club. The property owner said he had no objections to this, so a figure for the rent was agreed and hands were shaken to finalise the deal. Reggie *borrowed* the first three months' rent from car dealer Johnny Hutton and set about arranging the necessary paperwork and licence.

Sitting tenants occupied the top floor of the large three-storey building; the first floor was to be a boxing gym and the ground floor, the club. Situated only a short distance from *Bow Road Police Station*, the big house needed work to turn it into Reggie's vision. Fixtures and fittings were installed, including a bar, small stage, and dance floor. Furniture was bought, carpets laid, and the walls hung with red flock wallpaper – the last word in style in its day. Running low on cash, Reggie asked his brother Charlie if he would like to join him as a partner in the club for the price of stocking the bar with drink. Charlie agreed and the club – which was to be called *The Double R,* referencing *Rolls Royce*, synonymous with luxury and style, and of course the twins' initials – was registered on 6 May 1957.

East End drinking clubs at this time were grim, sparse, men-only establishments where dice and punches were thrown, but *The Double R* was to be something different and unique. Reggie's vision of an East End club with a touch of West End style – where nice people and couples could enjoy an evening out without the risk of trouble from rowdy hooligan types – was about to become a reality and, on a Wednesday evening in

May, the doors were opened.

The Double R Club was an instant hit and the locals were soon joined by a few curious West End types, plus a celebrity or two – including Barbara Windsor, Jackie Collins, George Sewell, and the East End's own blonde bombshell, Diana Dors. *The Double R* effectively opened a door for outsiders to safely visit the East End, and this *portal* into a slightly mysterious and undiscovered world soon began to attract journalists, who came and hung out in numbers, looking for a story. Upstairs was a fully kitted-out boxing gym with punch bags, speedballs, weights, and a full-size ring for local boxers to train.

Manning the doors at various times were Big Pat Connolly, an 18-stone Scotsman who would remain with the twins as a leading Firm member until their arrest in 1968; Tommy 'The Bear' Brown, ex-heavyweight boxer and friend of the Kray family; Alfred 'Limehouse' Willy, an ex-merchant seaman, professional gambler, and important Firm member throughout the '50s and early '60s; and Billy Donovan, who had nearly lost an eye after the fight with the twins in *The Coach and Horses* several years earlier. Remaining silent about the incident had earned Reggie's respect, and Donovan was given the job of head doorman at *The Double R*.

Once past the doormen, most guests were aware that it was not a good idea to misbehave inside the club, but on the odd occasion when a punter – due to drinking too much or just forgetting where he was – became rude or rowdy, Reggie would step in and deal with the situation. One polite warning was given, but if it went unheeded, a knockout punch and an unceremonious dumping outside would invariably follow.

Reggie was proud of his new club and easily slipped into the role of convivial host, welcoming the guests and often buying them a drink, which was generally returned. Live music was a regular feature at *The Double R*, and Fred Merry – a well-known pianist in the '50s – played most nights. Queenie Watts performed regularly and sang sentimental cockney songs in her inimitable style. Queenie would go on to become a well-known personality in the '60s and '70s, appearing in films and on television. During periods when the entertainment wasn't live, music was provided by the new jukebox – quite a novelty at this time. Opening hours were 3pm through to 11pm every night, except Sundays when the hours were 1-3pm and 7-10pm. After-hours drinking was not generally available; only a few close friends and family would occasionally remain behind after the doors were closed.

With Ronnie away in prison and Charlie stepping in to provide shared responsibility, Reggie was able to explore new possibilities – not just in business, but with other pleasures that life had to offer. Ronnie didn't like women; as far as he was concerned they were a waste of time, gave you diseases, and should be avoided, a viewpoint he expected Reggie to share and abide by. Now, without the overbearing influence of his twin brother, Reggie – with his good looks and alpha-male status – was able to enjoy the company of the many women who were attracted to him.

The Double R Club

145 Bow Road, London E3 3AA

Nearest TFL station: Bow Road underground.

On the north side of Bow Road, just a few yards east of Kit Kat Terrace – where the *Enterprise* car rental business meets the playground of the Phoenix Upper School – is the location of the former *Double R Club*. Opened in May 1957 by Reggie and Charlie Kray, while Ronnie was away in prison serving a three-year sentence for

GBH, *The Double R* occupied the ground floor of a large three-storey house and was the East End's most exclusive club. Nothing quite like it had existed before in the East End, and locals were joined by curious West End types, a few celebrities, and a pack of tabloid journo's sniffing around for a story. *The Double R* remained open and in business until 1960, when the police revoked the licence and closed the club down.

Sadly, this most iconic of locations in the story of the Kray twins has long since been demolished, and there is nothing to see except the spot where it used to be. However, on the opposite side of the road, just a few yards along in an easterly direction, is *The Bow Bells* pub; although not known as a regular Krays pub, it is little changed and very likely that the Krays crossed the threshold a time or two in the 1950s.

Between them, *The Regal* billiard club and *The Double R* were bringing in a regular legitimate income and, along with the earnings generated by *looking after* the security of the odd car pitch and other businesses, Reggie was making money. Shortly after opening *The Double R*, Reggie and Charlie further increased the inward flow of cash by opening several illicit gambling clubs (spielers), the first of which was in a rented house at number 8 Wellington Way, close to *The Double R* and just a few yards from *Bow Road Police Station*. This was the biggest money-spinner so far; the house cut from card games, dice, and an illegal bookmaking business was bringing in a minimum of £50 a night, well over £1,000 in today's money.

Within a short time, another club fell into Reggie's hands. On 5 August 1957, Stephen Martin opened a spieler at 1a Campbell Road, Bow, just a stone's throw from *The Double R* and the Wellington Way club. Reggie saw this as a liberty, particularly as Stephen Martin was the father of Charlie and Terry, whom Reggie saw as responsible for his brother's current incarceration.

One day, while Martin was enjoying a drink with a friend at the nearby *Bow Bells* pub, a group of men entered his club, punched the barman in the face, and proceeded to smash the place up. Despite the fact that illegal gambling was taking place at the club, Martin went to the police and suggested that the trouble could be connected with the Krays' animosity towards his family. Charlie and Reggie were brought in for questioning, but they both had alibis and there was no evidence to link them to the incident. Unsurprisingly, shortly afterwards, Stephen Martin told the police that he no longer wished the matter to be investigated. Reggie approached the owner of the premises, Anwar Haque, and took over the club – which from then onwards was known simply as *Anwars* by the Krays and their friends.

Wellington Way & Anwars

Nearest TFL station: Bow Road underground

In the early summer of 1957, Reggie Kray, helped by elder brother Charlie opened a spieler (illegal gambling club) in a rented house at number 8 Wellington Way, E3 4NE. Card games, dice and a bookmaking business brought in a tidy sum and added to the Krays' income from the nearby *Double R Club*. The house at number 8 no longer exists and a modern multi storey apartment building now occupies the spot.

Later the same year, Reggie took over another spieler known as *Anwars*, almost directly opposite the *Double R* at 1a Campbell Road E3 4DS. Still in existence today, the house on the west side of Campbell Road, close to the junction with Bow Road is a Sikh place of worship.

Both spielers along with the *Double R Club* were closed down by the police in 1960.

All three clubs were in close proximity to *Bow Road Police Station*. Situated at 111 Bow Road, the Grade II listed police station is unchanged and displays the iconic blue lamp at the entrance.

Charlie Kray was finding life in business with his younger brother satisfactory and financially rewarding, much more so than his previous means of making a living *on the knocker* buying and selling second-hand clothes and jewellery. Charlie's new-found affluence enabled him, his wife Dolly, and their young son Gary to move out of Vallance Road into a home of their own. Charlie found a vacant two-bedroom flat on the second floor of an apartment building – called *Brightlingsea Buildings* close to London Docks on Narrow Street in Limehouse – and the family moved in. Charlie's departure from Vallance Road was long overdue as, by all accounts, neither of the twins liked Dolly very much and referred to her as *'Snotty Nose '*or *'Skinny.'*[91] Charlie was helping to fill the void left by Ronnie's absence and, despite missing his twin brother, Reggie was becoming prosperous and enjoying himself. All was well with two of the Brothers Kray, but there was a problem looming on the horizon – a big problem.

91   Kray, Reg. *Born Fighter*. London: Century, 1990.

Brightlingsea Buildings

Narrow Street, Limehouse, London E14 8BP

Nearest TFL station: Limehouse DLR

Built in 1904 to help provide accommodation for the large number of people displaced by the construction of the Rotherhithe Tunnel that began in 1900, the large apartment building was severely damaged by bombing during the war – but it was repaired and remained standing until its demolition as part of the complete redevelopment of London's Docklands, which began in1981. Modern apartment buildings now occupy the site at the junction of Narrow Street and Brightlingsea Place where *Brightlingsea Buildings* once stood.

Charlie Kray moved into a second-floor apartment here in 1957, with his wife Dorothy and their six-year-old son Gary, and remained here until the family moved to a more spacious and modern apartment at 40 Thornfield House, Rosefield Gardens, Poplar in the early 1960s. Nancy, a daughter, was born in 1965.

Nothing remains of the original Brightlingsea apartment building, but a visit to the area is not without interest. Directly opposite where Charlie Kray and family once lived in Narrow Street is *The Grapes* pub, which dates back to the 16th century and is now part-owned by the actor Sir Ian McKellen. Two doors along from *The Grapes* at number 80 is the house where painter and friend of the Krays, Francis Bacon, lived and worked before moving to 7 Reece Mews, South Kensington in 1961.

Ronnie's general behaviour in *Wandsworth* was good, so the prison authorities decided to send him to a lower-category institution. On 19 June 1957, he was transferred to *HMP Camp Hill* on the Isle of Wight, a category C jail that operated a more relaxed and easy-going prison regime, but Ronnie was not happy there.[92]

Visits from family and friends became more difficult and less frequent due to the prison's location, and Ronnie had little in common with the other inmates whom he regarded with contempt, considering them to be a bunch of small-time nobodies. Ronnie became increasingly more unbalanced and his mental health was deteriorating fast. Eventually, the gauge on his pressure cooker of emotions went into the red zone and then, triggered by being denied permission to attend a gymnastics class, the explosion came. In a fit of uncontrollable rage, Ronnie began smashing up the games room, destroying the table tennis tables, lashing out at other prisoners, and screaming abuse at inmates and staff alike: *"You're all a load of fucking idiots!"*[93]

Following Ronnie's meltdown, he was deemed unsuitable for *Camp Hill* and – on 16 August 1957 – he was transferred to *Winchester Prison* in Hampshire. Winchester was a little nearer to London and, importantly, had a psychiatric unit where he was assessed and placed under observation. Ronnie's mood improved slightly but he was still extremely emotionally fragile. Also present in Winchester at the time was Bert 'Battles'

---

92   Built in 1912 and officially opened by Winston Churchill, *Camp Hill* was a category C men's prison. In 2008, *Camp Hill* – along with nearby *Albany* and *Parkhurst* prisons – were amalgamated to become a single large prison complex. The Camp Hill element of the newly named *HMP Isle of Wight* closed in 2013 and currently lies empty and unused.

93   O'Leary, Laurie. *Ronnie Kray: A Man Among Men*. London: Headline Publishing, 2002.

Rossi, an Anglo-Italian gangster from Clerkenwell serving time for his part in the attack on Jack Spot the previous year. Bert wrote a book with James Morton – *Bert Battles Rossi, Britain's Oldest London Gangland Boss* – which was published just before his death, aged 94, in 2017. In the book, Bert tells of how he met Ronnie Kray in the prison's mailbag shop and they became friendly. Also serving time in *Winchester* was a man by the name of George Cornell, and Ronnie Kray's arrival – according to Bert – made up a trio of pals from London.

Diagnosed with *prison psychosis* by the medical officer, Ronnie's mental health, once again, began to deteriorate. His behaviour was showing signs of paranoia and he was becoming increasingly more irrational. So, Ronnie was moved out of the general prison population and into the psychiatric unit, where he could be monitored more closely. Medicated and under the care of the staff in the unit, Ronnie slowly responded to treatment and his condition began to improve, but on 27 December, he received a letter from Reggie telling of the death, from leukaemia, of his beloved Aunt Rose. Receiving this news was catastrophic for Ronnie and he quickly slipped into a total and cataclysmic mental breakdown. To ensure the safety of other prisoners, staff, and himself, Ronnie – who had become incoherent and uncontrollably violent – was put into a straitjacket and placed in a padded cell.

Seven weeks after Rose's death, on 16 August 1957, Violet received some devastating news. A telegram arrived at Vallance Road stating, abruptly and to the point: "*Your son Ronald Kray certified insane.*"

HMP Winchester

Romsey Road, Winchester SO22 5DF

Built in 1850, the Victorian prison – which was the first of many designed with five blocks radiating from a central hub – still operates today as a category B men's prison and young offenders institution.

Ronnie Kray was transferred from *Camp Hill Prison* to *Winchester* in August 1957. After being admitted to the prison's psychiatric unit later the same year, Ronnie's mental health condition began to improve, but news of the death of his Aunt Rose triggered a catastrophic mental breakdown and Ronnie was certified insane.

Ronnie was transferred to *Long Grove Hospital* near Epsom in Surrey on 20 February 1958, where his condition could be treated. There was a family connection with the hospital through the twins' maternal great-grandfather. 'Crutcha' Lee, who suffered from psychotic episodes in later life, had ended his days at *Long Grove* a few years before the First World War. Around 2,000 patients, mostly from the London area, were resident at *Long Grove* during Ronnie's time there, only six of whom had come from prisons. Hospital policy was to make no distinction between prisoners and other patients; they were to be treated exactly the same. Ronnie was held in the secure Napier Ward, where trained staff kept patients under round-the-clock supervision and observation. Seriously ill and suffering from paranoid delusions, Ronnie would sit motionless and huddled over a radiator. Ronnie never forgot the terror of his first few days in *Long Grove* and later recalled:

"I thought the man opposite me was a dog and if I got

his name right he would come and jump in my lap. I'd have a friend then but I never got his name. Sometimes I thought I'd kill myself to stop someone else doing it first."

After observation and assessment, the doctor's report deemed Ronnie to be: *"A simple man of low intelligence, poorly in touch with the outside world."*[94]

Visits were upsetting for the family as Ronnie didn't appear to recognise them and would simply sit and stare blankly at them without saying a word. Mother Violet refused to believe that her son was insane and consoled herself with the thought that Ronnie was just playing up again to get one over on the authorities – like he did when he was in the army – and that it was the drugs they were giving him that were causing him to be like he was. Treatments for mental disorders prior to the '50s were limited and sometimes, by today's standards, inhumane, but recent advances had brought about the discovery of effective drug treatments. Stemetil – the brand name for one of many new antipsychotic drugs – was not a cure for conditions like Ronnie's but it was effective in helping patients recover from a breakdown and, taken thereafter, would continue to keep them stabilised.

Within a relatively short time, Ronnie began to respond to the Stemetil and his condition improved significantly. Doctors were so pleased with his progress that, by the end of March, he was moved from Napier Ward to M1 Block, where patients were less closely monitored and the security more relaxed. Ronnie began to spend his time reading and, when the family came to visit, he recognised them and appeared perfectly normal – even sharing a joke or two.

Time in *Long Grove* did not count as time off Ronnie's sen-

---

94   Pearson, John. *The Profession of Violence*. London: Weidenfeld and Nicolson, 1972.

tence and he was eager to be discharged and sent back to prison to finish his time – but, at the end of May, after being examined and assessed by two doctors, it was decided that, although greatly improved, a swift return to prison could bring about a recurrence of his symptoms. Therefore, he must remain in hospital for the full recommended period of 20 months. Ronnie was obviously unhappy about the situation and complained to Reggie that he was beginning to think he would never be free again. Reggie too was worried and, when he heard that Ronnie, while eating an apple, had been punched in the face by another patient, Reggie decided that this was the last straw and he needed to somehow get Ronnie out of there.

After some research, Reggie discovered that – according to procedure at the time – a patient certified insane remaining at large for a period of six weeks without incident would render the certification void. The plan was to spring Ronnie from *Long Grove* and keep him hidden for six weeks, after which time he would have the option of giving himself up to finish the remainder of his sentence.[95] A great idea in theory, but how exactly was he going to pull it off? Reggie hatched a rather ingenious plan to confuse the authorities over his and Ronnie's identical appearance; a stratagem used successfully so many times in the past.

On Sunday 26 May 1958, two carloads of men – including Reggie, George Osborne, and Curly King – left the East End and headed for Epsom, about an hour's drive away. During previous visits, Ronnie had been briefed about the plan and told what to wear on the day. A blue suit, grey checked shirt, red tie, and black shoes was the chosen attire, and of course Reggie would be wearing the same. Arriving at *Long Grove* around 2pm, Reggie put on a light fawn raincoat to cover his clothes.

---

95   Bennett, John. *Krayology*. London: Mango Books, 2015.

Only two visitors were allowed at one time, so Reggie – accompanied by George Osborne, and with visiting permits and an album of old photographs in hand – went inside.

Finding Ronnie in the visiting room, the three men sat together flicking through the pages of the photograph album, and Ronnie made a point of laughing uproariously. When tea time came, visitors were allowed to go and collect refreshments from the small canteen in the entrance hall. Just prior to this, when none of the staff were looking, Reggie took off his coat and Ronnie put it on. When the time came to go and get the tea, Ronnie – wearing Reggie's coat – walked unchallenged out of the visiting area, into the entrance hall, past the canteen, and out into the car park, where he climbed inside the waiting getaway car which pulled out and drove away.

Meanwhile, back in the visiting room, Reggie took over laughing at the photographs and it was some time before one of the guards realised there was something amiss. Walking over to the two remaining men, the guard looked at Reggie and said, *"You've pulled a flanker."*

"How do you mean?" asked Reg, pretending not to understand.

"You shouldn't have let him go to get the tea; you should have got it."

"Well, it's your job to look after him, not mine," said Reg nonchalantly.[96]

Alarms sounded and the police were called, but Ronnie was long gone. Reggie and George Osborne were detained and questioned for over an hour, but Reggie was able to confirm his identity by producing his driving licence – and the two men stuck to their story that they had simply waited for a cup of tea that never arrived. At 4pm, Reggie and Osborne were

---

96   Kray, Reg. *Born Fighter*. London: Century, 1990.

allowed to go, as there were simply no grounds on which they could be held.

Long Grove Hospital

Horton Lane, Epsom KT19 8PU

The hospital, originally called *Long Grove Lunatic Asylum*, was opened in June 1907. In 1918 it was re-named *Long Grove Mental Hospital* and, in 1937, the word Mental was dropped from its name. By 1960, the hospital accommodated over 2,000 patients and had gained an international reputation as one of the most advanced and pioneering psychiatric hospitals. Following a run-down period in the 1980s, the hospital finally closed in 1992 and stood derelict until 1998, when the site was redeveloped for housing. Many of the original buildings were demolished during the creation of the *Clarendon Park* housing development, completed in 2002, but some remain – including the former administration building, which is now an apartment block called *Prospect House*.

The entrance to *Prospect House* was once the main entrance to the hospital and, in February 1958, it would have seen Reggie Kray walk in and Ronnie Kray walk out after switching identities.

The next day, the story of the audacious breakout hit the headlines, reflecting the authorities' concern over the matter. Ronald Kray, as far as the police were concerned, was a violent criminal at large, suffering from a mental disorder that could make him a danger to the public. Reggie was again questioned by the police the following day, and afterwards spoke to a reporter from the *Daily Mirror*, the interview appearing in Wednesday's edition on 28 May 1958.

Reggie, playing the innocent, claimed: *"I was with him a few minutes before he disappeared from the hospital on Whit Monday afternoon. But I don't know how he escaped."* When asked about the fact that he and his brother were dressed identically, Reggie said: *"A coincidence. We are identical twins. We think alike."*

Ronnie was taken to Suffolk, where the twins' friend Geoff Allen had an isolated property with extensive wooded grounds. Reggie had first met crooked businessman Geoff Allen five years earlier at *The Vienna Rooms* when he took part in a rigged card game. Allen's farmhouse property was somewhere in the deep, mysterious Suffolk countryside, close to Sudbury and not far from the village of Borley – where Britain's most haunted house, *Borley Rectory*, once stood. In an area of secluded woodland was a four-berth caravan stocked with food, drink, and some of Ronnie's favourite books and records. Reggie and the family thought that the peace and tranquillity of the beautiful Suffolk countryside in the springtime would help keep Ronnie calm while he lay low for a while. Accompanying Ron as his live-in minder, cook, and housekeeper was Mad Teddy Smith – a fellow homosexual and one of the few friends Ronnie trusted completely.

Born in Islington in 1932 and embarking on a life of crime at an early age, Edward Richard Smith accumulated a string of convictions ranging from armed robbery to assaulting a police officer. Often violent and unpredictable, especially under the influence of drink, Mad Teddy Smith was a character of contradictions: a violent, dyed-in-the wool criminal on the one hand, and articulate, intelligent and creative on the other. Teddy Smith spoke several languages and wrote plays, one of which – a prison drama called *The Top Bunk* – was screened by the

BBC in 1967.[97]

As David Teale, fringe Firm member, said: *"He was the most charming, funniest, most entertaining thug you could ever meet."*[98]

Frank Kurylo, Kray associate, said of him: *"Teddy Smith, big fine lad, full of his own importance; could speak a few languages – I don't think he told the truth in any of them."*[99]

Mad Teddy Smith was a trusted member of the Krays' inner circle and would go on to become deeply involved in many of the twins' exploits and escapades to come – at least until late 1967, when he inexplicably disappeared completely. Many, including the police, thought Teddy Smith had been murdered by one of the twins and this was the assumption held for decades afterwards. Then, in 2017 – via a gangland memorabilia website, and further investigation by amateur crime researcher Ray Rose – it became apparent that Mad Teddy Smith had moved to Australia in the late '60s or early '70s and lived out his life there before returning to England shortly before his death, aged 74, in 2006. Another even more startling revelation came to light in 2019 when journalist Clare Campbell – with the help of former Kray associate David Teale – gained access to open MI5 files held in the National Archives and revealed that Mad Teddy Smith was 'probably' a mole in the Kray camp, passing information to the secret services.

Ronnie, at first, appeared to settle in at the caravan nice-

---

97   Teddy Smith's play was broadcast on BBC2 at 8.35pm on Monday 30 October 1967 as part of an anthology series called *Thirty-Minute Theatre. The Top Bunk* was the first of the series to be broadcast in colour.

98   Teale, David. *Surviving the Krays*. London: Ebury Press, 2021.

99   *The Gangster and the Pervert Peer*, TV documentary, Blakeway Productions, Channel 4, 2009.

ly, spending days relaxing or exercising, running, and playing games with Teddy Smith. Ronnie's favourite game was the *hunting* game, where they would stalk each other with air rifles. Teddy Smith probably enjoyed the game too – until Ronnie shot him in the corner of the eye, necessitating a trip to *Sudbury Hospital* to have the pellet removed. On one occasion, Teddy Smith borrowed a car from Geoff Allen and took Ronnie to the cinema; he wanted to see *Dracula*.[100] Most weekends, Reggie would arrive with a carload of food and drink, and sometimes a few trusted friends, for a party. Other times, knowing what was needed to keep Ron happy and calm, Reggie would bring a boy, leaving him for a day or two before picking him up and taking him back to London. Reggie soon began to question if this was such a good idea, as Ronnie would generally have a bit of a tantrum when the boy was taken away, and sulk for days afterwards. What Reggie and the family didn't really grasp was the fact that Ronnie was not cured; he was merely stabilised by the drugs he'd been given at *Long Grove*. There was no cure for his condition and, inevitably, as time went by Ronnie became more restless, anxious, and progressively more unbalanced. Alcohol in large quantities was Ronnie's only relief, drinking himself into a stupor until he eventually fell asleep. Teddy Smith could see the decline and told Reggie of his concerns. Also, Geoff Allen reported back to Reg that he was worried about Ronnie who, by now, no longer wanted to stay in the caravan and had moved himself into the house.

---

100 Released in May 1958, this was the first of a series of Hammer Horror films starring Christopher Lee as Dracula and Peter Cushing as Van Helsing.

Sudbury, Suffolk

In the late spring of 1958 – after swapping identities with Reggie – Ronnie Kray escaped from *Long Grove Hospital* and was hidden in a caravan, in woodland, somewhere deep in the Suffolk countryside.

Suffolk is a beautiful and slightly mysterious county, with miles of narrow winding roads lined with high hedges and trees that form tunnels through verdant woodland and serene countryside. Tiny villages, with ancient pastel pink or pale mustard yellow-washed thatched cottages and a crumbling medieval church, suddenly appear and quickly disappear in the rear-view mirror. Hidden somewhere in a corner of this picturesque and unfathomable piece of England, which seems to hide many-a-secret, was Ronnie's four-berth mobile hiding place.

Accounts vary considerably as to the precise whereabouts of the caravan, and the property owner Geoff Allen is not to be found on the electoral register at this time. John Pearson, in his book *The Profession of Violence*, says that it was near the small market town of Sudbury and not far from the tiny village of Borley, once the location of *Borley Rectory* – famously, Britain's most haunted house, until it was mysteriously destroyed by fire in 1939 and demolished in 1944.

To get a feel of Ronnie's surroundings in the spring of 1958, there is a pleasant 2.8-mile walk, much of it along a disused railway track by the River Stour, from Sudbury to Borley. The village is reached by leaving the track where it joins Hall Road (the only road that runs through Borley) and continuing for a further half-mile or so. Borley is tiny and without a pub or a shop, but it does have a small medieval church – parts of which date back to the 11th century. Directly across the road from the church is a gateway and sign: '*The Old Coach House.*' Just inside the gate of this private property, to the left, is an area of open ground where *Borley Rectory* once stood. Some say that the spooks left the rectory when it was destroyed by fire and now inhabit the church.

Good walking shoes and a change of underwear are recommended for this trip.

Ronnie pleaded to be taken back to London, and Reggie – thinking it might help him to have more contact with family and friends – made arrangements for Ronnie to take a few trips back to the East End, staying for a night or two in one of several flats at various locations. One of the flats was at Adelina Grove, just off the Whitechapel Road, opposite *The Blind Beggar* pub.

During these trips home, Ronnie put in an appearance or two at *The Double R*, and was able to attend a party celebrating Cousin Rita's engagement to the twins' friend Richie Smith. Sometimes Ronnie would dress as – and pretend to be – Reggie to take a walk or have a drink in a local pub. Occasionally, the services of Doctor Blasker were called upon; he was able to supply Ronnie with the drugs he needed. Ronnie failed to take the drugs regularly, however, and – coupled with the enormous quantity of alcohol he was consuming – the effect was minimal.

Doctor Morris Blasker, among his other duties, acted as resident doctor at the *Repton Boxing Club* and had known the twins since their time as young amateur boxers. Himself an ex-boxer and great fan of the sport, the good doctor could be relied upon by the criminal fraternity to stitch up slashed faces, remove bullets, and generally attend to wounds – without involving the police. *'Doc'* Blasker, who lived above his surgery at Manchester Grove on the Isle of Dogs, was a much-loved character who clearly judged no one and devoted his life to the care of others. Before the National Health Service came into being in 1947, medical treatment had to be paid for, but Doc Blasker – who never took a holiday – would regularly treat hard-up patients for free. His altruism knew no bounds and when, on one freezing night on his way home from work, he was asked why he had no overcoat, he explained that he had given his only coat to a man *"in more need of it than me."* Doc Blasker was at work in his surgery on the day he died. Suddenly taken ill, he passed away on 28 December 1974, aged 70. Fond memories of the good doctor and his selfless work in his local community resulted in a successful 2010 campaign to have a new riverside road named after him.[101]

Doc Blasker's House

2 Manchester Grove, Isle of Dogs, London E14 3BG

The private house, close to the junction with East Ferry Road, is the former surgery and home of Doctor Morris Blasker who, until his death in 1974, worked tirelessly attending to the sick and needy of his local community. 'Doc' Blasker, who was clearly not one to judge others, would often be called upon by the Kray twins to supply medication and *patch-up* injured members of the criminal fraternity without involving the police.

In 2010, a campaign was launched to honour the memory of the much-loved doctor, resulting in a new riverside road being named after him. *Blasker Walk*, on the north side of the river close to the SS Great Eastern's

---

101 islandhistory.wordpress.com

Launch Ramp (E14 3TD), forms part of the Thames
Path.

Back in Suffolk, Geoff Allen and Teddy Smith were the only
ones who really knew the extent of Ronnie's illness, and both
were worried to see that he was getting progressively worse.
After each trip to London, Ronnie would sink into a deep pit
of depression, with periods of restlessness and severe agitation.
Eventually, it became impossible to reason with Ronnie and he
announced that he needed to get away – and that he would kill
anyone who tried to stop him. Geoff Allen was not going to
stand in his way, so he phoned Reggie at *The Double R*, passed
the phone to Ronnie, and listened to him beg and plead to be
taken away. Reggie duly arrived and took Ronnie, who insisted
on travelling in the boot of the car, back to London.

The fantasy was finally over, and Reggie was scared by
the realisation that his brother was severely mentally ill. Now,
Reggie devoted all his time and energy to looking after Ronnie;
he became exhausted by the constant struggle to keep him calm
and convinced that he and the rest of the family, including his
mother, were not cleverly disguised impostors plotting to kill
him. Reggie moved Ronnie into a flat in Finchley and stayed
with him there in the hope that his round-the-clock presence
would help to keep his brother calm, but it made little difference. Nothing other than alcohol seemed to have any effect, but
the endless bottles of brown ale – and up to two bottles of gin
every day – were completely negating any good done by the ir-
regularly taken Stemetil supplied by Doctor Blasker.

Reggie, Charlie – and, by now, Violet – simply had to accept that there was nothing more they could do and that Ronnie
was in desperate need of help from professionals. After much
soul-searching, the family reluctantly decided to turn Ronnie
in. On the night of 25 October 1958, the day after the twins' 25th

birthdays, two policemen accompanied by two male nurses arrived at Vallance Road to take Ronnie away. Ronnie did not resist; he said he knew they had come to take him and went to get his coat.[102] Reggie was finding it difficult to reconcile breaking the unwritten law against *grassing*, but he knew he had no other choice and that it had to be done for Ronnie's own good.

Ronnie, whose certification of insanity had now expired, was taken back to *Long Grove* where he rapidly responded to treatment. Only three weeks later, on 18 November 1958, he was sent back to *Wandsworth* to complete his sentence. Interestingly, and much to everyone's surprise – despite the fact that he had spent time in *Long Grove*, escaped, and spent six months on the run – Ronnie was released only weeks later in early December 1958, just over two years after being given a three-year sentence in November 1956.

During Ronnie's time away, *The Double R Club* continued to grow in popularity and attract a diverse crowd. More of the West End set were venturing east for a taste of East End subculture, and a growing number of journalists were using *The Double R* as a watering hole in the hope of uncovering a story. Who exactly were these characters from the East End? How come they attracted celebrities into their circle, and what exactly were they up to? Among the pack of hungry journo's sniffing around for a story was crime reporter for the *Sunday Mirror*, Norman Lucas.

In 1994, Lucas was interviewed for an episode of the TV crime documentary series *Gangsters* with Martin Short,[103] in which he made some interesting revelations: Lucas claimed that he was present, in the getaway car, when Ronnie was

---

102 Kray, Charlie with McGibbon, Robin. *Me and my Brothers*. London: Grafton, 1988.

103 Chameleon Films, Carlton Television, 1994.

sprung from *Long Grove*. If this is true, he must have become very friendly indeed with Reggie and gained his complete trust – or perhaps Reggie was looking to document the event and have it publicised and written about at some point thereafter. Also, according to Lucas, he was instrumental in facilitating high-level negotiations with the Home Office to secure a surrender deal for Ronnie with no penalties attached. Lucas told Reggie that if Ronnie were to be given up immediately, he would *"go back there but not necessarily stay there."* Perhaps this goes some way to explain Reggie's decision to give Ronnie up when he did – and Ronnie's subsequent early release from prison.

Ronnie was now free but he was far from well. Pale and drawn with glazed eyes, he became reclusive and refused to go to his coming-out party at *The Double R*. Ronnie appeared detached and unaware of what was happening around him; he would sit in the kitchen at Vallance Road staring into space, smoking, and drinking endless cups of tea. Ronnie seemed to recognise and trust his mother Violet and father Charles, but he was suspicious of his brother Charlie – and even Reggie.

One evening, in an effort to cheer Ronnie up and bring a bit of normality into his life, the family took him for an evening out at the pub. But this evening out did not have the desired effect and Ronnie's behaviour became increasingly more strange and disturbing. Hoping that friends and familiar surroundings would bring Ronnie back to reality, the family moved on to *The Regal*, but Ronnie became anxious and began to prowl up and down, deep in a world of his own. Suddenly, Ronnie's body stiffened as if he had been given an electric shock, and then – after a few moments – went limp, causing him to sink to his knees. Terrified, shocked, and not knowing quite what to do, Reggie shouted for someone to call an ambulance. Ronnie was admitted to *St Clements Hospital* in Bow on 19 December 1958 and remained there until 4 January 1959.[104]

St Clements Hospital

2A Bow Road, London E3 4LL

Nearest TFL station: Mile End underground.

Built in 1874 as a workhouse, the building was used as such until 1909, when it closed, reopening in 1912 as an infirmary called the *City of London Institution*. In 1936, it became a psychiatric unit and was renamed *St Clements Hospital*. After services were transferred to *Mile End Hospital*, *St Clements* closed in February 2006. In 2014, work began to convert the old hospital into flats; it is now a large residential development of 252 homes. The original workhouse clock tower is visible from Bow Road.

Ronnie Kray was admitted to *St Clements* in December 1958 and spent just over two weeks here after his mental illness worsened, causing him to convulse and collapse one evening while at *The Regal* billiard hall. Ronnie recovered but was changed, and would need drug treatment for the rest of his life.

Ronnie had suffered a seizure from which he was lucky to survive mentally intact. It could so very easily have resulted in a complete and devastating mental breakdown from which he would never have recovered. Receiving the care and medica-

---

104   Bennett, John. *Krayology*. London: Mango Books, 2015.

tion he so desperately needed, however, Ronnie quickly began to feel better, and the family were relieved and happy to see Ronnie back to his *almost* normal self. From now on and forever, drugs would be a vital part of Ronnie's life. Fully accepting that he was ill and in need of medication to keep the paranoia at bay, Ronnie had no complaints about the monthly injection and the four different tablets to be taken every day.

Prior to this time, the twins were almost identical, and only those who knew them well were able to tell them apart, but Ronnie's illness – combined with drugs and huge quantities of drink – had caused a physical change. Although Ronnie had lost weight after being returned to prison, his eyes now appeared to bulge, and puffiness around his face had smoothed out his cheekbones and made his jaw line less defined. The Ronnie Kray who came back into the world to join his brothers in business in 1959 not only looked different, but his whole demeanour had altered. Ronnie's mind appeared numbed by his medication, his movements more ponderous and his speech slower and slightly slurred.

On December 14 1958, just under a week before Ronnie was admitted to *St Clements Hospital*, an event took place that would bring more problems for Reggie. Ronnie Marwood, a 25-year-old scaffolder from Islington, was on a heavy drinking night out with friends and visited *The Double R Club* before going to *Grey's Dance Hall* in Seven Sisters Road, where they expected trouble. *Grey's* was well known to Reggie; during their younger days, he and Ronnie spent many-a-night and had many-a-fight there. Marwood and friends left the *Double R Club* and, sure enough, violence erupted between rival gangs outside the dance hall. PC Raymond Summers – who was alone, walking his beat – saw the trouble and intervened to break up the fighting. Marwood stabbed PC Summers in the back and the 23-year-old policeman collapsed and died at the scene.

Marwood ran off and went into hiding, during which time the police thought that Reggie was providing sanctuary for the wanted man. In his book, *Born Fighter*, Reggie claims he was indeed hiding Marwood. When interviewed at *Bow Road Police Station*, Reggie, of course, denied harbouring the fugitive, and nothing to the contrary could be proven. Reggie was told, in no uncertain terms, that from then on, the police would be watching and keeping a very close eye on him indeed.

Eventually, on the evening of January 27, Marwood gave himself up and confessed to stabbing PC Summers. Later, in court, Marwood pleaded not guilty and denied having made the confession, suggesting it was made up by the police. Marwood was found guilty of capital murder, sentenced to death, and hanged at *Pentonville Prison* on Friday 8 May 1959.

Grey's Dance Academy

133 Seven Sisters Road, Finsbury Park, London N7 7PT

Nearest TFL station: Finsbury Park underground.

During the 1950s, *Grey's Dance Hall* was a popular gathering place for the youth of East and North London, and a setting for rival gangs to fight for dominance. The prospect of violence was an attraction for the young Kray twins, and *Grey's* was one of a number of dance halls that, as teenagers, they would often visit with their friends, looking for excitement. In December 1958, by which time the twins had outgrown the dancehall, *Grey's* was the scene of a tragic event. After stepping in to break up a fight outside the dancehall, 23-year-old PC Raymond Henry Summers was stabbed and killed by 25-year-old Ronald Marwood. Marwood went into hiding and Reggie Kray was suspected by the police of harbouring the wanted man. Eventually, after six weeks, Marwood turned himself in and was hanged for capital murder in May 1959.

Although much of Seven Sisters Road remains unchanged, the buildings on the stretch of road where *Grey's Dance Hall* was located have all been demolished and replaced by a modern housing development. On the north side of Seven Sisters Road – just a ten-minute walk from Finsbury Park underground station, between Newington Barrow Way and Sonderburg Road, and directly opposite *The Bedford Tavern* – is an open grassy area planted with trees, and it is here that *Grey's Dance Academy* once stood.

Things changed for Reggie and Charlie after Ronnie once more became involved in their lives and business. With Ronnie out of the picture, Reggie had been free to make his own decisions based on his keen business sense, but now Ronnie insisted that he was to be consulted on everything – which resulted in arguments. Ronnie had always been the dominant twin and, just like before, Reggie would, more often than not, give in and let Ronnie have his way. Reggie and Charlie's combined efforts were bearing fruit and bringing in good money, but with Ronnie around, profits were beginning to suffer. The till at *The Double R* became Ronnie's personal bank and he would simply help himself to as much as he wanted whenever he wanted… and then want to know why there was none left.

Just one month after Ronnie's recovery and re-immersion into the world of Kray enterprises, another little problem presented itself, this time involving Reggie. Daniel Shay – car dealer, gambler, small time criminal, and regular at the billiard hall – approached Reggie and asked him if he would like to come for a ride in his new sports car; he was going to Finchley to speak to a man about some business. Shay had provided some help while Ronnie was on the run, so Reggie agreed and asked Georgie Osborne – the friend who had been present during the switch at *Long Grove* – to come along also. On 4 February 1959 at 1.15pm, the car with the three men aboard pulled up outside a shop called *Swiss Travel Goods Ltd* at 267 Finchley Road, North London; a Jewish family business that made and sold leather goods. Shay, Reggie, and Osborne entered the shop and Shay then demanded that the shop owner, Murray Podro, pay him £100. Podro protested and, without further ado, Shay proceeded to punch him in the face. A scuffle began and Reggie stepped in, head butting Podro, causing bruising and a bloody nose.

In his book, *Born Fighter*, Reggie says that the purpose of the visit was to collect a gambling debt and that he did not set out with the intention of using violence. Podro later told the police that Shay demanded money, claiming that he'd been overcharged for a briefcase he'd collected from his shop, but not paid for, the day before.

Whatever the truth behind the reason for the visit, Shay – feeling like ten men with Reggie at his side – most probably saw this as an opportunity to play gangsters, and by joining in the game, Reggie had seriously implicated himself.

Believing he had put the fear of God into Podro, Shay told him he'd be back the following day for the money. Podro was no stranger to violence; he had been a leading member of the '43 Group', an anti-fascist organisation that had fought in the streets with Oswald Mosley's Blackshirts and other extreme right-wing groups following a resurgence after the war.[105]

---

105 Sonabend, Daniel. *We Fight Fascists: The 43 Group and Their*

Tough and willing to use violence for a cause Podro certainly was, but he was not a member of the criminal fraternity bound by the rule of silence; he was simply the co-owner of a small business and, just like most regular citizens, he reacted as one might expect – he went straight to the police.

Reggie, by this point, presumably wanted nothing more to do with it, and when Shay returned to *Swiss Travel Goods Ltd* the next day accompanied by another man, he was confronted and arrested by two policemen who had been hiding in the back of the shop. Reggie and Ronnie were also arrested as a result of Podro claiming that it was the 'Kray twins' who had accompanied Shay on the first visit. Ronnie was later released without charge after George Osborne came forward and it was established that it was he and not Ronnie who was present on the day in question. Reggie Kray, Daniel Shay, and George Osborne were all found guilty of demanding money with menaces and, on 10 April 1959, Reggie and Osborne were sentenced to 18 months' imprisonment; Shay received three years.

Reggie appealed and, due to legal complexities resulting in a delay in acquiring the transcript of the trial, he was given bail and released from *Wandsworth Prison* on 22 September 1959. It would be almost a year before Reggie's appeal would be heard, rejected, and Reggie recalled to prison to finish his sentence.[106]

Forgotten Battle for Post-War Britain. London: Verso Books, 2019.
106 Morton, James. Krays: *The Final Word*. London: Mirror Books, 2019.

Swiss Travel Goods Ltd

267 Finchley Road, London NW3 6LU

Nearest TFL station: Finchley Road underground.

The shop was a Jewish family business owned by the Podro family, who made and sold leather goods. Originally established by their parents, the business was run by sons Murray and Maurice, both of whom were leading members of the 43 Group, an organisation that fought against extreme right-wing, anti-Jewish, fascist groups that reappeared on the streets after the war.

In February 1959, Reggie Kray, Daniel Shay, and Georgie Osborne entered the shop and, after demanding £100, Shay assaulted Murray Podro. Reggie briefly joined in and was subsequently arrested, charged with demanding money with menaces, and given an 18-month prison sentence.

Swiss Travel Goods Ltd was among a row of shops on Finchley Road that were demolished in the early 1990s to make way for the O2 shopping and leisure centre, which now occupies the site.

Regulars at *The Double R* began to notice a change of atmosphere at the club with Reggie away in prison and Ronnie running the show. Outsiders were blissfully unaware of the ticking time bomb that was Ronnie Kray, but those who knew the twins personally – or even slightly – began to feel a little less relaxed knowing that one wrong word could bring big trouble. It was wise to walk on eggshells around Ronnie, to choose words carefully, and to be sure to know if anyone was out of favour, as just talking to them could be a mistake.

One evening when Ronnie – dressed in his smartest suit, collar, and tie – was playing the role of convivial host at *The Double R*, Micky Fawcett witnessed an event that was by no means unusual, and a typical example of Ronnie's unpredictable, hair-trigger temper. Micky Fawcett, a young criminal from the Silvertown area of East London, had for some time been using *The Double R* and had become friendly with Reggie. Although an independent operator, never choosing to be a member of The Firm, Micky Fawcett – whose speciality was elaborate frauds – would work closely with the Krays for some years to come.

Ronnie was circulating, greeting the guests and saying that he hoped they would have a pleasant evening, and to let him know if there was anything they needed – anything at all. After completing his tour of the club, Ronnie noticed one guest, a tough character from Hoxton, sitting near the door. He said politely, *"Hello Tony, I didn't see you sitting there. I've got bad eyes, you know."*

Obviously thinking that it was okay to joke and be a little bit cheeky in the relaxed atmosphere, Tony replied, *"You must have fucking bad, eyes Ron; I've been sitting here for20 minutes."*

This was a major faux pas, and Ronnie proceeded to smash him in the face, kick him off his seat, and stamp all over him in full view of the other guests. After the bouncers saved the hapless Tony from further punishment by throwing him out, Ronnie – out of breath and sweating profusely – circulated once again and apologised to each of the guests for the *slight disruption* to their evening. *"I'm terribly sorry about that. It doesn't happen very often."*[107]

107 Fawcett, Micky. *Krayzy Days*. Brighton: Pen Press, 2013.

Despite Ronnie's frittering of the profits and his presence creating an atmosphere of increased tension, the club continued to grow in popularity and attract the many and various. Several characters who would go on to play a part in the Krays' later story began drifting into *The Double R* at this time, among whom were Johnny Davis – a tough character from the Stratford area, introduced to the twins by Micky Fawcett and Alfie Teale, who was introduced by Mad Teddy Smith. Alfie Teale, along with his brothers David and Bobby, would become deeply involved with the twins and play a part in their eventual downfall.

In the summer of 1959, while Reggie was in *Wandsworth Prison* serving the first part of his sentence for demanding money with menaces, another well-known instalment from the annals of the Kray epic took place. There are several versions told of Ronnie Kray's 'shooting up' of the Italian club in Clerkenwell, and several reasons proffered as to why it happened. Leading Anglo-Italian gangster Bert 'Battles' Rossi was directly involved. He was there when it happened, and he told all in his 2017 book written with James Morton, *Bert Battles Rossi: Britain's Oldest London Gangland Boss*.

On a night off from *The Double R Club*, Ronnie – accompanied by the fixer and go-between, Tommy 'Red Face' Plumley – went to *The Central Club* in Clerkenwell where they found Bert Rossi, who was recently released from prison after serving a three-year sentence for the attack on Jack Spot. Ronnie and Bert had become friendly during their time served together at *Winchester Prison* in 1957. In keeping with the custom of helping fellow criminals get back on their feet after being released from jail, Ronnie gave Bert £200. Bert was grateful but recalls that Ronnie was "*still mad as a hatter.*"

Later, Ron and Bert were drinking together in Soho when a man approached them and told Bert that a partly crippled friend of his – whom he'd been asking about earlier – had been beaten up by a man named Tommy Falco, a member of a well-known family of villains from Clerkenwell. Bert was angry and told Ron that he was heading back to *The Central Club* to teach Falco a lesson. Ron insisted on coming along and they returned to the club to find that Tommy Falco was not there. Two of Falco's brothers and a number of their friends, however, were there. *"Where's that fucking brother of yours?"* shouted Bert and began threatening the group of men. It looked to Ronnie very much like a row was about to begin – with Bert on the losing end – so Ronnie pulled out a gun and started firing. There were around 30 men and women in *The Central Club* that night, but fortunately for all concerned, no one was hit.

The Central Club

127 Clerkenwell Road, London EC1R 5LP

Nearest TFL station: Chancery Lane underground.

The Central Club was an Italian social club and the meeting place of London's Anglo-Italian gangsters during the 1950s and 60s. During the mid-1950s, Billy Hill – in his campaign to oust Jack Spot from his position in the underworld – formed an alliance with Albert Dimes and the Italians. Hill, along with his number 1 henchman Frankie Fraser, regularly visited *The Central Club* at this time.

In 1959, Ronnie Kray fired several shots at a group of men in the club in support of his friend Bert 'Battles' Rossi, who was involved in an altercation with some of his fellow Italians. Fortunately, Ronnie – who may or may not have been shooting to kill – failed to hit anyone.

Sadly, the building in which *The Central Club* was located is now demolished, and *Greys Inn House* – a modern commercial building – now occupies the spot. Immediately next door to the new building is *The Griffin* at 125 Clerkenwell Road. The Griffin is an adult entertainment club but was formerly a pub of the same name – and headquarters of a previous generation of Italian gangsters: the notorious Sabini gang, headed by Darby Sabini and his brothers.

The end of the 1950s and the beginning of the Swinging Sixties marks a milestone in the lives of the Kray twins – who would soon be moving on to pastures new – but before closing the door on the '50s there is one other notable event recorded only by the Kray twins' most important biographer, John Pearson, in his excellent and now famous book, *The Profession of Violence.*

In the early spring of 1959, just a few weeks after leaving *St Clements Hospital* and his recovery from the worst of his mental illness, Ronnie called a meeting of old and new friends at *The Regal* billiard hall. The Colonel was back, and – flanked by his two favourite boys, a huge dog at his feet, and a gleaming cutlass in hand – he announced that there was going to be a showdown at *The Hospital Tavern* the following evening. The whole of the Watney Street Gang would be there – who, as far as Ronnie was concerned, were responsible for his ordeal over the last couple of years – and it was time for some payback. Reggie said nothing and, as was so often the case, went along with Ronnie's plan; besides, it had been a long time since they'd had a proper little war.

The next night, there was a battle royal at *The Hospital Tavern* on Whitechapel Road as the two gangs fought with knives, coshes, and knuckle dusters. Just like the old days, the twins fought as one invincible unit, and as the last of the Watney Streeters was fleeing or being dragged away, injured, Reggie – standing amid broken chairs on a carpet of smashed glass – reached for the pub microphone and shouted, "*If Watney Street wants any more, the Krays are ready for them!*"[108]

John Pearson is the only purely objective biographer to have been close to the twins during their heyday. He was invited into their world by the twins themselves, who wanted him to write a book about their lives. It is possible, but by no means certain, that he was fed a line on this particular event as there were no arrests made by the police and nothing in the newspapers.[109] Moreover, there is no mention of the event in any other book,

108 Pearson, John. *The Profession of Violence*. London: Weidenfeld and Nicolson, 1972.
109 Kirby, Dick. *London's Gangs at War*. Barnsley: Pen and Sword Books, 2017.

including those written or co-written by the twins themselves. If it did happen, it was the last full-scale gang fight in which the twins were involved. The violence, however, would continue and get worse – but on a much more personal level.

The Hospital Tavern

176 Whitechapel Road, London E1 1BJ

Nearest TFL station: Whitechapel underground.

The pub is the location and scene of the Krays' last ever full-scale gang fight in the spring of 1959 when Ron, Reg, and their mob fought and vanquished their arch-rivals, the Watney Street Gang. There is some doubt as to the historical validity of the event, but whether fact or fiction, the pub is very much on the Krays' manor and was visited by the twins on occasion. In his book, *Bullets, Blood And Broken Bodies*, renowned East End hardman Henry 'Buller' Ward tells of an incident in *The Hospital Tavern* where the young twins beat up and slashed a man called Ken Roode.[110] Built in 1876, the Victorian pub replaced an earlier pub built in 1753 to provide refreshment for the builders of the *London Hospital*. Today, *The Hospital Tavern* does the same for many of the NHS staff who work there. In contrast to the 1950s, the recently refurbished pub has a nice friend-ly atmosphere and provides an "*interestin*" (one of the twins' favourite words) range of beers and cocktails.

---

110 Ward, Henry and Weeks, David. *Bullets, Blood and Broken Bodies*. New Breed Publishing, 2008.

Reggie was released from prison on bail, pending his appeal in September 1959, after serving just over five months of his 18-month sentence for demanding money with menaces from shop owner Murray Podro. During his time in *Wandsworth Prison*, Reggie met – for the first time – two characters who would go on to play major roles in the twins' later story, and ultimately lose their lives as a result: Frank Mitchell and Jack 'The Hat' McVitie. Also around this time, the twins formed a solid alliance and friendship with South London's godfather of crime, Freddie Foreman, who would also go on to become deeply involved in the Jack McVitie and Frank Mitchell chapters of the Kray chronicles.

Freddie Foreman was a highly respected South London criminal who, along with his gang, specialised in robbery. Freddie first met and became friends with Charlie Kray through their mutual connection with a buyer of stolen goods and, in turn, he came to know the twins. After a van used in a robbery in Southampton was found by the police and traced back to Freddie, he *went on his toes* over the river to the East End to avoid arrest. The twins found accommodation for Freddie, his wife, and their two young boys, Gregory and Jamie, in a flat in Adelina Grove, Whitechapel; the same flat used to hide Ronnie on occasion after his escape from *Long Grove Psychiatric Hospital*.[111] During the two-year period that Freddie Foreman stayed in the East End, he came to know the twins well – and this friendship, along with his gratitude to the twins for helping him at this time, ensured that *Brown Bread Fred* (brown bread – cockney rhyming slang for 'dead'), as he would later become known, could be called upon in the future when the twins needed help.

---

111   Foreman, Freddie. *The Godfather of British Crime.* London: John Blake Publishing, 2018.

Adelina Grove

Mile End Road, London E1 3AA

Nearest TFL station: Whitechapel underground.

Adelina Grove is a short 0.2 kilometre stretch of road behind the buildings on the south side of Mile End Road, opposite *The Blind Beggar* pub. The Kray twins had a flat here that was used to hide Ronnie Kray for periods after his escape from *Long Grove Hospital* in 1958. South London gangster Freddie Foreman and his family were also given the use of the flat by the twins while Freddie was on the run from the police in early 1960.

There are no records of the actual address of the flat in Adelina Grove. *Ansell House*, a large apartment building on the north side, was completed in 1956 and could feasibly have been the location of the flat, but Freddie describes it as "*not in good nick*",[112] so the likelihood is that the flat was in one of the older apartment blocks on the south side. *Dron House* was built in 1922 and *Grove Dwellings* in 1910.

After Reggie's release from *Wandsworth Prison*, money was still coming in from *The Double R Club* and the spielers in Bow, but Ronnie's poor financial management had slowed down the flow and it was time to expand the business portfolio and increase income with more *protection* work. Pubs, cafes,

---

112 Foreman, Freddie with Kurylo, Frank and Noelle. *Running With The Krays*. London: John Blake, 2017.

car lots, and other legitimate businesses in the East End could often be persuaded to pay the twins to look after their security. In some cases, business owners – particularly pub landlords having problems with badly behaved customers – would approach the twins and *ask* to pay for their services. Heavy-handed tactics and extortionate demands were generally avoided as straight people were likely to go to the police. The preferred targets were businesses operating outside the law, where the twins could be as heavy-handed as they liked and demand whatever payment they saw fit.

Illegal gambling clubs were a prime target and one such establishment was *The Greatorex Club* on Greatorex Street,[113] and another *The Green Dragon Club* on Whitechapel Road. Shortly after the club opened, *The Green Dragon* was visited by a group of men who proceeded to smash the place up, then – after a brick was thrown through the window – the three club owners, George Mizel, Matty Constantino, and Bill Ackerman[114] were told by the Krays that it would be a *pony* (£25) a week to operate trouble-free.[115] This price was later doubled to £50.

Like most illegal gambling clubs, criminals made up the majority of the clientele and the club became a popular hangout and meeting place for the Kray crowd. Poker, kalooki, and dice were on offer for criminals to lose their easy come, easy go cash, but Reggie – who was in the club one night at the beginning of February 1960 – had no interest in gambling; he was there just to drink and socialise. Reggie was in the company of former Jack Spot man Bernard 'Sonny the Yank'

---

113   Situated at 25 Greatorex Street, E1 5NP, now City Hub Estate Agent.

114   Ackerman would later go on to work for the Krays.

115   Documentary, *Flesh and Blood: The Story of the Krays*, 4 Front, Chris Short, 1991.

Schack and, after a pleasant enough evening, was getting ready to leave. Reggie then did something that was more typical of Ronnie's behaviour than his own. Sonny called Reggie *"son"* and Reggie took offence. Perhaps it was the last straw after an evening of patronising behaviour by Sonny, or perhaps not, but Reggie head butted and punched the 58-year-old man, breaking his jaw.[116]

116　Kirby, Dick. *London's Gangs At War*. Barnsley: Pen and Sword Books, 2017.

The Green Dragon Club

25 Whitechapel Road, London E1 1DU

Nearest TFL station: Aldgate East underground

On the north side of Whitechapel Road – about five metres along from *The Nags Head Gentleman's Club*, tucked between a shop called *Fujifilm* and another called *Whitechapel Supermarket* – is the entrance to a small alleyway that leads to Green Dragon Yard where *The Green Dragon Club* and its sister club, *The Little Dragon,* were once located. *The Green Dragon Club* was at first an illegal gambling club (spieler) until the law changed and gambling was legalised in 1961. Throughout the 1960s – until their arrest in 1968 – the Krays took protection money from the club, and it was used by the twins and their associates as a regular hang-out and meeting place.

There is some anecdotal evidence that Ronnie Kray took a beating from George Cornell in *The Green Dragon Club*, an event that must have contributed towards Cornell's murder at Ronnie's hands in March 1966.

Green Dragon Yard was completely redeveloped between 1999 and 2001 and is now a modern apartment complex. The alleyway leading to the apartments is much the same as it was in the 1960s, though it is now gated and accessible to residents only.

The first ever television documentary about the Krays – *The Name is Kray,* made in 1969 – has a scene showing the interior of the club and the owner George Mizel talking about protection money paid to the twins. The documentary is not currently available on YouTube but can be purchased on DVD.

The next day, Reggie saw Sonny again when he went to the *London Hospital* to visit Billy Ambrose, an old friend from his boxing days. Sonny was in a bed in the same ward as Ambrose, who had been admitted to hospital the previous day after receiving a gunshot wound to the stomach during a fight at *The Pen Club* in Spitalfields – the aftermath of which was creating a stir in the London underworld.

In the late 1950s, Billy Ambrose and associate Jeremiah

Callaghan opened a drinking club on Duval Street, Spitalfields. *The Pen Club* was reputedly named after and financed by a robbery that had taken place some years earlier in November 1952. Ambrose and six other men had broken into *Conway Stewart and Co.* and stolen 2,970 fountain pens valued at £1,500.[117] Caught and convicted of the robbery, Ambrose – who was a talented middleweight boxer and likely-looking contender for the British title, was sentenced to five years in prison and lost his boxing licence. During his time in *Wormwood Scrubs*, he was reunited with his boxing pals the Kray twins, who were still in the army at the time and serving a month's sentence in a civilian jail for an assault on PC Roy Fisher. *The Pen Club*, which occupied two floors, was managed by the late Tommy 'Scarface' Smithson's former girlfriend, Fay Richardson, and was a popular night haunt for the criminal fraternity.

Around midnight on 6 February 1960, the manager of Billy Hill's wife's *New Cabinet Club* and promising middleweight boxer Selwyn Cooney entered *The Pen Club* accompanied by two friends. Shortly afterwards, Jimmy Nash – one of seven brothers who made up the notorious crime family from Islington – came into the club accompanied by friends Joey Pyle and John Read. Selwyn Cooney had, the night before, fought with Jimmy Nash's brother Ronnie and knocked him out. Inevitably, a furious fight ensued during which a gun was produced and Selwyn Cooney was shot in the head, killing him instantly. Club owner Billy Ambrose – who joined the fray in defence of Cooney – took a bullet in the stomach but survived and drove himself to the *London Hospital*. Jimmy Nash, Joey Pyle, and John Read were all arrested and charged with murder.

Shortly after the shooting, and before their arrest, Jimmy

---

117   Kirby, Dick. *London's Gangs at War*. Barnsley: Pen and Sword Books, 2017.

Nash and friends went to Vallance Road and asked the twins for help. They got help. Ron and Reg had a friendly relationship with the powerful Nash family and a long-held *understanding* over territorial ambitions. With the twins in solidarity with the Nashes', with South London godfather of crime Freddie Foreman representing Billy Ambrose, who was sticking to the unwritten code of silence, and with Billy Hill looking on with interest, London's underworld came together as one to ensure that Jimmy Nash, Joey Pyle, and John Read would escape the hangman's rope.

One by one, the 36 customers who had been present in *The Pen Club* at the time of the shooting, and had volunteered their services as witnesses, started to lose their memories of the night's events. Johnny Simons, who was in the company of Selwyn Cooney at the time of his murder, was attacked and slashed with razors in a cafe in Paddington in front of terri-fied women and children, and his pretty 22-year-old girlfriend – who had nothing whatsoever to do with the murder – was slashed across the face with a razor on two separate occasions. Witness intimidation, jury nobbling, and the best legal rep-resentation money could buy ensured that 28-year-old James Lawrence Nash – who was described as a *steeplejack* in police files and in the newspapers – was acquitted of murder and tried only for the beating that Cooney received prior to the shooting. On 9 May 1960, Nash was given a five-year prison sentence for GBH. Joey Pyle and John Read received 18 months each.[118]

The murder at *The Pen Club* and the subsequent events in which the Krays were clearly involved – along with the belief that Reggie Kray had harboured cop-killer Ronnie Marwood – stirred the Metropolitan Police into action. An in-depth in-vestigation into the activities of the Kray brothers was initiated

---

118   Ibid.

but it was clear that, due to the fear that the twins generated, it would be difficult if not impossible to find witnesses to give evidence in court and nail them for any specific crime. Until such time that they could, it seems the police intended to keep a very close eye and make life for the Brothers Kray as difficult as possible.

On 3 June 1960, the police swooped and raided *The Double R Club* and the spieler on Wellington Way. After evidence of illegal gambling was found at the spieler and *irregularities* with the licensing at *The Double R*, it was the beginning of the end of the twins' early career as club owners. By the end of the year, all their clubs – including *The Regal* – were closed.

The Pen Club

Duval Street, Spitalfields, London E1

Nearest TFL station: Aldgate East underground.

Opened in the late 1950s, *The Pen Club* occupied two floors of an old Victorian building on Duval Street and was a popular night haunt for the criminal fraternity. In the early hours of Sunday 7 February 1960, there was a shooting in the club in which one man – Selwyn Cooney – died, and another, Billy Ambrose, was seriously injured. The subsequent fallout from the event prompted the police to look more closely into the Krays' activities and resulted in the closing down of the twins' clubs.

The buildings on Duval Street were demolished in the 1960s to make way for a lorry park to service *Spitalfields Market*, and in the 2010s, redevelopment of the *Fruit & Wool Exchange* (1-10 Brushfield St E1 6EN) saw Duval Street built over and disappear completely.

A short distance from where *The Pen Club* once stood is the historic *Ten Bells* pub (84 Commercial Street E1 6LY) that is associated with two of Jack the Ripper's victims, Annie Chapman and Mary Jane Kelly. Mary Jane, the serial killer's last victim, was murdered and mutilated in 1888 at her lodgings in Duval Street – which, at the time, was called Dorset Street and known as the worst street in London.

Footage of the interior and exterior of *The Pen Club*, taken shortly after the murder, exists and can be seen on YouTube. The documentary, *The Underworld: Getting Away with Murder*, was first shown on BBC1 in Feb 1994.

The decade that would bring about great changes in British social history – the 1960s – was beginning, but the era that shook off the Victorian traditions and austerity of post-war Britain and welcomed pop music, new fashion, new ideas, and free love was a few years hence and yet to start swinging. Love, however, was in the air for two of the Brothers Kray.

Charlie Kray, who was involved in the day-to-day running of *The Double R Club* until its closure in the summer of 1960, was often joined at the club by his wife Dolly. Charlie noticed that Dolly was receiving a little more attention than usual from a man called George Ince. Dolly was an attractive woman and Charlie was neither surprised nor overly concerned about George Ince's obvious interest in his wife. According to Charlie, perhaps he should have been, because later – in *The Green Dragon Club* – he was told by the twins that Dolly had, for some time, been having an affair with Ince. Dolly denied the affair but, although not convinced, Charlie decided to stay with his wife for the sake of their young son, Gary.[119]

In February 1960, the musical comedy *Fings Ain't Wot They Used T' Be* opened at the *Garrick Theatre* in London's West End. Performing in the show was the East End's very own young starlet, Barbara Windsor. One evening, after the show, Charlie was taken backstage and introduced to Barbara by his actor friend George Sewell. Charlie decided to try his luck and asked Barbara if she would have dinner with him one night. Barbara said she would and an affair began that was to last several months. In her book *All of Me,* Barbara recalls that after finding out that Charlie was married, she decided to end the relationship. Barbara also reveals that, shortly afterwards, she accompanied Reggie on an evening out, which concluded with a one-night stand.[120]

Following his release on bail from *Wandsworth*, and while awaiting the court's decision on the appeal against his conviction for demanding money with menaces, Reggie began his courtship of 16-year-old Frances Shea, taking her out on a regular basis. Having first met the then 15-year-old schoolgirl Frances through her older brother Frankie the year before, Reggie – who was used to taking whatever he wanted – was in the process of making sure that the prettiest girl in the East End belonged to him.

Frankie, like his younger sister, was exceptionally good-looking and was picked out by Reggie to be his personal driver. After leaving school, Frankie was one of the lucky few from the East End to find an apprenticeship as a typesetter at a printing works. Printing during the '50s and '60s was the high-

119 Kray, Charlie with McGibbon, Robin. *Me and My Brothers*. London: Grafton, 1988.

120 Windsor, Barbara. *All of Me: My Extraordinary Life*. London: Headline Publishing, 2001.

est paid of all the trades and a route to the *respectable* life that Frankie's mother Elsie wanted for her son. Unfortunately, after being caught playing dice for money with some workmates, Frankie was sacked and began hanging around at *The Regal*. He soon strayed from the straight and narrow and became involved in low-level criminality, and the wheeling and dealing of used cars – a journey that led to him becoming involved with Reggie Kray and ultimately sealing the fate of his little sister.[121]

Father of Frankie and Frances, Frank Senior – who earned his living in the illegal bookmaking business – approved of his daughter's relationship with the impeccably mannered Reggie Kray and thought she would be treated with the utmost respect. Reggie offered Frank Senior a job running the bookmaking at the spieler in Wellington Way, which he accepted, but he was ignominiously scooped up by the police a short time later when the club was raided in June 1960. Frances' mother Elsie, to whom *respectability* was so important, was not so approving of the suave gangster who had turned up on her doorstep in Ormsby Street one day and dazzled her little girl with his immaculate appearance and oily charm.

---

121 In 2002, Frank gave an interview to the *East London Advertiser* in which he claimed that Reggie was in love with him and married his sister as an act of revenge after Frank spurned his advances. Frank, suffering from inoperable cancer, took his own life with a morphine overdose in 2011.

Home of the Shea Family

57 Ormsby Street, Hoxton, London E2 8JQ

Nearest TFL station: Hoxton overground.

Ormsby Street in Hoxton was, in the early 1960s, a typical East End street of humble Victorian terraced cottages situated between the Hackney and Kingsland Roads. Number 57 was the home of the Shea family. Reggie Kray first met 15-year-old Frances Shea in 1959 on the doorstep of the house when he called to see her older brother Frankie – who, at the time, was employed as Reggie's driver. Reggie, who was ten years older than Frances, began dating the teenager shortly afterwards. Frances' father Frank Senior was not unhappy about the relationship, but Frances' mother Elsie disapproved of her daughter's liaison with one of the East End's notorious gangster twins.

Nothing remains of the old Victorian houses which, like so many across great swathes of the old East End, were placed under compulsory purchase order and torn down as part of the massive slum clearance programme that began in the 1960s. The approximate location of the Shea household was on the east side of the street, close to the *Pearson Street Adventure Playground.*

Frances was swept off her feet and quickly fell under Reggie's spell. She was made welcome by the Kray family – especially the twins' cousin, Rita, with whom she got on well – but there was just one problem… that strange brother of his. Ronnie was not so welcoming and subtly made his disapproval of the relationship quite clear to Frances. Apart from those within his immediate family, Ronnie did not like women. As far as he was concerned, they were a waste of time and his brother's choice to become involved with one was a distraction from important business matters – and, worse still, a threat to the twins', until now, exclusive relationship.

1960 saw the entrance of a very important and influential character into the twins' story. Leslie Payne – *'The Man with the Briefcase'* or *'Payne the Brain'*– was a shady businessman who would open many-a- door for the twins… and direct a torrent of cash in their direction. Payne was probably the most important character in the cast in terms of shaping the twins' lives over the next few years, and certainly the most important in bringing about their eventual downfall.

Leslie Payne – a former soldier who had fought at the *Battle of Monte Cassino* in 1944 – first made contact with the twins during a dispute between his and another car sales business in the East End. Payne's adversaries in the dispute called in the Krays but the twins took Payne's side in the argument and, clearly impressed by the silver-tongued businessman, were keen to form a friendship. Payne concluded that the Kray twins were slightly less dangerous as friends than enemies.[122]

Payne and his sidekick – the dubious accountant Freddie Gore – worked alongside a man called Alexander Rapp, who ran a business called *Rapp Radio* on Dalston Lane in Hackney. Following several unexplained burglaries, Rapp sold an interest in the business to Payne, and then – after the twins and The Firm became regular visitors to the premises – Rapp ceased to have any connection with the business.[123]

---

122 Payne, Leslie. *The Brotherhood*. London: Michael Joseph Publishing, 1973.

123 Morton, James. *Krays: the Final Word*. London: Mirror Books, 2019.

Rapp Radio Ltd

181 Dalston Lane, Hackney, London E8 1AL

Nearest TFL station: Hackney Downs overground.

Delta Security locksmiths now occupy the site that, in 1960, was a business selling radios, televisions, record players, and records, run by Leslie Payne in partnership with Alexander Rapp. Following the intervention of Leslie Payne's new friends – the Kray twins – Rapp was pushed out, and from then onwards, Payne effectively became the twins' business manager.

Rapp Radio, later becoming the *625 Centre*, along with several of Payne's other dodgy businesses, was wound up in 1964 by court actions brought by creditors; in this case, *Decca* and *Pye Records*.

Payne operated a number of other shady businesses at various addresses including: *Carston Securities Ltd* at 143 Great Portland Street W1, *Dominion Refrigeration Ltd* at 258 Brixton Hill SW2, and *Carston Trading Co. Ltd* at 67-70 Dalston Lane E8. The premises at Great Portland Street and Dalston Lane have been demolished and rebuilt, but the commercial premises at 258 Brixton Hill still exist, and – at the time of writing – are up for sale.

The relationship between Payne and the twins was, for a while at least, mutually beneficial. Payne – who involved himself in any number of shady and downright crooked business dealings – knew that with the twins onside, he could operate outside the law without the interference of heavies muscling in and taking the profits. All the twins had to do was leave the business arrangements to Payne and sit back while the cash poured in.

Payne set up long firm frauds, the basic operation of which involves the setting up of an apparently legitimate company and buying goods, paid for promptly, to secure a good credit record. Once the relationship between the buyer and the supplier is well established, a big order of goods on credit is placed and the fraudsters disappear with the goods and any profits from the previous sales. Leslie Payne's organised LF frauds began to provide a source of income for the twins that required no effort and posed little risk of falling foul of the law. There was no need for the twins to be directly involved in the workings of the fraud and therefore no evidence to prove that they were; just the fear generated by their name was all that was needed.

On 26 July 1960, Reggie's appeal against his conviction for demanding money with menaces was heard by the court and rejected. Reggie was returned to *Wandsworth Prison* for another seven months to complete the remainder of his sentence.

The next major event in the lives of the twins was the acquisition of a smart West End club in Wilton Place, Knightsbridge called *Esmeralda's Barn*. There are many varying accounts of how the club was acquired, who was involved in the negotiations, and exactly when it happened. Some accounts suggest that the club fell into the twins' hands with the help of the notorious slum landlord and pimp Peter Rachman. Polish-born Rachman created a property empire in the 1950s centred around the Notting Hill, Paddington, and Bayswater areas by buying up run-down apartment buildings, dividing the rooms into smaller rooms, and letting them out to prostitutes and recently arrived immigrants at extortionate rents. Rachman employed a number of heavies to intimidate tenants and ensure that rent was paid in full and on time.

Ronnie Kray, so the story goes, wanted a slice of the pie and put the frighteners on Rachman's frighteners.[124] In order to get Ronnie off his back and focus his interest elsewhere, Rachman supposedly pointed Ronnie in the direction of *Esmeralda's Barn*, which was there for the taking.

Charlie Kray's account makes no mention of any involvement by Rachman and states that it was Leslie Payne who initiated the proceedings. According to Charlie, a meeting was held at the home of Hyman Diamond (Charlie calls him Drummond), a character who styled himself as an ex-naval officer and used the title *Commander*. Also at the meeting were Ronnie, Charlie, Leslie Payne, Freddie Gore, and the major shareholders in the club, Stefan De Faye and a gentleman called Burns. Reggie was not present, suggesting that the meeting took place while he was in prison between July 1960 and late February 1961. With the Brothers Kray involved in the negotiations, Payne's offer of just £1,000 for the controlling interest in the club was an offer that couldn't be refused.

Whatever the ins and outs of the acquisition, the Krays now had a club in the smartest part of London and the timing was ideal. On 1 January 1961, a new Act of Parliament came into force that essentially made gambling legal, and the club management was quick off the mark to install three tables for *chemin de fer* – a card game similar to baccarat – and a roulette table. For the first few weeks while Reggie was finishing his sentence in *Wandsworth*, Ronnie – alone, dressed in a dark blue Savile Row dinner jacket – would sit at the bar and watch with interest as the upper-class punters were parted from their money at the gaming tables. Ronnie hated gambling and he despised the over privileged, moneyed classes and the stuck-up young Guards officers with their dopey Sloan girlfriends. His

---

124   Teale, David. *Surviving the Krays*. London: Ebury Press, 2022.

new plaything, however, offered an opportunity to rinse them of their cash and place them in a position beholden to him.

Ronnie started granting credit, which enabled punters to lose even more money and place them in his debt. He was not overly concerned about recovering all the money – as it was pouring in – but he very much enjoyed the power he then held over the indebted punters. Payne and the Krays inherited the expert and astute gaming operator Alf Mancini as manager of *Esmeralda's*. Mancini was unhappy about the takeover and appalled by Ronnie's frivolous granting of credit; so much so that he offered Ronnie £1,000 a week to stay away. Ronnie didn't and, despite the money he had invested in the club, Mancini left and moved on, taking some of the high rollers with him.

Pauline Wallace – who ran Kray-protected chemin de fer parties at her flat in Hertford Street, Mayfair – was installed as manager, but this proved to be unsatisfactory and she was replaced by the twins' uncle, Alf. *Esmeralda's Barn* was nothing short of a gold mine and, with the help of Leslie Payne, the twins were raking in huge amounts of cash without having to do any work. In fact, there was no real need for them to be there at all, but – after Reggie's release from prison – they were there most nights, dressed in their matching blue dinner jackets, swanning around and enjoying the mastery of all they beheld.

Esmeralda's entrance was just inside an arcade on Wilton Place and occupied three floors. The casino was on the top floor; the first-floor area was opened in September 1962[125] as a no-alcohol club for music and dancing called *The Barn Twist Club,* managed by the twins' friend from childhood, Laurie O'Leary; and on the ground floor was the *Cellar Club,* managed by a woman called Ginette. Licensed to sell alcohol until midnight, the *Cellar Club* was a lesbian club open to people

---

125   *East London Advertiser*, 28 Sept 1962.

of all sexual persuasions. Music at the *Twist Club* was sometimes live and provided by artists and bands that, in some cases,
would go on to bigger things as the '60s began to swing. Eric
Clapton and his band *Casey Jones and the Engineers* played at
the *Barn* during the early days of his career.[126]

Leslie Payne suggested bringing a washed-up aristocrat
on board to add prestige to the management team. Mowbray
Henry Gordon Howard, 6th Earl of Effingham, enjoyed gambling, 'the ladies,' and a drink or two, but the family money
to support his life of leisure and excess had dried up years ago
and he was skint. Mowbray was offered, and happily accepted,
£10 a week to act as meeter and greeter at *Esmeralda's* – and
his name would of course look good on the *Barn*'s headed note-
paper and business cards. Ronnie very much enjoyed having
Lord Effingham at his beck and call and would joyfully tell
'Effy' to "*get the effing tea.*" Ron and Reg brought their friends
to *Esmeralda's,* and those who formed the upper echelons of
British society found themselves rubbing shoulders with cockney sparrows and broken-nosed gangsters. Some members of
the genteel classes rather enjoyed the novelty of mixing with
these rough and ready cock-er-ney types; others did not and
moved on. The twins' friends and associates knew better than
to bring violence into the club, and none took place except for
the occasional floorshow when a drunk and troublesome punter
was unceremoniously thrown down the stairs.

---

126 O'Leary, Laurie. Ronnie Kray: *A Man Among Men*. London: Headline
Publishing, 2001.

Esmeralda's Barn

50 Wilton Place, Knightsbridge, London SW1X 7RL

Nearest TFL station: Hyde Park Corner underground.

The buildings in Wilton Place where *Esmeralda's Barn* was situated were demolished in 1970 and replaced by the super-plush, five-star *Berkeley Hotel*, which opened in 1972.

The Krays took over the club in early 1961, just as new laws came into force which effectively legalised gambling in the UK. *Esmeralda's* occupied three floors: the upper floor was the casino; the first floor became a club for music and dancing in 1962 called *The Barn Twist Club*; and the ground floor was a lesbian night-club called the *Cellar Club,* open to all. Some of the up-per-class punters who frequented the casino on the up-per floor found the influx of tough-looking East Enders – brought west by the twins – rather novel and amusing. Others disliked the change in ambience and took their custom elsewhere. At first, the Krays earned a great deal of money from the gambling at the chemmy and roulette tables, but by the summer of 1964, the club had ceased to be profitable and was closed.

Esmeralda's attracted the West End's bohemian crowd and the artists Francis Bacon and Lucian Freud were regulars at the gaming tables. Among the fashionable, creative, and flamboyant Chelsea set was a character by the name of David Litvinoff. Born into a poor Jewish family in Whitechapel in

1928, Litvinoff was a complex character whose intelligence, ability to speak with eloquence on almost any subject, and razor-sharp wit could mesmerise all around him. Outrageous and charming with a sense of humour that could shock and delight, Litvinoff could be described as raconteur and court jester to the in-crowd. After Litvinoff ran up a £3,000 gambling debt at the *Barn* that he had no way of paying, Ronnie took payment by taking over Litvinoff's luxury flat in Ashburn Place, Kensington and moving in with Litvinoff and his boyfriend, the young and very good-looking Bobby Buckley. Bisexual Buckley, who worked as a croupier at the *Barn*, became Ronnie's favourite boy and would remain in close contact with the Krays until their arrest in 1968.

Litvinoff was later attacked and viciously cut across the mouth with a blade. Many, at the time, put the mouth-widening attack down to Ronnie, who had previously fallen out with Litvinoff and broken his nose. Ronnie never denied having done it, and the cutting was most probably the inspiration for a sickening scene in the first Krays movie, *The Krays,* starring Martin and Gary Kemp. Litvinoff was attacked again, this time at the behest of a former close friend whom Litvinoff had upset; so much so that the former friend paid hitmen to teach him a lesson. Litvinoff was beaten unconscious and came round to find himself bloody and bruised, with his hair cut off, and tied to a chair that was dangling from his balcony high above Kensington High Street. It has been said that artist Lucian Freud commissioned the attack. Freud was friends with Litvinoff for some years before falling out and, in 1954, painted his portrait. The painting – originally called *The Procurer* but now called *Man in a Headscarf* – was sold at auction to a private collector for £1,156,000 in 1999.

David Litvinoff's Flat

4 Ashburn Place, Kensington, London SW7 4JR

Nearest TFL station: Gloucester Road underground.

This was the home of David Litvinoff, a well-known character among the rich and fashionable Chelsea set of the '60s. Litvinoff ran up a gambling debt of £3,000 at *Esmeralda's Barn* that he had no way of paying so, instead, Ronnie took the use of his flat – and the company of his young lover, Bobby Buckley – in payment. Buckley worked as a croupier at *Esmeralda's Barn* and all three lived together in the flat for several months in late 1961 and early 1962. Most Kray accounts have Litvinoff living at Ashburn Gardens, but during research for his book *Krayology,* published in 2015, John Bennett consulted the electoral register of the time and found out that Litvinoff was registered as living in Ashburn Place.

David Litvinoff was the dialogue coach and script adviser for the 1970 film *Performance* starring James Fox, Mick Jagger, and real-life hardman, John Bindon. Some of the characters in the film are said to be based on the Krays and their associates.

While Reggie was away in prison between July 1960 and February 1961, and with Ronnie at the helm of Kray enterprises, *Esmeralda's Barn* was clearly the focus of his attention – but there were, as always, other interests and opportunities to exploit. Alfie Teale, a street trader who had first been introduced to Ronnie by Mad Teddy Smith at *The Double R Club,* was gradually drawn into the fold by Ronnie; he was invited to Vallance Road and on nights out to West End clubs with the Kray crowd. Alfie Teale let slip that his parents ran a drinking club in Islington called *The Tudor Club* – known by its regulars as *The 66 Club* due to its address, 66 Upper Street, Islington. *"Oooh, that's good,"* said Ronnie. *"I must come up there and meet your mum and dad. Do you mind? We'll take a couple of friends up and have a nice drink with them. That will be nice, won't it?"*[127] Within a short time, Alfie's younger brother David was enticed into the Kray clique, and the club – unsurprisingly – was completely taken over. Ron, and later Reg, liked the fact that the club was just a little outside their usual manor and used it for quiet drinks and discreet meetings with corrupt police officers on the take. Bobby Teale, a third brother, would soon be persuaded to leave his home and business on the Isle of Wight and return to London to join the Kray party.

127   Teale, David. *Surviving the Krays*. London: Ebury Press, 2022.

The 66 Club

66 Upper Street, Islington, London N1 0NY

Nearest TFL station: Angel underground.

Sandwiched between *Winkworth* estate agents and *Desperados* restaurant is a pink doorway (*Islington Green Dental Practice*) with stairs leading to the upper floors. This was the site of the Teale family's drinking club called *The Tudor Club*, also known as *The 66 Club* due to the street number. Ron and Reg Kray took over the club in 1961 and made it their own in all but name. Slightly out of the way of the usual Kray haunts, it was used for quiet drinks and discreet meetings. The three Teale brothers – Alfie, David, and Bobby – although never fully fledged members of The Firm, became deeply involved with the Krays during the '60s and played a significant part in their eventual downfall. The Teale brothers' story is a fascinating one, and two books written by Bobby and David Teale are a must-read for anyone with an interest in the Krays:

Teale, Bobby. *Bringing Down the Krays*. Ebury Press, 2012.

Teale, David. *Surviving the Krays*. Ebury Press, 2021.

Early in 1961, shortly after Reggie's release from *Wandsworth Prison* on 25 February, all three Kray brothers fell victim to spurious accusations of petty criminality. Unable to get the evidence they needed to charge them with anything serious, the police had to settle for making the Krays' lives as difficult as they possibly could.

Reggie was arrested for housebreaking and making off with jewellery to the value of £500. Witness to the alleged robbery was a woman in her seventies called Lilia Hertzberg, who claimed to have seen Reggie and another man running out of her Stepney home with the swag. This is unlikely to say the least, as the twins were at a financial high point in their career and money was pouring in from numerous enterprises including long firm frauds, protection rackets, and *Esmeralda's Barn*. The only interest the twins might possibly have had in petty crime was relieving the perpetrators of their profits. Mrs Hertzberg was offered and accepted £500 by Charlie Kray to tell the truth in court, the money to be handed over once Reggie was released. When she entered the witness box at *Thames Magistrates Court*, Mrs Hertzberg failed to positively identify Reggie and the case was thrown out. Reggie walked free and was awarded costs. Mrs Hertzberg, predictably, never received a penny.[128]

Thames Magistrates Court & Arbour Square Police Station

East Arbour Street, Stepney Green, London E1 OPZ

Nearest TFL station: Stepney Green underground.

Reggie Kray was held in the cells at *Arbour Street Police Station* and appeared in the adjoining magistrates court on a trumped-up charge of burglary in early 1961. Reggie was acquitted and awarded £92 in costs.[129] This was not the first time that Reggie had been held in the cells at *Arbour Street* and appeared before magistrates at the court. In early 1952, while on the run from the army, he and Ronnie were dealt with here and given a month's sentence in *Wormwood Scrubs* after assaulting PC Fisher.

In 1841 on the corner of Aylward Street and East Arbour Street in Stepney, a three-storey redbrick police station was built with a court beside it, which became *Thames Magistrates Court*. The building sustained damage from a German V1 flying bomb in 1944 but was repaired and remained in service until 1999, when the Metropolitan Police deemed the building surplus to requirements. After the building was vacated, it remained empty – becoming increasingly derelict and frequently

128 Kray, Charlie with McGibbon, Robin. *Me and My Brothers*. London: Grafton, 1988.

129 Morton, James. *Krays: The Final Word*. London: Mirror Books, 2019.

squatted in – until 2012, when it was sold to private developers and turned into residential apartments. The large early Victorian building remains and the original entrance to the police station on East Arbour Street can be seen. Around the corner on Aylward Street, the entrance to the former magistrates court can also be seen.

Thames Magistrates Court now occupies a modern building at 58 Bow Road, London E3 4DJ.

In the early spring of 1961, Ronnie and Charlie were also on the police radar. Until 1981, when the 'Sus Law' was repealed, the police had the power to stop and search anyone they believed to be a suspicious person. According to Charlie, he and Ronnie were travelling in a car driven by their friend Jimmy 'The Dip' Kensit when Jimmy stopped the car outside his Pritchards Row flat in Dalston to call in for something. After they pulled up outside the flat, a police car roared up and three police officers got out. A detective constable told Ronnie, Charlie, and Jimmy to get out of the car and began asking them who they were and what they were doing, while two uniformed officers searched the car. Ronnie, Charlie, and Jimmy were arrested, taken to *Dalston Police Station,*[130] and charged with loitering in Queensbridge Road with intent to commit a felony and trying the door handles of parked cars. Charlie claims that, while held at the police station, their homes were searched without warrants.[131]

Jimmy 'The Dip' Kensit – father of actress Patsy Kensit –

---

130 The former police station building still stands and is now *Cape House Hostel*, 39-41 Dalston Lane E8 3DF.

131 Kray, Charlie with McGibbon, Robin. *Me And My Brothers*. London: Grafton, 1988.

was from Bethnal Green and, like so many young men from an impoverished East End background, became involved in criminality at an early age. As a youngster he was regarded as one of the best pickpockets around, earning him his nickname. Through his involvement with boxing, Jimmy – who was 17 years older than the twins – had watched Ronnie and Reggie's progress in the ring and knew them very well indeed. Reggie was godfather to Patsy Kensit's elder brother Jamie, and can be seen in a well-known photograph holding the baby at the Christening celebration.

Jimmy was something of an independent operator, working with the Krays on the fringes of The Firm and, at the same time, running long firm frauds with the South London Richardson Gang. Somehow, Jimmy managed to straddle both camps and also, remarkably, work with his best friend and sworn enemy of the Richardsons, Charlie Mitchell.[132] Charlie Mitchell was a fearsome, violent character who involved himself in fraud, money lending, bookmaking, and all manner of nefarious criminal activities – including the doping of horses and dogs at the races. Mitchell would become involved with the twins a little later in their story and eventually give evidence against them at their 1969 *Old Bailey* trial.

Ronnie, knowing full well the implausibility of the charges, saw the coming court case as an opportunity to shame the police for what he saw as a clear case of victimisation. Ronnie wanted publicity so he made contact with the press to make sure that their unfair persecution by the police was shouted from the headlines. Next – through the twins' solicitors, Lincoln and Lincoln – the services of the country's most eye-catching young female barrister, Nemone Lethbridge, were engaged. Finally, just to make sure his case was watertight, Ronnie hired

---

132 Kensit, Patsy. *Absolute Beginner*. London: Pan Books, 2014.

private detective George Devlin and produced eight witnesses to swear that he was elsewhere at the time of the alleged *loitering*. The case was heard at *Marylebone Magistrates Court*, where witness testimony and the oratory skills of Nemone Lethbridge – in highlighting the improbability of the charges – ensured that the police allegations could not hold up. On 8 May 1961, the case was dismissed.

Marylebone Magistrates Court

179 Marylebone Road, London NW1 5BR

Nearest TFL station: Edgware Road underground.

Situated at the corner of Marylebone Road and Seymour Place, the early Victorian redbrick and white stone building is still there to be seen today – though nowadays it is used as offices for *Westminster Magistrates Court*, which occupies a large modern building next door at 181 Marylebone Road.

Charlie and Ronnie Kray appeared before magistrates at the court in early 1961, accused of loitering with intent and trying car doors. These were unfounded and unlikely charges brought by the police during a campaign to make life difficult for the Krays. Defended by Nemone Lethbridge, one of Britain's first female barristers, Ronnie and Charlie were acquitted on 8 May 1961.

It was May 1961 and all three Kray brothers were free and exonerated of all charges. To celebrate, a party was held at *Esmeralda's Barn*, to which the press were invited. Ronnie

wanted to ensure press coverage of the injustice they had suffered at the hands of the police who, Ronnie believed, were
clearly set on persecuting the two young, sporting, cockney
lads made good. Ronnie got his way and, on 17 May, the *Daily
Express* carried an article with pictures under the headline: *'It's
a Vendetta, say Freed Boxing Twins.'* The police must have
been aware that flimsy accusations of petty misdemeanours
would not seriously trouble the twins and, under the spotlight
of publicity, could be damaging to the careers of individual policemen and to the force as a whole. Police harassment ceased
and, from then on, the twins would enjoy a sense of untoucha-
bility that would continue – for a while, at least.

Nemone Lethbridge was, during the late 1950s and early '60s, one of the country's first female barristers. Despite a
lack of encouragement and, in some cases, downright hostility
from the male old guard of the esteemed profession, Nemone,
in 1958, secured a place in chambers as a practising barrister
at 3 Hare Court, Temple, London.[133] She was welcomed cour-
teously rather than warmly and soon discovered that many of
the benefits of working in chambers – that were enjoyed by her
male colleagues – were not available to her. Nemone was not
allowed a fair slice of the job cake shared by the dozen or so
other barristers at Hare Court, but one day – when a job came
up that no one else wanted – she was thrown a few crumbs. The
job was, of course, the defence of the Brothers Kray.

For the next year or so, Nemone would be the darling of the
Kray organisation, and – through the twins' solicitors, Lincoln
and Lincoln – she would be called upon frequently to represent
the twins' friends and associates appearing before the courts.
Nemone continued her work with the twins until 1962, when

---

133 The spectacular redbrick, late Victorian, Grade II listed building at 3
     Hare Court, Temple, London E4Y 7BJ is still a barristers' chambers.

she left the legal profession for a while and moved, with her husband, to the Greek island of Mykonos. The next time she would see the twins would be seven years later, from the public gallery at their *Old Bailey* trial.[134]

Nemone can be seen in the first ever film documentary about the twins – *The Name is Kray* – made in 1969. She has appeared in several documentaries since then and, most recently, at age 90, in the 2021 BritBox production, *Secrets of the Krays.*

Esmeralda's Barn gave the Krays a jumping-off point in the West End, from which they could extend their influence and move into London's glittering clubland – where big money could be demanded for looking after the security and *protecting* the interests of the many booming upmarket clubs and casinos. Two of the more prestigious establishments that the twins were *looking after* were *The Pigalle* at 196 Piccadilly and *The Starlite* at 5 Stratford Place, Mayfair. Other powerful gangs were operating in the West End – including Albert Dimes, Frankie Fraser and the Italians, the Nash brothers from Islington, and others – so when a new club opened, it was a good idea to get in first.

One such club was Peter Cook's *Establishment Club* in Soho. Peter Cook was famously half of the double-act Peter Cook and Dudley Moore, and a leading light in the genre of satirical comedy. Cook took over *Club Tropicana*, a seedy strip club in Greek Street, and turned it into a venue for jazz and uncensored satirical comedy acts. Shortly before opening – in the late summer of 1961 – the twins turned up at the club and, after

---

134 Lethbridge, Nemone. *Nemone: A young woman barrister's battle against prejudice, class and misogyny. Her controversial marriage*: Independently published, 2022).

telling Cook what a nice place he had, pointed out that it would be dreadful if the wrong element came in and started smashing the place up. The twins could, of course, offer a service to prevent that from happening. Peter Cook later recalled:

"I knew perfectly well that they were indeed the element that I didn't want to have in and so I said, 'Well thank you very much, that's very kind of you, but the police are just around the corner, so if there's any trouble, I'm sure we'll call them and they'll do their best.' Never saw them again."[135]

Cook did indeed never see them again, but it wasn't his words that caused the twins to back off. This was by no means the end of the matter. It was the kind of response that the twins expected and had heard before; it was just a matter of time before the pressure would be ramped up. Had it not been for Peter Cook's next move, he would have found himself with no choice but to pay the twins what they wanted or close the club. After asking for advice, including from the police, Cook was directed towards – and approached – Soho's most influential and feared hardman, Billy Howard. Cook was furious and adamant that he wasn't going to *"pay money to a couple of thugs in dark suits with the IQ of a park bench."* Billy Howard explained that everyone pays – it's the way things work in Soho – and if he wasn't going to pay the Krays, someone else would soon be knocking on the door. So, Cook chose to pay Billy Howard to look after him and the wheels were set in motion.

Billy Howard arranged a meeting with the twins at *The Dorchester* hotel and managed to convince them that threatening such a high-profile celebrity would alienate them from the

---

135 Interview with Clive James, *Postcard from London*, BBC TV, 31 July 1991.

celebrity circles they so enjoyed being a part of. Howard claims that the twins were paying him a percentage of the profits from their existing protection work, and he told them that the money they were expecting from Cook could be deducted from future payments. Very few people had the clout to change the twins' minds once they decided on something; they were used to taking what they wanted, and nothing or nobody could stand in their way. But, on this occasion, Billy Howard –'The Soho Don'– did just that. Ron and Reg agreed to back off, but there was one caveat; Cook would be hurt *"if he gets mouthy about giving us the knock back."*[136]

The Establishment Club

18 Greek Street, London W1D 4DS

Nearest TFL station: Covent Garden underground.

Opened in October 1961 by British actor, comedian, and satirist Peter Cook, *The Establishment Club* was a venue for jazz – featuring the Dudley Moore Trio and edgy, uncensored comedy performed by budding comedians and satirists.

Just prior to opening, Cook was approached by the Kray twins, who were looking to extort protection money. Cook engaged the services of gangster Billy Howard, and after negotiations with the twins – which included a financial incentive – Ron and Reg agreed to back off, a rare and possibly unique event indeed.

---

136 Connor, Michael. *The Soho Don*. Edinburgh: Mainstream Publishing, 2003.

In the book *Our Story* with Fred Dinenage, Reggie remembers a visit to *The Establishment Club* in the company of Judy Garland, who introduced him to the Beatles. According to Reggie, they spent a brief but pleasant time together and he believed that, given more time, he and the *Fab Four* could have become good friends.

The Establishment Club closed in 1964 and the site that was once the club is now *Zebrano* cocktail bar. The building has a green plaque on the wall at the first-floor level commemorating Peter Cook's founding of the club.

Leslie Payne, the twins' business manager, could see there was a problem; he felt that the presence of the twins and their gangster friends at *Esmeralda's Barn* was bad for business. Scarred, flat-nosed thugs brooding over the gambling tables were causing some of the upper-crust clientele to drift away. Payne realised that he needed to find something, somewhere else, to interest and occupy the twins. The solution to the problem was the acquisition of *The Kentucky Club* at 106a Mile End Road in the heart of the East End. On 11 September 1961, the twins became the registered owners and, after spending £2,000 on redecoration, the club opened for business in the early summer of 1962. Garishly decked out in red velvet flock wallpaper, crimson carpet, wall-to-ceiling mirrors, and gold-sprayed furniture, the club was an instant hit. In no time the club was packed out every night, with East Enders enjoying a touch of West End class and the West End set looking for a fashionable, exciting, and slightly edgy flirtation with cockney culture. Ron was in charge of booking the entertainment and the house band was regularly joined by special guests.

Eddie Calvert – the chart-topping *Man with the Golden Trumpet* – performed at *The Kentucky* one evening. Another time, *Billy Daniels* of *'That Old Black Magic'* fame showed up after his performance at *The London Palladium* and put on a show for free.[137] One of the regular acts appearing at *The Kentucky* was the midget performer *Little Hank*. Ronnie took great pleasure in emerging from the wings with a donkey on a leash, ridden by Hank – who wore an enormous cowboy hat, strummed his guitar, and sang cowboy songs. A close friend of the Krays, Little Hank – real name Royston Smith – was a remarkable character who toured the world as a midget wrestler, calling himself *Fuzzyball Kaye*. He also worked in show business as *Little Jimmy* and as a criminal in the London underworld, where he was known as *Little Legs* or *The Kernel*, jokingly based on Ronnie Kray's title, *The Colonel*. Royston once famously rendered gangster Tony Mella unable to sit down for a while after slashing a criss-cross pattern on his buttocks.

The Kentucky Club

106 Mile End Road, London E1 4NU

Nearest TFL stations: Whitechapel underground and Stepney Green underground.

Leslie Payne, the Krays' business manager, helped the twins open *The Kentucky Club* in the early summer of 1962. After spending £2,000 on decoration, fixtures, and fittings, the club opened and was an instant success with locals enjoying a taste of West End style – and the West End set, fashionably travelling east for a flirtation with

---

137 Kray, Charlie with McGibbon, Robin. *Me and My Brothers*. London: Grafton, 2008.

cockney culture. Filmed on location in the East End, the 1963 film *Sparrows Can't Sing* starring Barbara Windsor has a scene in which the interior of *The Kentucky Club* can be seen, just as it was at the time. Following the premiere of the film at *Mile End ABC Cinema*, the after-party was held at *The Kentucky Club*. The club was closed down after the police objected to the licence on 7 April 1963.

Equidistant from Whitechapel and Stepney Green underground stations on the south side of Mile End Road, in a row of Georgian townhouses, is the location of the former club. The street-level door at 106a is now the entrance to private residences, but it was once the entrance to the club. Immediately next door at 106 is *Grillzbase*, a halal grilled chicken restaurant.

Publicity was always important to the image-conscious twins, and 1962-3 was a time when great efforts were made to counterbalance all the spreading tales of violence and terror – through their charity work. Numerous charity events were organised at *The Kentucky Club* and other venues, and in January 1963 Reggie began promoting charity boxing and wrestling events at Bethnal Green's *York Hall*. The first event – attended by the mayor of Bethnal Green – was a great success, and local newspapers reported favourably on the philanthropy of the well-known local twin businessmen.

York Hall, Bethnal Green was familiar to the twins; they had boxed there during their amateur days, fighting each other in the finals of the London Schools competition. A more sinister event that took place there was revealed by the 1960s photographer of the famous, David Bailey, in his 2020 book, *Look Again*. One evening in 1952, when the twins were 19 and on the run from the army, they attended a dance at *York Hall* accompanied by a gang of friends. After they started misbehaving and throwing beer around, the organiser of the dance – assisted by a policeman friend – threw the unruly gang out. Later, when the dance had finished and the organiser was alone in the hall clearing up, the gang – who had sneaked back in – jumped down from the balcony where they'd been hiding and smashed a glass in the man's face. Reg Kray then slashed the man's face with a knife, causing a wound that required 68 stitches. The victim was David Bailey's father.[138]

York Hall

5 Old Ford Road, Bethnal Green, London E2 9PJ

Nearest TFL station: Bethnal Green underground.

Opened by the Duke and Duchess of York in 1929 and named accordingly, *York Hall* was originally purposed as a new public baths complex, offering first and second-class swimming pools, Turkish, Russian, and slipper baths, and public laundry facilities. In the 1950s, *York Hall* began hosting professional boxing and went on to become known as the sport's spiritual home in Britain. Threatened with closure in 2004, *York Hall* was rescued and refurbished in a joint project between Tower Hamlets Council and Greenwich Leisure, and today operates as a multi-purpose indoor arena and leisure complex.

According to Charlie Kray, the twins boxed at *York Hall* during their days as young amateurs, fighting each

---

138 Bailey, David. *Look Again*. London: Macmillan, 2020.

other for the third year running in the final of the London Schools competition. Ronnie had been victorious in their previous two encounters but, at *York Hall*, Reggie won.

In 1952 at a dance held at *York Hall*, 19-year-old Reggie Kray slashed the face of the father of the world's most famous photographer, David Bailey.

In the early '60s, the twins organised and held a number of charity boxing and wrestling events at *York Hall*, which generated some much-needed favourable publicity. Local papers hailed the twins as good-hearted and respectable businessmen.

During the summer of 1962, the feature film *Sparrows Can't Sing* – starring Barbara Windsor in her first major film role – was being filmed on location in Limehouse, Stepney, and Stratford in London's East End. Based on a play by Stephen Lewis (Blakey from *On the Buses*) and directed by Joan Littlewood, the film is a sentimental comedy of errors, attempting to provide a real-life representation of the cockney East End in the early '60s. Joan Littlewood intended to create an *authentic feel* of the East End by using real locations, actors who came from the area, and locals in bit-parts and as extras. Working on the film was the young Hungarian assistant director Peter Medak, who would later go on to direct the very successful 1990 film *The Krays* starring Martin and Gary Kemp.

On the first day of shooting, several large black cars arrived at the location and the film crew were asked, "*What's going on and who's in charge?*" Peter Medak was told that he needed permission to film in the East End.

"*We have permission from the police,*" was the reply.

"*No permission from us,*" said Ronnie Kray, "*without it, you could get into terrible trouble – you could be killed."*[139]

Barbara Windsor knew the Krays, of course, and had previously introduced them to the film's director, Joan Littlewood, who was able to smooth the situation over – but production costs, which now included protection money, increased significantly.

When Joan Littlewood decided to use a real East End club for a scene in the film, it's no surprise that the twins were asked if they could help, and – for a substantial fee – help they did. *The Kentucky Club* features in a later scene in the film and provides a fascinating glimpse of the club, just as it was in 1962. Real-life Firm members Limehouse Willy and Big Pat Connolly make a cameo appearance as club bouncers.

The film is a light-hearted comedy melodrama with a good pinch of social realism, which could be described as a fusion between a gritty kitchen sink drama and an Ealing comedy. *Sparrows Can't Sing* opened on 26 March 1963 at the *ABC Cinema*, Mile End Road, and was billed as the *East End's first Royal premiere*. Princess Margaret was due to attend, but was unable to do so as a result of coming down with the flu. Lord Snowdon, her husband, did attend – along with stars of the film Barbara Windsor, James Booth, Roy Kinnear, and Victor Spinetti. Guests at the premiere included Stanley Baker, Charlie Drake, Ronald Fraser, Richard Todd, and Roger Moore – who, at the time, was starring in the '60s TV hit, *The Saint*.

---

139 BFI YouTube Channel, The Krays Q&A with Martin and Gary Kemp, 2015.

The ABC Cinema

93-95 Mile End Road, London E1 4UJ

Nearest TFL station: Stepney Green underground

Built and opened in 1885, a 2,000-seat theatre occupied the site near Stepney Green tube station until 1938. Originally called the *Paragon Music Hall*, later renamed the *Paragon Theatre of Varieties* and then the *Mile End Empire Theatre*, the building was demolished to make way for a new Art Deco-style *ABC Cinema*, which opened in 1939. ABC sold the cinema in 1986 and, following two changes of ownership, it closed its doors in 1989. After standing derelict for a decade, the building was bought and reopened as the five-screen *Genesis Cinema* on 5 May 1999.

The twins' grandfather, Jimmy 'Cannonball' Lee, is reputed to have performed at the theatre during the 1920s, delighting audiences with a routine of song, dance, acrobatics, and feats of daring.

Sparrows Can't Sing, starring Barbara Windsor, premiered at the *ABC Cinema* on 26 March 1963, and the twins were joined by the stars of the film and a host of celebrity guests at the after-party held at *The Kentucky Club*. The film premiere was covered by British Pathe News and can be seen on YouTube: British Pathe Royal film evening 1963.

On 8 September 2015, a preview of the Kray twins' biopic *Legend* starring Tom Hardy was shown at the *Genesis Cinema* followed by a Q&A with the director, Brian Helgeland.

The Kentucky Club was straight across the road from the cinema and, after the film, many of the film's stars and guest celebrities made their way there for the post-premiere party. Waiting to meet them were their hosts, the twins, immaculate in evening dress. Lord Effingham was there to mingle with the guests, and the voice of Queenie Watts – who appeared in the film, playing herself – provided the entertainment. After the party, some of the guests continued the celebration late into the night at *Esmeralda's Barn*.

Sadly, for the twins, good times at *The Kentucky* were short-lived. The police objected to the licence and, on 7 April 1963, the club was closed down after less than a year.[140]

Another business fell into the twins' hands in the summer of 1963: *The Cambridge Rooms*, a roadhouse pub and restaurant in suburban New Malden on the Kingston bypass. Leslie Payne had negotiated a deal with the owners, Lanni Caterers, which, true to form, resulted in them being pushed out completely and The Firm moving in. Teddy Smith became the manager, Pat Connolly manned the door, Sammy Lederman took over the bar, and The Firm were there in the evening, eating and drinking – without paying.

In the late summer of 1963, world heavyweight boxing champion Sonny Liston was in England on a promotional tour, meeting people, attending events, and boxing in exhibition bouts. Sammy Lederman, through his theatrical agency – now joined by Charlie – had contacts in show business and sport, and Sonny Liston was booked to attend *The Cambridge Rooms*' official opening night in September 1963, billed as a charity event. Several other celebrities were present including Barbara Windsor, Lita Roza, boxer Terry Spinks, and actor

---

140 Morton, James. *The Krays: The Final Word*. London: Mirror Books, 2019.

Ronald Fraser. Also among the guests was Vice Admiral Sir Charles Evans. It is interesting to note that the then recently retired Deputy Supreme Allied Commander Atlantic was in attendance at a Kray twin's bash.

Ron and Reg had previously bought their mother Violet a racehorse, but *Solway Cross* had a poor track record and had never come close to winning a race. With no prospect of it ever doing so, the twins weren't quite sure what to do with it. Auction it for charity was the answer, which they did that evening at *The Cambridge Rooms*. Actor Ronald Fraser, who liked a drink, made the winning bid and – probably much to his regret – was now stuck with Dobbin. At the end of the evening, a very drunk Reggie insisted on driving Sonny Liston back to his Mayfair hotel. Reggie was not a good driver at the best of times and, after the hair-raising 12-mile journey, Sonny told Reggie that he was scared of no man – except Reggie Kray behind the wheel of a car.

After driving the regular customers away, exhausting all the suppliers' credit, and drinking the bar dry, the Krays and The Firm walked away from *The Cambridge Rooms* in late 1964, leaving nothing behind except a pile of unpaid bills.

The Cambridge Rooms

197 Burlington Road, New Malden, London KT3

Nearest station: Motspur Park, South Western Railway – approximately 22 minutes direct from Waterloo station.
London bus K5 stops at Motspur Park.

Situated in the South London suburbs, a good distance from the Krays' usual haunts, *The Cambridge*

Rooms was taken over by the Krays in the summer of 1963, run into the ground, and abandoned just over a year later. World heavyweight boxing champion Sonny Liston attended the opening night in September 1963.

Well-known photographs of the opening night show Sonny Liston signing autographs surrounded by a group of onlookers. One clearly shows Ronnie angrily pushing a man away who is trying to shake the heavyweight champion's hand. (Google: Krays/Sonny Liston/images)

Happily, the building still exists, and is currently a *Krispy Kreme* doughnut outlet.

Ronnie Kray was a paranoid schizophrenic and was totally dependent on antipsychotic drugs to control his mental condition. When taking the drugs regularly as prescribed, Ronnie was reasonably stable – though he could still be moody and unpredictable, resorting to extreme violence at the slightest provocation. Even when Ronnie was properly medicated, it was wise to assess his mood and tread carefully in his presence. If Ronnie, however, failed to take the drugs regularly – which happened sometimes – he was a danger to all around him.

One example of Ronnie's extreme violence took place in late September 1963 at a drinking club called *Le Monde* on the Kings Road in Chelsea. One night, the Kray crowd were drinking in the club when ex-boxer and friend of the twins, Johnny Cardew, jokingly suggested that Ronnie must be doing well as he had put on some weight.[141] Nothing happened immediately, but Ronnie began to brood over the comment before leaving the club to go for dinner at *The Cambridge Rooms*. Shortly after leaving, Ronnie told his driver to turn around and go back

---

141   Morton, James. *Krays: The Final Word*. London: Mirror Books, 2019.

to the club. Ronnie told Cardew that he wanted a word and then set about his face with a knife, slashing, hacking, and causing terrible injury. Cardew, with his head wrapped in towels, ran to the nearby *St Stephen's Hospital* to get his face put back together. After receiving over 70 stitches and a prolonged period of treatment, Cardew was left with severe scarring – which gained him the nickname 'Tramlines.'[142]

Sometime later, the same club saw another angry outburst from Ronnie but this time, fortunately, no one was seriously hurt. Long-time friend of the Krays, George 'Ossie' Osborne – the friend who had accompanied Reggie when Ronnie was sprung from *Long Grove* – began a relationship with the club's owner, a woman called Jamette. Together, they ran *Le Monde* and lived on the premises in the flat above. According to close Kray associate Micky Fawcett, Jamette was an 'evil woman' who, on her daughter's 16th birthday, asked Ronnie to deflower the girl. Ronnie duly obliged. Jamette claimed that she provided *services* to the Commissioner of the Metropolitan Police, Sir Joe Simpson – who, she said, was a masochist and enjoyed being whipped. This hold over London's most senior policeman, which Jamette may or may not have had, very much appealed to the twins.[143]

One evening, Ronnie and a group of associates arrived at the club and were told by Jamette's daughter, who was working behind the bar, that George and her mum were staying in tonight and wouldn't be coming down to the club. This infuriated Ronnie, who told the girl to *"get that arsehole on the phone."* Despite Osborne's apologies and insistence that no snub was intended, Ronnie told him to keep the phone to

---

142 Pearson, John. *The Profession of Violence*. London: Weidenfeld and Nicolson, 1972.

143 Fawcett, Micky. *Krayzy Days*. Brighton: Pen Press, 2013.

his ear and listen to what was about to happen to his lovely little club. Ronnie then told the customers present to sit still and that no one would get hurt. Then, beginning by throwing a glass soda siphon and smashing the mirror behind the bar, Ronnie proceeded to wreck the place.[144]

Ronnie's unbalanced personality regularly led to outbursts of furious temper and violence, totally disproportionate to whatever wrongdoing Ronnie perceived – real or imagined. It is often said that Ronnie Kray enjoyed hurting people and was not in the least bit troubled by conscience, allowing him to commit acts of violence that, even for a gangster, were extreme and all too frequent. Ronnie's mental illness is associated with a lack of empathy towards others, and therefore a lack of remorse. Much of Ronnie's violent behaviour would bear this out, but there were occasions – usually involving friends, and often when he had failed to take his medication – when Ronnie regretted his impulsive behaviour, and this was one of them. The next morning at Vallance Road, after discussing the previous night's events with Reggie, Charlie, and friend Eric Mason, Ronnie became tearful. He told Reggie to get Ossie on the phone and informed his old friend that he would pay for the damage to his club – no expense spared.

---

144   Mason, Eric. *The Inside Story*. London: Pan Books, 1994.

Le Monde

287 Kings Road, London SW3 5EW

Nearest TFL station: South Kensington underground.

Le Monde was a small and rather discreet gang-ster-friendly drinking club owned and run by a woman called Jamette, in partnership with the twins' old friend George 'Ossie' Osborne. Popular with the Kray crowd, the club – situated on the Kings Road in Chelsea – saw at least two examples of Ronnie Kray's vicious temper in the early 1960s.

Ex-boxer and friend of the Krays, Johnny Cardew, made the mistake of failing to assess Ronnie Kray's mood and jokingly said that he was putting on weight. Ronnie slashed Cardew's face repeatedly, causing dreadful injury and scars that gained him the nickname 'Tramlines.'

Sometime afterwards, Ronnie Kray arrived at the club with a group of friends and was unhappy to discover that his friend and co-owner of the club, 'Ossie' Osborne, was not there to greet him. Ronnie took this as a snub, lost his temper, and began smashing up the club. Ronnie later regretted his actions and offered to pay for the damage.

Formerly *The Harvey Club*, *Le Monde* occupied 287 Kings Road for a period between 1963 and 1966. In 1967, *Raffles* nightclub opened on the premises, and is today one of London's oldest and most exclusive clubs frequented by the well-heeled and the famous.

Those who knew Ronnie Kray personally, and those who lived in the East End and simply knew of his reputation, were careful how they behaved in his presence. The lively, relaxed atmosphere of an East End pub on a Saturday night could suddenly change if Ronnie Kray walked in. Laughter would stop and, with eyes lowered, people would begin drifting away – knowing that a chuckle, a glance, or any innocent gesture could easily be taken by Ronnie as an affront to him, resulting in serious consequences.

One of the many local pubs used occasionally by the twins and their friends was *The Green Gate* on Bethnal Green Road. Live music was a feature of the pub and one of the regular performers was the blind singer, and friend of the Krays, Lennie Peters. Later, in 1973 – after teaming up with singing partner Dianne Lee – Peters and Lee topped the British charts with the song '*Welcome Home.*'

One evening, Ron, Reg, and two friends were listening to the music of a band playing in the busy *Green Gate* pub which, on music nights, attracted people from all over London – including non-locals, which might go some way to explain what happened next. A group of five[145] rowdy young men began to irritate Ronnie. In his book, *Born Fighter*, Reggie says that two of the men were making rude comments about Ronnie, which begs the question – how probable is that? Even in the unlikely event that the men in question didn't know who the Kray twins were, surely four tasty-looking geezers sitting poker-faced at the bar would be the last people to target. Deliberately provoked or otherwise, Ronnie stood up and knocked the two men unconscious before returning to his bar stool and casually picking up his gin and tonic. Reggie then took hold of the collars of

---

145 Reggie says five in his book, *Born Fighter*; three in a telephone interview conducted in 1995.

the two unconscious men, dragged them outside, and left them on the pavement. Yet another example of the assertion that "*the Krays only hurt their own*" not necessarily always being the case.

The Green Gate

230 Bethnal Green Road, London E2 0AA

Nearest TFL station: Bethnal Green overground.

The Green Gate was a long-established pub, in existence since the beginning of the 19th century and finally closing its doors in 1995. During the 1960s, the pub became a venue for live music and was one of the few East End pubs visited by people from other parts of London. The blind singer Lennie Peters – friend of the Kray twins, uncle to Rolling Stone Charlie Watts, and famously one half of the duo Peters and Lee – performed regularly at the pub.

Situated close to the junction of Bethnal Green Road and Vallance Road, the pub was very much on the Krays' manor and, as such, was visited by the twins and their friends from time to time.

During a telephone interview from *Maidstone Prison*, broadcast on national television news in 1995 at the time of Ronnie's funeral, Reggie was asked about his memories of his twin brother. Reggie, to illustrate his brother's *sense of humour*, recalled an incident in *The Green Gate* pub when Ronnie knocked two men unconscious.

Today, the building that was once *The Green Gate* pub is the *Saver Plus* supermarket. If you look up to the first-floor windows of the building, to the left, part of the original pub sign is still in situ and can be seen.

After the lease on David Litvinoff's flat in Kensington had expired in early 1962, Ronnie moved back to Vallance Road, where Reggie was still living. Reggie's deep involvement with Frances and talk of marriage – and Ronnie's infatuation with Bobby Buckley, on whom he doted and showered with money and gifts – was often the source of arguments that regularly came to blows. Arguing and fighting between themselves was nothing new to the twins, but at this point in their lives, their relationship was particularly fractious. Within a short time Ronnie was sleeping in a caravan on a bombsite near Vallance Road and then, in the summer of 1962 – just as *The Kentucky Club* was opening – he moved into *Cedra Court*, a block of smart Art Deco-style flats in Clapton, occupied mostly by well-to-do Jewish families. Ronnie's flat, the lease to which was in Leslie Payne's name, was number 8 on the first floor.

Despite all their falling out and quarrelling, the twin brothers were inextricably bonded and could never be far apart for any length of time. By the early summer of 1963, just after the closure of *The Kentucky Club*, Reggie began renting the flat immediately below Ronnie's on the ground floor. Ronnie's apartment was ostentatiously decorated and decked out with Chinese and Persian carpets, stuffed birds in cages, antique weapons on the walls, a giant fish tank, and an enormous four-poster bed. Mirrors adorned the walls and ceilings, and the bathroom – with pink tiles and a black bath – had a peephole in the door.[146] After a trip to Africa in 1964, adornments included an elephant's foot and a metre-high ebony elephant with real ivory tusks.

146   Morton, James. *Krays: The Final Word*. London: Mirror Books, 2019.

Lorraine, a waitress from *Esmeralda's Barn*, was employed as Ronnie's house keeper. Her duties included washing, cooking, and cleaning, but there was one other service required of her that is more than a little surprising. Ronnie was of course gay, with a voracious sexual appetite, and he would rarely sleep alone – but, on the odd occasion when no boy was available to him, Ronnie would tell Lorraine to go and have a bath and then hop into bed with him.[147]

Sex parties first held at Litvinoff's flat in Kensington continued at *Cedra Court*, where the availability of rough-trade sex with boys was attracting some very high-profile guests.

Cedra Court

Cazenove Road, Stoke Newington, London N16 6AT

Nearest TFL station: Stoke Newington overground.

Built in the 1930s, the elegant block of Art Deco-style flats was lived in by Ron and Reg Kray for periods from the early to mid-1960s. Ron moved into flat 8 on the first floor in the summer of 1962 and Reg followed just under a year later, when he began renting flat 1, directly below Ronnie on the ground floor. Ronnie's ostentatiously decorated flat was the scene of sex parties attended by a number of well-known and influential guests. Reggie lived with his wife Frances in flat 1 for a short period after their wedding in 1965.

Possibly the single most iconic and well-known

---

147   Pearson, John. *The Cult of Violence*. London: Orion Books, 2001.

photograph of the twins as they stride together through the courtyard of *Cedra Court* was taken by a *Daily Express* photographer in 1964.

Cedra Court was used as a location and appears in several scenes of the 2015 Krays movie *Legend*, starring Tom Hardy.

Born in 1900, Lord Robert Boothby was educated at *Eaton* and *Oxford* before becoming a Conservative member of Parliament in 1924, and from 1926 to 1929 he served as private secretary to Winston Churchill. Boothby was raised to the peerage in 1958, becoming Baron Boothby of Buchan and Rattray Head and taking his seat in the House of Lords. During his political career, he was a prominent figure and commentator on issues of the day, popular and well-known to the British public through his frequent appearances on radio and television. Bob Boothby was a pillar of the establishment: a privileged, successful, highly respected, and much-loved public figure. So why on earth would such a man choose to have any kind of relationship with a psychotic East End gangster? Simply put, it was bi-sexual Boothby's private life and his sexual appetite that led him into situations that were not only inappropriate for a man in his position but also downright dangerous.

Since 1929, Boothby had been having an affair with Lady Dorothy Macmillan (formerly Cavendish), wife of the Conservative politician, and later – from 1957 to 1963 – wife of the British Prime Minister Harold Macmillan. Rumour has it that Macmillan's youngest daughter Sarah, born in 1930, was Boothby's love child. The affair was common knowledge among politicians and high society, who closed ranks against outside scrutiny. Such business did not reflect well on the establishment, and the story – with the cooperation of the press – was suppressed.

This was not to be the last establishment-led suppression of a story involving Boothby; it would be eclipsed later in 1964 by a full-blown government cover-up of his liaison with Ronnie Kray. Had the full story got out, it would have rocked the establishment to its very core and potentially caused the collapse of the British Government – and the main opposition party along with it. Even the Profumo affair of 1963, which had severely shaken the government and led to the resignation of Prime Minister Harold Macmillan, did not compare in magnitude to the damage that would have been inflicted by the exposure of the lies, debauchery and, at the time, criminality surrounding the Boothby affair.

The saga begins with prominent politician and former Chairman of the Labour Party, Tom Driberg. Driberg was a homosexual with a penchant for *cottaging* – the seeking out of sexual encounters with strangers in public toilets, or anywhere else that the opportunity may present itself. The excitement for Driberg was enhanced by danger; the greater the risk of getting caught, the greater the thrill. Driberg's sexual proclivities were well-known among colleagues in Westminster and even Fleet Street, but friends in high places – including the newspaper baron Lord Beaverbrook – had successfully prevented the facts about him from reaching a wider audience.

In 1963, Driberg was introduced to the Kray twins and their world at *The Kentucky Club* by their mutual friend, theatrical producer Joan Littlewood. Driberg began a sexual relationship with the villain – aspiring writer and close friend of the Krays, Mad Teddy Smith – and it is reputed that Driberg would give him the addresses of people he didn't like so that Smith could burgle their homes while they were away on holiday. Not the kind of behaviour one would expect from such a prominent left-wing man of the people, advocate of Christian values and all things fair and good.

In the 2009 TV documentary, *The Gangster and the Pervert*

Peer, Kray associate Frank Kurylo has this to say about Tom Driberg: *"Driberg was unbelievable – he just wanted to have oral sex. If you lined ten up he would give each one head, he would, unbelievable! There are so many things that haven't come out, so many things."*[148]

Despite Driberg and Boothby being at opposite ends of the political spectrum, they had much in common and were friends. For instance, both enjoyed gambling – after all, they were happy to risk their political careers and reputations for the prospect of illicit sex with young men. *Esmeralda's Barn* had it all: gambling, drinking, good-looking young men selected by Ronnie to work there, and upper-class toffs mixing freely with East End gangsters, creating a heady cocktail with a twist of danger. Boothby was no doubt more than happy to accompany Tom Driberg to *Esmeralda's Barn* to meet his new friends.

Leslie Holt was a good-looking young man from a poor family in London's East End. Formerly a boxer fighting under the name of *Johnny Kid,* he had built a successful life for himself as a cat burglar, male prostitute, and Swinging Sixties man about town. With a background and lifestyle such as this, it was just a matter of time before he became a blip on the radar of the lord and master of London's dark underbelly – Ronnie Kray.

Leslie Holt lived for a period at *Cedra Court,* and it may well have been here that he first caught the attention of the resident living in flat 8. Holt had all the credentials Ronnie required and he was set to work as a trainee croupier at *Esmeralda's Barn.* Some accounts suggest that Holt, in his capacity as a rent boy, already knew Boothby before the good Lord began frequenting *Esmeralda's Barn.* Other accounts state that they met there, but one way or the other, Ronnie Kray saw an opportunity to gain a hold over the powerful and influential Boothby.

---

148 *The Gangster and the Pervert Peer*, Blakeway Productions, 2009.

With a bit of manoeuvring and manipulating by Ronnie – or at least his blessing and encouragement – Boothby's passionate and, at the time, illegal and dangerous sexual relationship with Leslie Holt got underway.

Boothby fell in love with Holt and enjoyed introducing him to high culture, with evenings at the opera and French haute cuisine at London's finest restaurants. Boothby showered his young lover with money and gifts, one of which was a beautiful new E-Type Jaguar. Holt could regularly be seen cruising the streets of the West End in his new car, sometimes accompanied by his good friend, Profumo affair leading lady, Christine Keeler – not an altogether surprising friendship as they had much in common.

Boothby's mutually beneficial relationship with Ronnie Kray also flourished. They both had an all-consuming passion for gay sex but not, as is sometimes speculated, with each other; both were only interested in boys. Ronnie had snared a very influential friend indeed and was acutely aware that such a friend could prove extremely useful in the future. For Boothby, the appeal was certainly the endless supply of boys for sex, but also, being close to London's most powerful and feared gangster must have given him a sense of invulnerability. He was, perhaps mistakenly, secure in the knowledge that any of his misdeeds would be hushed up and taken care of by a wealth of friends at the highest levels, and any problems occurring at the lowest would also be swiftly dealt with. Confident that he could get away with anything, Boothby clearly found irresistible appeal in pushing the boundaries of acceptable behaviour. What could be more outrageous than inviting a known gangster to dine with him at that most hallowed of institutions, the House of Lords dining room? But this he did and, afterwards, on to *White's Club* in St James's – the most exclusive private gentleman's club in London, frequented by the crème de la crème of the British establishment, high society, and even royalty.

White's Club

37-38 St James's Street, London SW1A 1JG

Nearest TFL station: Green Park underground.

Founded in 1693 and occupying its current Grade I listed premises since 1778, *White's* is the oldest and most exclusive gentleman's club in London.

In 1963, Lord Robert Boothby – in defiance of convention and rather outrageously – took London's most feared gangster Ronnie Kray as his guest to the House of Lords dining room at Westminster, and afterwards to *White's Club*.

Today, *White's* – rather surprisingly – retains its traditions and remains a men-only institution.

Ron's reciprocal gesture was to invite Boothby along to several of his equally exclusive get-togethers for the crème de la crème of London's low life. Ron's Friday night sex parties at his *Cedra Court* flat were attended by many high-profile friends including Boothby, Driberg, and it is rumoured – although unsubstantiated – other well-known politicians, at least one TV celebrity, a prominent artist, a famous DJ, an equally famous music producer, and even a couple of clergymen. Sex with boys was the main attraction, plus drink, blue movies, and the opportunity for those so inclined to indulge their fantasies. Bob Boothby is said to have had a penchant for 'scat' sex, involving boys and the use of a glass-topped table – the less said about that the better, perhaps.

In early 1964, an overseas business project in which Leslie Payne had become involved was underway and beginning to take shape. The essentially legitimate scheme was a development project to build a new town in Enugu, Eastern Nigeria. Leslie Payne was convinced that there was easy money to be made and assured the twins that their participation would raise their profile to that of international businessmen. Payne considered that Ronnie's new friend – the esteemed Lord Boothby – would be the ideal front man for the enterprise, and possibly open the way for some financial backing from the government.

After Ronnie's initial meeting with Boothby to broach the proposition, Leslie Holt was instructed by Ronnie to arrange a second meeting at Boothby's Eaton Square apartment. Holt was already there when Ronnie arrived on an early summer's day in 1964, accompanied by Mad Teddy Smith and a photographer by the name of Bernard Black. Boothby agreed to a photo shoot, and several, now famous, photographs were taken of the assembled group. After giving the business proposition due consideration, Boothby – exercising prudence for once – decided not to invest. Although Boothby's involvement in the Enugu project never took flight, his new-found friendship with Ronnie Kray continued to flourish.

1 Eaton Square

Belgravia, London SW1W 9DA

Nearest TFL station: Victoria underground.

The fine white-fronted Georgian building at 1 Eaton Square was home to Lord Robert Boothby, where – in 1964 – photographs were taken of Boothby in the company of Mad Teddy Smith, Leslie Holt, and Ronnie Kray. This added fuel to a political scandal that, had it not been covered up by the government, would have eclipsed the

Profumo affair of the previous year. Ronnie Kray, who supplied Boothby with boys for sex, was a regular visitor to the Peer of the Realm's second-floor flat.

There is a blue plaque on the outside of the building that reads: *Robert, Lord Boothby, 1900-1986, Politician, Author and Broadcaster lived here 1946-1986.*

Also in early 1964, Michael Thornton – a young journalist working for the *Sunday Express* – was asked by his editor John Junor to write a piece on the ever-popular Lord Boothby. It was not difficult to arrange an interview at Boothby's Eaton Square flat as the peer was a close friend of the owner of *Express* newspapers, Lord Beaverbrook. Thornton was puzzled by Boothby's relationship with the young man who emerged from his bedroom (Leslie Holt), and even more puzzled by the arrival of a heavy-set character with shark-like eyes and a bone-crushing handshake. This, of course, was Ronnie Kray, and when he and Boothby embraced it was clear that they knew each other very well indeed. Several more visits to Eaton Square revealed to Thornton that Ronnie Kray was supplying Boothby with rent boys, some of whom were clearly unhappy about the arrangement but too terrified of Ronnie to refuse.

One evening, after dining with Boothby and Ronnie at the *Society* restaurant in Jermyn Street, Thornton was taken to *Esmeralda's Barn* where he met and spoke to Ronnie's lover and favourite boy, Bobby Buckley. Buckley told him that many young heterosexual men, including a well-known boxer and an actor, had been coerced against their will into having sex with Ronnie. Thornton realised, to his horror, that he was in a situation contrived by Boothby to place him on the menu for Ronnie. Ronnie wanted Thornton to go home with him and wasn't taking no for an answer, and when his touching and pestering became too much to bear, Thornton told Ronnie to "*fuck off.*"

Diana Dors was present in the club that evening and chipped in, saying, "*Babycakes, you're dicing with death here; don't get stroppy with him for God's sake.*"

Ronnie's eyes bulged with rage and he dragged Thornton into the corridor and pointed a gun at him.

Fortunately for Thornton, Reggie appeared and said, "*Leave it out, Ron. You can see the kid's not interested – and he's the fucking press!*" Reggie dragged Thornton out of the club, frog-marched him to a taxi, put a £10 note in his hand, and pushed him inside.

Thornton realised that Boothby's unwholesome relation-ship with Ronnie Kray could be his newspaper's scoop of the century, but the editor of the Tory-aligned *Sunday Express* wasn't about to print a story that had the potential to unseat the Conservative Government. "*You have much to learn,* "he said to Thornton. "*There are some stories that just don't get print-ed.*" For now, Boothby was safe from exposure, but it wouldn't be long before a more left-wing, less inhibited newspaper got wind of the story.[149]

The Society Restaurant

40 Jermyn Street, London SW1Y 6DN

Nearest TFL station: Piccadilly Circus underground.

The *Society* – with its magnificent chandeliers and carved wood-panelled interior – was Ronnie Kray's fa-vourite restaurant and he would entertain here regularly. Sometimes, Ronnie, as a treat, brought groups of Firm

---

149   Michael Thornton for the *Daily Mail*, 14 October 2006.

members to the restaurant. They would all follow suit after Ronnie ordered his favourite dish: double spaghetti Bolognese.[150]

There are two well-known photographs of Ronnie at the *Society*; one in which he is in the company of Lord Boothby, his manservant Goodfellow, an unidentified boy, Billy Exley, his wife, and Charlie Clark; and another where Christine Keeler can be seen sitting between Ronnie and Leslie Holt. Also sitting around the table is Jimmy Nash and Firm member Johnny Davis.[151]

In December 1969, the ground floor of the building at 40 Jermyn Street, which was once the *Society* restaurant, became the very exclusive *Tramp* nightclub; nowadays, a favourite haunt of London's glitterati.

Thornton's snubbing of Ronnie's sexual advances at *Esmeralda's Barn* occurred in May 1964. Over a year later, in July 1965, Thornton was the victim of a vicious assault outside his home in Bryanston Mews, Marylebone. Outside his flat, next door to the home of Mick Jagger,[152] he was grabbed from behind, hit on the head with a hard object, and – after falling to the ground – repeatedly kicked in the head and body. Thornton recalls hearing an East End voice saying, *"That will teach you to show some fucking respect to Ronnie."* Thornton was taken by ambulance to *Paddington General Hospital*, where he was found to have severe bruising, a broken cheekbone, a broken nose, and a gash in his head that required 22 stitches.

For some considerable time, the Krays and their associates

150 Fawcett, Micky. *Krayzy Days*. Brighton: Pen Press, 2013.
151 Google Images: Ronnie Kray at the Society Restaurant.
152 Jagger lived at 13a Bryanston Mews, East, Paddington, WC1.

had been under surveillance by C11, *Scotland Yard*'s intelligence gathering branch. Covert operations had revealed the comings and goings of many high-profile individuals at Ron Kray's *Cedra Court* flat. A comprehensive dossier of the Krays' activities – including fraud, protection rackets, and possible links with the American Mafia – had been built up and *Scotland Yard* was poised, ready for action, awaiting the thumbs up from Metropolitan Police Commissioner, Sir Joe Simpson.

The police were not the only ones watching the Krays and gathering information; so too was the Inland Revenue. Author of the first-ever Krays book, Brian McConnell, was working as a reporter for the *Daily Mirror* when – in the summer of 1964 – he was summoned, on behalf of the newspaper, to a meeting with a representative of the Inland Revenue tax investigation department. Bound by the Official Secrets Act, McConnell does not reveal exactly what happened at the meeting in the anonymous, unlisted revenue office near Shepherd's Bush, but it was certainly to do with the newspaper's disclosure of information about the Kray twins.[153]

It was the US Treasury Department – not the police department – that was finally able to nail Al Capone and end his criminal career. In 1931, Capone was found guilty of tax evasion, sentenced to 11 years, and sent to Alcatraz.

So, who would strike first, the police or the revenue? Perhaps a two-pronged joint operation? Did either or both have the evidence needed to make the charges stick? If it was to be a police operation, was Commissioner Joe Simpson prepared to deal with the inevitable repercussions following the arrest – or at least the exposure – of two of the country's most senior political figures? Whether or not a swoop was set to take place we

---

153 McConnell, Brian. *The Rise and Fall of the Brothers Kray*. London: David Bruce & Watson Ltd., 1969.

may never know, because something happened at this juncture that changed everything.

Chief crime correspondent for the *Sunday Mirror*, Norman Lucas, was one of Fleet Street's best known and most highly regarded crime reporters. Himself an ex-policeman, Lucas had maintained and nurtured relations with many useful contacts within the force, and – for the price of a nice dinner and a few drinks from time to time on the expense account – he could rest assured that he would be the first to know if anything interesting came up. Lucas also knew the Krays well, having been among the pack of hungry journos hanging around *The Double R Club* in the late '50s.

Imagine Lucas' utter amazement when he received a tip-off from a C11 contact that they had uncovered information about a number of public figures involved in a homosexual vice ring, and that Lord Boothby was having an improper relationship with Ronnie Kray. Pure gold! But the problem was, how to print the story without being sued? After discussions with the *Mirror*'s lawyer, Lucas penned an article – without naming names – which was approved by the *Mirror*'s editor, Reginald Payne, and then submitted to the higher-ups for final approval.

Mirror Group's editorial director Hugh Cudlipp was on holiday at the time, so responsibility fell to the Chairman of the International Publishing Corporation, Cecil Harmsworth King. King gave the article the go-ahead and, in so doing, began a sequence of events that almost toppled the whole of the British political establishment.

Sunday 12 July 1964

'Peer and a Gangster: Yard Probe' shouted the *Sunday Mirror*'s front-page headline. The article claimed that Metropolitan Police Commissioner Joe Simpson had ordered an investigation into an alleged homosexual relationship between a prominent peer who is a household name and a leading

thug in the London underworld involved in West End protection rackets.

Monday 13 July 1964

Bernard Black, the photographer present at the meeting at Boothby's Eaton Square flat, visited the offices of Mirror Group Newspapers and handed over the photographs of Boothby with Ronnie, Leslie Holt, and Teddy Smith for an undisclosed sum. Later the same day, Black returned to the newspaper's offices and asked for the photographs back, saying that they were not his to sell. Derek Jameson – the *Mirror*'s picture editor – refused to hand the pictures over, so Black quickly consulted lawyers and a writ was served, attempting to restrain the newspaper from publishing the photographs.

Tuesday 14 July 1964

Reg Payne – the *Mirror*'s editor – and Norman Lucas were interviewed by police and reminded that they had a duty to inform the police immediately if they had in their possession any information implicating a person in criminal activities. Only names were given at this point, and a promise to supply further information as the newspaper's investigation progressed.

Also on 14 July, Metropolitan Police Commissioner Joe Simpson issued a carefully worded statement in *The Times* newspaper, denying the commissioning of an investigation specifically interested in a homosexual relationship between a peer and a London gangster.

Friday 17 July 1964

Boothby, who had been holidaying in France when the Peer and the Gangster headline broke, returned to London in a state of near despair, knowing full well that he was the subject of the article. Not knowing quite which way to turn, he phoned his old friend Tom Driberg and begged him to do what he could to get him – possibly both of them – out of this pickle.

Saturday 18 July 1964

Boothby penned a letter to the Home Secretary, Henry Brooke, stating that he was not homosexual and that Kray and his lawyer had visited him by appointment about six months earlier to discuss a business proposition, and that Kray had returned with a friend for another meeting about a week later. *"I gave them a drink and before he left he asked me if his friend could take a photograph of us as he was a great fan of mine on radio and television."* Boothby claimed that this was the sum total of his relationship with Mr Kray and that he had never met him outside his flat.

Sunday 19 July 1964

The *Sunday Mirror* hit the newsstands with another bombshell of a headline : *'The Picture we Must Not Print.'* The article stated that the *Sunday Mirror* was in possession of a picture – of the highest significance and public concern – that shows a well-known member of the House of Lords seated on a sofa with a gangster who leads the biggest protection racket London has ever known.

Wednesday 22 July 1964

Following further pressure from the police, the photographs were handed over, delivered by the *Mirror*'s editor Reg Payne to a senior officer. One of the images was of Ronnie Kray, Boothby, and Leslie Holt sitting together on a sofa. The police had yet to identify Holt, and Assistant Commissioner Ranulph 'Rasher' Bacon is noted in the Home Office file as describing: *"An ill-dressed beatnik youth also sitting on the sofa."*[154]

---

154 Morton, James. *Krays: The Final Word*. London: Mirror Books, 2019.

Tuesday 28 July 1964

The German news magazine, *Stern* – not subject to British liable laws and having somehow laid their hands on the information – ran an article naming Boothby and one of the homosexual Kray twins.

Wednesday 29 July 1964

With less than three months until the October general election, the government called a crisis meeting. After the Profumo affair of the previous year, Alec Douglas-Home and his Conservative Government could not possibly survive another sex-based scandal. Opposition leader Harold Wilson was fully aware of the sexual misdemeanours of his old and trusted friend in politics – Tom Driberg – and his perilous involvement with Boothby and Ronnie Kray. It was certainly not in the interest of the Labour Party if this was to come out, as it surely would if something wasn't done to keep a lid on the situation. And so began interparty machinations to find a way of making the problem go quietly away.

Enter Arnold 'Two Dinners' Goodman, the Labour Party's most highly respected lawyer and Mr Fixit. Goodman was a big man, both in terms of his presence and influence in politics and his physical size, earning him his nickname. Moving quickly and decisively, Goodman first managed to persuade the *Sunday Mirror* that it would be in their best interest to drop the story and take it no further. Quite what he said and did we will never know for sure, but drop it they did. Next, Goodman instructed Boothby to pen a letter to *The Times*, denying all the *Sunday Mirror*'s accusations.

Saturday 1 August 1964

Boothby's 500-word letter appeared in *The Times* newspaper, repudiating all the *Mirror*'s claims against him. *"In short, the whole affair is a tissue of atrocious lies,"* wrote Boothby.

All the *Mirror*'s allegations were of course true, and it was Boothby's letter that was in fact a tissue of atrocious lies.

Goodman's next move was to engage the services of another Labour heavyweight, Sir Gerald Gardiner, QC, and with Gardiner acting as Boothby's council, Goodman was able to exert huge pressure on *The Mirror* and make it clear to them that their best and least expensive course of action would be to retract all the allegations and print an apology to Lord Boothby. Also, explained Goodman, bearing in mind the suffering that these outrageous falsehoods must have caused Lord Boothby, they would be looking for a significant compensation payment.

Tuesday 4 August 1964

Rubbing salt into the *Sunday Mirror*'s wounds, Boothby and Ronnie Kray gave permission for the *Daily Express* to run the story of their *completely innocent* business meeting. The front-page headline read '*Boothby with Kray*' and it must have sold like hot cakes thanks to the *Mirror*'s tantalising prelude. Directly below the front-page picture of Ronnie and Boothby having a nice chat about business on a sofa is the first appearance of the now-famous and iconic picture of the twins walking majestically through the front courtyard of *Cedra Court*.

Sunday 9 August 1964

The *Sunday Mirror*'s front-page headline read '*Lord Boothby, an Unqualified Apology.*' Signed by the Chairman of the IPC, Cecil King, the article retracted the newspaper's allegations and stated: *"I am satisfied that any imputation of an improper nature against Lord Boothby is completely unjustified. In these circumstances I feel it my duty to sign this unqualified apology to Lord Boothby, and to add the personal regret of myself and the directors of the IPC that the story appeared."*

Adding insult to injury, after being forced to make a grovelling apology and to state that their allegations were false when they knew them to be true, Mirror Newspapers paid Boothby £40,000 in compensation; close to a million in today's money. Ronnie had to make do with just a printed apology, but if Boothby thought he was going to keep the whole £40,000, he had another thing coming. Reg Payne, the newspaper's editor, was scapegoated and sacked and the *Mirror*'s ongoing crusade against gangsterism and protection rackets in the capital came to an abrupt halt. Fleet Street as a whole would, from now on, take the view that the Kray twins were a subject best left alone. Even *Scotland Yard* backed-off – but, at *Commercial Street Police Station* in the East End, there was an ambitious young police officer by the name of Leonard 'Nipper' Read waiting in the wings.

Arnold Goodman – described by Krays biographer John Pearson as "*the lavatory attendant of British politics*"– orchestrated and executed a devious cross-party cover-up that saved Boothby and, more importantly, averted a scandal that could have brought about the downfall of the Conservative Government… and destroyed the credibility of the Labour Party to boot. Had the scandal erupted and burst forth, who knows what would have emerged from the wreckage of Britain's traditionally structured political establishment? It is interesting to ponder how close Ronnie Kray came to becoming the main protagonist in the complete destruction of the British political system.

Recently released documents held at the National Archives reveal that *Scotland Yard*'s C11 branch was not alone in monitoring Lord Boothby's activities. Prime Minister Sir Alec Douglas-Home's government had, for some time, been aware and concerned about Boothby's lifestyle and the damage that could be done if his (then illegal) homosexual pursuits were to come to light. Prior to the scandal erupting in the newspapers, it had been brought to the government's notice that Boothby and Driberg had been seen 'importuning' young men at *White City* dog track, and keeping company there with known criminals. MI5, Britain's domestic security and intelligence agency, were watching Boothby and gathering information on his activities and liaisons. Protecting the good name of the government, and those within it, was not really part of MI5's remit, but monitoring individuals with access to classified information who were leaving themselves wide open to blackmail by foreign powers certainly was.

Although Boothby did not have direct access to state secrets, a man of such high standing and influence within the British political establishment could be seen by the Russians as a source from which useful information could be extracted, given the right amount of pressure. The Cold War was at its height during this period and the KGB was active in seeking out individuals in important positions with something to hide. MI5 files that were made public in 2015 disclose that, unbeknown to all, Leslie Holt was on regular speaking terms with an MI5 informer referred to only as *Source,* who would regularly report back with details of their conversations. *Source* is described as a man linked to the press. Could Leslie Holt have been speaking to a journalist – there must have been a few sniffing around – or could he simply have been chatting with Mad Teddy Smith?

According to an article in the *Daily Mail*, writer Clare Campbell – after researching open MI5 files – concludes that Teddy Smith was *probably* an MI5 mole. Kray associate David Teale, in his 2021 book *Surviving the Krays*, tells how he is now convinced that Smith was passing information to the authorities.[155] There is no conclusive proof that Teddy Smith, who died in 2004, was working undercover for the Secret Intelligence Service – only speculation.

---

155   dailymail.co.uk, Nick Craven for *The Mail on Sunday*, 23 Feb 2019.

MI5 Headquarters

Leconfield House, Curzon Street, London W1J 5JA

Nearest TFL station: Green Park underground.

Built in 1939 and situated in the heart of Mayfair, *Leconfield House* was the headquarters of MI5, Britain's internal security service, from 1945 to 1976.

In 1964, Sir Roger Hollis – Director General of MI5 – authorised covert surveillance of Lord Boothby who, due to his association with Ronnie Kray and, at the time, his illegal homosexual activities, was deemed to be a potential threat to national security. During the Cold War period, the Russian KGB were on the lookout for people with access to information who had something to hide and could be blackmailed.

Recently released MI5 files held at the National Archives reveal that someone close to the Krays, referred to in the files as *Source*, was passing information to MI5.

Leconfield House still stands and is currently an office building. In 1976, MI5 moved its headquarters to 140 Gower Street (building now demolished) and then, in 1994, it moved to its current location at *Thames House*, Millbank, close to Lambeth Bridge.

On 27 July 1964 – just after the *Sunday Mirror*'s *Peer and the Gangster* editorial – newly promoted Detective Inspector Leonard 'Nipper' Read, serving at *Commercial Street Police Station*, was told by Area Chief Superintendent Fred Gerrard to "*get a little team together and have a go at the Krays.*" Read, originally from Nottingham, was a career policeman and police boxing champion who had risen quickly through the ranks. He set to work; the first and most immediate thing he needed to do was to find out what the Krays actually looked like.

He learned that Ronnie was scheduled to have a meeting with television journalist Michael Barratt at *The Grave Maurice* pub on Whitechapel Road. Nipper knew that the meeting was to take place sometime in the early evening after 6pm. So, dressed in scruffy workclothes, wearing a cloth cap, and carrying a copy of the *Evening News*, he bought a pint and a sandwich, took a seat in the pub with a good all-round view, opened the newspaper, and proceeded to wait. Within half an hour, a large American car pulled up outside. First out of the car was Colin 'Dukey' Osborne, hand inside his jacket to give the impression he was carrying a gun. Upon entering the pub, Osborne ignored Read, the pub's only customer. He glanced around furtively, checked the toilets, went back outside, and gave a nod in the direction of the car. Wearing a full-length American gangster-style coat, flanked by minders and looking immaculate, Ronnie Kray walked in majestically and took a seat in one of the pub's booths.

Within a short time, Barratt – who at the time was working as a reporter and presenter for the *Panorama* television programme – arrived and was escorted to Ronnie's booth. Drinks were collected and delivered and the minders waited patiently in the next booth as Ronnie spoke to Barratt. After the interview, Osborne and the others went outside, checked the street, and gave the all-clear. Ronnie hurried to the car, bringing the curtain down on the show that was clearly put on to impress the man from the TV.

In his book, *Mr Nationwide,* Michael Barratt makes no mention of his meeting with Ronnie but he does recount possibly an earlier meeting, with Reggie. Barratt describes meeting Reggie in a pub, most probably *The Grave Maurice*, just a short walk from Whitechapel station:

"I was then treated to a long harangue about all the charity work he and his brother Ronald organised in the area. He showed me lots of pictures of them at charity boxing matches and much else besides, then insisted that nothing like 'protection' took place."[156]

The Grave Maurice

269 Whitechapel Road, London W1 1BY

Nearest TFL station: Whitechapel underground.

Built in 1873 and opened in 1874, the pub was a *Truman*'s *Brewery* house – and, in the early '60s, it became one of the twins' favourite pubs and meeting places. When not using the pub's separate booths for business meetings, Ronnie would sit at the bar with a brown ale or a gin and tonic, where he could see everyone who came and went. In 1964, after being given the task of bringing the Krays to book, DI Nipper Read disguised himself in work clothes and waited in the pub to get a first look at his quarry, knowing that Ronnie had a scheduled meeting with TV presenter Michael Barratt.

Sadly, *The Grave Maurice* closed its doors in 2010 and was turned into a *Paddy Power* betting shop, but above the first-floor windows, the words '*Rebuilt, The Grave, Maurice, AD 1874*' can be clearly seen.

Morrissey was photographed standing in front of *The*

---

156 Barratt, Michael. *Mr Nationwide*. Birmingham: Kaleidoscope Publishing, 2012.

Grave Maurice for the cover of his 2003 album, *Under the Influence.*

It was summer 1964 and the star that was *Esmeralda's Barn* was fading fast and nearing the end of its life. Simple mismanagement by the twins – Ronnie in particular – was the cause. Treating the club as a plaything for themselves and their friends, rather than a business, resulted in a gradual decline. It didn't help matters when Ronnie, on a whim, decided that the *Cellar Club* should be closed; Ronnie, who took a dislike to lesbians, told Laurie O'Leary to close the club. Much against Reggie's wishes and Laurie's advice, Ronnie, as usual, got his way, and the *Cellar Club* – which put £500 a week into the twins' pockets – was closed down.[157]

Esmeralda's lost customers, lost money, and – in the end – the twins lost interest. Reggie offered the *Barn* to associate Micky Fawcett to "*see if he could do anything with it*" but the club was dead. The punters had gone for good and, apart from taking a couple of the waitresses out to dinner, there was nothing Micky Fawcett could do.[158] *Esmeralda's Barn* was wound up with outstanding tax liabilities of £1,400 in September 1964.[159]

One night, just before the *Barn* closed, Reggie, Micky Fawcett, and a man called *Coxie* were drinking in the West End when Reggie decided they should visit the very exclusive *21 Club* casino in Chesterfield Gardens, Mayfair. None of the group were members and they were refused entry by the

157 O'Leary, Laurie. *Ronnie Kray: A Man Among Men*. London: Headline Publishing, 2001.

158 Fawcett, Micky. *Krayzy Days*. Brighton: Pen Press, 2013.

159 Bennett, John. *Krayology*. London: Mango Books, 2016.

maroon-and-gold-liveried doormen. Reggie Kray reacted as one would expect and floored one of the doormen with a left hook; his colleague was dealt with in similar fashion by Micky Fawcett and Coxie.[160]

Billy Hill, although nominally retired from front-line crime and spending much of his time relaxing abroad, still had interests and influence in London. Casinos and gambling was Billy Hill's area of interest and the *21 Club* was one of a number of casinos where Billy was working a sophisticated card scam in league with the *Unione Corse* (the French Mafia), which significantly reduced the odds in the punters' favour, adding thousands to his already considerable fortune. After the incident at the club, Reggie and friends went to see Billy Hill at his Moscow Road flat. Far from being annoyed about the attack on the doormen, he gave Reggie £300 in brand-new notes and explained that it would have cost him more than that to hire someone to "*liven the place up*" and enable him to squeeze more protection money out of Harry Meadows, the *21 Club*'s owner.

Billy may well have upped the cost of his services to Harry Meadows, but the most important issue was to avoid trouble with the twins. Billy Hill maintained a friendly relationship with Ron and Reg – which would last for the rest of their time as free men – but should any *unpleasantness* have occurred at this point, interrupting business, the twins may have found themselves with a few problems on their hands. The *Unione Corse* was a secretive, powerful, and very dangerous international criminal organisation with connections worldwide – including the American Mafia.

---

160 Fawcett, Micky. *Krayzy Days*. Brighton: Pen Press, 2013.

The 21 Club

8 Chesterfield Gardens, London W1J 5BQ

Nearest TFL station: Green Park underground.

Widely regarded as the most exclusive casino in London in the '60s, the *21 Club* with restaurant and rooms was owned and operated by Harry Meadows, who also owned *Churchill's*, a hostess club in Bond Street. Billy Hill had an interest in the club and was lining his pockets by operating a sophisticated card scam in collaboration with the *Unione Corse* (the French Mafia). In 1964, Reggie Kray and two friends were refused entry to the club. Reggie punched and floored one of the doormen and his colleague received similar treatment from his two friends. In an effort to keep good relations, Billy Hill gave Reg £300 and thanked him for enabling him to increase Harry Meadows' protection payment.

Turning into Chesterfield Gardens from Curzon Street, the last doorway on the right – before the street comes to an abrupt end – is number 8, the entrance to the fine Georgian Grade II listed building that was once the *21 Club*.

In the autumn of 1964, not long after the furore of the Boothby affair had died down, Leslie Payne and his business partner Freddie Gore were languishing in a squalid African jail.

This particular episode of the Krays' story had begun back in late 1962, when the twins were busy with the newly opened *Kentucky Club*. Payne was introduced to Ernest Shinwell, son of the eminent politician Manny Shinwell, who was looking for investors in a business project to build 3,000 houses and a shopping centre on a 654-acre site in Enugu, the new capital of Eastern Nigeria.[161] Payne was interested, for once, in what was essentially a legitimate and above-board business opportunity.

Following an initial trip to Enugu with Shinwell, to take a look and meet some Nigerian dignitaries involved in the project, Payne concluded that the scheme was sound and introduced the proposal to the twins and Charlie. Available money from LF frauds and other enterprises would be invested and, with very little effort on their part, the return would be big piles of easy money. All three brothers poured money into the Great African Safari – GAS for short – confident that Payne had hit on a winner. Several more trips to Enugu followed. During the first one, Leslie Payne and Freddie Gore were accompanied by Ron and Reg, who very much enjoyed their VIP treatment. They were chauffeured around Enugu in luxury cars escorted by motorcycle outriders, taken to meet the President of Eastern Nigeria, Dr Mike Okpara, and put up in Enugu's most exclusive hotel, the newly built five-star *Hotel Presidential.*

When it was time for the next trip, Reggie stayed in London to take care of business and Ronnie, Payne, and Gore made the journey. Ronnie made the most of his time in Africa; he enjoyed escorted trips into the jungle and to see the sights, he sampled the local food and drink, and he was enchanted by the young, athletic African boys. When asked what he would like to do next, eyebrows were raised when Ronnie said he would like to see the local prison; the conditions there, as Ronnie discovered, made *Wandsworth* look like a resort hotel. Brother Charlie accompanied Payne and Gore on the next trip and collected £5,000 – money paid by one of the contractors to secure

---

161 Payne, Leslie. *The Brotherhood*. London: Michael Joseph Publishing, 1973.

the right to build an agreed number of houses on the proposed site. Charlie trousered the cash and flew back to London to give the twins their share.

Later on, Payne, Gore, and Charlie once again travelled to Enugu, but this time there was trouble. Payne had discussions with the contractor who had paid the £5,000 and, when discussion turned into argument, the contractor demanded his money back. Payne refused – he, of course, didn't have the money, and the furious contractor said he was going to the police, with whom he had family connections. Charlie was not yet an official representative of GAS – he was just there as a tourist – and therefore escaped arrest, but Payne and Gore were arrested and thrown in jail. Charlie phoned the twins from the hotel and told them he needed £5,000 in a hurry.

Ron, Reg, and The Firm set about scraping the money together, and a combination of donation and extortion quickly produced the desired amount, which was sent to Charlie by wire transfer. After frustrating and complex dealings with the police and local officials, Payne and Gore were released. Both were in a terrible state – particularly Payne, who appeared close to a nervous breakdown after enduring the diabolical conditions in the jail for several days. With losses amounting to £60,000, that was the end of the Great African Safari – and the beginning of the end of Payne's, until now, fruitful relationship with the Krays.

Enugu

After Nigeria gained its independence from the British Empire in 1960, the country was divided into states and Enugu became the capital of the new East Central State. In May 1967, tribal differences resulted in Enugu becoming the capital of the self-declared independent Republic of Biafra. After the ensuing Biafran War (1967-70) – a conflict that claimed the lives of over a million people, the vast majority through starvation – Enugu once again became the capital of the East Central State. Today, after further adjustments to the geopolitical boundaries, Enugu is the capital of Enugu State, an area in South-East Nigeria with a population of approximately 4.5 million.

In 1964, Leslie Payne involved Ron, Reg, and Charlie in a business venture based on a proposed construction project in Enugu. All three brothers visited Enugu and stayed at the newly built luxury five-star *Hotel Presidential* – Reg once, Charlie twice, and Ron twice. Ron is said to have particularly enjoyed his trips to Enugu. The scheme was a complete failure, resulting in financial losses of £60,000 (over 1.5 million in today's money), and Leslie Payne spending several terrifying days in a squalid African jail.

The *Hotel Presidential* was abandoned during the time Governor Sullivan Chime was in office between 2007 and 2015, and today lies empty and increasingly derelict.

Footage of the derelict hotel can be viewed on YouTube (Presidential Hotel || Abandoned Five Star Hotel in Enugu City, Nigeria)

1964 saw changes to The Firm and some new blood was hired – people who would go on to occupy senior positions in the hierarchy. The 18-stone Glaswegian Big Pat Connolly had been with the twins since the days of *The Regal* and was effectively their second in command. Big Pat and Ronnie are said to have enjoyed schoolboy humour together and regularly held farting competitions. Quite which of the two heavyweight gangsters was the foremost fabricator of flatulence is nowhere to be found in the annals of Kray history.

Towards the end of 1964, Big Pat was joined by fellow Scotsmen Ian Barrie and Jack Dickson. Barrie, an ex-soldier, and Dickson, a former Royal Marine, had become disenchanted with life in their home city of Edinburgh, so had teamed up and moved to the bright lights of London. Eventually they found their way to a gambling club, above a shop on the corner of Brick Lane and Fashion Street in the East End. *The 20th Century Club* was run by Billy Kray, the youngest of the twins' father's brothers. Barrie and Dickson became regulars at the club, and Uncle Billy thought his nephews would be interested in meeting the two handy-looking lads from Edinburgh. Introductions were made, the twins liked what they saw and, after a time, both were recruited to work for The Firm. Following a period of probation, Ian Barrie was given the position of Ronnie's personal minder and became known as *Ronnie's man.* Jack Dickson became Ronnie's driver.

The 20th Century Club

39a Brick Lane, London E1 6PU

Nearest TFL station: Shoreditch High Street overground.

On Brick Lane at number 39 is a hairdressers' shop called *HWDK*. Just around the corner, on Fashion Street, is a graffiti-covered door numbered 39a. This was the entrance to a Kray-controlled drinking and gambling club on the first floor called *The 20th Century Club*, run by the twins' father's youngest brother, William (Billy) Kray.

> In 1964, Ian Barrie and Jack Dickson left their native Edinburgh and headed to London to see what life in *The Smoke* might hold for them. Eventually, they found their way to *The 20th Century Club*, where Uncle Billy Kray introduced them to his nephews, the twins. *Scotch Ian* became Ronnie's personal minder and *Scotch Jack* his driver.

Another man who would become an important Firm member and be given the position of Reggie's personal minder was recruited in late 1964. The story of how Albert Donoghue, a tough Irishman, became involved with the twins – eventually becoming a leading Firm member – is more than a little surprising. Harry Abrahams, a friend of the twins from childhood, ran his own team of thieves, among which were Albert Donoghue and a man called Lenny Hamilton. One evening in 1962, Lenny was drinking in a club in Stoke Newington called The *Regency*, in a group that included Big Pat Connolly and a young man called Bonner Ward. Ward took exception to Lenny calling his girlfriend 'love' and a fight ensued in which Ward came off second best, leaving him with a broken nose. Lenny was worried about repercussions as Bonner was the son of the twins' friend and associate, Henry 'Buller' Ward.

Late one evening, Lenny's flatmate – doorman at *Esmeralda's Barn*, Andy Paul – told Lenny that Ronnie wanted to see him immediately at the *Barn*. On arrival, Lenny was taken into the kitchen, held down in a chair, and then tortured by Ronnie with glowing red-hot knife-sharpening steel. Lenny suffered burns to the face and damage to one eye. Harry Abrahams' crew were outraged when they saw Lenny's blistered and swollen face and asked who had done this to him – but Lenny wouldn't say. *"Well, if they'd done that to me,"* said Albert Donoghue, *"I'd have blown their fucking heads off."*

Then, later in 1962, Albert received a three-year sentence for a payroll robbery and was sent first to *Wandsworth* and then later to *Pentonville Prison*. In the meantime, word reached the twins that Albert had threatened to 'blow their heads off', but of course he hadn't; he'd made the remark not knowing who had burnt Lenny Hamilton. After serving two years of his sentence, Albert was released from prison and soon found out that Kray Firm member Limehouse Willy had left word at his local pub, *The Black Swan,*[162] that the '*other two*' wanted to see him. Unsure what it was about, and rather than waiting for the twins to find him, Albert decided to enter the lion's den and catch the twins by surprise.[163]

On 15 September 1964, Albert walked into *The Crown and Anchor* on Cheshire Street, just behind the Krays' Vallance Road home. As expected, the twins were there – along with a good crowd of friends and Firm members including Dukey Osborne, Billy Maguire, Uncle Alf, and the ever-faithful Bobby Ramsey. After shaking hands with a few familiar faces, Albert noticed a space forming around him as people moved away. Then… bang! Reggie, who had approached from behind, shot Albert in the lower leg. Following a period in hospital, during which he was interviewed by the police, Albert heard from the twins' runner Bill Ackerman that the twins wanted to see him. Without waiting for a meeting to be arranged, and with his leg in plaster, he went unannounced to see the twins at Vallance Road – to clear the air and find out whether or not that

---

162 Situated at 148 Bow Road, the original pub, built in 1871, was destroyed by a bomb dropped from a German Zeppelin during the First World War. The Black Swan was rebuilt in 1920 and demolished in 1970 during the widening of Bow Road.

163 Donoghue, Albert and Short, Martin. *The Krays' Lieutenant*. London: Pan Books, 1996.

was the end of it.

It was; as far as the twins were concerned, Albert had taken his punishment well and they were impressed by his stoicism and the fact he'd said nothing to the police. So impressed, in fact, that Albert was offered, and accepted, a position in The Firm. Rather an odd selection and recruitment procedure, perhaps, but this was not unusual for the twins; Albert's brother-in-law Billy Donovan had been welcomed into the brotherhood under similar circumstances. Hospitalised after fighting with the twins in *The Coach and Horses* pub in the early '50s, Billy Donovan's refusal to talk to the police impressed the twins and he was later given the job of head doorman at *The Double R Club*.

Another notable, this time happier, event took place in *The Crown and Anchor* just a few weeks later in November 1964. After making an early connection with the American Mafia the previous year – a relationship that would develop further in the coming months – the twins were given the opportunity to look after the security of some American celebrities while they were in London. Among the biggest stars in the world at that time was Judy Garland, who – along with her daughter Liza – was performing for two nights at *The London Palladium* on 8 and 15 November 1964. Judy Garland loved the company of the twins – Reg in particular – and one evening between the two shows, she accompanied them to a get-together in their local pub, *The Crown and Anchor*. Judy was with her soon-to-be husband number four, Mark Herron, but she had eyes for Reg.

"Reggie could have married Judy Garland. She truly loved him, fawned all over him, and was always trying to persuade him to stay at her house in Hawaii. But Reg only had eyes for Frances Shea".[164] Locals looked on in sheer amazement and

164 Kray, Charlie with McGibbon, Robin. *Me and My Brothers*. London: Grafton, 2008.

disbelief when the Hollywood star, in the company of Ron and Reg, came into their modest little boozer. Kray associate David Teale remembers the occasion:

"Someone put 'Somewhere Over the Rainbow' on the juke-box, and she starts singing. The place was packed by now and she came over to me and sat on my lap. The whole pub went wild. I was twenty-one years old at the time and didn't have a clue who she was."[165]

---

165 Teale, David. *Surviving The Krays*. London: Ebury Press, 2021.

The Crown and Anchor, Cheshire Street

147 Cheshire Street, London E2 6HZ

Nearest TFL station: Bethnal Green overground.

Cheshire St.before redevelopment in the early 1970's

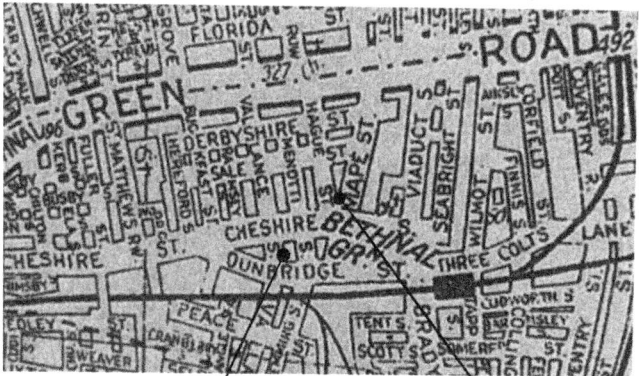

Fort Vallance   The Crown & Anchor

The pub was closed and demolished in 1972 during the redevelopment of the area, which cut off Cheshire Street at the point where it now joins Dunbridge Street at the junction with Vallance Road. *The Crown and Anchor* was the nearest pub to the twins' Vallance Road home and stood on what is now the corner of Chester and Kelsey Streets.

On 15 September 1964 in *The Crown and Anchor*, Reg shot Albert Donoghue in the leg. Impressed by Albert's staunch adherence to the code of silence, the twins offered Albert the opportunity to work for The Firm. Albert accepted and became Reggie's personal minder.

> In November of the same year, Ron and Reg stunned locals in the pub by bringing Judy Garland along for an evening with friends in traditional East End style.
>
> (Google Images: *The Crown and Anchor*, Cheshire Street)

The 19-stone Mafia man Eddie Pucci – who had once played guard position for the Washington Redskins – was Frank Sinatra's personal bodyguard. He was the connection through which the twins were given the opportunity to meet and chaperone a number of American celebrities visiting London in the '60s, including actor George Raft, singers Billy Daniels and Tony Bennett, ex-world heavyweight champion Joe Louis and, of course, Judy Garland. In December 1963, Frank Sinatra's son was kidnapped and released after two days on payment of $240,000 ransom money. Frank Junior was sent to England to be out of trouble's way for a while, with Pucci looking after him in London.

Eddie Pucci asked Reg if he would be able to arrange for American ex-world heavyweight champion Joe Louis to make a few guest appearances in the UK; the former world champion boxer was down on his luck and needed to earn some money. Reggie said that he could, and Louis duly arrived in England. Reg and Ron knew the Levey brothers – owners of Newcastle's premiere night club *La Dolce Vita* – and had, on a previous occasion, escorted American singing star Billy Daniels to Newcastle to appear at the club. The Levey brothers were happy to book Joe Louis for a week of nightly appearances at *La Dolce Vita* – talking a little about his life, shaking hands, and signing autographs. So, Ron, Reg, Joe Louis, and a few friends boarded a train at King's Cross station and journeyed to Newcastle. After barely two days in the city, however, the local police arrived at their hotel and ordered the twins and their friends to leave. Joe Louis stayed on but Ron, Reg, and their companions were put on a train with a police escort and sent back to London.

Shortly afterwards, Ron, Reg, and some of The Firm took a trip to Manchester to meet some of the local club owners. Arranging appearances for Joe Louis was ostensibly the purpose of the trip, but while they were there, the possibility of some *business* was to be explored. Following their arrival in Manchester, the Krays' man in the provinces, Eric Mason, introduced the twins to several of the city's club owners, and arrangements were made for a meeting the next day in the lounge of *The Midland Hotel*. The meeting, as far as the twins were concerned, was not a success; none of Manchester's club owners were interested in anything the twins had to say and, within a short time, the police arrived in force. Ron, Reg, and The Firm were escorted to the railway station and, once again, put on a train back to London.[166]

The Provinces

In the mid-1960s, the Kray twins and friends took the former world heavyweight boxing champion Joe Louis to Newcastle to make several appearances at the city's *La Dolce Vita* nightclub. Within two days of their arrival, the local police turned up and put the twins and their friends on a train back to London.

Opening in February 1963, *La Dolce Vita* – situated at 38-42 Low Friar Street in the centre of Newcastle – was, for a time, one of the country's top entertainment venues, hosting some of the biggest stars in showbusi-

---

166   Mason, Eric. *The Inside Story*. London: Pan Books, 1994.

ness. Owners the Levey brothers sold the club in 1967, after which there followed several changes in the club's name and identity. Finally, in 2001, then called *The Playrooms*, the club closed its doors for the last time. Today the site is occupied by luxury flats.

Shortly after their ignominious ejection from Newcastle, the twins and friends paid a visit to Manchester to meet some of the city's nightclub owners and discuss business. A meeting was arranged in the lounge of *The Midland Hotel* but within a short time the police swooped in, escorted the Londoners to Manchester Piccadilly station, and put them on a train home.

Built by the Midland Railway company and opened in 1903, the magnificent Edwardian hotel at 16 Peter Street in Manchester city centre, where the Kray twins once briefly stayed, still stands and operates as a hotel.

Many major cities in England have mythical tales circulating about the day that the local gangsters *ran the Krays out of town,* but there is no evidence that this ever happened. The local police, however, in the case of Newcastle and Manchester, did just that.

Nipper Read and his team were busy in the East End looking for evidence of the twins' criminal activities, but they were finding the wall of silence impenetrable; no one was talking. Nipper took the view that persistence would eventually pay off and, in the meantime, he was taking a heavy-footed approach to let the twins know that eyes were on them. Unmarked police cars parked outside the twins' homes at Vallance Road and *Cedra Court* were unmistakable and sent a clear message.

The twins needed a bolt-hole, and a quiet little hotel in a Victorian house in Finsbury Park was just the ticket. Run by

Phoebe Woods and her partner – who, for the sake of appearances, called himself Mr Woods – *The Glenrae Hotel* catered for travelling businessmen and had a small drinking club in the basement. One evening in September 1964, fighting broke out in the club during which windows were smashed and Mrs Woods'21-year-old son James was attacked. Such was the shock left by the violence at the normally quiet and respectable club, the decision was made to close it down. Three weeks later, three men came into the hotel brandishing knives and told Mr Woods he had better reopen the club or else. Mrs Woods reported the incident to the police at *Highbury Vale Police Station*. A short time afterwards, a man turned up at the hotel and once again told Mr Woods to open the club before punching him to the ground. Mrs Woods' son intervened and, between the two of them, they were able to subdue and hold the man until the police arrived.

This frightening cycle of violence left the Woods in near despair – until the middle-aged and genial Sammy Lederman made himself known. Lederman said he would run the catering at the club for them and bring in a barman who could take care of any trouble – and, "*Oh yes, just to be on the safe side,*" he knew just the man to keep an eye on the door until things calmed down. Kray Firm member Billy Exley was the barman and Bobby Ramsey the doorman. Within a short time, Ron and Reg moved into rooms 1 and 2 at the hotel and The Firm took over the club. Despite a promise to pay for bar bills and accommodation at a later date, no money, of course, was forthcoming, and by Christmas 1964 the realisation dawned on the Woods that their business had effectively been hijacked.

The Glenrae Hotel

**380 Seven Sisters Road, Finsbury Park,
London N4 2PQ**

Nearest TFL station: Manor House underground.

The hotel – mainly used by commercial travellers –
occupied a large Victorian house, and in the basement
was a small drinking club. In late 1964, the Krays, in
keeping with their usual business model, orchestrated violence at the club and then moved in and took over completely. Ron and Reg took up residence in rooms 1 and 2
and The Firm drank for free in the bar.

In January 1965, the twins were arrested at the hotel
and charged with demanding money with menaces.

Midway between Finsbury Park and Manor House

underground stations on the east side of Seven Sisters Road – between Alexandra Grove and Brand Close – is the location of the former hotel. The original building was demolished in the 1990s and a modern apartment building now occupies the site.

It was 1965, the midpoint of the decade that changed everything, and the '60s were well and truly swinging. Beatlemania was sweeping the nation, Mary Quant introduced the miniskirt from her shop *Bazaar* on the Kings Road in Chelsea, and the word 'fuck' was heard for the first time on British television, uttered by theatre critic Kenneth Tynan. More importantly, the death penalty for murder was suspended for five years pending a review and replaced with a mandatory sentence of imprisonment for life.

Ron and Reg Kray, now aged 31, were experiencing a period of depleted finances. The cash cow that was *Esmeralda's* was now gone and the debacle that was the Enugu venture had swallowed up thousands. Leslie Payne's long firm frauds provided some income but Ronnie, impatient with the long process necessary to complete a successful fraud, often took a *bird in the hand* approach and helped himself to all the ready cash in the bogus businesses, effectively closing them down before they could yield their full potential. Other LF fraud operations had come under the scrutiny of Nipper Read and his team and were terminated accordingly.

Some arrests were made but the twins were deliberately remote and their involvement could not be substantiated. The wall of silence was proving impossible to breach and, despite their efforts, Nipper and his team – based at *Commercial Street Police Station* – were no nearer arresting and charging the twins with anything than they had been at the beginning of the investigation the previous year.

Protection, as ever, was the mainstay of Kray business and with little else to line their pockets at this time, the twins were on the lookout for opportunities.

Commercial Street Police Station

Commercial Street, Spitalfields, London E1 6BA

Nearest TFL station: Shoreditch High Street overground.

Built in 1875 and with an additional floor added in 1906, the redbrick and white stone Grade II listed building on the west side of Commercial Street – between Elder Street and Fleur De Lis Street – is one of the few remaining buildings related to the case of Jack the Ripper. Investigations into the Whitechapel murders were carried out by Detective Chief Inspector Frederick George Abberline and officers based at *Commercial Street* in 1888.

In July 1964, Detective Inspector Leonard 'Nipper' Read, serving at *Commercial Street*, was given the task of bringing the Kray twins to justice. This first investigation into the twins' activities ultimately failed when Ron and Reg were acquitted of demanding money with menaces and walked free from the *Old Bailey* in April 1965.

Today, the building – now converted into apartments – is owned by a housing association and is called *Burhan Uddin House*. Above the central doorway the words *POLICE STATION* and the motto *DIEU ET MON DROIT* (motto of the UK monarch, 'God and my right') can still be seen. Just a five-minute walk from *Old*

Spitalfields Market, the former police station is close to the *Commercial Tavern* at 142 Commercial Street.

Nipper Read was concerned that the lack of progress – and the obvious impatience of Commander Ernie 'Hooter' Millen, head of the CID at *Scotland Yard* – would result in the investigation being closed down… but then, in January 1965, came what Nipper considered to be an amazing piece of luck. He was informed by a colleague at *Marylebone Police Station* that he had been approached by a West End club owner who was being pressured to pay protection money to the Krays.

Hew McCowan, homosexual son and heir of Baronet Sir Cargill McCowan, enjoyed the lifestyle afforded him by his family's wealth. His apartment at Marble Arch – flat 8, number 23 Great Cumberland Place – was a lavish affair with antiques, a quilted bar, and a bank of slot machines for guests to play. McCowan was a regular at a little club near Piccadilly Circus called *The Music Box,*[167] where he would pick up boys and take them back to his flat. The next morning, after the boy had left, the discovery that he had been robbed became almost routine and McCowan would report the incident to the police – but invariably fail to press charges.

In July 1964, when the Boothby affair was raging in the headlines and Leslie Payne was looking for investors in the Enugu project, Payne visited McCowan to see if he was interested in investing. McCowan – fortunately for him, as it turned out – did not invest, but a man named John Francis, who had accompanied Payne at the initial meeting, continued to visit McCowan at his flat for a while afterwards. During one of these

---

167 Situated at 37 Panton Street, Haymarket, St James's, the *Sagar* Indian restaurant occupies the site that was, in the 1960s, *The Music Box* club.

visits, McCowan – who enjoyed dabbling in business – happened to mention that he was in the process of opening a new club in Soho called *The Hide-A-Way*. Francis told McCowan that his friends, the Kray twins, would be a huge asset to his new venture – and, with their backing and their contacts in the world of show business, his club couldn't fail to become a huge success. Never having heard of the Krays and completely unaware of their reputation, McCowan agreed to meet the twins.

Several meetings took place at *The Grave Maurice* in November 1964, during which the twins upped the cost of their services – most importantly, security – from 25 to 50 percent of the takings. McCowan's club manager and adviser, Sydney Vaughan, became exasperated by the manner in which demands were being made, and called Ronnie a cunt. Fortunately for Vaughan, who clearly didn't realise who he was dealing with, Reggie stepped in and managed to calm the situation. No deal was made at this point in the proceedings but, for the twins, it was by no means the end of the matter. Of course it wasn't; this is what they did, and they never let go until they got what they wanted.

McCowan's club had been previously owned by a man called Gilbert France, in partnership with gangsters Frankie Fraser and Albert Dimes, and had been called *The Bon Soir*. In the early autumn of 1964 – after the club had ceased to be profitable – Fraser and Dimes walked away, leaving France with the liabilities. McCowan – who knew *The Bon Soir*'s young manager, Sydney Vaughan – was introduced to France and, in October 1964, an agreement was signed whereby Sydney Vaughan would continue to manage the club and £150 per week would be paid to France's company, Gerrard Enterprises.

After parting with an undisclosed sum for his controlling share, McCowan spent £4,000 redecorating the club and opened for business on Saturday 19 December 1964. A table for ten was reserved for the twins and their guests, but they failed to show up. Complaining about this to Johnny Francis, McCowan was told that the twins were disappointed and wanted an interest in the place, not to be just guests. One night shortly afterwards, a drunken Mad Teddy Smith wandered into the club at around 2am and started causing trouble. After smashing a few glasses and punching Sydney Vaughan in the face, McCowan arrived on the scene and Teddy Smith began hurling abuse: "*Fuck you, McCowan, you know who I am and you know who my friends are!*" Smith was bundled out of the door by staff and driven away in a taxi, still shouting.

McCowan did indeed know who Teddy Smith was, and he certainly knew who his friends were. Shortly after, Johnny Francis first suggested that the twins would be good business partners. McCowan had been invited to *The Cambridge Rooms* and went along with Muriel Belcher, owner of *The Colony Room Club*, her barman, Ian Board, and a crowd of the club's regulars. McCowan and everyone in the group were very drunk that night and, after becoming rowdy and swearing loudly in customary *Colony Room* style, the equally drunk manager of *The Cambridge Rooms*, Teddy Smith, threw them out.[168]

The Colony Room Club

41 Dean Street, Soho, London W1D 4PY

Nearest TFL station: Leicester Square underground.

Not to be confused with the 1960s Mafia-run *Colony Club* in Berkeley Square, *The Colony Room Club* was founded in 1948 and run by Muriel Belcher until her

---

168   Teale, David. *Surviving the Krays*. London: Ebury Press, 2021.

death in 1979. In late 1964, Muriel Belcher and a crowd of *Colony Room* regulars were thrown out of the Kray-run *Cambridge Rooms* for rowdiness. Although not a major landmark in any tour of the Krays' London, it is certainly worthy of note. The twins are said to have visited *The Colony Room Club* on occasion and it was an icon of London's avant-garde subculture in the 1960s and beyond.

Frequented by Soho's Bohemian crowd, the tiny drinking club in a first-floor room was the haunt of musicians, writers, artists, actors, and intellectuals with a penchant for the louche lifestyle, witty banter, and seriously heavy drinking. Regulars in the '60s included George Melly, Daniel Farson, Tom Driberg, Christine Keeler, Lucian Freud, and many more famous names – including *The Colony*'s most regular of regulars, Francis Bacon. Muriel Belcher greeted those she liked with a friendly "*hello cunty*" and strangers wandering into the members-only club would be told politely to "*fuck off.*" After Muriel's death, the club was run by her equally caustic barman Ian Board, until his death in 1994, and then by his barman Michael Wojas until *The Colony Room* closed in 2008.

Just to the right of the entrance to *Ducksoup* restaurant at 41 Dean Street is a doorway, behind which are the stairs that led to Soho's most celebrated den of iniquity.

Shortly after New Year 1965, McCowan and Vaughan met the twins once again, this time at *The Glenrae Hotel*. McCowan brought up the subject of Mad Teddy Smith's threatening, abusive, and violent behaviour less than two weeks earlier. Reggie assured him (untruthfully) that Smith was a *former* employee, and went on to explain that it was just the kind of thing that could be prevented if he were to agree to a revised offer of 20 percent of the takings. McCowan asked for a written agreement and was told he would get one at the next meeting on Wednesday 6 January, when arrangements would be finalised. McCowan, by now, was under no illusion and fully aware that this was a blatant attempt to extort money from him. So, on the morning of 6 January, he picked up the phone and called the police.

DI Nipper Read, moving quickly, took statements from McCowan and Vaughan and, at 9.15pm on 6 January, accompanied by DSI Gerrard and DS Hall, he entered *The Glenrae Hotel*. Ron and Reg were there, along with elder brother Charlie and several members of The Firm. Arrested and cautioned, the twins were taken to *Highbury Vale Police Station,*[169] where they were charged with demanding money with menaces. Ronnie was found to be carrying a sheath knife in his hip pocket, and when questioned about it, he replied:

"*It's just one of those things. That will be a bit more aggravation I suppose…I just have it, you know – it's nothing.*"[170]

Appearing at *Old Street Magistrates Court* the next day, the twins were refused bail and remanded in custody at *HMP Brixton*. When the arrests were made, Phoebe Woods – proprietor of *The Glenrae Hotel* – in a state of hysteria threw herself at Read's feet and cried, "*Take them away and never let me see them again. You've saved my life. Please take them away.*" The poor woman was in such a state that Read decided not to take a statement there and then but to leave it until the next day.

---

169 Built in 1903, the police station remained in use until 2013. Following its closure, the building at 209 Blackstock Road N5 2LL was converted into an apartment block.

170 Bennett, John. *Krayology*. London: Mango Books, 2016.

Imagine his surprise and disappointment when Phoebe turned up the next day at *Old Street*, dressed to the nines, saying she was more than happy with the arrangements at the hotel with Messrs Kray and that she would gladly stand bail for her good friends.[171]

Aware that he would be wanted by the police, Johnny Francis telephoned Read on 7 January looking for an assurance that he wouldn't be tied in with the menaces charge. Read gave no such assurances and insisted that he was to come in and see him immediately. Knowing that arrest would be the likely outcome if he did, Francis went on his toes and began a globe-trotting journey that would end in America. Johnny Francis would reappear a little later on in the Krays' story, when the Mafia came to town.

Teddy Smith was tracked down and arrested on 14 January. Denying any involvement with the Krays, he made light of the alleged incident at *The Hide-A-Way* and admitted he'd "*done up a club,*" but said it was just a drunken brawl and that he'd got the worst of it. Teddy Smith was charged with demanding money with menaces.

Following the arrests, the police searched the twins' rooms at *The Glenrae Hotel* and their apartments at *Cedra Court*, looking for incriminating evidence to support the charges and possibly bring about further prosecutions. Among the letters, notes, and papers that they found were the contact details of a surprising number of celebrities and public figures, including Tom Driberg MP and Lord Boothby; actors Barbara Windsor, Diana Dors, Ronald Fraser, and Victor Spinetti; singers Billy Daniels, Lita Roza, and Lennie Peters; composer Lionel Bart; pianist Winifred Atwell; artist Francis Bacon; and boxers Ted

---

171 Read, Leonard with Morton, James. *Nipper Read: The Man Who Nicked the Krays.* London: Macdonald Publishers, 1991.

'Kid' Lewis, Terry Spinks, and Sonny Liston. Surprising indeed, but perhaps the most remarkable discovery of all was the personal contact details of one of the world's biggest superstars – Judy Garland.

On 20 January, three days before the committal proceedings were due to begin at *Old Street Magistrates Court*, Nipper Read received a message that his most important and reliable witness was *going down the road*. Sydney Vaughan had had a change of heart and was claiming that his original statement was, in fact, false, and that it had been made as a result of pressure from McCowan. It was clear to Nipper Read that this development significantly weakened his case against the Krays; in fact, it was positively falling apart. The case now depended solely on McCowan's testimony, and Nipper knew that McCowan's homosexuality (illegal in 1965) would be used by the defence to cast doubt on his reliability as a witness.

Sydney Vaughan, rather than Read's star witness for the prosecution, had now become a hostile witness and needed to be treated as such at the upcoming committal proceedings. Vaughan now insisted that no demands had been made directly by the Krays and that the whole thing had been cooked up by McCowan. Nevertheless, Ronnie, Reggie, and Teddy Smith were committed for trial at the *Old Bailey* on 1 February 1965 – but, from Read's point of view, it was an unsatisfactory state of affairs.

Old Street Magistrates Court

335-337 Old Street, Shoreditch, London EC1V 9LL

Nearest TFL station: Old Street underground.

Built and opened in 1905, the eastern half of the Grade II listed building was a police station with accommodation for officers (section house), while the western half contained two courtrooms with a public entrance on the street front.

On 7 January 1965, the Kray twins and Mad Teddy Smith appeared before magistrates at *Old Street* charged with demanding money with menaces. They were refused bail and remanded in custody at *HMP Brixton*. Several more applications for bail were heard at the court and refused. Following committal proceedings on 23 January, the twins and Mad Teddy Smith were sent for trial at the *Old Bailey* on 1 February 1965.

The magistrates court closed in 1999 and the police left the building in 2008. In 2016, after a £40 million refurbishment, the former courthouse and police station opened as the luxury 128-room *Courthouse Hotel Shoreditch*. Many of the building's original features have been retained, including several of the court's holding cells – complete with steel-reinforced doors – now forming a bar area.

It's not too difficult to figure out why Sydney Vaughan retracted his original statement. On 20 January, three days before the committal proceedings, Vaughan went to the Krays' house at Vallance Road and explained to the local vicar, who just happened to be there, that he'd had a crisis of conscience and had experienced some kind of *revelation* that made him realise he'd made a big mistake by not telling the truth – and that he bitterly regretted accepting money from McCowan to commit perjury. Police statements were taken from Sydney Vaughan, Charlie Kray, Reverend Albert Foster, and ex-policeman and private investigator, William Nobel, who also just happened *quite by chance* to be at Vallance Road when Vaughan arrived.

Years later, in 2002, Sydney Vaughan appeared in the television documentary *The Krays: Their Empire Behind Bars,* in which he alludes to the fact that he went on to work for the Krays and states that Ronnie was extorting money from the Beatles manager, Brian Epstein.[172]

Prior to the committal proceedings, repeated bail applications were made and refused. It is likely that word reached Lord Boothby that the twins wanted him to do something about it, because he took a course of action that in retrospect seems quite bizarre. Boothby had no power to overturn the decision of a magistrate, but he clearly felt the need to be seen to be doing something, so he let it be known that he would bring the matter of the twins' lengthy incarceration without bail before the House of Lords. Boothby no doubt knew that such an intervention was against established protocols – and wholly inappropriate – but the knowledge that the twins knew so much about him and most probably had evidence of his *peccadilloes* must surely have influenced his decision to speak.

So, on 11 February, Boothby rose to his feet and tabled a question in the House of Lords. He asked the Lord Chancellor: *"Was it the government's intention to keep the Kray twins and Edward Smith in prison on remand indefinitely?"* Considering

---

172 *The Krays: Their Empire Behind Bars.* Real Life Media Productions, 2002.

that a trial date had, at this point, been fixed, his question was not only unconstitutional but completely absurd. Boothby's question was met with outrage from the assembled peers and cries of *"Order! Order!"* as Boothby floundered and tried to justify his question with some nonsense about *"bringing to light a general problem with the legal system."* The fiasco eventually concluded with the words of Lord Longford: *"My Lords, I think the Nobel Lord will regret that intervention when he reads it in cold blood."*

On March 8 1965, the trial began at Court Number Two at the *Old Bailey*. McCowan conducted himself convincingly in the witness box, sticking firmly to the story given in his statement to the police and successfully enduring a penetrating cross-examination by the three barristers acting for the twins and Teddy Smith.[173] After lunch on the second day, following McCowan's testimony, witnesses were produced to support the twins' claims that McCowan had approached them with a business proposition and that, subsequently, he had made threats against Vaughan and another man called Peter Byrne. The thrust of the defence was to discredit McCowan, and much was made of his homosexuality and apparent double life. On 18 March, the jury retired but were unable to reach a unanimous decision, leaving the judge with no choice but to order a retrial, which was to begin on 29 March.

Many years later, in his book *Born Fighter*, Reggie Kray gave an insight into the reason why the jury could not come to a unanimous decision – The Firm had been at work and the jury had in fact been nobbled.

Just before the second trial, the twins were asked by their solicitor Manny Fryde (pronounced 'free-di') for another

---

173   Read, Leonard with Morton, James. *Nipper Read: The Man who Nicked the Krays*. London: Macdonald Publishing, 1991.

£1,500 to cover the mounting legal costs. Charlie was duly dispatched to go and see Lord Boothby and ask for more money from the £40,000 he had received in compensation from Mirror Newspapers. Charlie describes himself as *shell-shocked* when Boothby said, *"I'm sorry, my dear boy. The forty thousand's all gone. I owed so much."*[174] Much, most, or possibly all of the money had already found its way into Ronnie's pocket, and perhaps Boothby saw this as a point to dig his heels in. After all, there was a good chance that the twins would go to prison and he would be rid of them at last.

On 29 March, a new jury was sworn in and the second trial began. By this time, the twins had hired private detective George Devlin to thoroughly investigate McCowan's background and dig up as much dirt as possible. McCowan – now the only witness for the prosecution – admitted that he had, in the past, alleged blackmail in three previous cases and, in 1953, had been placed on probation for three years after being convicted at *Edinburgh High Court* on four counts of sodomy. He had served four months in 1956 for breaking the terms of his probation and 30 days the previous year for having unlawful relations with a male person.[175]

Two new witnesses were called to discredit McCowan, but with his integrity in such doubt and his character so severely blackened, the outcome of the trial was a foregone conclusion. On 5 April, the case against the Krays and Teddy Smith collapsed and the judge told the jury that *"if they did not trust the word of McCowan, they should acquit."* After only ten minutes of deliberation, the jury did just that and Ron, Reg, and Teddy Smith were discharged.

---

174 Kray, Charlie with McGibbon, Robin. *Me And My Brothers*. London: Grafton, 1988.

175 Morton, James. *Krays: The Final Word*. London: Mirror Books, 2019.

After the trial, the twins returned in triumph to Vallance Road and were greeted and cheered by friends and family as conquering heroes returned from the fray. The press were, of course, in attendance and, as Reggie embraced the lovely Frances, he said to reporters, *"We hope to marry very soon – yes, maybe next week."* Press photographers captured the jubilant scenes including the now famous image of Kray family unity; the twins' and Charlie's three-way handshake.

Later that evening, Ron and Reg – accompanied by their solicitor, Manny Fryde – made their first ever appearance on television. In an interview conducted by Tom Mangold for *BBC News*, they were asked about the cost of the trial, the perceived *toughness* of London clubland, and what they intended to do now it was all over. Reg speaks of his intention to get married as soon as possible and Ronnie explains that he would like to go abroad for a short while – and then he'd like to be left alone. The interview is easily accessible online (YouTube) and is a must-see for anyone with an interest in the Krays; the footage gives a brief but fascinating look at the twins during a time that could be considered as their heyday. Reggie, with his often-spoken-about *quizzical* expression, appears relaxed and talks with a softly-spoken, old-fashioned cockney accent. Ronnie, on the other hand, appears more intense, and it is not difficult to imagine him as dangerous. The most surprising aspect of the interview is Ronnie's voice; not the gruff tones one would expect of a violent gangster, but instead a touch high-pitched, soft, and very slightly slurred.

1965 was the year that the Krays were established as icons of the Swinging Sixties and became as much a part of the decade's counterculture as the Beatles, Twiggy, and the Mini Cooper. Publicity surrounding the Boothby and McCowan affairs had brought the twins to the notice of the general public, and even the disinterested had at least vague notions of gangsters and protection rackets in London. Then, in March 1965, two journalists – Cal McCrystal and Lewis Chester – wrote a full-page article which appeared in *The Sunday Times*. Aware that the mention of crimes and violence could bring trouble from above, the article focused on Ron and Reg – the two charismatic cockney characters who were so much a part of the culture of the old East End. Described for the first time as *Legends* and folk heroes, the twins were photographed in the parlour of their quaint and humble home in Bethnal Green.

Following the article, Francis Wyndham – writer for *The Sunday Times* magazine – met the twins and was keen to follow the newspaper article with a feature in the magazine. Wyndham arranged for photographs to be taken by the famous fashion photographer David Bailey who, at this time, had no idea that Reggie Kray was responsible for the knife scar on his father's face. *The Sunday Times*, however, decided that the twins had been given enough attention already and the feature never appeared, but the photographs – taken in the studio of *Vogue* magazine – were put to another use.[176] Shortly afterwards, David Bailey released his now famous *Box of Pin-ups,* a collection of 36 individual portraits of 1960s icons including John Lennon, Paul McCartney, Lord Snowdon, Michael Caine, Andy Warhol, Jean Shrimpton, Rudolf Nureyev, and others, with text on the back of each by Francis Wyndham. The collection of 37 x 32 cm prints was boxed with a portrait of Mick Jagger on the lid. Included in the collection was the well-known picture of Ronnie facing front and Reggie standing behind, looking over his shoulder, and another of Ron, Reg, and Charlie gazing into the distance.

The inclusion of the Krays in the *Box of Pin-ups* sealed forever their place in the pantheon of '60s icons, but it caused a stir in some quarters. Lord Snowdon objected strongly, and it

---

176   Pearson, John. *The Cult of Violence*. London: Orion, 2001.

is thought that this is the reason why there was only ever one print run. The box as a whole was priced at £10 – expensive at the time – so the collection was often broken up and the prints sold individually. Today, a complete boxed collection in good condition can sell for anything up to £20,000.

In April 1965, Reggie and Frances finally tied the knot at the *Church of St James The Great* on Bethnal Green Road. Reggie asked the twins' old friend, Father Hetherington – who had moved to a parish in Ealing – to marry them, but he declined. He would not give a reason, but explained as gently and tactfully as he was able that he could not conduct the service for a wedding he believed should not take place. Father Foster, the incumbent vicar of *St James's*, had no such qualms; he had just given evidence in court on the twins' behalf.

A friend of the Kray family, Maureen Flanagan, was at Vallance Road on the morning of the wedding, helping with preparations and tending to Violet's hair. Maureen watched with concern as Reggie nervously paced up and down and Ronnie grumbled about the marriage – at one point declaring that he wasn't going.[177] Tensions were high but, fortunately, before the brothers came to blows, the cars arrived to take Ronnie and the rest of the family to the church. Reggie decided to walk.

Maureen first met Violet when she was 15, working as a hairdresser. From then onwards, she became Violet's personal hairdresser and close friend to the Kray family. Maureen remained close from then on and regularly visited the twins and Charlie during the prison years. Maureen was involved in the organisation of all three brothers' funerals.

When Maureen was 18, she was spotted by a photographer

---

177 Flanagan, Maureen with Hyams, Jacky. *One Of The Family, 40 Years With The Krays.* London: Century, 2015.

and began a successful modelling – and, later, acting – career. Maureen was one of Britain's first Page Three girls and has appeared in films and on television shows including *Monty Python's Flying Circus* and *The Benny Hill Show*. Maureen's memoir, *One of the Family: 40 Years with the Krays,* was published in 2015. Recently, Maureen – who nowadays involves herself in charity work – appeared in the 2022 ITV BritBox documentary, *Secrets of the Krays*.

On a cold, grey morning on 19th of April, Reg, best man Ron, family, friends, flat-nosed gangsters, and a handful of celebrities gathered in the church to await the bride. David Bailey had agreed to take the photographs as a wedding present and arrived in a blue Rolls Royce, matching his blue velvet suit. Elsie Shea, the bride's mother, hated Reggie and wore black for the occasion; something that Reggie would never forgive. When the hymn singing began, Ronnie – who became annoyed by the congregation's half-hearted attempts at chorale rendering – walked up and down the aisles, hissing, "*Sing, fuck you, sing!*"

After the service, a fleet of cars headed to the reception held at *The Glenrae Hotel* in Finsbury Park. David Bailey was busy snapping away, capturing the event on camera, but he found himself in a bit of an awkward spot:

"I had Ron making a pass at me and the bride making a pass at me as well. So I was being very butch with him and very gay to her. Talk about being between a hard place and a rock."[178]

Some accounts suggest that the East End's 'wedding of

---

178   David Bailey for the *Daily Mail*, 18 Oct 2020.

the year' was not the joyous occasion with hugs, kisses, and beaming smiles that one would expect, but more of a stilted, staged-managed performance for the benefit of the press, dominated by fearsome-looking characters unknown to some of Kray family, let alone the small contingent of Shea relatives and friends. Later that afternoon, Reg and Frances said their goodbyes and were driven off in their hired Daimler. Athens awaited the newlyweds, the destination chosen for their week-long honeymoon.[179]

St James The Great Church

331 Bethnal Green Road, London E2 6LJ

Nearest TFL station: Bethnal Green underground.

On 19 April 1965, 31-year-old Reggie Kray married his fiancée, 21-year-old Frances Shea at the *Church of St James The Great*. Frances wanted a quiet, modest wedding, but that was never going to happen; her wishes were completely disregarded and the large redbrick church on Bethnal Green Road became the venue for the East End's wedding of the year. Small numbers of family and friends on Frances' side were hugely outnumbered by the cast of the Kray show. Reggie's family and friends were joined by a large posse of scrubbed-up gangsters in their best suits, wearing buttonholes, as well as several well-known boxers and a few famous faces – including actress Diana Dors, MP Tom Driberg, and the popular American tap-dancing duo, the Clark Brothers. David

---

179 Hyams, Jacky. *Frances: The Tragic Bride*. London: John Blake, 2015.

Bailey was there, taking the wedding photographs, and the press – who had, of course, been notified – were there in force. Rather than a joyous, heart-warming, intimate family occasion, the wedding was remembered – even by some close Kray family relatives – as a rather contrived and stage-managed publicity event.

Tragically, two years later, in June 1967, Frances 'funeral service was held at the same church.

Built in 1884, *The Red Church* – as it was known – served the community until 1987, when it was converted into apartments. A one-bedroom flat in *St James Court*, as it is now known, will cost the buyer something in the region of half a million quid.

Just a day or two after the McCowan trial was over, the twins 'bought' *The Hide-A-Way* club and renamed it *El Morocco.* Now in the hands of Ron, Reg, Charlie, and their good friend from South London, Freddie Foreman, the club opened the day after Reggie and Frances returned from their honeymoon – on 29 April – with a party to celebrate the twins' acquittal. Along with friends, family, and Firm members' wives and girlfriends, the glamorous guest list included celebrities Lita Roza, Edmund Purdom, and Adrienne Corri, as well as Victor Spinetti and Roy Kinnear – both of whom had appeared in *Sparrows Can't Sing* and, more recently, the Beatles' new movie *Help!*, which was due to be premiered in the West End in a few weeks' time.

Nipper Reade, who considered the result of the trial an unmitigated disaster, decided he would go to Gerrard Street to take a look at The Firm gathered in celebration and make a note of who was there for the intelligence records. Read and two colleagues took up positions opposite the club, but Read – who was in a telephone box – was spotted by the Krays' private detective George Devlin, who opened the booth door and said, *"If you want to see who's here, why don't you come inside?"*

Finding himself in a bit of a spot, Nipper agreed, left his colleagues outside, and went into the club. Ronnie was clearly furious and kept a distance, but Reggie was more relaxed and didn't seem to mind very much. Understandably, the atmosphere became a bit tense so Read had a quick look around, to mentally log as many faces as he could for the records, and then promptly left. The *Daily Express* printed the story that Nipper had attended the party along with a picture of him supposedly enjoying a drink with the Krays. Read was apparently quite flattered to see that the picture was not of him at all but was in fact Edmund Purdom, the star of the 1954 epic film, *The Egyptian.* Contrary to what has been written many times, there was no Yard inquiry into the incident or any disciplinary proceedings. Read was promoted to Detective Chief Inspector a year later and transferred to *West End Central Police Station* on Savile Row.

Following the Boothby affair, Fleet Street was steering clear and giving the Krays a wide berth, knowing that the terrible twins could bring trouble down upon them from high places. The police also moved their sights, for a while at least, away from the Krays. Ron and Reg must have felt untouchable and were in fact more powerful at this point than they would ever be again. As far as the twins were concerned, the police were soundly beaten, humiliated, and impotent against them. This was – to some extent, at this juncture – true, but it was of course only a temporary state of affairs. It wouldn't be too long before they would meet Det Supt Leonard 'Nipper' Read once again.

The Hide-A-Way

16 Gerrard Street, London W1D 6JE

Nearest TFL station: Leicester Square underground.

In the heart of London's Chinatown on Gerrard Street is the site of the former Kray-controlled nightclub, *The Hide-A-Way*. In January 1965, the previous owner of the club, Hew McCowan, reported to the police that he was being pressured by the Kray twins to pay protection money. The twins and Mad Teddy Smith were arrested and sent for trial at the *Old Bailey*, charged with demanding money with menaces. Witness intimidation and jury nobbling ensured that the twins walked free and, immediately after their release in April, they *acquired* the club for themselves and changed its name to *El Morocco.*

Among the performers and entertainers appearing *at El Morocco* was a young man called David Essex, just beginning his career as a singer.

Today, Gerrard Street is in the heart of London's Chinatown, but in 1965 London's Chinese community was still mainly based near the docks in Limehouse. The present Chinatown did not become established until the 1970s, and Gerrard Street in the mid-'60s was a slightly run-down area of Soho.

The building at number 16 that was once the Krays' club is now home to *Dumplings' Legend* Chinese restaurant. On the outside wall is a green plaque commemorating the site of the *Mont Blanc Restaurant* – a meeting place for leading writers in the early 20th century. Just to the left of the plaque, in the space between the first and second of the three first-floor windows, faint marks on the brickwork can be seen where the *'HIDE-A-WAY'* sign was attached to the wall.

Newlyweds Reggie and Frances returned from their honeymoon in Athens on 28 April 1965 where, it is often said, their union as man and wife was not consummated. There is much speculation about Reggie's sexuality and possible Madonna complex – placing Frances on a pedestal way above the slightly sordid business of sex – but whatever the reason for the lack of, or at best very infrequent, lovemaking, there was clearly something very wrong with the relationship. Father Hetherington, who declined to perform the wedding ceremony, would soon be proved right. He knew full well that the liaison was toxic and that the couple were embarking on a disastrous journey – with dire and devastating consequences for them both, particularly Frances.

Married life began with Reggie and Frances moving around like nomads for several weeks, staying for periods at Vallance Road, Reggie's friend Charlie Clark's bungalow in Chingford, a flat in Finsbury Park, and another in Sussex Gardens near Marble Arch. Wherever they were, Frances would be left alone all day and most of the night until Reggie returned, drunk and frequently abusive, at some ungodly hour. Occasionally, Reggie would take Frances to parties or nightclubs, but alcohol-soaked evenings surrounded by the usual crowd of besuited gangsters, hangers-on, and the odd celebrity were little short of an ordeal for Frances, and only increased her sense of isolation. She had nothing in common with these people and could not join in the drunken banter even if she wanted to. Frances would often clam-up, retreat into herself, and talk to no one. Only Mad Teddy Smith, character that he was, could coax a smile from Frances and occasionally make her laugh.

In the early summer of 1965, the couple moved into Reggie's

newly decorated and furnished flat below Ronnie's at *Cedra Court*. Living in such close proximity to Ronnie – who made no secret of the fact that he didn't like Frances – did nothing to improve her state of mind, and Reggie, who spent more time in Ronnie's flat than their own, showed no signs of changing his lifestyle. Frances was trapped in a joyless and oppressive marriage where drunkenness, blazing rows, and threats of violence towards her family – whom Reggie blamed for all their ills – were becoming the norm. Isolated from her family and friends and already emotionally fragile, Frances was fast sinking into a pit of misery and depression.

In need of a rest, and without objection from Reggie, Frances travelled alone to Ibiza on 4 June and stayed until 14 July. Two weeks later, she travelled to Torremolinos, where she stayed from 2 to 15 August. On her return to England, she stayed alone for periods in the Marble Arch flat and hotels in Finsbury Park and Stamford Hill. Medical attention had been sought by this time and she was taking antidepressant drugs. Unhappy that the drugs appeared to be doing nothing to improve his new wife's mood, Reggie arranged for Frances to see a Harley Street psychiatrist. Dr Clein changed her medication and suggested a recuperative stay at *Greenways Nursing Home* in Hampstead.[180] Frances stayed for a week at *Greenways* and then, on 29 October – despite the doctor's recommendation that she stay longer – she left and went back to Ormsby Street to stay with her parents.[181]

---

180 Situated at 11 Fellows Road, Hampstead, London NW3 3LY, *Greenways* saw Frances Kray stay for one week in October 1965. Three years later, on 28 November 1968, the much-loved children's author Enid Blyton, aged 71, died at the nursing home. Now demolished, modern apartment buildings occupy the site.

181 Hyams, Jacky. *Frances: The Tragic Bride*. London: John Blake, 2015.

After just seven months, the marriage – much of which was spent apart – was effectively over, but it was by no means the end of the story.

Manor Lea

Flat 6, 295 Green Lanes, Finsbury Park, London N4 2EU

Nearest TFL station: Manor House underground

Just a short walk from Manor House underground station, on the west side of Green Lanes, is a modern block of ten flats – which must have been newly built when newlyweds Reggie and Frances stayed at flat 6 for a brief period in the spring of 1965. *Manor Lea* is one of a number of addresses where the couple stayed before moving into Reggie's flat, below Ronnie's, at *Cedra Court* in Clapton.

Reggie also stayed at *Manor Lea* with Bobby Teale for a period in 1966 after the murder of George Cornell in *The Blind Beggar* pub.

The American Mafia were present in London in 1965, but why were they there and what exactly were they doing?

Back in 1959, Meyer Lansky – the Mafia's accountant and financial genius – watched in dismay as the mob's huge money-generating project in Cuba came to an abrupt end. Havana, the capital, had for some years been under development as a very lucrative Mafia-controlled gambling destination. With the Cuban president's cooperation – and just a short flight from Miami – Havana's hotels, nightclubs, and casinos were bringing in millions of dollars and lining the pockets of America's top mobsters. In 1959, Fidel Castro and his rebel army toppled the regime of President Batista and assumed military and political control. Castro seized the casinos and threw all American companies off the island, including the mob. The American evacuation from Cuba was hurried and everything was left behind – including the American's cars, which even today are a feature on the streets of Havana.

Lansky needed to start work on developing alternative destinations for the mob's gambling and casino enterprises, and his sights were set on England. Britain's gambling laws were about to change – in fact, there is some suggestion that the mob had a hand in effecting that change – and work was done to pave the way for an American invasion. The General in Chief of the

Mafia's invasion force was the Caporegime (Boss) of the powerful Philadelphia crime family, Angelo Bruno. Unlike some of his counterparts, Bruno was known for his preference for conciliation over violence and, wherever possible, he would seek to further his interests through negotiation.

The Kray twins were known to the Mafia as a significant force in London's underworld, and therefore needed to be taken into account. Including the Krays in the syndicate's expansion plans would avoid conflict and – more importantly, as far as the Mafia were concerned – the attention of the police. Violence was always an option for the mob – they were experts – but a mutually beneficial arrangement with the local gangsters was the preferred choice. Kept onside, the Krays could be called upon if required and might prove useful as local muscle.

The twins had a number of meetings with Bruno in the 1960s. The first one was back in 1963 at the *Hilton Hotel*, where Bruno explained that there would be, in the near future, financially rewarding opportunities in the security and protection of Mafia-run casinos, and the minding of rich Americans flown into London to spend their money in them. On his trips to London, Angelo Bruno was regularly accompanied by his good friend Rocky Marciano – yet another world heavyweight boxing champion that the twins would meet. The charm and charisma of the powerful but genial Mafia Don impressed the twins and they got on well. One of Bruno's favourite sayings – "*If you kick the dog you kick the master*" – struck a chord with Ronnie and he would repeat it all the time. Bruno promised to look at other big money opportunities he would soon be putting their way, and the meeting ended with the promise of further business and an agreement that they would meet again soon.

On 25 July 1965, 46-year-old former world light heavyweight champion boxer – and much-loved radio, film, and television personality – Freddie Mills was found dead in his car, parked behind his nightclub, *The Freddie Mills Nite Spot,* in Goslett Yard off Charing Cross Road. Mills had been shot once in the eye and was found on the back seat of his Citroën car with a fairground rifle resting against his legs. The coroner's inquest concluded that the angle of the bullet was consistent with a self-inflicted wound and ruled his death as a suicide. But there were inconsistencies and many, to this day, remain convinced that he was murdered.

Numerous books have been written about the life and death of Freddie Mills offering differing, sometimes compelling, theories as to how and why he died. One book, *The Secret Life of Freddie Mills* by former journalist Michael Litchfield, alleges that Mills was the still-unidentified serial killer known as *Jack the Stripper,* responsible for the deaths of eight women whose naked bodies were found in the Hammersmith area in 1964-65. According to Litchfield, Mills – fearing that he was about to be exposed – took his own life. Another interesting book, *Mafialand* by Douglas Thompson, published in 2012, claims that after threatening to blow the whistle on one of the Mafia's most important men in London – boxing promoter Benny Huntsman – Freddie was *whacked* by Mafia assassins who made his death *look* like suicide.

Countless other theories, explanations, and *facts* concerning Freddie's death abound, but one of the most interesting is that he was murdered by the Kray twins. In his 1995 book, *Freddie, My Friend,* Peter McInnes is firmly of the opinion that Freddie was murdered by the twins for refusing to pay protection money – and even claims that his own life was put in danger following an angry confrontation with Charlie. It is impossible to discount the claims outright without knowing the full truth of Freddie Mills' story, but we do know that boxers – especially world champions – were the one group of people that the twins truly respected and whose company they enjoyed above all others.

One night in Freddie's club, Freddie's wife Chrissie was looking a bit anxious about the presence of the twins and a group of their friends. She told her husband that she'd heard the Krays were responsible for everything rotten in London. In response, Freddie took his wife by the hand and led her to the Krays' table to meet his good friends. Freddie Mills laughingly told Ronnie Kray that his wife had heard bad things about him and his brother. *"I wouldn't believe the rumours,"* said Ronnie before bursting into laughter. *"Don't worry, Fred. We wouldn't do anything to you. You're too much of a handful for even us two. Let's have a picture!"*[182]

The Freddie Mills Nite Spot

143 Charing Cross Road, London WC2H OLA

Nearest TFL station: Tottenham Court Road underground.

In 1946, three years before his eventual retirement from the ring, world light heavyweight champion Freddie Mills opened *The Freddie Mills Chinese Restaurant* in Charing Cross Road. By 1963, the restaurant was no longer profitable and it was converted into a nightclub. *The Freddie Mills Nite Spot* – which opened in May of that year – was an initial success, but by 1965, Freddie was in financial difficulty.

On 25 July 1965, Freddie was found dead in his car in Goslett Yard behind his nightclub. His death was caused

---

182 Evans, Christopher. *Fearless Freddie*. Durrington: Pitch Publishing, 2017. Google Images: 'Freddie Mills and the Krays'.

by a single gunshot to the eye but there was, and still is, much uncertainty about the circumstances; was it suicide or was it murder? One of the many purported theories is that the Kray twins, who were regulars at his club, murdered Freddie Mills.

The original Victorian buildings on this part of Charing Cross Road have all been demolished, and the building that housed the Freddie Mills Nite Spot disappeared along with them. The newly built *@sohoplace* theatre occupies the space where Freddie Mills' club once stood. Goslett Yard still exists but the once cobbled backstreet is much changed; most of the buildings that surrounded Goslett Yard in 1965 have been demolished and replaced. Just in front and to the right of *The Royal George* pub at the end of the yard is the spot where Freddie was found dead in his car.

Freddie Mills' connection with the Jack the Stripper case is speculation, but in 1965, Cornelius (Connie) Whitehead – a man with a genuine link to the case – joined the Kray Firm. Whitehead was a casual labourer and dock worker with several criminal convictions, including one for assaulting a police officer. His CV demonstrated an aptitude for violence and included experience of running a few girls as a pimp. After an altercation with one of his girls, prostitute Gwynneth Rees, she left him and was found dead on 8 November 1963. Cornelius Whitehead was, for a while, the chief suspect, but there was no evidence linking him to the murder. Whitehead was Ronnie's driver for a time and his involvement with Firm business in the later years was significant. Much to the annoyance of Ronnie, Connie Whitehead, while working for The Firm, continued to operate independently. Whitehead was frequently thrown off The Firm and then reinstated, but he was there at the end and was sentenced to eight years in prison as a result.

In early 1965, the Krays' *consigliere* Leslie Payne was approached by a representative of the American Mafia and told that the syndicate had two million dollars in negotiable bearer bonds stolen in the USA and Canada. The bonds were in Canada, but not negotiable (cashable) there, as they were too *hot* and the authorities would be on the lookout. Selling the bonds on the European market through the Mafia's London contacts would be safer, and would still bring a return for the syndicate while providing the Krays with a money-making opportunity as promised by Angelo Bruno.

Beating the rap with the McCowan case and making connections with people of influence (Boothby) impressed the Americans and, at this point, they were keen to nurture relations. Bonds were available for 25 percent of their face value and the first batch would be handed over on credit, payable after they'd been sold. Payne was interested and put the idea to Charlie, the only Kray he could bear to speak to by this time. Once Payne had explained exactly what bearer bonds were, Charlie put the proposition to the twins, and – after they had absorbed the idea – they were eager to buy a lot of bonds.[183]

Negotiable bearer bonds are shares without registered owners that were issued and sold by American corporations from the mid-1800s until 1982. Just like cash, whoever holds the bond is the owner. Printed from engravings like a bank note, the bond is a certificate displaying the value of the shares in the holder's possession. The term *negotiable* simply means that the bonds have a monetary value of the amount displayed and may be sold, used as currency in business transactions, or – once the

---

183   Payne, Leslie. *The Brotherhood*. London: Michael Joseph Publishing, 1973.

bond reaches its maturity date printed on the bond itself – exchanged for its cash value plus interest.

Following a trip to Canada to meet the representative of the local Mafia Don, Payne returned to London and then went to Paris, where he took delivery of over $50,000 in bonds. Although the essence of a bearer bond is that the holder is anonymous, the fact that they were stolen presented problems in turning them into cash. Eventually, the crooked bookmaker and fraudster Charlie Mitchell bought the bonds for £8,000, and – with the help of a complicit bank manager – was able to cash the bonds through his own bank in London. Payne had made a small profit on the first batch, but the twins were becoming impatient and a better way of converting the bonds into cash was required. Some centre of dubious financial expertise was needed and soon found in the form of a small private bank with offices in Mayfair called the European Exchange Bank – specialists in shady dealing and all manner of financial jiggery-pokery.[184]

Charlie Mitchell, during his search for a means of cashing the bonds, had come into contact with Heinz Pollman – the bank's owner – and his associate, Alan Bruce Cooper. Charlie Mitchell introduced Cooper to Charlie Kray,[185] and this was the beginning of an intriguing and eventful three-year relationship between Cooper and the Krays that would play a significant part in their eventual demise.

Within a short time, Leslie Payne received word from Gordon Andersen – a Canadian lawyer with mob connections who had been involved in the ill-fated Enugu affair – that more bonds were available for collection from Montreal. Payne made a second trip to Canada, this time accompanied by

184 Ibid.

185 Morton, James. *Krays: The Final Word*. London: Mirror Books, 2019.

Gordon Andersen, Charlie Mitchell, Charlie Kray, and his close friend Bobby McKew, but on arrival in Montreal the five men were thrown in jail and put on a flight back to London the next day.[186] All was not lost, however, as a week later a Canadian syndicate representative arrived in London with two $25,000 bonds – which were promptly cashed in Hamburg through Alan Bruce Cooper and the European Exchange Bank.

During the next year, Charlie and Payne travelled to various European destinations including Paris, Geneva, Hamburg, and Amsterdam to collect more bonds from couriers sent by the Mafia from Canada. In November 1965, Charlie was informed by the twins that there was a large batch of bearer bonds to be collected from Paris and that he should accompany Payne – and the new boy to bond collection, accountant Freddie Gore. They would be staying at the *Hotel Claridge* on the Champs-Élysées,[187] where the pick-up was to be made.

Two Mafiosi, Artie and Tony, arrived and met Charlie, Payne, and Gore in the hotel bar, where the package containing the bonds was handed over. Remaining together for the evening, the five men enjoyed wining and dining French-style and a good sampling of Parisian nightlife until the early hours of the morning, when the three Englishmen said goodbye to their new Mafia pals and turned in for the night. The next morning, Charlie opened the package and found that they had bearer bonds to the value of $250,000 in their possession, a far larger amount than expected.

Returning to London on the 5pm BEA flight from *Orly*

---

186   Fry, Colin and Kray, Charlie. *Doing the Business*. London: John Blake Publishing, 2011.

187   Situated at 74 Avenue des Champs-Élysées, Paris, the classical old-style luxury hotel built in 1914 survives as an apartment-hotel called *Fraser Suites Le Claridge Champs-Élysées.*

Airport, Freddie Gore became nervous. It had been previously arranged that he would carry the package through customs at London airport, but now he was refusing to do it. Payne likewise refused, so Charlie angrily said that he would do it himself. Stopped by a customs official on the way through, Charlie was relieved to find that the official was not interested in the paperwork, only in hearing if he had any cigarettes. When told of the incident, the twins were far from happy, and it was clear to them that Payne and his associate were becoming superfluous to requirements; another nail in the coffin of the Payne/Kray relationship.

There was worse to come; the next morning Charlie received a call from Artie, apologetically telling him that the bonds were *"just too hot"* and he needed to get rid of them. Later that day, Charlie burnt $250,000 worth of negotiable bearer bonds in the backyard at Vallance Road.[188]

Payne also realised that his relationship with the twins was on the rocks; he could barely bring himself to speak to either of them. During the course of the dealings in Europe with the Mafia, Payne had made more contacts and broadened his business dealings to include forged savings stamps and currency. It was clear to him that the twins contributed little – apart from gaping pockets – and that he would be far better off as a lone operator. Consequently, Payne drifted away and his position as the brains of the Kray organisation was taken by Alan Bruce Cooper.[189]

Interestingly, Ernest Shinwell – the *straight business man* who had introduced the Enugu scheme – was arrested in August

---

188 Fry, Colin and Kray, Charlie. *Doing the Business*. London: John Blake Publishing, 2011.

189 Payne, Leslie. *The Brotherhood*. London: Michael Joseph Publishing, 1973.

1964 and charged with issuing forgeries of 14,000 Quaker Oats stock shares and fraudulent dealings in Woolworth Co. shares. In February 1965, Shinwell was sentenced to three years in prison for forgery and fraud.[190]

During 1965, more Mafiosi were arriving in London – including Meyer Lansky's close associate and Mr Fixit of the casino and gambling world, Dino Cellini. In September 1965, Cellini instigated the takeover of the already existing *Colony Club* in Berkeley Square, which became *The Colony Sports Club*, the Mafia's flagship for London operations. George Raft – the veteran Hollywood actor with mob connections – was brought in as frontman and his profile was raised by appearances on television, including *Sunday Night at The London Palladium* hosted by Jimmy Tarbuck. *The Colony* became *George Raft's Colony Club*, emblazoned in Las Vegas-style neon over the entrance. Class, style, and conviviality were important in creating an environment where high rollers would be made to feel comfortable – and entitled to spend, and lose, as much money as possible.[191]

The Kray twins – known as the *Brothers Grimm* among casino workers – were of course active in the West End, shaking down many of the clubs for protection money. So, before the inevitable *Colony* versus the Krays confrontation loomed, Angelo Bruno was brought in to defuse any trouble before it even started. A meeting was brokered by former Kray associate Johnny Francis who, strangely enough, was now working with the American Mafia. Francis had skipped the country in January 1965 to avoid arrest for his part in the McCowan affair,

---

190 *New York Times*, August 14 1964 and February 10 1965.

191 Thompson, Douglas. *Mafialand*. Edinburgh: Mainstream Publishing, 2012.

and – with the help of connections in America – he had moved from Spain to California, where he became chauffeur to one of the mob's favourite entertainers, Nat King Cole. After a time, Francis moved to Philadelphia to work as a driver for Angelo Bruno. Ron and Reg already knew and liked Bruno, who offered a simple deal: stay out of *The Colony Club* in return for a weekly payment of £1,700.[192] Not a bad deal as far as the twins were concerned; all they had to do was send Albert Donoghue to make the weekly collections.

Harold Wilson's Labour Party Government was fully aware of the mob's infiltration into Britain, and it was decided that it must not be allowed to continue. In January 1967, the scuppering of the Mafia's plans began by declaring George Raft – at this point back at home in Beverly Hills – an undesirable alien and refusing him entry back into the country. A purge followed, and Angelo Bruno – along with other leading members of the Cosa Nostra – were likewise banned from Britain. *The Colony* was left in the hands of English manager Alf Salkin, and the hands-on responsibilities of Dino Cellini and Angelo Bruno were left to English associates Benny Huntsman and Albert Dimes. In 1968 the government introduced amendments to the Gambling Act and, following a police raid on *The Colony Club* in December, irregularities were found and gaming equipment was confiscated. Shortly afterwards, *The Colony Club* went into voluntary liquidation and was closed on 31 January 1969.

---

192   Ibid.

George Raft's Colony Club

Berkeley Square, London W1J 6ER

Nearest TFL station: Green Park underground.

Taken over by the American Mafia in 1965, *The Colony Sports Club* was the first of many prestigious casinos and gambling destinations planned for London. In 1966, the veteran Hollywood actor George Raft was drafted in as the frontman for the club, which was re-named *George Raft's Colony Club*. In order to create the kind of classy ambience that the Mafia bosses wanted – and, at the same time, nurture good relationships with the local gangsters – the Krays were offered, and accepted, a generous weekly payment to stay out of *The Colony Club*. In January 1967, George Raft – whose underworld associations were common knowledge – was banned from Britain. *The Colony* remained open for a further two years in the hands of the mob's English associates until January 1969, when the doors were finally closed.

Situated at the southern end of Berkeley Square, *George Raft's Colony Club* was located close to what is now the main entrance to *Lansdowne House*.

December 1965 saw a meeting between members of London's top underworld gangs at *The Astor Club* just off Berkeley Square in Mayfair. *The Astor* was a glitzy nightclub that attracted royalty, landed aristocrats, the well-to-do, numerous celebrities, and gangsters flashing their grubby cash. Present at the meeting were the Krays, who controlled much of East London, the Nash brothers, whose interests were mainly in North London, Freddie Foreman, who was very influential in South London, and the Richardsons – also very powerful and increasingly successful south of the river. The issue at stake was the West End, and the purpose of this gangsters' summit meeting was to come to some kind of understanding and agreement on how it would be divided up to their mutual benefit.

Charlie and Eddie Richardson expressed that they had no interest in an alliance and would continue to operate where and how they wanted. This of course caused friction, argument, and ill-feeling, particularly between the Krays and the Richardsons; a situation that was unlikely to be resolved peacefully. It is said that during an argument at this meeting – or another around the same time – the Richardsons' henchman, George Cornell, in front of everyone and to his face, called Ronnie Kray a "*fat poof.*"

The Astor Club

Lansdowne Row, Off Berkeley Square, London W1

Nearest TFL station: Green Park underground.

First opened in the 1930s and later taken over by businessman and manager of show business performers Bertie Green, *The Astor Club* was perhaps the most prestigious of a number of *hostess* clubs operating in London in the 1960s. Aristocrats, celebrities, and gangsters rubbed shoulders at *The Astor* in an atmosphere of luxury, glamour, and Champagne-drenched decadence. Many famous artistes performed at *The Astor* in their early careers including Shirley Bassey, Engelbert Humperdinck, and Tom Jones. It is said that there was an underground passageway connecting *The Astor* to the nearby *Colony Club*, where the hostess girls could move from one club to the other and work both on the same night. Managed by Sulky Gower, *The Astor* paid protection money to both the Nash brothers and the Krays, who were regulars at the club and treated as VIPs when they arrived.

During a gangsters' summit meeting at *The Astor* in late 1965, Richardson Gang member George Cornell is said to have called Ronnie Kray a *"fat poof."*

It was at *The Astor Club* that Ron and Reg spent their last night of freedom before they were arrested in May 1968.

Following the emergence of the discotheque-style of nightclub in the 1960s, the popularity of *The Astor* and many clubs like it gradually began to decline. *The Astor* club eventually closed in the late 1970s.

The 1930s building called *Morris House*, which separated Lansdowne Row from the southern end of Berkeley Square, disappeared in the 1980s – and *The Astor Club* along with it. *Morris House* was partially demolished, redeveloped, and replaced by *Lansdowne House*. *The Astor Club* was located on Lansdowne Row, approximately where *Moffats* newsagent and shop is today.

The South London Richardson Gang – so-called rivals of the Krays – were better organised, more financially successful, and probably even more dangerous than the Krays. Brothers Eddie and Charlie Richardson operated both legitimate businesses and criminal enterprises from their power base in Camberwell, South London. Charlie made money in the scrap metal business and had interests in the mining of pearlite in South Africa. Eddie too was involved in the scrap business and also imported slot machines from America, which were installed in pubs and

clubs in South London and the West End, automatically bringing the premises under Richardson protection. Racketeering,
handling stolen goods, smuggling, and long firm frauds were
just some of the activities that made up the Richardson business
portfolio, and anyone threatening their interests – or who was
suspected of skimming money from the organisation – would
be dealt with ruthlessly.

Charlie Richardson wielded power over others through fear.
He would also preside over mock trials, after which the victims
would be stripped naked and subjected to prolonged beatings,
sometimes lasting for hours. If it was felt that a victim was
lying or withholding information, various methods of torture
were employed, including attaching wires to sensitive body
parts with bulldog clips and delivering electric shocks from
a hand-cranked generator. Frankie Fraser is reputed to have
crushed teeth and lacerated gums while trying to perform tooth
extractions with a pair of pliers.

Mad Frankie Fraser was among several of London's most
feared men of violence in the ranks of the Richardson Gang,
which also included hardman George Cornell and the very dangerous Jimmy Moody. Fully aware of the Richardson Gang's
reputation for violence, members of the Kray Firm rarely ventured into what they called 'Indian country' – south of the river
– and, if they did, it wouldn't be without a gun.

Charlie and Eddie Richardson saw themselves as businessmen first and foremost, and it is likely that any rivalry between
the Richardsons and the Krays was cooked up in Ronnie's
mind. Ronnie was envious of the Richardson success and saw
their expansion into the West End, and their running of at least
two protection rackets and one long firm fraud in the East End,
as a direct threat.

The Richardsons, on the other hand, saw the Krays as a bit of
a nuisance – fame-seeking amateurs not to be taken too seriously – but, if trouble came, the Richardsons were well equipped

to deal with it. Both Eddie and Charlie Richardson were intelligent, shrewd operators and deliberately avoided unnecessary exposure. In fact, prior to the infamous *Torture Trials* in 1967, very few people – apart from other criminal gangs and those who lived in their local area – had ever heard of them. Despite operating under the radar they did, like the Krays, have celebrity friends, including Diana Dors and actor Stanley Baker, who starred alongside Michael Caine in the 1964 feature film *Zulu*.

Peckford Scrap Metal

50 New Church Road, Camberwell, London SE5

Nearest TFL station: The Oval underground.

Kray Firm rivals Charlie and Eddie Richardson owned several scrapyards, but New Church Road was their main centre of operations, and it is here that they are said to have tortured victims using various sadistic methods including electric shock. Charlie and Eddie always strongly denied this – claiming that it was pure fantasy and a fit-up – but in 1967, the brothers, along with Frankie Fraser, were convicted at what came to be known as the *Torture Trials* and given long prison sentences.

Nothing remains of *Peckford Scrap Metal* in Camberwell, and the site at the junction of New Church Road and Sears Street is now occupied by a modern block of flats called *Leslie Prince Court*.

Ronnie Kray hated the Richardsons with a passion and, by early 1966, the feeling had become mutual. Frankie Fraser crossed the river on a few occasions to talk with the twins, but nothing changed and both sides made preparations for what looked like the inevitable war. The Colonel took charge of the planning and Kray Firm members were issued with guns, allocated a specific Richardson Gang member, and given as much information as was known about the places where they were likely to be found. London was teetering on the edge of a full-scale gang war – but whether or not the order to 'Go' would have been given, and whether or not Firm members would have obeyed their orders to kill will, due to a dramatic change in circumstances, never be known.

In the early hours of Tuesday 8 March 1966, most of the leading members of the Richardson Gang were arrested and jailed following a shoot-out with another South London gang in a Catford nightclub. Originally called *The Savoy Rooms*, the club was taken over in 1965 by Manchester businessmen and tough guys Owen Ratcliffe and Paddy McGrath. On the street level was a live music venue, which was renamed *The Witchdoctor*; and downstairs a nightclub and casino called *Mr Smiths*.

Before moving on to the details of the shoot-out, it is worth looking at the club's renaming which, if not intentional, must be the daddy of all coincidences. In 1962, a scandal surrounding the doping of racehorses hit the headlines. Bookmaker William Roper organised a gang of horse dopers who operated in the late '50s and early '60s, netting tens of thousands for Roper and his accomplices. Gangsters and bookmakers Charlie Mitchell and Albert Dimes were both deeply involved. In March 1962, an attempt to nobble one of the royal horses alerted the police and most of the gang were arrested. Dimes escaped arrest and Charlie Mitchell was freed following an appeal, but Roper and other gang members – including Roper's beautiful Swiss mistress Micheline Lugeon – served time in prison. Before the trial, word reached the gang's ears that the supplier of the phenobarbitone used to dope the horses was set to give evidence against them. While on remand in *Lewes Prison*, Edward Smith – known by the gang as the *Witch Doctor* – mysteriously fell from an upper landing and later died.[193]

According to Eddie Richardson, the club's new owners contacted Billy Hill and asked him to help arrange the security. Billy Hill in turn contacted Eddie Richardson and asked him to look after the security on the door and inside *Mr Smiths* – where, as a bonus, he would be able to install slot machines supplied by his business *Atlantic Machines.*

On Monday 7 March, Eddie Richardson and friends went to the club during the day to take an initial look, liked what they saw, and arranged to return in the evening to sign off the deal. Unbeknown to Eddie Richardson, another gang of local hard cases – headed by brothers Billy and Harry Hayward – had taken it upon themselves to *protect* the club and, when Eddie and friends, who weren't expecting trouble, returned in the evening, the Hayward Gang were there in force. Also unbeknown to Eddie Richardson and friends was that two of the Hayward Gang were carrying guns.

Inevitably, sometime after 2am, fighting broke out and, in the ensuing mayhem, four of the Richardson Gang were shot. Eddie was blasted with a shotgun and injured in the buttocks and leg, Ronnie Jeffreys received a shotgun blast to the groin and stomach, Harry Rawlins was shot in the arm with a .45 bullet, which ruptured an artery, and Frankie Fraser's femur was shattered after being shot in the leg with the same gun. Hayward Gang member Dickie Hart was firing the .45 pistol but, somehow, in the chaos, the gun was turned on him and he was shot in the chest. Supposedly a friend of the Krays, Dickie Hart – who had just been released from prison after serving

---

193 Reid, Jamie. *Doped*. Newbury: Racing Post Books, 2013.

a sentence for GBH – died later the same day in *Lewisham Hospital*.

Most of the Richardson Gang who were present at *Mr Smiths* were arrested, charged with causing an affray, and sent to prison on remand. Frankie Fraser was charged with Dickie Hart's murder. Two important members of the Richardson Gang were not involved in the incident and remained free: Charlie himself, who was in South Africa at the time, and George Cornell.

Mr Smiths and The Witchdoctor

75 Rushey Green, Catford, London SE6 4AF

Nearest station: Catford Bridge, Southeastern Railway.

Built in 1910, *The Savoy Ballroom* became a venue for live music in the early 1960s and was known as *The Savoy Rooms*. In 1965, *The Savoy Rooms* was taken over and the music venue at street level was renamed *The Witchdoctor*. Downstairs, a nightclub – with a restaurant, casino, cabaret, and a drinks licence until 2am – was opened and called *Mr Smiths*. In the early hours of Tuesday 8 March 1966, a fight broke out between the Richardson Gang and another local gang led by Billy and Harry Hayward. After the fight – during which Hayward Gang member and friend of the Krays, Dickie Hart, was shot and killed – most of the leading members of the Richardson Gang were arrested and jailed, thus ending the Kray/Richardson war before it even started.

The Rolling Stones and Gene Vincent are said to have played at *The Savoy Rooms* and, after the venue became *The Witchdoctor*, many pop groups and artists of the era played there. Regularly appearing were The Gaylords who, after changing their name to Marmalade, had several hits including a number 1. In 1966, The Who played at *The Witchdoctor* and, on 28 April and 8 October of that year, David Bowie appeared.

Happily, the building still exists and is now a furniture store called *Istikbal*. Upstairs is the *Elim, Right Now Jesus Centre*.

George Cornell (real name George Myers) was an East Ender who grew up in the same streets as the Kray twins. He was from the Watney Street area and, in his youth, was a member of the Watney Street Gang – traditional enemies of the Bethnal Green boys. Ronnie Kray knew Cornell, if not from the East End as youngsters, then certainly later in 1957 when they served time together at *Winchester Prison*. Later in life, Cornell met and married Olive Hudd, a South London girl, and he left the East End and moved south of the river. Cornell was a tough and violent man with a reputation as a formidable street fighter, and his natural talents and abilities were put to use on his new home turf as a leading enforcer with the Richardson Gang.

Masterman House

New Church Road, Camberwell, London SE5 7HX

Nearest TFL station: The Oval underground.

In 1966, George Cornell was living with his wife Olive and his two children in the newly built block of flats on Camberwell's *Elmington Estate*. On Wednesday 9 March 1966 George returned home around 4.30 pm after an afternoon's drinking with friends and stayed for a couple of hours before going out again. George Cornell never returned home and this was the last time that Olive would see her husband alive.

The imposing 17-storey tower block built in the early 1960s still stands and is just a two minute-walk from the site of the Richardsons' scrapyard at 50 New Church Road.

Much has been written about the infamous and now legendary murder in *The Blind Beggar* and, although some accounts vary in detail, the sequences of events leading to George Cornell's death from a 9mm bullet through the brain are well documented. Perhaps the only remaining aspect of the killing that is still open to some speculation is exactly *why* it happened. Many theories have been chewed over as to why Ronnie Kray shot George Cornell, but there was likely no single, definitive reason but rather a number of contributory factors.

First and foremost was Ronnie's mental illness; he suffered from paranoid schizophrenia, an incurable condition kept barely under control by antipsychotic drugs. Ronnie's illness – which often caused him to become delusional, irrational, and impetuous – was made worse by his failure to take the drugs on a strict and regular basis. His mood swings could be extreme, often leading to acts of explosive and dreadful violence for reasons that most people would consider trivial. Such was the ferocity of Ronnie's violence, it is a wonder he hadn't killed anyone before this point in his life.

George Cornell was fearless and brash to the point of arrogance, and was one of only a small number of individuals who held little or no regard for the Krays' reputation for violence or their standing as rulers of the East End. Cornell was a regular drinker in many of the pubs used by the Krays and made no secret of his utter disdain for Ronnie's homosexuality and his choice to surround himself with young boys. Cornell was casual in bad-mouthing and belittling Ronnie regardless of the company. As far as George Cornell was concerned, Ronnie Kray was a bit of a joke and he didn't particularly care who was listening when he spoke about it. Although uncertain, it is widely believed that George Cornell called Ronnie Kray a *fat poof* in company and to his face. On balance, the likelihood is that it did happen and most probably in *The Astor Club*.

Ronnie Kray considered himself untouchable by anyone – including the police. Traditional East End culture dictated that no one, no matter what the circumstances, must ever give information to the police. *Grassing* was a cardinal sin in the East End and anyone breaking the unwritten rule would be treated as a social pariah or worse. This ingrained tradition – coupled with the vice-like grip of fear imposed by the Krays – gave Ronnie the assurance that no matter what he did or where he did it, there would be no witnesses to give evidence against him in a court of law. The Krays further increased their immunity by letting it be known that they had contacts in the police and, should anyone for whatever reason, speak to the police about Kray business, they would know about it within a very short time. Ronnie Kray was confident that no one would dare speak out against him and therefore felt assured that he was free to do whatever dark deeds he chose with impunity.

Leslie Payne, the Krays' business manager, in his book *The Brotherhood,* tells of another incident that must have added fuel to the fire. According to Payne, George Cornell was operating a protection racket in the East End and demanding money from a warehouseman. The man went to the Krays and asked them to get Cornell off his back. The Krays told the man that they would kill Cornell for £2,000 and the money was handed over. With no intention of carrying out the killing, the twins approached Cornell and told him that there was a new arrangement and that, from now on, they were protecting the man's business. Cornell refused to back off and said that he intended to continue getting his money. After being told by the twins that they had accepted £2,000 for his murder, Cornell said that they'd better earn it. With that, Cornell promptly went back to see the warehouseman and beat him up.

Into the mix must also go Ronnie's American gangster complex. He liked the idea of being a gangster and styled himself as an American Mafioso: the walk, the talk, and the clothes. In order to play the part to the full – and further increase the fear, power, and respect he so loved – he wanted to be known as a killer. In Mafia terms, he wanted to 'make his bones'; he wanted his 'button'. Ronnie's homicidal fantasies involved the keeping of a list of those he planned to bump off, and anyone finding themselves out of favour – often for the most trivial of reasons – could find their name on Ronnie's deadpool list. George Cornell's name must surely have been on the list.

Legend has it that sometime prior to his murder, George Cornell beat the living daylights out of Ronnie in a fist fight. There is some anecdotal evidence to suggest this did happen – particularly that of the twins' biographer John Pearson who, in his book *Notorious*, tells of a conversation between Ronnie Kray and his old friend Wilf Pine that took place many years later when Ronnie was interned in *Broadmoor*. Among Ronnie's reflections of the events surrounding Cornell's murder are two important declarations:

"I'll be honest with you, Wilf; Cornell kicked the shit out of me that night."

"Yeah, once he did call me a fat poof and a couple of other things I won't repeat."[194]

Some accounts say that Ronnie's beating took place in

---

194 Pearson, John. *Notorious*. London: Century Publishing, 2010.

or outside *The Brown Bear* pub on Leman Street, but John Pearson's very reliable and informed writing tells us that it happened in *The Green Dragon Club* on Whitechapel Road.

After the battle in the *Mr Smiths* club, in which the twins' friend Dickie Hart had been shot and killed, there was only one important Richardson Gang member left still at liberty (apart from Charlie Richardson who was in South Africa), and there he was the following evening enjoying a drink with a couple of friends in *The Blind Beggar*.

'*The Beggars*' was very much on Kray turf, right in the middle of their manor, and – along with all other pubs and clubs in the East End – a source of income. Although only occasionally used by The Firm, it was just a few yards from *The Grave Maurice*, very much a Krays pub and one of The Firm's favourite meeting places. Cornell was in fact a regular drinker in *The Blind Beggar* and his presence there that evening was probably not an act of deliberate provocation – more an indication of his lack of fear of the Krays and his complete disregard for their authority in the area.

All things considered, it's no great surprise that on the evening of 9 March 1966, Ronnie Kray readily set out to commit murder. It could be argued that George Cornell's presence in *The Blind Beggar* on that fateful night was just the opportunity he'd been waiting for.

On the night of the shoot-out at *Mr Smiths*, George Cornell – who generally worked with Charlie Richardson rather than Eddie – was in *The Jack of Clubs*, a West End nightclub below *Isow's* restaurant in Brewer Street, Soho.[195] The next day, Wednesday 9 March, Cornell spent much of the day drinking with brothers Billy and Ron Webb in *The Old Basing House*

---

195 Powell, Nosher with Hall, William. *Nosher*. London: Blake Publishing, 1999.

pub in Haggerston.[196] After the pub stopped serving at 3pm, as they did in 1966, arrangements were made to meet the following day in *The Ten Bells* pub in Spitalfields, and Cornell made his way home.[197]

Around 6.30pm, Cornell left his home, and – along with his friend Albert Woods – went to the *London Hospital* on Whitechapel Road to visit Jimmy Andrews, who was receiving treatment for a gunshot wound to the leg. According to Eddie Richardson, Andrews had been shot "*over some fucking love triangle.*"[198] After the hospital visit they decided to go for a drink in *The Blind Beggar*, which was just across the road. George Cornell and Albie Woods were joined by another friend, Johnny Dale, and by around 8pm the three men were enjoying a drink together in the saloon bar of *The Blind Beggar*.

Meanwhile, less than half a mile away, Ronnie, Reggie, and some of The Firm were gathered in their latest meeting place of choice, *The Lion* pub on Tapp Street. Ronnie, who had started drinking early, was joined by more of The Firm gradually drifting in and, by 8pm, there was quite a crowd. Around 8.15pm, Ronnie – who had ears and eyes everywhere in the East End – was informed that Cornell was drinking in *The Blind Beggar*. Ronnie told Reggie that he was going for Cornell and Reggie said it would be better to wait and think it through before doing anything rash – but, as ever, when Ronnie made his mind up to do something, there was no talking him out of it. Ronnie gave

196 Situated at 25-27 Kingsland Road, E2 8AA, the former pub – now simply called *Basing House* – hosts electronic music events on Friday and Saturday nights.

197 Webb, Billy. *Running With The Krays*. Edinburgh: Mainstream Publishing, 1993.

198 Richardson, Eddie. *No Handcuffs*. London: John Blake Publishing, 2019.

orders and strode out of the pub, with Jack Dickson and Ian Barrie following obediently behind.

The Lion

8 Tapp Street, Bethnal Green, London E1 5RE

Nearest TFL station: Bethnal Green overground.

Just a short walk from the site of the twins' former home in Vallance Road, next to Bethnal Green overground station, is Tapp Street. Under the railway arch and out the other side to the right is the building that was once one of the Krays' favourite pubs, *The Lion*.

Built and opened in 1853, the pub occupied a spot in what was then one of the poorest and most deprived areas in the East End. The Krays and The Firm began using *The Lion* regularly in the mid-'60s and, by 1966, it was their meeting place of choice. Run by 'Marge' – the widow of the former licensee – *The Lion* was affectionately known by The Firm as *Madge's, The Widow's, or The Merry Widow's*. Downstairs were two bar rooms, one of which was exclusively used by The Firm, and upstairs was a private room that Marge let Ron and Reg use for meetings.

On the evening of 9 March 1966, The Firm were gathered in *The Lion* when Ronnie heard that George Cornell was in the nearby *Blind Beggar* pub. Ronnie left, accompanied by Scotch Ian and Scotch Jack, and set out to commit one of the most infamous murders in British history.

It was believed for a time in early 1966 that the Richardson Gang were planning an attack on *The Lion*.

This may or may not have been so, but either way it never happened, possibly due to the arrest of the leading Richardson Gang members following the incident at *Mr Smiths*.

The pub was closed in 2002 and converted into residences. The original *Truman's Brewery* sign can still be seen on the outside wall.

Jack Dickson was ordered to drive to nearby Fort Vallance and Ronnie went inside, returned a few moments later, and jumped back in the car. Ronnie then told Jack Dickson to drive the half-mile or so to *The Blind Beggar* and wait outside in the car. Ronnie gave Ian Barrie a gun – a .32 automatic – and the two men entered the saloon bar of *The Blind Beggar* at approximately 8.35 pm.

George Cornell, who was sitting at the far end of the bar with his two friends, looked up and said, *"Well look who's here."* Ronnie marched to within a few feet of Cornell, pulled a 9mm automatic from his coat, pointed the gun, and fired a single deafening shot, which hit Cornell in the centre of his forehead. The force of the bullet knocked Cornell off his bar stool and he fell to the floor with blood spurting from his head. Ian Barrie then fired two more ear-splitting shots randomly into empty space, presumably to frighten the small number of potential witnesses who were in the pub that night. Frances, the terrified barmaid – thinking that she too would be shot – ran and jumped down the cellar steps, hurting her back.[199] After a couple of minutes, hearing nothing but silence, she emerged into the haze and smell of gun smoke and the sound of the record player, which was stuck in a groove and repeating the same line of the Walker Brothers' song over and over: *"The sun ain't gonna shine anymore."*

Cornell's companions left the scene quickly before the police could arrive and Cornell was left lying on the pub floor in an ever-growing pool of blood. Patrick 'Patsy' Quill – the owner of the pub – was upstairs when he heard the shots. He came down quickly, phoned the emergency services, and then he and Frances the barmaid tried to do what they could for the stricken man. A 9mm bullet had passed straight through Cornell's head, but he was groaning and somehow still alive.

Cornell was taken by ambulance to *Mile End Hospital* on Bancroft Road where he was examined and found to be in need of emergency brain surgery, which was only available at spe-

---

199 Kelly, Patricia and Morton, James. *Calling Time on the Krays, The Barmaid's Tale*. London: Little, Brown and Company, 1966.

cialist units. Even though there was only a slim chance that Cornell's life could be saved, he was transferred by emergency ambulance to *Maida Vale Hospital*, where he was prepared for surgery – but before the operation could begin, George Cornell's heart stopped and, despite cardiac massage, he was declared deceased at 10.29pm.[200]

The Blind Beggar

337 Whitechapel Road, London E1 1BU

Nearest TFL station: Whitechapel underground.

No tour of the Krays' East End would be complete without a visit to this most iconic of destinations where Ronnie Kray shot and killed rival gangster George Cornell on the evening of 9 March 1966.

Built in 1894, the pub takes its name from the ballad and legend of *The Blind Beggar of Bethnal Green* and was the brewery tap for the *Mann's/Albion Brewery*. Next door, it is possible to see the original wrought iron entrance arch to the brewery, which – until its closure in 1979 – was famous for the production of the first modern brown ale, Ronnie Kray's favourite tipple.

In 1966, the pub was divided into three separate rooms: the saloon bar to the left where the shooting took place, a smaller public bar to the right, and a room at the back called the *dark bar* or *snug*. The pub has clearly undergone refurbishment since 1966 but the outside facade is much the same. Although the bar occupies a similar

---

200   Bennett, John. *Krayology*. London: Mango Books, 2016.

position, it has been moved to the right, closer to the east wall, taking up the space that was once the public bar. The interior of the *Beggars* retains some similarity but the decor and atmosphere are definitely modern; a far cry from the seedy East End boozer it once was.

If asked, the staff may show you a bullet hole in the ceiling, but whether or not it was made on the night of 9 March 1966 is open to some debate. The 9mm bullet that killed George Cornell was found by the police in the snug bar, and holes consistent with having been made by the two .32 calibre bullets fired by Ian Barrie were found in furniture.[201]

There is some uncertainty over the make of the German 9mm automatic pistol that Ronnie used. Some accounts say a Luger, others a Mauser. So, when visiting the pub, does one piss the bar staff off by ordering a *'Luger and Lime'* or piss them off even more by asking for an obscure sherry-based cocktail called a *'Mauser'*?

Ronnie, Jack Dickson, and a very shocked Ian Barrie returned to *The Lion* pub and, when someone came in shortly afterwards and shouted, *"There's been a shooting in the Whitechapel Road,"* it was obvious to all who was responsible. Reggie was bordering on frantic and realised that they needed to get off the manor with some urgency. Cars were commandeered and Ronnie left in a car full of Firm members, driven once again by Jack Dickson. Reggie travelled with the three Teale brothers – Alfie, Bobby, and David – who had earlier been summoned to join the party at *The Lion* and arrived just as the mass exodus was about to begin.

---

201 Ibid.

The Firm make ready to leave *The Lion* and '*get off the manor.*'

A fleet of cars full of gangsters left Bethnal Green – heading in different directions to avoid the notice of the police – and made their way towards a rendezvous in Walthamstow, a spieler called *The Stow Club* in Hoe Street, run by Firm members Limehouse Willy and Charlie Clark. Ronnie gave the two guns to Charlie Clark and told him to get rid of them.

For many years it was not known what happened to the gun that Ronnie Kray used to shoot George Cornell. Then, in 1997 – two years after Ronnie's death – Kate Howard, who married Ronnie in *Broadmoor*, wrote and published a book in which she claims that almost three decades after the shooting, Charlie Clark gave her a box which contained the gun, a 9mm Mauser. According to Kate, she arranged for the gun to be deactivated and then placed it in a bank safety deposit box.[202]

Next, the group moved to the nearby *Chequers* pub, run by an ex-policeman called Charlie Hobbs, who ushered them into a private bar room and began dispensing the drinks. An ill-fitting change of clothes was found for Ronnie and he scrubbed his hands and arms clean using Vim sink cleaner. When it was announced on the television news that a man had been shot in the head in a Stepney public house, there was cheering, laughing, and a mood of celebration among The Colonel's loyal troops.

The Chequers

145 High Street, Walthamstow, London E17 7BX

Nearest TFL station: Walthamstow Central underground/overground.

Ron, Reg, and The Firm used the pub occasionally, particularly for *off their manor* clandestine meetings with corrupt police officers. On 9 March 1966, immediately after Ronnie shot George Cornell in *The Blind Beggar*, the twins and The Firm needed to get out of

---

202   Kray, Kate. *Ronnie Kray: Sorted.* London: Blake Publishing, 1997.

the East End fast; they headed for *The Chequers*, where they gathered and stayed drinking until approximately 11.30pm.

The Chequers is one of the oldest pubs in Walthamstow, dating back to the 18th century. The original building burnt down in 1791 and the current building was erected not long afterwards. Sadly, the original front-entrance portico was removed in 2003 and, in July 2012, the pub was voluntarily closed due to its association with the dealing and use of drugs. Happily, *The Chequers* reopened less than a year later – remodelled, renovated, and revamped with a welcoming atmosphere. Sorted!!

By 11.30 pm, The Firm had outstayed their welcome in *The Chequers* and somewhere else, away from the East End, needed to be found to continue the party. Roland Tarlton, a brewery driver and regular at *The Chequers*, lived in a flat with his wife and daughter above a row of shops in nearby Palace Parade, and had a bar set up in his front room for after-hours drinking. Tarlton was apparently happy to welcome the 30 or 40-strong Kray crowd into his home, but things became a little difficult around 1.30am when his wife returned from her job as a waitress at the *Cafe Royal* and began screaming hysterically for them to "*get out.*"

Somewhere else needed to be found quickly, and – much to the dismay of David Teale, who lived in a small two-room flat with his pregnant wife and two young daughters – Reggie said to him, *"Right Dave, we're going to stay round your house."* David Teale's objections were overruled and The Firm descended on the tiny flat and continued drinking. A radio played in the background and, when the news came on, everyone hushed to hear what was being said. When it was announced sometime in the early hours that the victim of the shooting in an East End pub had died, Ronnie cheered – and the rest of The Firm, keen to express their loyalty, joined in.

"*You're a cold-blooded killer, Ronnie,*" declared Sammy Lederman, and Ronnie laughed heartily; he was clearly enjoying the moment and not in the least bit troubled by remorse. Drinking and high spirits continued until, eventually, every chair and every inch of floor space was taken up by sleeping gangsters.

Nothing short of a nightmare followed for David Teale and his family, as their very humble little abode became home base for The Firm and a hub of activity for the next two weeks. Some of the Kray troupe would stay, and others were in and out – Scotch Ian, Scotch Jack, Nobby Clark, Pat Connolly, Fat Wally Garelick, Bobby Buckley, Connie Whitehead, Billy Frost, Charlie Kray, Sammy Lederman, and Harry 'Jew Boy' Cope were just some of the characters among the throng that overwhelmed the little family home. David, his wife Christine, and his two brothers, Bobby and Alfie, were not allowed to leave without permission from Ronnie – and, if they did, it was only for a short time and for what Ronnie considered to be a good reason. Ronnie knew that with the children present, the police were unlikely to come in heavy-handed, so the flat in Moresby Road effectively became the scene of a siege in which the children were being used as human shields.

---

51 Moresby Road

Clapton, London E5 9LE

Nearest TFL station: Clapton overground.

Less than a ten-minute walk from *Cedra Court*, the ground floor of number 51 was, in 1966, home to fringe

Firm member David Teale, his wife, and two young daughters. Following the murder of George Cornell in *The Blind Beggar* - in the early hours of March 10 – and much against the wishes of David Teale – Ron, Reg, and The Firm descended on the tiny family home and used it as a hideout for two weeks. Ron effectively held the family hostage, believing that the presence of the children would deter the police from raiding the address.

Something happened at Moresby Road that would have far-reaching repercussions for the Teale brothers and ultimately play an important part in ending the Kray twins' time as free men. David, Bobby, and Alfie Teale's kid brother, Paul – aged 11 at the time – came from his mother's home at nearby *Cedra Court* to visit Aunty Christine and his two little cousins at Moresby Road. He, of course, had no idea what was going on and was not going to be allowed to leave. Ronnie Kray took an unhealthy liking to the boy, and it was clear to Bobby Teale that Ronnie was interested in having more than just a friendly chat with his little brother. When Ronnie said he was going to take the boy for a *lie-down* and was leading him towards the bedroom, Bobby Teale blocked Ronnie's way, looked him in the eyes and, with iron resolve, told him, *"No."* Unbeknown to Ronnie, Bobby had a gun, and he'd decided to use it if things went too far. Ronnie must have sensed something, because he simply made light of the situation and backed off.

This was the last straw for Bobby Teale; he decided that Ronnie Kray – who he now saw as a psychotic, murdering paedophile – must be stopped... and his enabling brother along with him. Bobby was allowed to leave the flat for a short time under the pretence that he was going to *Cedra Court* to visit his mother. Ron and Reg had, by this time, all but abandoned their flats there. Instead, Bobby Teale went to a phone box some distance away, phoned *Scotland Yard*, and asked to speak to the famous Detective Superintendent Tommy Butler. Amazingly, he was put through, and he spoke directly to Butler, telling him he had information about the Krays.

A meeting was arranged for that afternoon, during which Bobby told Butler that Ronnie Kray had killed George Cornell. He also gave him the address of where he and the rest of The Firm were hiding. Much to Bobby Teale's disappointment, Butler explained that he was not going to make any arrests at this time, as he first needed more information. Bobby was given a phone number to memorise, the name of his police contact, and was told to choose a code name for himself. He chose *Phillips*. Now it was time to return to the flat, and he did so knowing that he might possibly have just signed his own death warrant.[203]

Meanwhile, in the East End, The Firm were at work making sure that witnesses to Cornell's murder were keeping quiet. It was, by now, common knowledge in the East End that Ronnie Kray was the killer – everyone knew, including the police, but unsurprisingly no one was talking. Detective Superintendent Axon and his team from *Arbour Square Police Station* took statements from the dozen or so witnesses in *The Blind Beggar* that night, but no one had seen anything – including the barmaid, who knew full well who was responsible but was too terrified to say. John Dale – one of Cornell's two companions in the pub – did, in fact, give Ronnie's name, but refused point-blank to include it on his signed statement, let alone stand as a witness in court.

After two weeks of misery for David Teale and his family, Ron, Reg and The Firm finally left the flat in Moresby Road. Reggie had discovered that the police were aware of

203   Teale, Bobby. *Bringing Down The Krays*. London: Ebury Press, 2013.

their whereabouts. Bobby Teale had, of course, told the police, and the information had no doubt been fed back to Reggie
through his paid contacts on the inside. Ron, Reg, and some
of The Firm – including the Teale brothers, under duress –
decamped to Firm member Jack Dickson's flat in nearby
Clissold Road, Stoke Newington, staying there for the next two
weeks. Throughout their time laying low at Moresby Road and
Clissold Road, the twins and The Firm ventured out regularly
to local pubs and even put in an appearance or two at their regular haunts in the East End.

The American Mafia was still present and active in London
in 1966, conducting business and carefully avoiding unnecessary problems with the authorities and the police. Their association with the Kray twins, who had just committed a very public murder, must have been the cause of some concern. When
Mafia man Eddie Pucci – Frank Sinatra's bodyguard – paid a
visit to Clissold Road, he was taken for drinks to the nearby
Albion pub.

The Albion

2 Clissold Road, London N16 9EU

Nearest TFL station: Rectory Road overground.

Happily, the distinctive Georgian pub building on the
corner of Clissold Road and Albion Road still stands,
though the pub was closed in 1972 and converted into
residences.

In late March 1966, following the shooting of George
Cornell in *The Blind Beggar*, the Kray twins left their
hideout in Moresby Road and, along with some of
The Firm, moved to Firm member Jack Dickson's flat

---

in nearby Clissold Road. They stayed for around two weeks and, while there, they were paid a visit by Frank Sinatra's Mafia bodyguard, Eddie Pucci. They took him for a drink in *The Albion*.

The life of a Mafia man can be cut short at any time, and Eddie Pucci was shot and killed on a golf course in Chicago in 1972. Later, in 1980, the twins' friend, Mafia boss Angelo Bruno, was shot dead in his car outside his home in Philadelphia.

During this time, several other watering holes were used by The Firm, including *The Coach and Horses* on Stoke Newington High Street. Jack Dickson was a regular there and knew the landlord – 'Blondy Bill' – well. From around 1964, The Firm had been using the pub for meetings – something that the landlord was none too happy about. He was also powerless to do anything about it. Jack Dickson had a frank discussion with his friend Ian Barrie in the pub; he tried in vain to persuade him to get out of town and go back to Scotland, before he was arrested along with Ronnie and charged with murder. Ian Barrie decided to stay-put in London, in a flat he shared with his girlfriend in Kilburn, rented under the name of Davidson.[204]

204 Morton, James. *Krays: The Final Word.* London: Mirror Books, 2019.

The Coach and Horses, Stoke Newington

178 Stoke Newington High Street, London N16 7JL

Nearest TFL station: Stoke Newington overground.

Not to be confused with another pub of the same name in the Krays' story – the now-demolished *Coach and Horses* at Mile End – this pub survives, still dispensing good cheer today. Originally a coach house, the pub – built in 1826 – is Grade II listed and is one of the oldest remaining public houses in the borough of Hackney.

From 1964 onwards, Firm member Jack Dickson's local – *The Coach and Horses*, run by landlord 'Blondy Bill' – was used for occasional meetings by the Kray twins and The Firm. In the spring of 1966, following the murder of George Cornell in *The Blind Beggar*, Ron, Reg, and some of The Firm were laying-low at addresses in the area, and the pub was used more frequently.

A week after the twins' arrest in May 1968, Jack Dickson was arrested in *The Coach and Horses* by Chief Inspector Harry Mooney and his team.

In early spring 1966, Ronnie was becoming increasingly confident that the police would get nowhere with their investigation – but he still chose to keep away from the East End and, along with Ian Barrie, he moved into a bungalow in Chingford. Friend of The Firm Charlie Clark owned the residence and lived there with his wife and 12 cats. Charlie Clark was known as the *Cat Man* due to his former career as a cat burglar of renown – and his choice to share his home with a dozen feline friends.

Charlie Clark's Bungalow

3 Loxham Road, Chingford, London E4 8SE

**Nearest TFL station:
Walthamstow Central underground.**

The 1930s-built black and white-fronted bungalow-was, in 1966, home to friend of the Krays Charlie Clark, his wife, and lots of cats. Charlie Clark's home was used as an occasional meeting place for The Firm and, in the spring of 1966, Ronnie moved in with Ian Barrie – staying for several weeks before moving to a flat in Leyton in July of that year.

From Walthamstow bus station, take the 97 bus towards Chingford and alight at Rowden Road (stop CT). Loxham Road is just a two-minute walk away.

Reggie moved into the flat at Manor Lea, Green Lanes in Finsbury Park, which he had briefly shared with his estranged wife Frances after they were married the previous year. Bobby Teale moved in along with him and, together, they made the most of bachelor life; enjoying parties and the company of many a young lady. Reggie also found himself a more regular girlfriend around this time – 21-year-old croupier Christine Boyce. Bobby Teale was of course in regular contact with the police, feeding them information, and the fun that he had at *Manor Lea* must have been tempered by some troubling thoughts.

In the second week of April, the twins – along with Bobby Teale, Scotch Ian, Scotch Jack, and Albert Donoghue – took a break from London and went to see their old friend Geoff Allen, who could always be relied on to help in times of difficulty. Geoff Allen – who, at the time, was living in a grand house in Saffron Walden – booked the Kray party into a local hotel called *The Saffron*.[205]

After taking over the bar and demanding to be served out of hours, a row broke out and the troublesome gangsters were asked to leave. Ron, Reg, and the others moved on to Cambridge and stayed at the *Garden House Hotel*, where the presence of the shady-looking bunch of characters from London aroused suspicion and came to the notice of the local police. It is likely that some members of the public – and certainly the police – knew exactly who they were. Ron and Reg Kray, the two gangster twins from London, weren't exactly unknown; in fact, they were unmistakable. The British public had, over the past few years, been bombarded with pictorial news-

---

205 Situated at 12 High Street, Saffron Walden, the 16th century Grade II listed *Saffron Hotel* continues to provide refreshment and accommodation for visitors to the historic market town.

paper articles covering the twins' exploits, and they had even appeared on television. Cambridge police must surely have informed *Scotland Yard* of the Krays' presence in the city, and were likely told to keep a low profile as the Krays were currently the subject of a major ongoing investigation.

Garden House Hotel

Mill Lane, Cambridge CB2 1RT

In April 1966, Ron and Reg – accompanied by four members of The Firm – took a break from London to visit their friend, the wealthy fraudster and arsonist Geoff Allen. After trouble with the management at their hotel in Saffron Walden, the group moved to Cambridge and stayed at the *Garden House Hotel*. Suspicion was aroused by the dubious-looking group of characters from London and the local police watched from a distance.

Dating back to the 18th century, the historic Cambridge hotel that played host to the Kray twins in 1966 was destroyed by fire six years later in 1972. Rebuilt the following year, the hotel became the *Double Tree Hilton Hotel* and then, in 2020, *The Cambridge Hotel.* Following a major refurbishment in 2021, the hotel was renamed *The Graduate Cambridge.*

There was another long-standing place of refuge available to the twins, which they used for regular short breaks away from London during the spring and summer of 1966. For the past five years, come the warmer months, Ron, Reg, and their parents – separately or together – spent many a weekend at their family caravan at *Steeple Bay* in Essex. Reggie spent time there with Frances and had first proposed to her while there in 1961. Later, and rather more sadly, Mitzi – Reggie's beloved Pekingese dog – was run-over and killed on the caravan site.

David Teale was encouraged by the twins to get a caravan, and when he did, the much bigger mobile home was placed next to the Krays' caravan. Of course, the twins promptly claimed it for themselves. Kray associate Micky Fawcett described *Steeple Bay* as: "*The most boring place on earth. I couldn't think of anything worse – you'd send me there as some kind of punishment.*"[206] But the twins seemed to like it, and members of The Firm would often be invited for weekend parties at the seaside.

Violence was a part of everyday life for the twins; beatings, cuttings, and shootings were almost routine, and too many to mention, but a few stand out – one of which took place at *Steeple Bay*. It was notable not for the level of violence used, but more for the fact that it took place where ordinary folk went with their kids to enjoy a family holiday.

One of the regulars in the site clubhouse and bar was a man who might be described as having a bit of a swagger – a bit *cocky* perhaps – and one evening he had apparently pushed past Violet without an "*excuse me.*"After an evening in the clubhouse, the Kray party were heading back to the caravans for another drink when Ronnie turned around, slipped back into the clubhouse, and proceeded to smash into the man and knock him unconscious. The next day, Alfie Teale discovered that the man had been taken to hospital by ambulance. He mentioned it to Ronnie, who shrugged his shoulders and said, "*He was only a cunt.*"[207]

---

206   Fawcett, Micky. *Krayzy Days*. Brighton: Pen Press, 2013.

207   Teale, Bobby. *Bringing Down the Krays*. London: Ebury Press, 2013.

Steeple Bay Caravan Site

Canney Road, Steeple, Southminster CMO 7RS

Situated close to the town of Maldon, on the River Blackwater in Essex, *Steeple Bay* was the site of the Kray family caravan which, from 1961 onwards, was used by the twins and their parents for weekends and occasional longer breaks. Reggie first proposed to Frances at *Steeple Bay* when she was 18. Some years later, Reggie met a girl here called Carol Thompson, who was in his company the night Jack 'The Hat' McVitie was murdered in October 1967. Charlie Kray and his wife Dolly also had a caravan here on the opposite side of the bay. Fringe Firm member David Teale leased the caravan next to the twins and members of The Firm would regularly be invited to join the twins for weekend breaks.

Now called *Steeple Bay Holiday Park*, the site is open from March to October and caters for families.

The management at *Steeple Bay* were extremely helpful in trying to locate the exact position of the Krays' caravan, but sadly this information appears to be lost to history.

It was summer 1966 and the country was in the grip of World Cup football fever. England reached the final and, on 30 July, beat Germany 4-2 at Wembley to win the tournament. On the same day, it was 'all over' for Charlie Richardson, who was arrested, charged with GBH, and remanded in custody. Following the infamous *Torture Trials* of 1967, Charlie was sentenced to 25 years in prison – and his brother Eddie and Frankie Fraser each had ten years added to the sentences they were already serving for affray, following the incident at *Mr Smiths* nightclub in Catford.

Also in July, the twins, Ian Barrie, and Bobby Teale moved into a flat owned by Charlie Clark, above *Adams* barber's shop in Lea Bridge Road, Leyton. Through their contacts in the police, the twins were aware that someone close was supplying information to *Scotland Yard*. They even knew the informer's code name, *Phillips*. Bobby Teale was under suspicion and his continued health and well-being was looking far from assured.

Bobby told his police contact where the twins and Ian Barrie could now be found, described the layout of the premises, and then prayed they would take action, arrest the twins, and end his nightmare. The police did take action and, on 4 August at 1.50am, armed Flying Squad officers swooped on the flat in Lea Bridge Road using ladders and sledge hammers. Ron and Reg were arrested and, along with them, Ian Barrie, Mad Teddy Smith, and Tommy Cowley. Ronnie and Ian Barrie were taken to *Commercial Street Police Station*, while Reggie, Teddy Smith, and Tom Cowley went to *Leyton Police Station*.[208]

Ronnie was interviewed by DSI Tommy Butler and, later that day, put on an identity parade. Albie Woods – George Cornell's companion on the evening of his murder – failed to pick Ronnie out, and another man present in *The Blind Beggar* at the time of the shooting *couldn't be sure*. Frances – the barmaid, who had been advised that talking to the police was not in her best interest – lost her nerve and failed to show up. The next morning, Friday 5 August, all were released and the press were there waiting. Pictures were taken of the twins at the Lea

---

208 Built in the 1930s, Leyton Police Station – at 215 Francis Road, E10 6NJ – was sold off and converted into an apartment building called *Met House* in 2012. Six carvings of bobbies from history can be seen around the main entrance.

Bridge Road flat, and the now famous low-angle picture of the twins – in suits, ties, trousers with buttoned pockets, and braces, with a mirror and woodland print wallpaper in the background – appeared on the front page of the *Daily Mirror* the next day.

The public were now aware that the renowned Flying Squad detective Tommy Butler – famous for solving the case of the 1963 Great Train Robbery – was now targeting the Krays. From Butler's perspective, this was nothing short of a huge fail; no one was talking and there was little else he could do except put the enquiry on hold and wait for any possible developments. The twins had done it again: humiliated the police and literally, as Ronnie believed at this point, got away with murder. Ronnie must have felt invincible at this time – completely untouchable and free to do whatever he chose. Reggie, on the other hand, always a little more circumspect, was not quite so sure.

471 Lea Bridge Road

Leyton, London E10 7EA

Nearest TFL station: Leyton Midland Road overground.

Ron, Reg, and some of The Firm were holed-up in the two-room flat above a barber's shop when the Flying Squad swooped in and arrested all present in the early hours of Thursday 4 August 1966. Ron, Reg, and the others were released the next day without charge. The press were waiting and a now well-known picture of the twins taken in the Lea Bridge Road flat appeared on the front page of the *Daily Mirror* on Saturday 6 August.

Number 471 in the parade of 1930s-built shops with

flats above was, in 1966, *A. Adams Barbers*. Today, the shop premises are occupied by *Al Madinah* travel agents.

Bobby Teale's situation was now desperate. If he ran and disappeared, it would be obvious that he was the grass, and his two brothers – who had no idea what Bobby was doing – would without-doubt bear the brunt of Ronnie's anger. Staying around and trying to look innocent was his only option, but the twins were becoming more and more suspicious of Bobby Teale and he was running out of time. He had already told the police that he was in mortal danger and asked them to spread some false information that would hopefully get back to the twins and take their focus off him – anything at all to protect him and his brothers from the wrath of the Kray twins, which was surely just around the corner.

Something was done; the police did act. They knew that all three Teale brothers were in danger of being killed and that, for their safety, they needed to be quickly removed from the situation. So, on 8 August, all three brothers were lured into a contrived set of circumstances by a character who called himself *Wallace,* and arrested on dubious charges of demanding money with menaces. Bobby Teale had a good idea of what was going on and why, but his two brothers had no clue and were completely baffled. All three Teale brothers would remain in prison until the twins were arrested and brought to trial two years later.

Less than a week after the Lea Bridge Road incident, Ronnie became involved in another confrontation with the police – but this time it was of a very different nature. Detective Sergeant Leonard Townshend, based at *Hackney Police Station*, came across Ronnie and several members of The Firm drinking in *The Bakers Arms* on Northiam Street, Hackney. Townshend clearly saw an opportunity to earn himself a little bit extra on the side, and put it to Ronnie that he and his friends could con-

tinue using the pub whenever they liked without any kind of interference from the police. That was, of course, if Ronnie was
happy to come to some kind of pecuniary arrangement. Ronnie
– seeing an opportunity to hit back at the police – agreed to the
idea in principle, explained that he needed to discuss the matter
with his brother, and promised to talk further a couple of evenings hence on Thursday 11 August.[209] Ronnie quickly sought
the help of private investigator George Devlin, and a plan was
hatched to trap the cheeky copper and cut him a big slice of
trouble.

Townshend arrived for the meeting – accompanied by a detective constable – and a discussion took place, the essence of
which was a demand for £50 a week to guarantee police-free
drinking in the pub. Little did Townshend know that Devlin
had rigged up a hidden microphone in Ronnie's jacket and the
whole conversation was captured on a concealed tape recorder.
After Townshend and the detective constable left, Ronnie and
company moved to the nearby *Kenton Arms* for a celebratory
drink.[210]

The next day, the incriminating tape was delivered to
Scotland Yard by the twins' solicitor and – with the help of
the landlord of *The Bakers Arms*, who agreed to be the go-between – Townshend was caught red-handed accepting money
on Monday 15 August. Townshend was immediately suspended from duty and there was nothing more for Ronnie to do except enjoy the moment and leave Townshend to his fate at the
hands of the Met's internal disciplinary department. Job done,
thought Ronnie, but he was wrong in thinking that this was the
end of the matter; there was more to come.

209 Bennett, John. *Krayology*. London: Mango Books, 2019.
210 Teale, David. *Surviving the Krays*. London: Ebury Press, 2021.

The Bakers Arms

75 Northiam Street, Hackney, London E9 7HX

Nearest TFL station: Cambridge Heath overground.

In the summer of 1966, the pub was adopted as a meeting place by the twins and The Firm. Ronnie was approached by a local policeman, Detective Sergeant Leonard Townshend, who offered Ronnie the assurance that he and his friends could continue to use the pub and would not be bothered by the police if money was paid to him. A later conversation confirming the arrangement, during which Ronnie was wearing a hidden microphone, was captured on tape and handed over to the police. Townshend was later caught in the act of accepting money and was immediately suspended from duty pending a court case.

After the conversation was successfully taped in *The Bakers Arms*, Ronnie and friends moved to *The Kenton Arms* to bask in their smugness and enjoy a celebratory drink.

The Bakers Arms opened in 1826 and was demolished in 1971. Modern housing now takes up the whole of Northiam Street but, happily, *The Kenton Arms* – also used by the Krays – is still open and trading. Situated around 20 minutes' walk from Northiam Street at 38 Kenton Road, the pub – now known simply as *The Kenton* – boasts '*a genuine Norwegian moose head*'… reason enough to visit.

On 13 September 1966, Ron, Reg, and Ian Barrie chartered

a flight and went to Tangier, Morocco to see their old friend Billy Hill, who was now spending most of his time there. This was not their first trip to Tangier; Ron had visited the city twice before and Reg had taken Frances for a short holiday in 1963. Both twins enjoyed foreign travel and had been abroad on many occasions, visiting several different countries already. Reggie took Frances to Greece, Spain, Italy, and France for short breaks, and Ronnie too had visited several foreign destinations including Africa, Spain, and Turkey.

Billy Hill, who shared a luxury apartment on the outskirts of the city with his girlfriend Gypsy, welcomed them. Billy arranged for the twins and Ian Barrie to stay in an apartment on the edge of Tangier, 100 yards from the beach, and after a few days they were joined by Reggie's new girlfriend Christine Boyce. Swimming, sunbathing, and relaxing was the order of the day, and sometimes they would drive in Billy Hill's white MG to Tangier's best hotel, the *El Minzah*, and spend the day around the hotel's outdoor swimming pool. Billy Hill's successful criminal career had left him sitting on a pile of cash and he was busy investing it in property in Tangier and elsewhere. He had recently bought a villa near the quiet fishing village of Marbella in southern Spain, planting a seed that would eventually blossom into Spain's *Costa del Crime.*

Billy also bought Tangier's biggest nightclub, *The Polo Room*, renamed it *Churchill's*, and gave it to girlfriend Gypsy to manage. Gypsy ran *Churchill's* nightclub from the opening night in July 1966 – said to have been attended by actor Kenneth Williams – until the mid-'70s. Tangier in the 1950s and '60s was not subject to the strict rules and regulations of other countries, and the relaxed and tolerant regime gave rise to a unique bohemian culture where all manner of illicit pleasures could be enjoyed.

Ronnie found the free and easy attitude towards homosexuality particularly appealing. Good-looking young Arab boys willing to sell *services* to Western men knew that there was much money to be made. Ronnie indulged himself to the full and fell in love with one particular boy he planned to take home to London. After around two weeks, the relaxing days in the sun and fun nights at *Churchill's* and other bars and clubs came to an abrupt end. *Scotland Yard* knew of the twins' whereabouts and contacted the authorities in Tangier; after which the chief of police appeared and, albeit reluctantly, explained that they'd been deemed undesirable aliens and had 24 hours to leave. Ian Barrie, Christine Boyce, Reg, and Ron – without the new love of his life – caught a scheduled flight back to London.

Tangier, Morocco

Between 1925 and 1956, Tangier was the centre of a part of Morocco called the *International Zone*; it was governed separately from the rest of French Morocco by a loose and complex amalgamation of countries including France, Spain, Britain, Portugal, the Netherlands, Belgium, and the USA. Due to a less than rigid rule of law and a relaxed and tolerant attitude towards homosexuality, drugs, and all other sinful pleasures, Tangier became a centre for smuggling and international espionage – and a mecca for artists, writers, musicians and, of course, criminals. Such freedoms and diversity created a unique, exotic, bohemian culture that inspired the likes of William Burroughs, Truman Capote, Allen Ginsberg, Francis Bacon, and the Rolling Stones. Morocco gained its independence from France in 1956 and Tangier came under the governance of Morocco. For several years after independence, Tangier retained much of its character and cultural identity, but by the mid-'70s the hedonistic *interzone years* were a thing of the past.

In the late summer of 1966, Ron and Reg – accompanied by Ian Barrie and Reggie's new girlfriend Christine Boyce – spent two weeks in Tangier in the company of their old friend Billy Hill and his girlfriend Gypsy. Billy Hill now spent most of his time in the Moroccan city and shared a luxury apartment with Gypsy at Boulevard Hassan II.

Tangier's biggest nightclub, *Churchill's*, was owned by Billy Hill and run by Gypsy until the mid-'70s. The twins spent evenings in the club located in the centre of Tangier, just outside the Medina and close to the Petit Socco (Small Square). Days were spent relaxing around the pool of the five-star *El Minzah Hotel*, located at 85 Rue de la Liberte and still very much there today.

After *Scotland Yard* informed the Moroccan authorities of the twins' presence in the city, Ron, Reg, Ian Barrie, and Christine Boyce were deemed as undesirable aliens and made to leave.

When the era known as the *interzone years* came to an end in the 1970s, Tangier went into a period of decline and became run-down, slightly dangerous, and unattractive to visitors. However, following a government programme beginning in 2010 to restore the city as a tourist destination, Tangier today is a vibrant, tourist-friendly place.

Arriving at London's *Heathrow Airport*, the twins half-expected to find a police reception committee waiting for them. There wasn't and, with some relief, the group collected their baggage and strolled out of the airport. There was, however, another problem with the police just around the corner. Sergeant Leonard Townshend had been summoned to appear in court on charges of corruption following his attempt to extort money from Ronnie in *The Bakers Arms* pub. Ronnie discovered, through his solicitors, that he would be called as a witness to give evidence in court; something he was not prepared to do. It was one thing dropping a copper in the proverbial, but giving evidence against someone in court – even a copper – was beyond the pale. Ronnie did not attend when Sergeant Townshend appeared at *Old Street Magistrates Court* on 13 December and pleaded not guilty to charges of corruption. Ronnie, however, was needed as the prime witness for the prosecution, and a warrant was issued on the same day, compelling him to attend court. With absolutely no intention of doing so, Ronnie went into hiding.[211]

Frank Mitchell knew both the twins from the different times they'd served along with him in *Wandsworth Prison*. Frank thought of both twins as his friends, but Ronnie – who had first befriended and looked out for Big Frank in jail in 1956 – was a special friend whom he idolised and trusted completely. Born in Canning Town in 1929, Frank spent most of his youth in and out of detention centres and borstals, usually for shop breaking and theft. By the time he reached adulthood, the die was cast and Frank was trapped in a life of criminality. Prison, reoffending, and more prison became his way of life. Within the prison system, Frank became notorious for his rebellion against authority and his violence towards prison officers and other prisoners. He was birched and flogged with the cat-o'-nine-tails for attacks on warders and, in 1955, he was certified insane.

After escaping from *Rampton Secure Mental Hospital* in 1957 and attacking a man in his home, Frank was sentenced to nine years. Within months he was recertified and, this time, sent to *Broadmoor*. However, in July 1958 he escaped again

---

211   Bennett, John. *Krayology*. London: Mango Books, 2016.

and held an elderly couple hostage in their home with an axe. Tom Bryant – journalist for *The Sunday People* and regular in *The Double R Club* – dubbed Mitchell *The Mad Axeman*, something Ronnie was none too pleased about, and he issued instructions that Bryant was to be ignored.[212]

In 1958, Frank was sentenced to life imprisonment and sent to *Hull Prison* where, in 1962, he was birched for slashing a prison officer. Later that year, he was sent to *Dartmoor*. During his time in *Dartmoor*, Frank's behaviour changed for the better and the scourge of the prison system became a calm, compliant, model prisoner, due in no small way to the sympathetic ear lent to him by the prison governor. Frank had not been given a release date, and the governor promised to speak to the Home Office and see what he could do. In the meantime, Frank would be treated as a trusted prisoner and, in September 1966, he became part of the minimally supervised Honour Party – prisoners who were allowed outside the prison to work on the moor, mainly repairing fencing and *Dartmoor*'s granite dry stone walls. Such trust was put in prisoners to demonstrate their suitability for release, but still there was no release date for Frank.

HMP Dartmoor

Princetown, Devon PL20 6RR

High on Dartmoor, the granite walls of the prison at Princetown dominate the surrounding landscape and provide a foreboding and eerie sight on a misty day. Construction began in 1806 and the prison was opened in 1809, with the purpose of holding French prisoners of

---

212 Fawcett, Micky. *Krazy Days*. Brighton: Pen Press, 2013.

the Napoleonic Wars. After 1812, the French were joined by American sailors; prisoners of the concurrently running American War. When all hostilities ceased in 1815, the prisoners were repatriated and the building remained unused for the next 35 years.

In 1850, the prison was partially rebuilt and recommissioned for use as a high-security civilian prison. Frank Mitchell – dubbed by the newspapers as *The Mad Axeman* – was among Britain's most notorious and rebellious prisoners, but after being sent to *Dartmoor* in 1962, his behaviour gradually improved. Eventually, by 1966, Mitchell had earned the trust of the prison's governors and he became a member of the Honour Party; a small group of loosely supervised trustees allowed to work outside the prison. Ron and Reg Kray made arrangements for Mitchell's escape and, on 12 December 1966, he absconded from the Honour Party, met two members of The Firm at a pre-arranged spot, and was driven to a hideout in East London.

In 2002, *Dartmoor* became a category C prison for less violent offenders. It was announced in 2019 that *HMP Dartmoor* would close in 2023, but plans were revised and it was later confirmed that the prison would remain open for the foreseeable future.

Dartmoor Prison Museum – once the prison's dairy – is open to the public seven days a week, and the interesting collection of artefacts provides a fascinating insight into prison life over the past 200 years.

Frank was a huge, good-looking, powerful man, immensely strong with a magnificent physique that he kept toned by performing hundreds of press-ups in his cell each day. Prison officers were wary of Frank and treated him with respect, knowing that should his behaviour change and he once again became the Frank of old, they would have a very difficult situation on their hands.

Personality-wise, Frank was different, considered by some to have the mental age of a 13-year-old boy. He was placid and childlike if people were nice to him and he was happy, but he was subject to temper tantrums and capable of extreme violence when he wasn't. Frank kept and tended to budgerigars in his cell, and spent time exercising and making models. When out with the Honour Party on the moor, he and the others could be left unsupervised for hours, and Frank would regularly visit the nearby pubs for a few pints. On one occasion, he phoned for a taxi to take him to Tavistock to buy a new budgie. Money sent to him by the twins was plentiful, and it is said that he met a woman in one of the pubs and they would have sex in a nearby farm building. All in all, for a prisoner, life wasn't too bad for Frank, but he desperately needed a release date. Be it soon or be it not, he just needed a date to keep despair at bay and enable him to focus his mind on the future. But still none came.

The Elephant's Nest Inn

Horndon, Mary Tavy, Tavistock, Devon PL19 9NQ

From September 1966 until his escape on 12 December, Frank Mitchell – *The Mad Axeman* – worked outside *Dartmoor Prison* with a small group of loosely guarded trustees called the Honour Party. Usually in the company of another prisoner, Mitchell regularly visited two local pubs close to where the Honour Party was working: *The Elephant's Nest Inn* and *The Peter Tavy Inn*. Each pub was visited once or twice a week and Mitchell would stay for around 45 minutes; he would down a few pints and, with money provided by the Krays, buy bottles of spirits, wine, beer, and cigarettes to take away. On one occasion, on 29 November, Mitchell phoned for a taxi from *The Elephant's Nest Inn*, which arrived at the pub and took him to Tavistock to buy a budgerigar.

Sadly, *The Elephant's Nest Inn*, dating back to the 15th century, did not reopen as a public house when lockdown restrictions were finally lifted in 2021. Hopefully, this is a temporary measure, and *The Elephant's Nest* – currently operating as a bed and breakfast hotel – will one day reopen its doors to locals and thirsty travellers.

Around two miles from *The Elephant's Nest* is the other pub visited by Frank Mitchell during this time. The charming 15th-century *Peter Tavy Inn* in the pretty village of Peter Tavy – two miles north of Tavistock on the Okehampton Road – is still very much open for business. (Peter Tavy, Tavistock PL19 9NN.)

Throughout the summer of 1966, Ron and Reg had been sending members of The Firm to visit Frank in *Dartmoor Prison*, and when word came back of his growing despair at not having received a release date, a plan was hatched to spring Frank from prison. The rather bizarre scheme was contrived to bring the attention of Frank's plight to the public and demand that the government give Frank a release date; after which he would give himself up and return to prison to finish his sentence. Quite why the ill-thought-through plan was hatched is something of a mystery. It is possible that Ronnie, in one of his ever-changing moods, felt sorry for his friend and possibly saw an opportunity to vent his anger against authority, highlight yet another injustice within the system, and garner the respect and admiration of the criminal fraternity.

On Monday 12 December 1966, Frank Mitchell was out on the moor with the Honour Party, repairing a fence on *Bagga Tor*. Due to the poor weather, the half-dozen convicts – under the supervision of just one guard – spent most of the day sheltering and drinking tea in a hut. Mitchell, at some point in the late morning, asked permission to go and feed the Dartmoor ponies in a field some distance away. This was not an unusual request from Frank, and he was told that he could do what he wanted – providing he made sure to be at the usual meeting point in good time for the pick-up later that afternoon. When the rest of the Honour Party arrived at the pick-up point at 4.20pm, the transport was there waiting but there was no sign of Frank.

Hours earlier, Frank had made his way to a pre-arranged meeting point at a phone box close to *The Elephant's Nest* pub and found Teddy Smith and Albert Donoghue there waiting for him. Mitchell climbed inside the hired grey Humber Hawk and the three men were back within the borders of London before the car radio broadcast a newsflash - that the 37-year-old *Mad Axeman* had escaped. Television news showed footage of Royal Marines from their nearby base at Lympstone – and a helicopter from the *Royal Naval Air Station Culdrose* in Cornwall – searching the moor for the dangerous fugitive. But they were too late: Frank was long gone, safely ensconced in a flat in East London.

Lennie 'Books' Dunn ran a stall in the Whitechapel Road selling new and second-hand paperback books and magazines – including the popular, mildly pornographic, men-only publications of the day. Lennie was in awe of the Krays and did what he could to ingratiate himself into their circle, enabling him to boast that he knew Ron and Reg well. In fact, the twins hardly noticed Lennie – other than to register him, along with all the other sycophants, as someone who could be used if the need arose. Dunn, having split up with his wife, lived alone in a flat in East Ham, and when he was approached by Reg and offered £500 to put-up Frank Mitchell in his flat for a few days, he was more than happy to oblige.

Frank took the main bedroom of the small ground-floor flat and the other was used by various members of The Firm, taking turns to stay and keep Frank company until it was decided what would happen next. Lennie Dunn had to make do with the settee. Frank was a little disappointed with the arrangements, having expected a hero's welcoming party with his good friends, the twins, there to greet him, but all he found awaiting him was a poky flat with a few strangers in attendance, giving him repeated messages that the twins would be along to see him in good time.

Much to their dissatisfaction, Albert Donoghue, Jack Dickson, and ex-boxer Billy Exley were given the job of staying at the flat on a rota – and making sure that at least one of them was there at all times to look after Frank and keep him company. Lennie Dunn did the cooking and, between them, the three Firm members did what they could to keep Frank amused. Card games and listening to music helped pass some of the time, and Frank would exercise constantly, breaking off from time to time to obsessively clean his teeth. By midweek, Frank was becoming increasingly frustrated by the twins' failure to show up, and troubled by the growing feeling that he'd just swapped one cell for another.

Ronnie Kray, meanwhile – to avoid being arrested and forced to appear in court as a witness against DS Townshend in *The Bakers Arms* case – was holed-up in a flat in Finchley, drinking heavily, listening to recordings of Churchill's wartime speeches, and working on his list of people who needed to be killed. Ronnie's plan was to remain in hiding until the case was heard and the warrant for his arrest expired. Eventually, after a few days, Reggie put in a brief appearance at the Barking Road flat, apologised for not having come earlier, and explained the reason for Ronnie's absence. Reggie assured Frank that Ronnie would be coming along just as soon as he could. This made no sense to Frank; Ronnie was his best friend and he saw no reason why he couldn't make the trip to see him now.

After a week, Mad Teddy Smith – who fancied himself as a bit of a wordsmith – arrived to help Frank compose a letter to the newspapers. Teddy Smith dictated, and Frank – who was barely literate – painstakingly, wrote the words down on paper. After several failed attempts the letters were completed, marked with Frank's fingerprint, and posted on Monday 19 December: one to the *Daily Mirror* and one to *The Times*. The letter, which told of Mitchell's *unhappy plight* and his willingness to give himself up if only he would be given a release date, appeared on the front page of the *Daily Mirror* on Wednesday December 21.

Reggie had promised to send Frank some female company and he was becoming impatient. He wanted a *bird* and declared that if the twins didn't send one soon, he would go out and find one for himself. Mitchell's demands were beginning to annoy the twins, and his ever-darkening moods were unsettling his minders. Female company, therefore, needed to be found with some urgency, and would hopefully be the solution to keeping Frank calm and happy – for a while, at least.

Firm member Tommy Cowley was a regular at *Winston's* nightclub,[213] and knew many of the hostesses who worked there. Lisa Prescott, a well-built, attractive blonde woman from Leeds, was singled out as the perfect partner for Frank. Lisa was told by Reggie that she would have the gratitude and respect of everyone in the East End – and, of course, a generous financial reward – if she would look after the needs of a friend

---

213 Owned by Bruce Brace and protected by gangster Billy Howard, *Winston's* was situated at 10 Clifford Street in Mayfair.

for a few days. Despite feeling somewhat press-ganged, Lisa agreed and was taken in a taxi – accompanied by Reggie, Tom Cowley, and Albert Donoghue – straight from *Winston's* to the Barking Road flat, arriving at 3am on Tuesday 20 December. Lisa quickly realised who Frank was but decided to proceed with the arrangement; a decision possibly made a little easier by the fact that Frank was an extremely handsome chap. Frank was clearly thrilled to see the lovely lady, and the two of them enjoyed drinks and a getting-to-know-you chat for about an hour before disappearing into the bedroom together and closing the door.

Apart from a quick escorted trip home for a change of clothes, Lisa would remain at the flat for the next four days, most of which was spent in the bedroom. Lisa's arrival had the desired effect and Frank was calm and content for a while, but after a couple of days, he once again became agitated and annoyed about his confinement – and the fact that Ronnie still hadn't been to see him.

When Frank received word from the twins that, now that the letters were sent, he should think about giving himself up, he became angry. Frank declared that the twins should tell him themselves and, if they didn't come to see him very soon, he would go to Vallance Road to see them. The twins took this as a threat. Frank was like a caged tiger and everyone in the Barking Road flat was tense, nervous, and living on tenterhooks. Albert Donoghue had better things to do than babysit a dangerous maniac; Jack Dickson's plans to go home to Scotland for Christmas had been scotched by Ronnie; Billy Exley was sick and tired of being used by the twins; and Lennie Dunn hadn't received the money he was promised – and he never would. There was only one positive: Lisa was a great cook and the food was much improved.

Frank announced that he would not remain cooped-up for much longer; he wanted to see his family and he wanted to have a drink in a pub. But, most worryingly, he was now saying that he would never give himself up and that he would kill anyone who tried to stand in his way. It was now clear to both twins that their over-hasty, ill-considered plan to spring Mitchell had been a big mistake. Nothing had come of the letters to the newspapers, and he was now making threats and refusing to give himself up under any circumstances. Mitchell was fast becoming a liability, and his behaviour was threatening to expose the twins' involvement in his escape.

Something had to be done quickly to make this problem go away and, following a meeting between the twins, Charlie, and Freddie Foreman at Harry Hopwood's flat, it was decided that the only viable solution was to make Mitchell go away – permanently. In the meantime, the twins needed to keep a lid on the situation and word was sent to reassure Frank that plans were in hand and everything was going to be just fine. All Frank needed to do was remain patient and calm for just a little while longer.

It was Christmas Eve 1966, 12 days after Frank Mitchell's escape from *Dartmoor Prison*. Albert Donoghue, the most trusted of Frank's minders, arrived at the Barking Road flat and explained that a van would be arriving later that evening to take Frank to the country to join Ronnie in a safe house, where they would spend Christmas together.

By now, Mitchell had fallen in love with Lisa and insisted that she was to come along with him. Lisa had grown fond of Frank and felt sorry for him, but she certainly didn't love him and wanted very much to go home and return to her own life. Eventually, Frank was persuaded that it would be safer for Lisa not to travel with him and that she would be brought along to join him later.

Albert Donoghue returned to the flat at 8pm the same evening and told Frank, who was packed and ready, that there was a van waiting around the corner to take him to the country to see Ronnie. Once again, Frank insisted that Lisa was to come with him and, once again, he was talked into letting Lisa follow on later. Frank gave Lisa a long kiss farewell, said good-bye to the others, and then followed Albert to the waiting van in Ladysmith Avenue.

Just after leaving the flat, nerves jangled as Frank and Albert saw a policeman on his beat, walking towards them. Much to their relief, however, the policeman strolled past the two men and continued on his way. Jeremiah Callaghan, a South London gangster, opened the rear doors to the van and ushered Frank inside, where he found Alfie Gerrard and Freddie Foreman sitting on a wheel arch. Frank was greeted and told to sit on the opposite wheel arch.[214]

Albert Donoghue was asked to give directions to the Blackwall Tunnel, so he climbed up-front so he could speak to the driver. Callaghan closed the rear doors and climbed into the passenger seat.[215] Almost immediately after setting off, Gerrard and Foreman produced guns and fired a volley of bullets into Frank's body. Despite being riddled with bullets, Frank appeared to still be alive, so Freddie Foreman performed the *coup de grâce* and finished Frank with two or three more shots to the head. There ended the sad and tragic life of Frank Samuel Mitchell, *The Mad Axeman.*

---

214 The police believed that the driver and fourth member of the team was Freddie Foreman's good friend, Ronnie Oliffe. Callaghan, Gerrard, and Oliffe did not appear at the Frank Mitchell murder trial at the *Old Bailey*, as all three could not be found.

215 Donoghue, Albert and Short, Martin. *The Krays' Lieutenant*. London: Smith Gryphon, 1995.

Barking Road Flat

206a Barking Road, East Ham, London E6 3BB

Nearest TFL station: Upton Park underground.

After escaping from *Dartmoor Prison* on 12 December 1966, Frank Mitchell was hidden by the twins in the small ground-floor council flat owned by Lennie 'Books' Dunn for 12 days. Within a short time, Mitchell grew unhappy with his incarceration in the tiny flat – and with the fact that Ronnie Kray had not been to see him. Frank became agitated and began issuing threats that he would break out and kill anyone who tried to stop him. Ron and Reg realised they had made a mistake in springing *The Mad Axeman* from jail and decided to solve the problem by having him killed. On Christmas Eve 1966, Frank Mitchell was led to a van parked around the corner in Ladysmith Avenue, under the pretence that it was going to take him to the country to spend Christmas with Ronnie. Once inside the van, Mitchell was shot to death by two South London gunmen. His body was never found.

Situated about 15 minutes' walk from Upton Park tube station, the early 1960s-built low-rise block of flats occupies a position on the corner of Barking Road and Ladysmith Avenue.

Travelling along Ladysmith Avenue, the van turned right into Central Park Road and then right again and back onto Barking Road, where it pulled up for Albert Donoghue to get out. Having witnessed the murder, Albert Donoghue walked towards the flat half-expecting to receive a bullet in the back, but – much to his relief – this didn't happen. Donoghue phoned Reggie and said, "*That dog won*"– code to confirm that the deed had been done. Having heard several bangs as the van pulled away, it was clear to all what had happened, and Lisa – who was shocked and distraught – could not be consoled by the dismissal of the bangs as a car backfiring.

Next, Albert Donoghue, Jack Dickson, Lennie Dunn, and Lisa set about cleaning the flat to remove any possible evidence of Frank's presence. Once the work was done, Connie Whitehead arrived to take Albert and Lisa to Sammy Lederman's flat in Whitechapel to report to Reggie. Prior to Whitehead arriving, Albert Donoghue explained to Lisa that she must not mention hearing any *bangs,* otherwise she too would be in danger of being killed. Despite her shocked and terrified emotional state, Lisa performed well during Reggie's grilling, and after being told in no uncertain terms that harm would come to her if she spoke to anyone about Frank Mitchell, now or at any time in the future, she was given a bag of money.

Lisa was taken along to a party held at the home of Winnie Harwood on Evering Road, Stoke Newington. Winnie Harwood was a friend of The Firm and lived at number 113, just a few doors along from the basement flat that, less than a year later, would become the scene of the brutal murder of Jack 'The Hat' McVitie. Lisa spent the night with Albert Donoghue, and the next morning she was driven home by Connie Whitehead – who warned her once again of the danger she'd be in if she spoke to anyone about the events of the previous evening.

In his 1996 autobiography *Respect* with John Lisners, Freddie Foreman admits to shooting Mitchell at the behest of the Krays, and tells how his body was taken to Newhaven, wrapped in chicken wire, weighted down, and dumped in the English Channel.

After the murders of George Cornell and Frank Mitchell,

some of the long-standing members of The Firm and friends of the twins began to dissociate themselves and drift away. Billy Donovan, Micky Fawcett, Limehouse Willy, Bobby Ramsey, Johnny Davis, and Johnny Squibb are some of the names heard less at this point in the twins' story. Leslie Payne also cut ties and distanced himself from the twins. Big Pat Connolly and Tommy 'The Bear' Brown took a back seat, and the ever-loyal Billy Frost and Teddy Smith disappeared altogether.

Ron and Reg were always on the lookout for new blood. Ex-soldier and dock labourer Ronnie Bender, a big powerful man with no previous criminal record, joined The Firm in the mid-'60s. Ronnie Hart, an ex-merchant seaman, petty criminal and family relation turned up at the twins' door one day and asked to join their gang. Hart, who was looking for excitement and adventure in his life, was taken on and became a key member of The Firm. Partnered with Albert Donoghue, Hart was actively involved in Kray business during The Firm's latter years. Hart's grandmother was sister to the twins' maternal grandmother, Mary Ann, and although he was in fact a second cousin to the twins, nine years their junior, he referred to them both as *uncle*.

Chris Lambrianou, born in 1938, was the eldest of five brothers from a Greek Cypriot/Irish family and, along with his younger brother Tony, had gained a reputation for violence and criminality in the Dalston and Haggerston areas of the East End. Inevitably, the brothers attracted the attention of the twins, and when Tony was released from prison in November 1966 after serving two years of a 30-month sentence for attempting to rob a Wimpy Bar, he became a junior member of The Firm. Chris was very much an independent operator but, by early 1967, he too had formed an association with the Krays.

Another very important character in the story of the Krays emerged in the mid-'60s. After his release from prison in November 1965, Jack 'The Hat' McVitie began working for the twins on an occasional basis. McVitie would never become a full member of The Firm, but he was a tough and violent character who the twins kept around as a useful pair of hands – or fists – if required.

Born in 1932, Jack Dennis McVitie had been involved in crime since his teenage years and had served time in *Borstal* and six years in prison for possessing explosives and weapons. Jack 'The Hat' was heavily built and heavily tattooed (by the standards of the day) and gained his nickname on account of the fact that he was never seen without the trilby hat he wore to hide his baldness. Many of his contemporaries spoke highly of Jack – who possessed a devil-may-care attitude to life and liked to enjoy himself – but his penchant for amphetamines and alcohol often led to outrageous and sometimes violent behaviour in pubs and clubs that would annoy members of the criminal fraternity and shock regular folk. When off his head on booze and drugs, which was much of the time, Jack was a loose cannon, causing havoc and thoughtlessly shooting his mouth off wherever he went – exactly the kind of behaviour that could get him in trouble.

One of the jobs given to McVitie by the twins was the pedalling of *pep pills* and, with such easy access to an endless supply, he developed a serious habit. During the mid-'60s, the use of amphetamine pills with street names such as Purple Hearts, Dexies, and Black Bombers became popular with the young and played a big part in the emerging *Mod* culture. Prior to the mid-'60s, amphetamine pills were marketed as a pick-me-up or an aid to weight loss and could be bought over the counter. After new laws were introduced in 1964, they became available by prescription only and criminals stepped in to supply the ever-growing demand. Pharmaceutical warehouses and chemists were robbed, and it is said that the twins were involved with an illegal drug factory in Essex, churning the pills out by the thousand.[216]

Home of Jack 'The Hat' McVitie

42 Hartland Road, Newham, East London E15 4AH

Nearest TFL station: Maryland (Elizabeth Line)

Jack McVitie was released from prison in November 1965 after serving six years for unlawful possession of

---

216 Pearson, John. *The Profession of Violence*. London: Weidenfeld and Nicolson, 1972.

explosives and possessing a flick knife. Following his release, he moved into the Victorian terraced house in Stratford with his girlfriend Sylvia Barnard, and later they were joined by a baby daughter. Unlike his portrayal by actor Tom Bell in the first Krays movie starring the Kemp brothers, Jack was a big, powerful, dangerous character – just a year older than the twins – liked and feared in equal measure. Sylvia saw Jack for the last time on the late afternoon of Saturday 28 October 1967, when he left the house, never to return. She waited two weeks before going to *West Ham Police Station* and reporting Jack as a missing person.

Jack 'The Hat' McVitie's former home is 13 minutes' walk from Maryland station or 16 minutes from Plaistow underground station.

By 1967, Alan Bruce Cooper – known as 'ABC' or 'The Yank' – had, to some extent, taken Leslie Payne's place as the brains of the Kray organisation. Stolen bearer bonds supplied by the American Mafia were still flowing with regularity across the Atlantic, and Cooper was the man who turned them into hard cash for the Krays. Cooper was a 40-something American citizen who, by the 1960s, had clearly made a great deal of money and was living and operating in Europe. He had flats in various European cities and his home in London was a luxurious apartment at *Campden Hill Court* in Holland Park, where he lived with his beautiful wife Beverley, young daughter Leslie, and Sam, their Yorkshire Terrier.[217]

London-based business was conducted from an office at the European Exchange Bank in Dean Street, and another in

217   Pearson, John. *Notorious*. London: Century Publishing, 2010.

Albemarle Street – to which he would travel in his chauffeur-driven Rolls-Royce Silver Cloud. Cooper was something of an enigma, and exactly how he operated and made his money is a mystery, but it was certainly criminal; gold smuggling, narcotics, arms dealing, and the international trade in stolen securities and forged currency were just some of the activities within his portfolio of nefarious business interests. Cooper spoke with a noticeable stutter, and his physical appearance gave no clue as to how he lived his life; he was small in stature and slight of build, with thinning hair and a wispy moustache. It may be that he knowingly used his lack of inches and unimposing presence to his advantage, enabling him to stay under the radar, go unnoticed by potential enemies, and move with stealth through the world of big-time crime. Clever and canny Cooper surely was, and he knew that his method of covert criminality might not always be enough to prevent him from becoming prey to other criminals. He needed a little insurance, and what better way to get it than cosying up to the most feared and dangerous exponents of violence in London?

Ronnie was mesmerised by the enigmatic American with a seemingly encyclopaedic knowledge of organised crime, and impressed by his big, way-out money-making schemes – among which was a fully worked-out plan to kidnap the Pope. Cooper played along with Ronnie's homicidal fantasies and suggested that the formation of a worldwide murder syndicate could become a reality; in fact, it could be called *Murder International*.

Reggie and Charlie had reservations and didn't fully trust Cooper, who had appeared out of nowhere and was seemingly intent on ingratiating himself into their world. When Cooper first came on the scene there was probably no reason not to trust him but, later on, something happened to justify Reg and Charlie's misgivings; Cooper was *turned* and began working for the police.

366

In early 1967, Cooper and his father-in-law David Nathan were arrested for their involvement in the production and distribution of LSD. Admiral John Hanley, a senior member of the US Secret Service based at the American Embassy in Paris, was responsible for monitoring the Mafia's activities in Europe. Intelligence gathering revealed a connection between the Mafia and the Kray twins in London. When Hanley received a report that Cooper, an American citizen, had been arrested in the UK, he recognised Cooper's name as an associate of the Krays with Mafia connections.

Hanley saw an opportunity and contacted Deputy Assistant Commissioner John Du Rose at *Scotland Yard* to suggest a joint operation to infiltrate the Kray gang and the Mafia. Consequently, Cooper was made an offer that he would find very difficult to refuse. His father-in-law would be charged with narcotics offences, but Cooper was given another option: either face similar charges with the likelihood of a long prison sentence, or go to work as an undercover agent for Uncle Sam and the Queen. Predictably, Cooper chose the latter.[218] When, later in the year, Nipper Read began his investigation into the Krays, Du Rose failed to tell him that he had Cooper in his pocket; something Read would not discover until Cooper was arrested the following year in 1968.

Cooper was walking a tightrope without a net; whichever way he fell would mean disaster. If he was unable to prove his worth as a double agent, he was in big trouble, and if the twins began to suspect he was a spy, he was in even bigger trouble.

Having let slip that he'd been involved in arms dealing, Cooper was faced with demands from Ron to provide some hardware for Murder International. Ron wanted some assurance that Cooper wasn't just talk; he wanted to see some guns.

---

218   Pearson, John. *Notorious*. London: Century Publishing, 2010.

After discussing the situation with John Du Rose, the DAC agreed to provide Cooper with a couple of .32 Mauser automatics – but the guns would first need to be immobilised and rendered harmless by removing part of the firing mechanism. It is said that the twins were also in possession of two machine guns. Accounts vary and the guns have been named as Browning, Thompson, Sten, and Bren guns, but if they came via Du Rose, it is likely that they were Sterling submachine guns; the semi-automatic Mark 6 version was issued to police forces in the 1960s.

Ever since Reggie's wife Frances had left him in 1965 and returned to live with her parents, Reggie had continued to visit her at the Shea's house in Ormsby Street, convinced it was just a matter of time before she would come back to him. Both of Frances' parents now hated Reggie and he was not allowed into the house. Instead, he would stand outside on the pavement and talk to Frances as she leaned out of her bedroom window. Despite this, nothing was changing, and Reggie – who was used to getting everything he wanted – was becoming ever more frustrated and unhappy. Frances even more so; she just wanted to be left alone to forget the ordeal of her disastrous marriage. There were occasional lighter moments when Reggie even made Frances smile, but she was emotionally fragile, damaged by the relationship, and deeply depressed.

On 17 October 1966, Frances was admitted to *St Leonard's Hospital* after taking an overdose of barbiturates bought from a street dealer. On 30 January 1967, she attempted suicide a second time – this time barricading herself in the front room at Ormsby Street and turning on the gas from the fire after swallowing a large quantity of barbiturates. Frances' father found her just in time to save her life and, once again, she was hospitalised.

At this point, Frances' brother Frank stepped in and suggested that Frances come to live with him, his common-law wife *Bubbles,* and their baby daughter in their flat, less than a mile away at *Wimbourne Court.* Frank was desperate to help his little sister and also his parents, who he could see were at the end of their tethers and close to utter despair. Frances adored her little niece – also called Frances – and, Frank thought, perhaps leaving Ormsby Street, with all its unhappy past associations, would help bring a little light into his sister's life, lifting her spirits and enabling her to look to the future.

Frances, who had by now changed her name by deed poll back to Shea, moved into the flat at *Wimbourne Court* in the spring of 1967 and, on the surface at least, she seemed a little happier. Frank, by this time, had fallen out with Reggie, who had borrowed £1,000 from him and was refusing to pay it back. There was some tension between the two men, but Reggie would visit regularly and Frances seemed happy enough to let him. Reggie even managed to persuade Frances to agree to a holiday together on the island of Ibiza, and booked the tickets with a travel agent. Frances was completely broken and had nothing left – not even the strength to do anything other than go along with whatever Reggie said. There were no choices left for Frances; there was only one option available to end her agony and, on 7 June 1967, she took it.

Frances appeared to be sleeping when her brother Frank took her a cup of tea in the morning and left it on her bedside table before going out. Returning at lunchtime, Frank found Frances just as he had left her, the tea untouched and stone cold. Frances' third attempt at suicide was tragically successful; she had died, aged just 23, after taking a massive overdose of phenobarbitone sleeping pills.

Wimbourne Court

Flat 34, 59 Wimbourne St, London N1 7HD

Nearest TFL station: Old Street underground.

Following the break-up of her marriage to Reggie Kray in 1965, Frances moved back to her parents' home in Ormsby Street, Hoxton. Frances had long suffered from an emotional disorder but her mental health had worsened significantly after just a few months of marriage to Reggie Kray. In October 1966, and again in January 1967, Frances attempted to take her own life by swallowing large quantities of tranquillisers. In the spring of 1967, Frances moved into her brother Frank's *Wimbourne Court* flat, which he shared with his partner *Bubbles* and their baby daughter. The hope was that a change of scenery would help lift Frances' spirits, but it was to no avail and she attempted suicide for a third time. This time, after taking a huge quantity of sleeping pills, she sadly succeeded – 23-year-old Frances was found dead in bed by her brother Frank on 7 June 1967.

Wimbourne Court is an early 1960s-built 11-storey apartment block on the *Wenlock Barn Estate* in Shoreditch. Getting there by tube means a 15-minute walk from Old Street, the nearest underground station. Taking the bus is perhaps a better option, as Mintern Street bus stop (Stop XQ) is just a two-minute walk from *Wimbourne Court*.

Frances' death obviously came as a huge blow to Reggie, and his anguish was all-consuming, but rather than bonding with the Shea family in shared grief, he turned his pain into anger and blamed them for Frances' death. In Reggie's eyes, they had turned their daughter against him and it was them and only them who were responsible for the tragedy. Reggie was incapable of accepting responsibility for any of the ills in his life; no matter how big or small, the blame always lay with someone else and they would become the focus of his anger. Reggie's egocentric personality and innate lack of empathy for anyone was key to his success as a feared gangster, but in this instance, the focal point of his self-serving hatred was a shattered family who had lost their baby daughter.

Reggie proceeded to plunder all of Frances' possessions from the *Wimbourne Court* flat: clothes, trinkets, letters, photographs, bank book, the lot. Frances' family had no right to any of it, he thought; he was her husband and everything belonged to him. The Shea family's wish for a quiet family funeral was completely disregarded and Reggie set about arranging a spectacular display of public mourning, befitting of the beloved wife of a man of his status. Funeral arrangements were made with *Hayes & English Funeral Directors* in Hoxton and the service, conducted by the twins' old friend Father Hetherington, was held at the *Church of St James The Great* on Bethnal Green Road. Father Hetherington had, of course, refused to perform the marriage ceremony less than two years earlier, believing that the liaison would lead to unhappiness and eventual disaster. He was right.

Hayes & English Funeral Directors

148 Hoxton Street, London N1 6SH

Nearest TFL station: Hoxton overground.

In June 1967, 23-year-old Frances Shea sadly committed suicide, and the funeral arrangements were made with *Hayes & English*. Reggie decided that his wife was to be buried wearing her wedding dress; Frances' mother Elsie persuaded the funeral directors to dress Frances in a slip and a pair of tights so that the hated dress would not touch her skin. Elsie was also able to ensure that her wedding ring was removed and replaced with a ring that Frances wore as a young girl.

The Hayes family and the English family were both established funeral directors when they formed a partnership in the early 20th century, and their premise on Hoxton Street – still there today – dates back to the 1930s.

Reggie bought a plot in *Chingford Mount Cemetery*, and an expensive Italian marble headstone. He also decided that Frances was to be buried in her wedding dress – and, despite the fact that Frances had changed her name back to Shea, she was his wife and therefore the headstone would bear the name Kray.

Among the solemn-faced gangsters dominating the graveside scene were a number of police officers mingling with the mourners in the hope that Ronnie would show up. Ronnie was still in hiding and smart enough not to be caught like this, so he merely sent a large wreath of carnations. Reggie gave Albert

Donoghue the task of checking to see who had sent floral trib-
utes and, more importantly, who hadn't; something Donoghue
would later describe as "*pretty sick.*" Reggie wept openly as
Frances' coffin was lowered into the grave, and when the first
spadeful of earth thumped against the casket lid, he tipped the
gravediggers and walked away.

Leonard 'Nipper' Read's continuing successful police career took an upward turn when, in the summer of 1967, he was
promoted to Superintendent and posted to the elite Murder
Squad. DSI Read left *West End Central Police Station* to
take his place at *New Scotland Yard*; the headquarters of the
Metropolitan Police. At the age of 42, he had achieved his ambition and made it to where he wanted to be – but his elation
was short-lived.

Just a few days after his promotion, Read's happiness evap-
orated when he was told by Assistant Commissioner Peter
Brodie, "*Mr Read, you're going to get the Krays.*" Having tried
and failed once before to nail the East End gangster twins, Read
was fully aware of the seemingly insurmountable difficulties of
the mission before him. Nevertheless, deflated but determined,
Read began making preparations to begin the laborious task of
finding a chink in the twins' armour. Corruption was rife in the
Met at this time, and Read knew that one of the many problems
he faced was keeping the investigation a secret – and preventing information from being fed back to the twins.

Nipper consulted the file on the Krays and was amazed
to find that no additional information had been added since
his own investigation that had ended with the McCowan trial
in the spring of 1965 – not one single scrap of new information. There was no record of Detective Superintendent James
Axon's initial investigation into the murder of George Cornell,
in which Ronnie Kray was the chief suspect. No record of
Tommy Butler's follow-up investigation, during which he had

arrested the twins and put them on an identification parade in August 1966. And there was no record of Bobby Teale passing information to Butler's team between March and August 1966, something Read wouldn't find out about until the Krays' trial in 1969. There was also nothing in the file added by Detective Superintendent Ferguson Walker, who had later been put in charge of the investigation by DAC John Du Rose.

It appears that Nipper Read's concerns about an *enemy within* were justified. In his 2019 book, *Krays: The Final Word*, Nipper Read's biographer James Morton reveals that Ferguson Walker was corrupt and passing information to the Krays.

New Scotland Yard (current location)

Victoria Embankment, London SW1A 2JL

Nearest TFL station: Westminster underground.

In the summer of 1967, DCI Leonard 'Nipper' Read was promoted to Superintendent, given an office on the 17th floor of the *New Scotland Yard* building, and told – much to his disappointment – that his first task was to *get the Krays.*

Nipper Read's posting came just as the Met moved headquarters into a new 22-storey, steel-clad and glass building at 8-10 Broadway, Westminster, London SW1H 0BG, near *St James's Park*. Between 1890 and 1967, *Scotland Yard* occupied buildings on the Victoria Embankment overlooking the Thames. The first of the two distinctive Victorian Romanesque buildings in banded redbrick and white Portland stone, designed by architect Norman Shaw, was completed in 1890 and the second in 1906. The two buildings were linked by a bridge over what was then a public road. A third building, designed by architect William Curtis Green, was added in 1940. When *Scotland Yard* was moved in 1967, the two redbrick buildings known as the *Norman Shaw Buildings* were refurbished and, from 1979 to the present, used as parliamentary offices. The 1940 *Curtis Green Building* was retained by the police and became a sub-HQ for the force's territorial department.

In 2016, the police moved out of the 1967 building and it was demolished. Six modern apartment, office, and retail buildings known as *The Broadway Development* – completed in 2022 – now occupy the site.

After the 1967 building was vacated by the Met, the refurbished and extended 1940 *Curtis Green Building* on Victoria Embankment became, and is still today, the home of *New Scotland Yard*. The iconic revolving *New Scotland Yard* sign, brought from the 1967 building, can be seen today outside *Scotland Yard*'s much downsized current location.

Overseeing Read's investigation was Deputy Assistant Commissioner John Du Rose. *Four-Day Johnny* was a bit of a legend among the Met's detectives, and so-called because of his reputation for solving murder cases within that time. Du Rose understood Read's concerns about information being leaked to the Krays, and granted his request to conduct the investigation away from *Scotland Yard*, across the river at *Tintagel House*. It would be some time before the twins would meet DSI Read again – but meet him again they surely would.

Tintagel House

92 Albert Embankment, London SE1 7TY

Nearest TFL station: Vauxhall underground.

Detective Superintendent Read needed to keep his investigation into the Krays secret for as long as possible – away from the eyes and ears of corrupt police officers in the pay of the twins, and away from the rumour mill that was *Scotland Yard*. Consequently, Nipper Read was given permission to use *Tintagel House* on the South Bank of the Thames as a base for his investigation.

Beginning in the late summer of 1967, Read was at first assisted by just two sergeants, but after three months he was able to assemble a team of trusted officers. After the twins were arrested on conspiracy charges in May 1968, work began to bring murder charges against them – and all associates, suspects, and witnesses were interviewed at *Tintagel House*.

Built in 1960 and occupied by the Metropolitan Police for half a century, the 12-storey building close to Vauxhall Bridge was the home of the first police computer. The police left *Tintagel House* in 2011 and the building remained empty and mouldering for several years. Following a major refurbishment, *Tintagel House* reopened in 2018 as a modern office block.

Following Frances' death, Reggie went into a steep decline and began drinking heavily to try and ease the pain of his loss. The thought that he himself might bear some responsibility for what happened to Frances was simply too unbearable to acknowledge. Huge quantities of gin drank throughout the day helped nullify and banish feelings of guilt and replace them with anger – simmering, festering anger that needed a release. The first to feel his fury, he thought, should be those whom Reggie held solely responsible for his wife's death – the Shea family.

One evening, Reggie told new Firm member Tony Lambrianou to drive him to *The Victory* pub in Hoxton.[219] Reggie knew that Frank Shea drank there, and it became clear to Tony Lambrianou – who had known Frank Shea since childhood – that Reggie intended to shoot him. Sitting in the car parked opposite the pub, Tony did his best to talk Reggie out of shooting his old friend and, after half an hour or so, he succeeded in calming Reggie down.

Frankie Shea looked very much like his sister – and Tony Lambrianou believed that Reggie, on seeing Frankie face to face, could not have gone through with the shooting. More likely, he would have seen Frances' eyes, broken down, slipped Frankie a few quid, and walked away.[220] Frank Shea literally dodged a bullet that night, but letting him off the hook did nothing to quell Reggie's anger and, over the next few months, others would become the focus of the grieving gangster's gin-soaked fury.

One evening in the summer of 1967, Tony Lambrianou, Jack 'The Hat' McVitie, and a couple of friends were drinking

---

219 *The Victory* was situated at 24 Murray Grove, N1 7FB. The pub was demolished in 2008 and a multi-storey apartment building now occupies the site.

220 Lambrianou, Tony. *Inside The Firm*. London: John Blake Publishing. 1991.

in *The Mildmay Tavern,*[221] and at closing time they moved on to a new club that had recently opened at Highbury Corner in Islington. *Club Tempo* was opened and owned by a Newcastle-based businessman called Ray Grehan, and he installed Freddie Bird – an associate of the twins – as manager. Jack The Hat, true to form, soon started making a nuisance of himself by standing in front of the stage and heckling the female singer. When Freddie Bird came over – accompanied by doormen from Newcastle – and asked Jack to turn it in, Jack began re-monstrating about the fact that he was using Geordies from out of town as bouncers. Arguing led to a scuffle and Jack was thrown out and barred. Jack returned the following evening with a gun and began shouting and making threats, but once again he was thrown out without shots being fired.

Amazingly, and probably much to his regret, Freddie Bird later readmitted Jack to the club – a decision that predictably led to more trouble. Dorothy Squires, wife of Roger Moore – star of the hit '60s TV show *The Saint* – was singing on stage when Jack began shouting questions about the Saint's prowess in bed. Dorothy Squires – who was known to like a drink and was clearly inebriated at the time – rose to the bait and drunk-enly shouted back. Roger Moore is said to have been present at the time and, when the crowd began shouting, "*Get The Saint up!*" he apparently left – quickly. Although officially married to Dorothy Squires until 1968, Roger Moore split with his wife in 1961, so his presence on the night in question is subject to some doubt.

Jack The Hat continued to cause problems and, when the next act came on – another female singer – Jack stood in front of the stage and dropped his trousers. This was the last straw

---

221 Situated at 130 Balls Pond Road, N1 4AD, it was closed and partially demolished in 1987. A *Costcutter* supermarket now occupies the site.

for Freddie Bird and, this time when he intervened, punches were thrown.[222] Reggie Kray telephoned Ray Grehan and advised him that his non-London doormen didn't know the local villains and that it would be in his best interest to employ door staff supplied by him. *"You can have Big Pat* [Connolly] *at £100 a week,"* said Reggie.

Knowing that this was the thin end of the wedge, Grehan resisted, but within a short time, the trouble started. One of the doormen from Newcastle had an ear cut off and, shortly afterwards, two men with shotguns shot up the bar while customers cowered under tables. Reggie was clearly in no mood for negotiation and when a demand for protection money was not immediately met, Freddie Bird – who had known the twins for years – was shot in the knee.[223] *Going way back* held no sway with Reggie during this time, and he would go on to vent his anger on at least two more friends of old.

Club Tempo

20-22 Highbury Corner, Islington, London N5 1RD

Nearest TFL station: Holloway Road underground.

Built and opened as a temperance billiard hall in the early 1900s, it remained open until 1966 and gained a reputation for serving tasty meat pies. Newcastle-based entrepreneur Ray Grehan acquired the building and opened *Club Tempo*, a nightclub with cabaret, in May 1967. Topping the bill on the opening night was Lonnie

---

222   Ibid.

223   Facebook, Islington Archaeology & History Society.

Donegan. Trouble started shortly after the club opened when Jack 'The Hat' McVitie began making a nuisance of himself by heckling the performers – which included Dorothy Squires, wife of actor Roger Moore – and dropping his trousers in front of the stage. Within a short time, the Krays moved in to extort protection money and manager Freddie Bird was shot in the knee. Violence continued and, less than three months after opening, Grehan shut up shop and returned to the North East.

The building today is home to *The Garage*, a live music and club venue that opened in 1993 and hosts big-name bands and artists.

Ex-flyweight boxer and founding member of The Firm, Nobby Clark, had – at some point – said something, probably unintentionally, about Frances that Reggie took as a slight. Now, due to his unbalanced emotional state brought on by grief and almost constant drinking, Reggie made Nobby Clark the focus of his anger. Fringe Kray gang member 'Fat' Wally Garelick was summoned in the dead of night and told to bring his van to an address where Ron, Reg, and some of The Firm were gathered, drinking. Reggie told Jack Dickson to come along too and, together, the three men drove to the block of flats where Nobby lived. Reggie banged on the door and, shortly after it was opened, he shot his old friend in the leg.

After Detective Sergeant Leonard Townshend was cleared of corruption charges on 18 July 1967, the warrant for Ronnie's arrest expired and he was free to join his twin for business as usual. Once again, The Colonel was back. Ronnie had long been the impetuous, irrational, and ultra-violent force in the relationship, and Reggie – for reasons of pragmatism rather than conscience – had been the voice of reason, attempting to moderate and temper Ronnie's excesses. But this was no longer the case; Ronnie was and always had been the dominant twin and Reggie, who was teetering on the edge of a breakdown, had neither the strength nor desire to resist his brother's dominance. Now, instead of one unhinged homicidal crazy-man wreaking havoc in London's underworld, there were two – and it soon became common knowledge that the Krays were totally out of control.

The Regency Club in Stoke Newington had, since the days of the twins living at *Cedra Court*, been a hang-out and meeting place of choice for the twins and The Firm. Opened in 1960 by brothers John and Tony Barry, the nightclub was popular with the criminal fraternity and considered something of a neutral zone. On the first floor of *The Regency* was a Chinese restaurant, with music and dancing on the ground floor, and a private bar in the basement. The twins had their claws well and truly into *The Regency* and they were paid protection money by the Barry brothers. Ron and Reg used the basement bar for private parties, and during the day it was used for meetings – and as a court to dispense justice, criminal-style. Anyone who had displeased the twins could be summoned to *The Regency* for disciplining, which – if they were lucky – could just mean a tongue-lashing. If the accused was not so lucky, they could be made to hurt someone, demand money from a business, or – worse still – take a beating or a cutting.

The Regency was the scene of several well-known violent incidents, one of which occurred In the mid-'60s and involved a man called George Dixon. Ronnie held a gun to Dixon's head and pulled the trigger. Fortunately for Dixon, the gun jammed and Ronnie was restrained by Reggie and Freddie Foreman, enabling Dixon to make good his escape. It is said that Ronnie made-up with Dixon and gave him the bullet that could have killed him. George Dixon, it is said, had the bullet mounted on a chain and wore it around his neck.

Later – in 1967, after Frances' death – Reggie carried out a particularly vicious attack in *The Regency* against the respected hardman and friend of the Krays, Henry 'Buller' Ward. Buller was in the company of a man called Tony Maffia one evening in *The Regency* when the twins and their entourage walked in. Buller knew that, at some point previously, Tony Maffia had incurred the twins' displeasure and so he told his friend to make himself scarce – quickly. Reggie was angry that Buller had clearly sided with Maffia and, after an exchange of words, Reggie threw a right-hander – but Buller saw it coming and rode the punch. "*You'll have to do better than that, Reggie boy,*" said Buller, and with that, Ron, Reg, and their cohorts began raining blows onto their lone victim. Finally, Tommy Cowley cracked Buller on the head with a cosh from behind and he dropped to the floor.

"*I lay on the floor and tried to cover up but then I felt something sharp stabbing into my thigh and I saw something glistening in Reggie Kray's hand. He kneeled over me with a crazed look and began slicing away at my face like a maniacal butcher hacking away at some tough meat.*"[224]

Buller's face was put back together with 110 stitches, and he recovered, but as far as Buller was concerned, there was unfinished business and the twins were going to pay – with their lives. Quite how he would kill the twins was mulled over during his recovery and he decided that his best option was a bullet from a rifle with a telescopic sight.

From a vantage point on the railway arch overlooking Vallance Road, Buller spent several nights waiting for the right moment to come – but before it did he received a phone call from Charlie Kray to tell him he'd been seen and was now on the twins' hit-list. So, Buller put his plan on hold for the time

---

224   Ward, Henry and Weeks, David. *Bullets, Blood and Broken Bodies*. New Breed Publishing, 2008.

being. He would bide his time and wait for an opportunity; after all, the twins weren't going anywhere… or so he thought.[225]

The Regency

240a Amhurst Road, Stoke Newington, London E8 2BN

Nearest TFL station: Rectory Road overground.

The Regency was a nightclub and restaurant in Stoke Newington, opened in 1960 and owned by brothers John and Tony Barry. Ron and Reg Kray took protection money from the club, and the basement bar was used for private Kray parties, meetings to discuss business, and as a court – where anyone who had incurred the twins' displeasure was disciplined, sometimes violently. Popular with the criminal fraternity from North and East London, the club was the scene of several well-known violent incidents, including the attempted shooting of George Dixon by Ron and the cutting of Henry 'Buller' Ward by Reg. On Saturday 28 October 1967, Jack 'The Hat' McVitie was drinking in *The Regency* before being lured to a flat in nearby Evering Road and murdered by Reg Kray.

The Victorian civic building of red brick and white stone, built in the 1880s, is typical of the period. From the 1940s until it was converted into a nightclub in 1959, the building was the headquarters of the local 'Jewish Lads Brigade.' Following the closure of *The Regency* in

---

225   Ibid.

1970, the premises continued to be used as a nightclub – firstly called *Willows* and later *Trendz*. Troubled by drugs and violence, the licence was revoked in 2008 and the building was converted into a high-end residential apartment block.

A few hundred metres from *The Regency* – along Amhurst Road in an easterly direction, at number 277 on the corner of Foulden Road – is an apartment building recognisable as a former pub. This was *The Farleigh Hotel*, a pub used by the Krays in the 1960s.

Unhappy with the twins' ever-increasing and often unnecessary and gratuitous violence, Leslie Payne had distanced himself from the twins the previous year. Having the effrontery to walk away and continue to do illegal business without them infuriated the twins and could not go unpunished. After all, Payne possessed knowledge of the inner workings of The Firm and the twins themselves – knowledge that gave him the power, should he choose to use it, to go to the police, tell them all he knew, and bring about the twins' demise. This was a situation that could not be tolerated, and there was only one solution to the problem: Payne must be killed.

Jack McVitie – stupefied by drugs and alcohol most of the time and, as far as the twins could see, easily persuaded to do their bidding – was the ideal man for the job. McVitie was given an advance payment of £100 to kill Payne and told there would be £400 more once the job was done. Firm member Billy Exley drove McVitie to Payne's House in Tulse Hill, South London, and – armed with a concealed gun – McVitie knocked on Payne's door. Perhaps he lost his nerve, or perhaps – as he later told the twins – Payne wasn't at home, but either way the hit did not take place and McVitie did not return the money paid to him. The possibility of a second attempt could explain why the twins made no effort to recover the money at this point, but they didn't, and McVitie disappeared with a pocketful of cash.

This was not the only time that McVitie took money from the twins and failed to deliver on a promise. On one occasion, he was given the job of taking his van to a warehouse in Kent, collecting stolen merchandise, and delivering it to another address in London. Instead of carrying out the task as instructed, McVitie took a detour, sold some of the gear to a contact of his own, and pocketed an amount of cash for himself. Yet another event indicative of McVitie's total irreverence was the acceptance of a batch of Purple Hearts from the twins on credit – and his failure to pay for them. All this must have been a vexation to the twins, and even more so when word came back that McVitie was going around boasting about the fact that he'd had one over on the Krays and they weren't doing anything about it. Worse still was when McVitie heard that the twins were unhappy with him and he began broadcasting in public places that he wasn't bothered what they thought or did and that the shotgun he was carrying would ensure that at least one of them would go down with him if they tried anything.

One day, McVitie managed to upset the twins' close friend and ally Freddie Foreman by misbehaving and pulling a knife on a croupier in Freddie's South London nightclub and casino.[226] Upsetting Freddie Foreman, by default, meant upsetting the twins. On another occasion, McVitie turned up at the door of *The Regency* waving a shotgun around and threatening to shoot any members of The Firm that might be inside. Tony Barry, one of the club's owners, received word that his door-

---

226 *Hamilton House* at 211 Balham High Road, SW17 7BQ was, in the 1960s, the location of Freddie Foreman's nightclub and casino, *The 211 Club*. Today, the early 19th-century building is home to the *Polish White Eagle Club*.

man was having trouble, and fortunately he was able to defuse the situation, but making threats and causing trouble in a Kray-protected establishment was yet another reason why the thin ice McVitie was skating on would eventually crack.

It is surprising that McVitie was allowed to continue his antics for as long as he did and that nothing was done sooner. Perhaps the twins saw McVitie as someone not to be taken seriously; no real problem, just a drunken, drugged-up joker who, if kept around, could easily be manipulated into committing murder on their behalf. Useful to the Krays or not, McVitie was clocking up a litany of misdeeds that were bringing him ever closer to the point where they could no longer be ignored. Ever since Ronnie killed George Cornell, he had been goading his brother into killing someone; "*I've done mine now you do yours.*" This, along with Reggie's unbalanced state of mind and pent-up anger following the death of Frances, was leading him steadily towards the ultimate act of violence. Someone soon was going to be sacrificed at the altar of Reggie's now unbridled rage, and the most likely candidate was Jack 'The Hat' McVitie.

On the evening of Saturday 28 October 1967, there was a party in *The Carpenters Arms*. Tuesday of that week had been the twins' 34th birthdays, and Saturday night was the time to celebrate with family and friends. Mum Violet, Dad Charles, and Brother Charlie – together with his wife Dolly – were all there. The entire inner circle were also in attendance, suited, booted, and unusually, accompanied by their wives and girl-friends, their hair done and dressed in their best. Reg – accompanied by the new love of his life, Carol Thompson – was in a good mood, drinking moderately, welcoming the guests, and playing the convivial host. Ron, also enjoying the occasion, had invited two young friends along: Terry and Trevor, both 17-year-old local lads from Bethnal Green. Music, laughter, cigarette smoke, and beaming smiles filled the bar room of the little Cheshire Street pub, where all present were enjoying the relaxed atmosphere and an altogether pleasant evening. But for some of the guests, what began as a pleasant evening would soon degenerate into a nightmare of sickening brutality and sheer horror.

The Carpenters Arms

73 Cheshire Street, Bethnal Green, London E2 6EG

Nearest TFL station: Bethnal Green overground.

In 1967, Ron and Reg bought the little Cheshire Street pub – close to their Vallance Road home – for £2,000, and used it for social get-togethers and as a meeting place for The Firm. It is often said that they bought the pub for their mum – and Violet was, of course, free to use it anytime and involve herself in the running of the business if she chose to do so, but Violet was not the licence holder. Due to the twins' criminal records, they would not be granted a licence to sell alcohol, so the son-in-law of Harry Hopwood – the twins' father's friend – became the legal tenant, and he and his wife moved into the flat above and saw to the day-to-day running of the pub. Firm member Billy Exley worked behind the bar.

On the evening of Saturday 28 October 1967, the Kray twins' friends and family were gathered in *The Carpenters Arms* for a party to celebrate the twins' 34th birthdays. Later, in the early hours of Sunday morning, Reggie murdered Jack 'The Hat' McVitie in a flat on Evering Road, Stoke Newington.

Built in 1871, the Victorian pub on the corner of

Cheshire Street and St Matthew's Row closed in 2006 and almost went the way of so many others – converted into residences. Happily, the pub was saved, reopened in 2009, and is still open and trading today. Although refurbished and brought up to date, the pub's interior layout is much the same as it was in the 1960s and is one of the more important Kray destinations still in existence.

Footage exists of the interior of *The Carpenters Arms* – taken in 1969 for the television documentary *The Name is Kray* – and provides a fascinating glimpse of East End pub culture as it once was. An old girl sings accompanied by a geezer, fag in mouth, bashing away at the old *Joanna* (cockney rhyming slang for piano).The clip has been used in other, more recent documentaries, including *The Underworld: The Krays*, first shown on BBC1 in 1994 and available to watch on YouTube.

Cheshire Street

Nearest TFL station: Bethnal Green overground.

When visiting *The Carpenters Arms* or the twins' junior school, *Wood Close* (now *William Davis Primary School*) on Cheshire Street, there are a couple more places of interest.

In January 1965, the twins' friend and ally Freddie Foreman was looking to avenge his brother, who had been shot and injured by small-time villain Jimmy Evans. Foreman's brother George was allegedly involved in an affair with Evans' wife, so Evans knocked on his door one evening and blasted him in the groin with a shotgun. George Foreman was seriously injured, but fortunately, 'all' was not lost. Freddie Foreman, Alfie Gerrard, and two other men in a car caught up with Evans, who was accompanied by his friend Tommy 'Ginger' Marks, in Cheshire Street. Shots were fired from the car and Ginger Marks was killed. More shots were fired at Evans as he ran along Cheshire Street, keeping his head low to make himself a smaller target. Evans describes bullets hitting the wall in front of him, creating brick dust as he ran. Slipping left into Wood Close, Evans narrowly escaped death by rolling under a parked van, unseen by his pursuers. Having lost Evans, the car turned around and Marks' body was pulled inside before it drove away.[227] Ginger Marks' body was never found. In 1975, Freddie Foreman, Alfie Gerrard, Jeremiah Callaghan, and Ronnie Everett were acquitted of Marks' murder under the direction of the trial judge.

Looking towards *The Carpenters Arms* from Cheshire Street – just to the right, attached to the fence surrounding the playground of the twins' old school – is a sign: *William Davis Primary School.* Directly underneath the sign, in the brickwork of the wall below, are several holes said to be made by bullets fired at the time Ginger Marks was killed – and when Jimmy Evans narrowly escaped with his life.

A few metres further to the right, on the corner of Wood Close, is a residential building recognisable as a former pub. This, until it closed in 1996, was *The King and Queen*. What makes this pub remarkable is the fact that, despite its close proximity to the twins' Vallance Road home (only *The Crown and Anchor* was closer),

---

227   Evans, Jimmy and Short, Martin. *The Survivor*. Edinburgh: Mainstream Publishing, 2002.

there is no mention of it whatsoever, anywhere, in the reams of published literature written about the twins. It is a reasonable assumption, however, that the twins must have crossed the threshold at some point, and it is fair to assume that they accepted some payment for the pub's protection.

As the party in *The Carpenters Arms* was getting underway,

Kray associates Chris and Tony Lambrianou were enjoying a drink with friends Alan and Raymond Mills, just over a mile away in *The Brown Bear* pub in Leman Street, Aldgate.[228] Chris Lambrianou knew Ray Mills and Tony knew Alan. The plan was to have a few drinks together to get to know one another, and for the Mills brothers to be introduced to the twins a little later on. The four men then made their way to *The Carpenters Arms* to find the party in full swing, and the Mills brothers were duly introduced to the twins.

Eager to visit more pubs before closing time, the Lambrianous and the Mills brothers left *The Carpenters Arms* and headed for *The Queen's Arms* on Hackney Road.[229] After another round or two of drinks, Tony proposed moving on to *The Regency Club* in Stoke Newington. Arriving at *The Regency* not long after 11pm, they went downstairs to the Saturday night jazz club and saw a familiar face in the crowd, beaming from under the rim of his brown trilby hat and moving towards them – it was Jack 'The Hat' McVitie.

Meanwhile, back at *The Carpenters Arms,* it was closing time and some of the guests were beginning to drift away. For others, however, the night was still young and there was talk of a party at Blonde Carol's Evering Road flat in Stoke Newington. 'Blonde Carol' Skinner – so-called to distinguish between her and Reggie's red-headed girlfriend, Carol Thompson – knew the twins, having worked for a time as a cloakroom attendant

---

228 Situated at 139 Leman Street, E18EY, *The Brown Bear* pub – built in 1830 – is sometimes cited as the location where George Cornell beat Ronnie Kray in a fist fight. If it happened at all, the more reliable anecdotal evidence suggests that the incident took place in *The Green Dragon Club* on Whitechapel Road.

229 *The Queen's Arms* was situated at number 288 Hackney Road. The pub closed in 1971 and was demolished shortly afterwards.

at their club *El Morocco,* and through having her flat regularly commandeered for after-pub parties. George Plummer, her
boyfriend, worked at *The Green Dragon Club* in Whitechapel
and, when told by the twins, *"We're going to have a party at
your girlfriend's flat tonight,"* like it or not, there wasn't a great
deal he could do about it.

Reggie announced that he was taking his girlfriend Carol
for a meal, but this never happened because soon after 11pm,
Reggie and Carol, Ronnie Hart and girlfriend Vicky James,
and Ronnie Bender with his new girlfriend Bubbles, turned
up at *The Regency.* Bubbles had recently split up with Frank
Shea (Frances' brother). Reggie spoke to Tony Barry, the club's
owner, and discovered that the Lambrianou brothers and Jack
McVitie were in the downstairs bar. Tony Lambrianou was
summoned to Tony Barry's office and told by the now drunk
and angry Reggie to go back downstairs, get McVitie drunk,
and bring him to the party at Blonde Carol's later on. Before
leaving, and much to the club owner's dismay, Reg produced a
.32 Mauser automatic and told Barry to look after it.

It was now 11.30pm and Blonde Carol Skinner was casually
watching television in the basement sitting room of her flat at
Evering Road, awaiting the return of her boyfriend, who was
bringing guests to a party of her own. Carol Skinner, although
not expecting them on this particular evening wasn't completely surprised when the doorbell rang and there were the Kray
twins and a group of friends looking for a party. Reggie, Hart,
Bender, and the girls must have rendezvoused with Ronnie
and the others at some point between leaving *The Regency*
and turning up at the Evering Road flat because – according to
Carol Skinner's later statement to the police – Ron, Reg, and
friends arrived at her flat at the same time.[230]

---

230   Statement by Carol Ann Skinner, DPP 2/4583, National Archives.

She made no attempt to turn them away; she just allowed them in and thought about asking her friend Kitty Collins if she and her boyfriend George could bring their party to her flat across the road at number 76.[231] Having taken over the use of the TV, the uninvited guests changed the channel to BBC2 to catch the end of the heavyweight fight between Jerry Quarry and Floyd Patterson – the first-ever boxing match broadcast live by satellite from America. The commentator was Harry Carpenter and the fight ended at 11.56pm with a points victory for Quarry. During the boxing, Blonde Carol popped across the road to see her friend Kitty Collins; she explained the situation and was relieved to hear that Kitty was happy to host the party at her place. On the way back, she saw boyfriend George and a group of friends heading towards her flat and redirected them to number 76.

Saturday night changed to Sunday morning and the group now gathered at number 97 consisted of Ron, Reg and girl-friend Carol, Ronnie Hart and Vicky James, Ronnie Bender – alone now as Bubbles had left – Connie Whitehead and wife Pat, Geoff Allen and girlfriend Annie, Big Pat Connolly, and Ronnie's two young friends, Trevor and Terry. Ronnie ordered Ronnie Hart and Connie Whitehead to go back to *The Regency* to collect more drink and, while there, Hart was to instruct Tony Barry to bring the gun to the Evering Road flat. Tony Barry strongly protested but, fearing the likely consequences of a refusal, he drove his car to Evering Road and delivered the gun to Ronnie at the doorstep, thus implicating himself in the murder that would soon take place.

By now, Geoff Allen and Annie had left. Ronnie Bender left to give Pat Connolly a lift somewhere, and Ronnie Kray told

---

231   76 Evering Road was demolished at some point between 1967 and 1975 to make way for *Heatherley Court* flats (HM Land Registry).

Connie Whitehead to take his wife home and come straight back. Vicky James and Carol Thompson, the only two remaining women, were told to go over the road and join the party at number 76. This left only Ron and Reg Kray, Ronnie Hart, and the two youths, Terry and Trevor, who were dancing to music from the record player and probably unaware of the situation unfolding around them. Ronnie Hart was told to go upstairs and keep a lookout from the ground-floor window and to shout down when he saw the Lambrianous and McVitie arrive. There was no love lost between Ronnie Hart and Jack McVitie; they had argued in a club sometime earlier and McVitie had called Hart's girlfriend Vicky James a slag.[232]

Just after 12.30am, the shout came from Ronnie Hart that they had arrived, and Terry and Trevor were told to turn up the volume on the record player. Hart opened the door and in walked Jack, followed by Chris and Tony Lambrianou and the Mills brothers. Together, they walked through the hallway and down the stairs to the basement rooms. Drunk, loud, and exuberant as ever, Jack 'The Hat' shouted, *"Where's the party then? Jack's here!"*

Exactly what happened next – the sequence of events and the actions of those involved – will probably never be known for certain. Statements made to the police at the time of the twins' arrest the following year, statements made from prison on appeal, memoirs, and television interviews all contain differences and contradictions. That said, it is possible to give a good general overview of the catastrophic events that followed:

Ronnie Kray attacked McVitie, smashing him in the face with a small glass. Reggie Kray then pointed the gun at Jack's head and pulled the trigger. Nothing happened – the gun failed

---

232 Lambrianou, Tony. *Inside the Firm*. London: John Blake Publishing, 2009.

to go off – and the same thing happened when Reggie pulled the trigger for a second time. The gun had been supplied by associate Alan Bruce Cooper who was, of course, working for the police. This gun, along with other weapons given to the twins, had been modified to render it useless.

Ronnie Bender and Connie Whitehead returned to find the twins and Hart attacking Jack with their fists, and it was at this point that Jack punched the window, breaking the glass. Chris Lambrianou – shocked by the realisation that he and his brother had unwittingly delivered Jack into a perilous situation – became visibly upset, and at some point during the chaos, Ronnie told Connie Whitehead to take him home. As the vicious and drawn-out assault on McVitie continued, something happened that caused the situation to take a dramatic turn for the worse. Somebody produced a knife[233] and passed it to Reggie. Ronnie Kray and Ronnie Hart then grabbed and held McVitie. *"Go on, Reg, kill him!"* said Ronnie Kray as Reg plunged the knife repeatedly into McVitie's body. While McVitie lay on the floor, dying or already dead, Reg performed a *coup de grâce* and pushed the knife through McVitie's neck.

Reggie had cut his hand badly at some point during the frenzied attack and, according to a later statement made by Ronnie Bender, this was a result of him intervening to try to wrestle the knife out of Reggie's hand.

Ronnie Bender later described the killing:

"It was terrible. Savagery at its utmost. Reggie was foaming at the mouth like a raging bull. Have you ever seen a bull's eyes before the toreador finishes him off? He was like that.

---

233   It is uncertain where the knife came from. It may have been brought to the Evering Road flat by Hart or Bender. In her statement (DPP2/458, National Archives) Carole Skinner recalls Ronnie Bender taking something out of his pocket and placing it on top of her kitchen cabinet.

Absolutely gone. Blood everywhere."[234]

Terry, Trevor, and Tony Lambrianou left the scene as soon as the furious knife attack began, and the Mills brothers – having seen enough – quickly left the house too. Jack's body was now lying doubled up on the floor of the blood-drenched room and Ron, Reg, and Ronnie Hart were set to leave, leaving Ronnie Bender alone to deal with Jack's body. *"What can I do with it, Ron?"* pleaded Ronnie Bender.

"Chuck it over the railway at Cazenove Road," replied Ronnie Kray as the three of them left, taking the knife and the inoperative gun with them, wrapped in a towel.

97 Evering Road

Stoke Newington, London N16 7SL

Nearest TFL station: Rectory Road overground.

Between midnight and 1.30 am on Sunday 29 October 1967, Jack 'The Hat' McVitie was lured to a party at 'Blonde Carol' Skinner's flat and stabbed to death by Reggie Kray.

27-year-old Carol Skinner had lived in the flat since 1963 and knew the Krays from her time working as a cloakroom attendant at their club, *El Morocco*. Regardless of whether she liked it or not, her flat was regularly taken over and used by the Krays and The Firm for after-pub parties. When the twins and friends turned up late on Saturday 28 October 1967, she moved her own party guests across the road to the home of her friend,

---

234   Morton, James. *Krays: The Final Word*. London: Mirror Books, 2019.

Kitty Collins.

Jack McVitie was brought from the nearby *Regency Club* to Evering Road by the Lambrianou brothers, and was thereafter set about and brutally murdered in a frenzied and horrific knife attack by Reggie Kray.

The basement flat of the large Victorian end-terrace house at number 97, where the murder took place, is one of the most-visited Kray tourist destinations.

Just a few doors along from 97 Evering Road – on the same side at number 113 – is the former home of friend to the Krays, Winnie Harwood. Winnie was a tall blonde woman around the same age as the twins and known to the Kray Firm from the club and pub scene. Winnie was responsible for making sure there were always plenty of pretty girls at Kray parties. After splitting up with his wife, long-time Firm member Big Pat Connolly rented a front room at Winnie Harwood's house.

The house where Jack McVitie was murdered is just a short distance from Rectory Road overground station and close to other places of interest, including *The Regency Club* and *Cedra Court*.

Sometime after the twins and Hart had left, Chris Lambrianou returned to the Evering Road flat where, shortly after his arrival, his brother Tony reappeared. Both brothers were shocked and appalled by what had happened and wanted to walk away, but they simply couldn't ignore Ronnie Bender's pleas for help. So, the three men began doing what they could to clean away the evidence of the slaughter. Carol Skinner's two children were sleeping in a bedroom that they shared with their mother on the ground floor; Chris Lambrianou tiptoed inside, carefully removed the bedspread from the empty double bed, and took it downstairs.

The party at Kitty Collins' place was, by now, winding down, and Carol Skinner and a very drunk George Plummer crossed the road back to their flat. On entering, they were met by Ronnie Bender who told them they couldn't go downstairs as there had been a bit of trouble and they were just cleaning up. Carol Skinner saw Chris Lambrianou, wearing a pair of socks on his hands, coming up the stairs and carrying a bowl of bloody water to be poured down the toilet. The couple were told to wait in the ground-floor bedroom; there was nothing to worry about, but on no account were they to go downstairs.

Jack's body was placed on the bedspread, rolled up like a sweet wrapper, and carried upstairs to the ground-floor landing. Hart and the twins had taken Ronnie Bender's Mini; Chris Lambrianou's car was parked and blocked in back at *The Regency*, and Jack's car, a clapped-out cream and blue Ford Zodiac Mark II, was parked outside. After finding that Jack's body wouldn't fit in the boot, it was, with some difficulty, deposited on the back seat.

It was now after 2am and, with Jack's body safely stowed away out of sight, Carol Skinner was told she could go downstairs if she wished. She did, and when she saw the blood-stained carpet folded up in the middle of the floor, the mess, and the remaining bloodstains on the walls and surfaces, it was clear to her that there had been more than a *bit* of trouble. Connie Whitehead reappeared around this time and involved himself in the clean-up operation. Ronnie's instruction to dump the body on nearby railway lines was clearly a bad idea, so it was agreed that they would drive the body to South London and dump it somewhere there, well away from Kray territory.

Chris went back to *The Regency* to get his car – which, thankfully, was no longer blocked in. Tony Lambrianou volunteered to drive Jack's car with his body inside, a risky business made worse by the fact that only one headlight was working. Chris Lambrianou and Ronnie Bender followed in Chris' Ford

Corsair. It was a worrying drive through East London towards the Blackwall Tunnel, and nerves jangled when a police car pulled out of a side road and settled between the two cars. Chris felt for the gun he was carrying, but – after a time and much to his relief – the police car pulled off into Dalston Lane and headed away towards Stoke Newington. It was now 2.45am,[235] and instead of heading towards the Blackwall Tunnel as Chris thought had been agreed, Tony appeared to be heading towards the Rotherhithe Tunnel, and Chris lost him. Unsure what to do next, Chris and Ronnie Bender took the Rotherhithe Tunnel and drove around the area immediately south of the river in the hope that they would find Tony. Hardly able to believe his luck, Chris spotted Tony walking along the street towards him. Tony had left Jack's car in a quiet, little, confetti-covered, cobbled back street outside the *Church of St Mary's*, Rotherhithe.

St Mary's Church

Saint Marychurch Street, London SE16 4HZ

Nearest TFL station: Rotherhithe overground.

Built on the site of an older church in 1715 by Christopher Wren's associate John James, *St Mary's* is worthy of a visit in its own right. Situated on the South Bank of the River Thames, the handsome brick and white stone church has historic maritime associations. Captain Christopher Jones and crew members of the *Mayflower* – the ship that took the Pilgrim Fathers to

---

235 Lambrianou, Chris with McGibbon, Robin. *Escape From The Kray Madness*. London: Pan Books, 1996.

America – are buried in the churchyard. The altar and bishop's chair are made from timber salvaged from *The Fighting Temeraire*, a ship made famous by Turner's celebrated painting that now hangs in *The National Gallery*. The 250-year-old church organ is original and a unique musical instrument of historic importance.

In the early hours of Sunday 29 October, Jack 'The Hat' McVitie's car – with his body inside – was left outside the church in the narrow cobbled street, which was strewn with confetti from the previous day's wedding. Just as day was breaking, the car was found by Freddie Foreman and driven to a lock-up garage in Camberwell. From there, Jack's body was taken to Newhaven and disposed of at sea.

After leaving Ronnie Bender alone at Evering Road to clean up the mess and get rid of Jack's body, Ronnie Hart drove the twins, in Ronnie Bender's Mini, to the home of Harry Hopwood at Ravenscroft Road in Bethnal Green. Both twins needed to get out of their bloodstained clothes and take a bath. Due to his badly cut hand, Reggie needed help to wash his hair, and Harry Hopwood duly obliged. Ronnie Hart was instructed to take Harry Hopwood with him and drive to Vallance Road, where fresh clothes were always ready to be collected from Aunt May's house at number 174. On the way, they were to throw the gun and the knife into the Regent's Canal from the bridge at Queensbridge Road.

On 23 August 1968, the gun – a German Mauser .32 calibre automatic – was retrieved from the Regent's Canal by a police diver. Some vital parts of the gun's mechanism were missing, preventing the gun from working. The gun is now held in the *Police Crime Museum*. The knife was never found.

When Hart and Hopwood returned with fresh clothes, and

having disposed of the weapons, the twins changed into clean trousers, shirts, and jackets. Their paper money was burnt in the kitchen and their jewellery thoroughly cleaned. It was now approaching 3am and Harry Hopwood, not having a phone, was told to go to the nearest phone box, call their brother Charlie, and tell him to come over straight away. Charlie arrived shortly afterwards and was horrified to hear what had happened. Angry, shocked, and wanting nothing more to do with it, Charlie left around 3.45am to return home.

While Charlie was at Harry Hopwood's flat, Ronnie Bender was dropped off by the Lambrianous close to Charlie's flat in Poplar. Ronnie Bender knocked and the door was answered by Charlie's wife Dolly, who told him that Charlie had gone out without telling her where or why. Bender, probably without thinking it through, told Dolly that the twins had killed Jack 'The Hat'. Clearly shocked by what she heard, Dolly reached for the phone, called Tommy Cowley, and explained what had happened. Cowley arrived a short time later and Ronnie Bender informed him of all that had occurred – and where the body had been left. Then Charlie returned, anxious and agitated as a result of what he now knew, to find Ronnie Bender and Tommy Cowley at his home. Charlie, despite wanting nothing to do with yet another diabolical mess that the twins had created, knew he had no choice but to try to do something. Charlie and Tommy Cowley had a grave situation on their hands that needed to be addressed with some urgency. Giving Ronnie Bender a lift home was not high on the priority list, so he was left to walk the two miles from Charlie's flat in Rosefield Gardens, Poplar to his home in Cubitt Town on the Isle of Dogs.

Charlie's phone had been tapped by the police, and both the call from Harry Hopwood and Dolly's call to Tommy Cowley were recorded. Clearly aware that there may have been a tap on Charlie's phone, the conversations were guarded and cryptic, but it was apparent from Hopwood's call that *something* had happened, and clear from Dolly's call that it involved *"the others"* and the *"man with the hat."*[236] This information was passed to Nipper Read who was, at the time, quietly working away and gathering information.

Harry Hopwood's Flat

Ravenscroft Street, Bethnal Green, London E2 7QQ

Nearest TFL station: Hoxton overground.

The twins clearly weren't too concerned about involving and implicating old Kray family friend Harry Hopwood in a murder when they turned up at his flat shortly after killing Jack McVitie. Following the murder in the early hours of 29 October 1967, the twins were driven by Ronnie Hart to Hopwood's flat on Ravenscroft Street, just off the Hackney Road in Bethnal Green. While there, the twins bathed and sent Hart and Hopwood for fresh clothes – and to dispose of the malfunctioning gun and the murder weapon, a knife, in the Regent's Canal.

This rather important location in the Krays' story is also the scene of a meeting that took place in December 1966 – attended by Ron, Reg, Charlie, and Freddie Foreman – where the fate of Frank Mitchell was decided.

On the east side of Ravenscourt Street is a building that is clearly a former pub. *The Ravenscroft* pub (previously *The Victoria*) closed in 2014 and is now *Silas Yard Public Farmhouse*. Next to it is a two-storey block

---

236   Morton, James. *Krays, The Final Word*. London: Mirror Books, 2019.

> of maisonettes built in 1957 called *James Brine House.*
> Harry Hopwood lived in flat 3 on the ground floor.

Jack's body was dumped on Freddie Foreman's manor and it needed to be moved before the morning light came and it was discovered. Charlie Kray and 'Ginger Tom' Cowley knew that 'Brown Bread' Fred,[237] also known as 'The Undertaker' and 'The Godfather of British Crime,' was something of a Mr Fix-it who was highly respected and highly efficient in dealing with problems. Making bodies disappear was just one of Freddie's areas of expertise and he had, in the past, helped the twins with this particular problem (Frank Mitchell). Freddie Foreman – as far as the Krays were concerned – was always happy and willing to help, but when Tommy Cowley rang the bell on the door of his pub on Lant Street in the early hours of Sunday 29 October, he was far from happy:

"Now I've got this little ginger bastard, Tommy Cowley, ringing my doorbell, getting me out of bed at fucking three o'clock in the morning [it was probably later] *to tell me about Jack The Hat."*[238]

According to Freddie, two cars arrived at his pub: Ronnie Bender's Mini, in which the twins and Hart had left the murder scene, and another driven by someone unseen needed for the return journey. Freddie was not overly pleased that the Mini, bloodstained from Reggie's cut hand, was left outside his pub for him to clean.

In 1969, Ronnie Hart – who gave evidence against the twins at their trial – was interviewed by journalist Norman

---

237 Brown bread – cockney rhyming slang for 'dead'.

238 Foreman, Freddie and Lambrianou, Tony. *Getting it Straight: Villains Talking.* London: Pan Books, 2002.

Lucas and, playing down his own involvement in the killing, he gave a different version of events before, during, and after the murder. Hart stated that he drove the Mini to Freddie Foreman's pub followed by Charlie driving his blue Austin 1800, and that it was Charlie who roused and spoke to Freddie Foreman.[239]

Freddie waited until just before daylight and then, accompanied by his good friend Alfie Gerrard, found the car outside the church in Rotherhithe. Jack's body was clearly visible, wrapped in a candlewick bedspread on the back seat. *'Oh, that's fucking nice!'* thought Freddie to himself. It was raining and, after managing to break into the car and get it started, he was dismayed to find that the windscreen wipers didn't work. With Alfie Gerrard following in a car behind, Fred drove the clapped-out Zodiac – which, it turned out, also had a non-functioning tail light – to a lock-up garage in Camberwell. Jack's body was later taken out to sea from Newhaven to join that of Frank Mitchell at the bottom of the English Channel.

The Prince of Wales

23 Lant Street, London SE1 1QP

Nearest TFL station: Borough underground.

Freddie Foreman bought the pub for £5,000 in 1965. Charles Dickens lodged in Lant Street in 1824 and, in tribute, the pub's wood-panelled and red flock-wall-papered interior walls were adorned with pictures of Dickens' characters. *The Prince of Wales* was a busy pub

---

239 Lucas, Norman. *Britain's Gangland*. London: Pan Books, 1969.

attracting a diverse clientele, which included some well-known personalities of the day. Captain of England's World Cup-winning football team, Bobby Moore, was among the regular crowd, which also included Cat Stevens, Manfred Mann, Barbara Windsor, and other stars of the *Carry On* films. Freddie Foreman's criminal friends and associates drank there and the twins, of course, visited the pub on occasion. Freddie's wife Maureen sold the pub in the early '70s when Freddie was serving a ten-year prison sentence for his part in disposing of Jack McVitie's body.[240]

The Prince of Wales was demolished in January 2005 and the site – just a few minutes' walk from *Borough Market*, on the corner of Weller Street (east side) – is now occupied by a modern apartment building.

Freddie Foreman's son Jamie Foreman is an acclaimed actor who has appeared in numerous successful and well-known films. Jamie has played memorable roles in many a TV drama and appeared as Derek Branning in *EastEnders* from 2011 to 2012.

Ron, Reg, and Ronnie Hart left Harry Hopwood's flat early on Sunday morning and went to Tommy 'The Bear' Brown's flat in Tottenham to plan their next move. Orders were issued and work continued at Blonde Carol's flat to clean away evidence of the previous night's terrible events; in the following days, the bloodstained carpet and furniture were removed and replaced, and Albert Donoghue was called in to redecorate the room from top to bottom. Hush money was paid and threats were made – or both – to keep anyone from talking,

---

240   Foreman, Jamie. *On The Run*. London: John Blake Publishing, 2009.

and false rumours were deliberately spread to explain Jack's disappearance.

Ron and Reg decided to take a break and get out of London for a week or so. Taking Ronnie Hart with them, they travelled first to Cambridge, staying at the *University Arms Hotel*,[241] and then to the picturesque village of Lavenham in Suffolk, where they stayed at *The Swan Hotel*.[242]

The Swan Hotel

High Street, Lavenham, Sudbury CO10 9QA

Friend of the twins, Geoff Allen, made the bookings and, at the end of October 1967, the twins and Ronnie Hart checked into *The Swan Hotel* and stayed for around a week. While there, the twins and Hart attended the local Hunt Ball held at the hotel and spent days rambling, horse riding, and relaxing at Geoff Allen's country mansion in the nearby village of Gedding.

Beginning life as a coaching inn in the 15th century, *The Swan* is now a wonderfully preserved luxury hotel complete with low oak beams and original features. Lavenham became prosperous as a hub for the wool trade, but when the bottom fell out of the business in the late 16th century, fortunes were lost and there was no money to upgrade the old buildings. As a conse-

---

241 Regent Street, Cambridge CB2 1AD. Opened in 1834 and still operating today, the historic hotel played host to the Kray twins for a night or two in October 1967.

242 Lucas, Norman. *Britain's Gangland*. London: Pan Books, 1969.

quence, Lavenham is something of a time-capsule and among the best preserved Tudor villages in England.

Suffolk, with its beautiful countryside and childhood associations, was a much-loved place of refuge for the twins. They had visited the countryside shortly after the murder of George Cornell and now, following McVitie's murder – and perhaps seeking a little peace of mind – they were drawn there once again. Geoff Allen, the twins' friend of old who bought and sold properties in and around Suffolk – and sometimes set fire to them – had recently bought a fabulous 16th-century mansion, eight miles from Lavenham in the village of Gedding. While staying at *The Swan Hotel*, the twins spent time with Geoff Allen at *Gedding Hall* – and they were certainly there eight days after McVitie's murder, to greet a very important guest.

Gedding Hall

Gedding, Bury St. Edmunds IP30 0QD

Ron and Reg spent time at *Gedding Hall* as guests of their old friend – businessman and fraudster, Geoff Allen – in the autumn of 1967, immediately after the murder of Jack McVitie.

It was during this time at *Gedding Hall* that the twins first met the author John Pearson; the man whose book, *The Profession of Violence,* would become responsible for the creation of the Kray *Legend.*

Little of the redbrick Elizabethan manor house is

original, having undergone major refurbishment and enlargement in the 19th century. *Gedding Hall*, happily, did not go the way of many of Allen's other properties – reduced to ashes. Instead, in 1968, Allen sold *Gedding Hall* to ex-Rolling Stone Bill Wyman, who lives there today.

Geoff Allen first met the twins in 1953 and, having something of a gangster complex himself, continued the association until the twins' imprisonment in 1969. During the 1960s, Allen aroused suspicion because many of his heavily insured properties were going up in flames. Eventually, in 1977, he was convicted at *Norwich Crown Court* and jailed for seven years. Geoff Allen died in 1992 and was dubbed *Godfather* on his gravestone, which resides 500 metres south west of *Gedding Hall* in the grounds of *St Mary's Church*.

On the morning of 5 November 1967, the twins waited at *Gedding Hall* to meet the man who, more than any other, would become responsible for the wide-spread interest in the Krays that exists today. Had journalist and author John Pearson not entered the twins' lives at this point, it is possible that interest in the Krays would have gradually faded as the prison years passed by. Instead, John Pearson's bestselling book, *The Profession of Violence* – first published in 1972 – not only kept interest in the twins alive but sparked a public fascination that would lead to innumerable books, newspaper articles, television documentaries, and two major feature films. Interestingly, there was an excellent book about the twins called *The Rise and Fall of the Brothers Kray* by journalist Brian McConnell, published just after their trial in 1969, and the Krays took up a chapter of fellow journalist Norman Lucas' book *Britain's Gangland,* also published in 1969, but it is through John Pearson – who came

to know Ron, Reg, and many of their family and friends inti-
mately – that the secret world of the Krays and insight into their
true character was revealed for the first time.

   In the autumn of 1967, John Pearson was living comforta-
bly in Rome, enjoying a lifestyle provided for by the success
of his recent book – a biography of James Bond's creator, Ian
Fleming. Aware that he would soon need to consider possibilities for his next project, his interest was aroused when he was
contacted by New York publisher and film producer, Frank
Taylor, and told about a pair of twin gangsters who lived in a
country mansion and ruled London. They were looking to have
a book written about their lives. Ron and Reg, in fact, wanted
a film made about their lives, and the idea had found its way
to Frank Taylor through Alan Bruce Cooper's Mafia-connected
American contacts. While on a business trip to London, Frank
Taylor was invited to meet the twins at *Gedding Hall*, and he
explained that the chances of a movie becoming a reality would
be greatly increased if first there was a book. Taylor was enthu-
siastic and told John Pearson that an all-expenses-paid trip had
been arranged for him to meet the twins at their country mansion. If he thought there was a book in them, he would publish
it, and if things worked out, there could be a movie too.

   John Pearson found pre-paid tickets waiting for him at
Rome airport and he flew first-class to London, where he
checked into *The Ritz* hotel on Piccadilly, the bill already
having been paid. The following morning, John Pearson was
met at the hotel by Tommy 'The Bear' Brown and Tommy
Cowley, who chauffeured him, in a Mercedes, to an impressive
Elizabethan country mansion surrounded by a moat with black
swans a swimming. Ron, Reg, Geoff Allen, and Charlie were
there to greet him and, after some talk and a lunch of tinned
cold meat, salad, and light ales, it was agreed that John Pearson
would come to London to see life in the East End and to meet
the twins' family and friends. John Pearson noticed Reggie's

bandaged hand and, when he asked him how he got the injury, "*Gardenin '*" was the reply.[243]

Some weeks later, on a cold, rainy Sunday in late November 1967, John Pearson arrived in London and took a taxi to the East End to begin his research for the book. He had previously asked if accommodation could be arranged for him, and when he was shown, by Tommy Cowley, to a squalid and dingy apartment in the dilapidated *Blackwall Buildings*, close to Vallance Road, he was a little surprised:

"The last time I'd seen a room like this was in a slum in Calcutta."[244]

He was even more surprised to find out, a little later on, that the twin gangsters who apparently *ruled London* didn't own and reside at *Gedding Hall* but lived most of the time with their mum in a tiny Victorian terraced house that had seen better days.

Blackwall Buildings

Fulbourne Street (now Castlemain St.)
London E1 5DA

Nearest TFL station: Whitechapel underground.

Perhaps it was Ronnie's idea of fun to give the twins' biographer John Pearson a taste of *the real East End* by accommodating him in a squalid, run-down apartment in the dilapidated *Blackwall Buildings*. The twins and The Firm referred to the flat as *The Dungeon,* and it was used

---

243 Pearson, John. *The Cult Of Violence*. London: Orion Books, 2001.
244 Ibid.

occasionally for meetings or as a place for friends to crash after a night's drinking. John Pearson arrived in the East End in November 1967 and, undaunted, began work on his book, staying for short periods in his rather insalubrious accommodation.

Built in 1890 to accommodate the area's poor who'd been displaced by railway construction work, the *Blackwall Buildings* consisted of four large four-storey tenement blocks. Anecdotally, George Cornell is said to have lived there at some point. By the mid-1960s, the buildings had fallen into disrepair and many of the apartments were boarded up and unoccupied. Along with the majority of the area's Victorian buildings, the *Blackwall Buildings* were demolished in 1969 as part of the huge slum clearance programme of that time.

The buildings stood close to what is today the junction of Castlemain Street and Lomas Street on the north side of Vallance Gardens. *St Peter's Hospital* (also demolished in the 1960s) faced directly onto the east side of Vallance Road, where *Lister House* is now, and the four *Blackwall Buildings* were immediately behind.

After a clearly embarrassed Tommy Cowley showed Pearson his rooms and quickly left, there was a knock on the door and Pearson was greeted by two rather unglamorous prostitutes; Tess and Trixie had been sent by Ronnie, surely to amuse himself, to *keep him company.* Cups of tea and a friendly chat were all that followed before the girls left, leaving Pearson to unpack, set up his typewriter, and await Reggie – who, he was told by Tom Cowley, would call for him around 8pm.

Reggie duly arrived and John Pearson's introduction to the world of the Krays began at the twins' latest meeting place and pub of choice, *The Old Horns* on Warner Place in Bethnal

Green. There gathered to meet him was the 1967 version of The Firm and many of the twins' friends of old. Those he spoke to all seemed to be singing from the same pre-rehearsed song sheet, telling stories of the twins' charity work and what simply marvellous chaps they were. It would be some time before John Pearson would manage to gain an insight into who the twins *really* were – and discover the shocking truth of their monstrous and grotesque violence.

John Pearson's description of his first glimpse into the world of the Kray twins in *The Old Horns* pub conjures a vivid picture:

"When I followed Reg into the crammed saloon bar, it was like stepping back in time to a tougher, rougher London, which has gone forever. It seemed packed with hefty-looking characters, most of them in their Sunday best. The tobacco smoke was powerful enough to fumigate a polecat. The noise was just as powerful, most of it coming from a tiny hunchbacked pianist in horn-rimmed spectacles pounding away at the pub piano like a mad percussionist."[245]

Landlord of *The Old Horns* was ex-boxer Teddy Berry, son of the twins' old boxing trainer, Harry 'Kid' Berry, and elder brother of the twins' long-time friend, Checker Berry. Until he suffered a detached retina and lost the sight in his right eye in 1949, Teddy Berry had been one of Britain's most promising boxers, winning all 19 of his professional fights and was widely tipped for the British lightweight title. In 1964, Teddy was shot in the leg and it was so badly damaged that the leg had to be amputated. There has, over the years, been much speculation as to why Teddy was shot and by whom. One story – believed by

---

245   Ibid.

some and refuted by others – is that Ronnie Kray shot Teddy Berry and, afterwards, feeling some remorse and by way of compensation, bought *The Old Horns* for him.

In the 2014 book *Fighting Men of London* by Alex Daley, Teddy gives his account of what happened.

On the evening of Friday 10 January 1964, Ted was walking in the street – about 200 yards from his home at the *Hadrian Estate*, Hackney Road, Bethnal Green – when a car containing two men pulled up alongside him and he was shot in the leg with a 12-bore shotgun. His assailant then got out of the car, stood over him, and fired another shot – hitting him close to his right knee. The shooting came as a result of a fight he and his brother Checker had been involved in a few weeks earlier. During the fight, two unnamed Kray associates were given a severe beating. Reggie Kray agreed to take the matter no further but not so Ronnie, who Teddy later discovered paid professional hitmen, possibly from abroad, to carry out the shooting. Money to help Teddy was raised by the people of Bethnal Green through collections and boxing shows, and Teddy was given enough money to buy a pub; firstly *The Bridge House* in Bow and then, two years later, *The Old Horns*.[246]

It's hard to imagine a charity boxing event taking place in Bethnal Green without the twins' participation, and it is most probable that, to make amends, the twins were indeed involved. Clearly, the Krays and the Berrys reached some kind of reconciliation as *The Old Horns* became the Kray's most-used pub in the late '60s.

After *The Old Horns* was adopted by the twins, it predictably became the scene of several violent incidents – but one in particular, remembered by Billy Webb as *The Battle of the Old*

---

246 Daley, Alex. *Fighting Men of London*. Durrington: Pitch Publishing, 2014.

Horns, stands out. Billy Webb – known to the twins since the days of *The Tottenham Royal* and their time on the run from the army in the early '50s – was a notable criminal character operating mainly in North London. Billy and his team were involved in a very lucrative racket, protecting a smuggling operation bringing pornography and handguns into the country from Denmark. When the twins heard about it, naturally it attracted their interest, and they were intent on muscling in and taking a cut for themselves. Consequently, Billy and his brother Ron were invited to a meeting at *The Old Horns* in the spring of 1968 to discuss business and come to some kind of arrangement – but the meeting, as far as the twins were concerned, was not a success. Billy Webb was not willing to hand over any share of his business; he neither needed nor wanted the suggested partnership with the twins and flatly refused to discuss the matter any further.

Ronnie made the first move and threw a punch, which missed. Soon, like a pack of dogs unleashed, Ron and most of the many Firm members present were attacking the Webb brothers with fists, chairs, and bottles. Scotch Jack Dickson, the Lambrianou brothers, and a couple of Firm members who were friendly with the Webbs remained on the sidelines, but they were vastly outnumbered and fighting for their very lives. Giving almost as good as they got and trying to stay on their feet, the brothers fought their way towards the door. Tommy Cowley went for Ron Webb with a knife but he was deterred by a stool being thrown at him. Fighting back desperately against the overwhelming onslaught, they managed to reach the door and make good their escape. Both were suffering from head injuries but Ron Webb's wounds were worse and he went on to be troubled by frequent, severe headaches for the rest of his life. Billy Webb blamed Ronnie Kray for his brother's early death in 1984 and, shortly afterwards, while visiting Ronnie in *Broadmoor*, he made the papers by punching Ronnie in the face.

The Old Horns

68 Warner Place, Bethnal Green, London E2 7DA

Nearest TFL station: Bethnal Green underground.

The Kray twins and The Firm began using *The Old Horns* as a regular meeting place towards the latter days of their reign in 1967. Ex-boxer Teddy Berry, son of the twins' old boxing trainer Harry 'Kid' Berry, was the landlord. A well-known photograph of the famous 1960s photographer David Bailey sitting between Ron and Reg was taken in *The Old Horns*. The twins spent their last night as free men in the pub before their arrest on the morning of 8 May 1968. Teddy Berry remained landlord of *The Old Horns* until he retired in 1979.

In the early '80s, the pub's name was changed to *Warners,* and then in 1990, it changed again to *Jeremiah Bullfrog*. After a period of gradually decreasing custom, the pub closed in 1997. There has been a pub on the site since Victorian times, but the current building was constructed in the 1940s and, happily, still exists.

The former pub is now *Bethnal Green Montessori School*. Situated just a short walk from *Pellicci's* cafe and many other Kray-related places of interest, no walking tour of the Krays' Bethnal Green manor would be complete without a visit to the building that was once the pub where the twins spent their last night of freedom.

Several more visits to *The Old Horns* over the coming months gave John Pearson the opportunity to meet – and form an impression of – most of the characters playing a part in the

Kray story. After meeting Alan Bruce Cooper and his wife Beverley in *The Old Horns* for the first time, John Pearson was interested to see them again about a week later, accompanied by a character who seemed to him to be somehow out of place:

"This time they were accompanied by a weird young man who was as tall and silent as a stick of human celery. When I tried to engage him in conversation he looked desperately around him and seemed scared out of his wits. I asked Reg about him afterwards and he told me that the man's name was Elvey. 'What does he do for a living?' I inquired. 'He says he kills people,' Reg replied. 'And does he?' I asked. Reg looked at me and shrugged."[247]

Eugene Paul Elvey – usually known as Paul – was an interesting and rather mysterious character who, via Alan Bruce Cooper, entered the story of the twins in the middle of 1967 and would go on to play a significant part in events to come – and in the twins' eventual downfall in the spring of 1968. In order to understand exactly how Elvey became a part of the story – and, more importantly, *why* – it is necessary to go back a few years to 1964.

In the summer of 1964, a pirate radio station called *Radio Sutch* – named after its initial founder, pop musician *Screaming Lord Sutch* – began broadcasting from an abandoned WWII sea fort called *Shivering Sands,* situated just outside British territorial waters in the mouth of the Thames Estuary. In 1965, Sutch lost interest in the radio station and left it in the hands of his manager, music producer Reg Calvert, who changed the name to *Radio City*. Paul Elvey was hired as a technician and sometimes acted as host DJ on some of the radio shows. Calvert con-

---

247   Pearson, John. *Notorious*. London: Century Publishing, 2010.

tinued to develop the business, secure more advertising revenue, and beam Radio City – *"Your Tower of Power"* – into more British homes. It must be remembered that unlicensed broadcasting from ships and abandoned wartime offshore structures was a concern for the government at this time due to the lack of control over what could be brought to the ears of the British public. Until new legislation was introduced in 1967, there was little that could be done, as Radio City and other pirate stations were operating from outside British territorial waters and therefore weren't subject to the laws of the land.

Reg Calvert began negotiations with another company with interests in pirate radio, called Project Atlanta, and a merger was proposed. Subsequently, a more powerful transmitter was delivered to the platform, but it was found to be unusable. Thereafter, the merger agreement fell apart but the transmitter was never collected. Reg Calvert then considered a merger with another pirate radio operator, but before any deal could be finalised, something rather dramatic happened.

In the early hours of 20 June 1966 – at the behest of a businessman called Major Oliver Smedley, who claimed ownership of the transmitter – *Shivering Sands* was boarded by a raiding party and the radio station was silenced. It was later discovered that a hatch had been opened, giving access to the raiders, and the person responsible for opening it was Paul Elvey. The next day, Reg Calvert went to Smedley's home in the village of Wendens Ambo in Essex to confront him, but there was to be no civilised discussion; Smedley pointed a shotgun at Calvert and shot him dead. Smedley was charged with murder, but the charge was reduced to manslaughter and then, at the trial, he was acquitted; a surprising result to say the least when the evidence is considered in retrospect. The trial judge was none other than *hanging Judge* Sir Aubrey Melford Stevenson, who would of course go on to preside over the Kray twins' *Old Bailey* trial in January 1969.

418

Following her husband's death, Dorothy Calvert took over the running of Radio City and immediately sacked Paul Elvey. Surprisingly, shortly afterwards she received a visit from a police officer who requested that she reinstate Paul Elvey as he was claiming he'd been unfairly dismissed. Since when did the police get involved in unfair dismissal cases? More surprising still is that no interview with Dorothy Calvert about her husband's death, the trial, Radio City, or anything else was ever printed or broadcast. Dorothy Calvert, it turned out, was the subject of a government 'D-notice': a government gagging order on the press and media requiring them not to publish or broadcast certain information for reasons of *national security!*

After new legislation was introduced in 1967, Radio City and other pirate radio stations were forced to close down. Interestingly, shortly afterwards, Dorothy Calvert was approached by Reggie Kray, taken to *The Astor Club*, and asked by Reggie to continue broadcasting:

"I understand you run Radio City?"

"Yes I did, but it's closed now. We had a court action against us a couple of weeks ago."

"Yes I heard, but I'd like you to carry on running it."

Dorothy, taken by surprise, shook her head. *"I can't. It would be breaking the law."*

"You don't need to worry about that. You can start broadcasting whenever you like and you'll be all right. I'll make sure of it."

"No, I'm really sorry, I can't. I'd be fined £100 a week if I went back on air."

"No, they won't prosecute you. I've got the government in my pocket."[248]

---

248   Moore, S.K. *Shivering Sands: 1960s Pirate Radio*. Coventry: Fillongley
       Publications, 2017.

Dorothy Calvert would not change her mind, and Reggie eventually conceded defeat and left it at that. One can only speculate as to why Reggie wanted control of Radio City. Much is known about the life and times of the Brothers Kray, but Reggie's brief meeting with Dorothy Calvert goes to show that there are still, and no doubt will always be, a few mysteries and unanswered questions.

Shivering Sands

On a clear day, looking out to sea from Shoeburyness beach near Southend, six (originally seven) weird-looking structures can be seen rising out of the sea, some 15km distant. The once interconnected towers are one of three *Maunsell* forts, named after their designer and positioned in the Thames Estuary during World War II. The towers are anti-aircraft gun and searchlight platforms and were constructed in 1943 to provide defence against Luftwaffe aircraft flying up the Thames to bomb London. *Shivering Sands Fort* was decommissioned in the '50s and finally abandoned in 1958.

During the 1960s, *Shivering Sands* became the operational base of a pirate radio station called *Radio City*. On 20 June 1966, after a dispute over the ownership of a transmitter, the sea fort was boarded by a raiding party and broadcasting temporarily ceased. One of Radio City's crew – a technician and DJ called Paul Elvey – secretly opened a hatch that allowed the raiders on board. Paul Elvey would mysteriously turn up later in the Krays' story as a supposed contract killer, playing an important part in the events leading to the Krays' arrest. Elvey was probably a spy, but quite who he was working for remains a mystery to this day.

Shivering Sands Fort still stands rusting today, though it can be difficult to see. The *Red Sands Maunsell Fort*, with all its seven towers intact, was likewise occupied by a pirate radio station in the '60s and is only 8km offshore. A third fort called *Nore* was dismantled in 1959 after being hit and badly damaged by a Norwegian ship in 1953. *Red Sands Fort* can be seen from the shore at Whitstable and, for a closer look, boat trips to see both remaining forts are available.

Even now, nearly half a century later, it is still not clear in just whose pocket Alan Bruce Cooper could be found or for whom he was working. (James Morton)[249]

We now know, at least, that Alan Bruce Cooper was working for a branch of the American Secret Service and certainly

---

249   Morton, James. *Krays: The Final Word*. London: Mirror Books, 2019.

for *Scotland Yard*, and that Paul Elvey was brought to the Kray party by Cooper. It appears likely that Elvey too was a plant working for a higher power; perhaps higher than the police. It is interesting that the head of *Scotland Yard*'s Murder Squad, John Du Rose, failed to tell Nipper Read that he had Cooper in his pocket, leaving Read to find out for himself much later on. Perhaps Du Rose was running a concurrent investigation and seeking some glory for himself, or could it be that he was directed to keep quiet about Cooper unless *absolutely necessary?*

In his role as *agent provocateur,* Cooper – assisted by Elvey – was instrumental in giving the police the means to bring about conspiracy to murder charges. Charges that enabled Read to make the initial arrests and keep the twins in custody until more serious charges of murder could be brought. During the committal proceedings at *Bow Street Magistrates Court*, of all the many charges levelled against the twins only the conspiracy charges involving Cooper and Elvey were dropped. Perhaps this was due to "*insufficient and confusing evidence*" as the magistrate stated, or perhaps – once murder charges were brought – it was thought no longer necessary to pursue the conspiracy charges and preferable to keep Cooper and Elvey away from the spotlight and scrutiny of an *Old Bailey* trial.

In the summer of 1967, a bizarre murder plot was hatched to kill Jimmy Evans – the man who had, in 1965, shot and injured Freddie Foreman's brother George. Most probably as a favour for their old friend and helper Freddie Foreman, the twins talked about killing Evans, and Alan Bruce Cooper stepped in with a plan. Cooper knew the former world-class speedway rider and gold smuggler Squire 'Split' Waterman who, at Cooper's request, made and supplied an ingenious murder weapon: a briefcase with a cyanide-filled vile inside and a needle that would spring out and deliver the poison when the case was swung against the victim's leg.

It was known that Evans was due to appear at the *Old Bailey* in June 1967 on a charge of robbery with violence, and the usually crowded entrance hall to the court was the chosen place to deploy the deadly device. *Expert killer* Paul Elvey was the man to carry out the hit. Elvey was provided with a photograph of Evans but, after two supposed attempts, he reported back that he was unable to positively identify his target. Hardly surprising considering Evans was not on bail at this time and was delivered directly from *Brixton Prison* to appear in court before being taken directly back again.[250]

One evening towards the end of February 1968, John Pearson was in the company of Ronnie Kray, Ronnie Hart, and an old-time criminal friend of Ron's called *Fat Steph* in a Turkish restaurant and club called *Gallipoli* near Liverpool Street station. Ron and Reg were taking protection money from the club and, along with The Firm, used it regularly. While enjoying an early evening drink and watching the gyrations of an ageing belly dancer, Pearson discovered something that came like a bolt from the blue. Ronnie mentioned that he knew Lord Boothby well – that he was a friend and that he had dined with him at the House of Lords. This was something of a bombshell and, if true, the implications were staggering. As far as Pearson and the rest of the world knew, Ronnie had simply had a couple of business meetings with Boothby in 1964, and accusations by the press that there was more to the relationship were subsequently found to be false, culminating in a grovelling apology from Mirror Newspapers – who admitted printing libellous lies and who were made to pay Boothby £40,000 in compensation.

---

250 Evans, Jimmy and Short, Martin. *The Survivor*. London: Mainstream Publishing, 2002.

Gallipoli

7-8 Bishopsgate, Churchyard, London EC2M 3TJ

Nearest TFL station: Liverpool Street underground.

In January 1967, *Gallipoli* – a Turkish club and restaurant with *sensual* entertainment (belly dancing)– opened and, soon afterwards, caught the attention of the Krays. Protection money was extorted and Ron, Reg, and The Firm adopted the club as a meeting place. One evening in February 1968, Ronnie – while in the company of biographer and journalist John Pearson – let slip that he was, and had been for some time, a close friend of Lord Boothby. This revelation, at this time, led to the eventual exposure of the top-level government cover-up behind the Boothby scandal.

Tucked in between towering glass office blocks in the City of London, close to Liverpool Street station, is a delightfully incongruous, ornate, Victorian kiosk. This was the entrance to the below-ground Turkish baths, built and opened in 1895. Following the closure of the baths in the 1950s, the subterranean space was used for storage until it became the *Gallipoli* club in 1967. *Gallipoli* was succeeded by further restaurants and clubs and today is a private party and function venue called *The Victorian Bath House*.

Pearson began digging. As a former journalist he knew Norman Lucas, the *Mirror*'s crime correspondent who had first broken the Peer and the Gangster story, and Lucas told him all he knew. Pearson spoke to a senior police officer involved in the surveillance of the Krays and discovered that Boothby, Driberg, and other well-known persons had been seen attending suspected sex parties with young boys at Ronnie's *Cedra Court* flat. After the twins' arrest in May, former Kray associates became much more talkative and he discovered the sordid details of Boothby's sexual shenanigans at *Cedra Court*.

Violet, the twins' mother, gave Pearson photographs and letters to Ronnie from Boothby dated well before Boothby's supposed *"three only brief business meetings with Mr Kray."* Then, in 1969, Pearson interviewed Boothby himself, who told him that Prime Minister Harold Wilson was responsible for sending the Labour Party's top lawyer and Mr Fixit, Arnold Goodman, to his aid. It was glaringly obvious that there had been a cover-up of epic proportions perpetrated and sanctioned at the highest level of the British Government.

John Pearson was set to publish his book in which he would reveal all he knew but, perhaps unsurprisingly, there was a problem. His home and his literary agent's office were broken into and copies of his manuscript were stolen. Thereafter, he received a phone call from Arnold 'Two Dinners' Goodman himself, who advised Pearson that it would not be in his best interest to go ahead and publish. *The Observer* newspaper, in which the book was to be serialised, pulled out of the deal and his publisher dropped the book like a hot rock. Pearson was left high and dry, with no book deal and no income. Happily, however, he was able to find another publisher and *The Profession of Violence* – with a dumbed-down version of the Boothby business – was published in 1972. After Boothby's death in 1986 and the release of government papers in 1994, later editions of *The Profession of Violence* – along with another book, *The Cult of Violence,* in 2001 – revealed most of the important facts. In the 2009 television documentary *The Gangster and the Pervert Peer,* the full story in all its fascinating glory, including the bullying and the stifling of John Pearson, was finally disclosed.

In April 1968, Ron and Reg took possession of a large country house in the Suffolk village of Bildeston. Gone were the days of plenty, in the early '60s, when the twins were riding high on a wave of easy money; now they were strapped for cash so, to buy the house, they turned to their friend and personal banker Geoff Allen, who lent them the money. The twins bought *The Brooks* in their mother's name for £11,000.[251] Work needed to be done to bring the house up to scratch and builders were hired to do most of the work, but the twins pitched in with painting and decorating. Mum Violet and Dad Charles moved into the gatehouse cottage and Violet would cook Sunday dinner up at the house for Ron, Reg, girlfriend Carol Thompson, friends, and members of The Firm who were invited to spend the weekend. Some of Bildeston's residents must have known who the twins were and word must have spread ("*Guess who's got The Brooks?*"), but Ron and Reg got on well with the locals and enjoyed evening drinks in the nearby *Red Lion* and other local inns. Ron was happy and in his element, playing the role of country squire and entertaining the idea of retiring there – with just the occasional trip back to London for business. Reg, on the other hand, was tense and anxious at this time. Deep down, he knew that sooner or later their luck would run out and the police would come crashing into their lives, bringing it all to an end. *Sooner,* as it turned out; the twins had just a few short weeks left before Nipper and his team would swoop in.

The Brooks

High Street, Bildeston, Suffolk, IP7 7EB

With the help of their friend Geoff Allen, Ron and Reg bought the elegant cream-painted Edwardian villa for £11,000 in the early spring of 1968.

Situated just behind the high street in the serene Suffolk village of Bildeston, the seven-bedroom prop-

251 Pearson, John. *The Cult of Violence*. London: Orion Books, 2001.

erty set in six acres of land also included a separate cottage, which was used for country breaks by the twins' parents, Violet and Charles. Ronnie, who particularly enjoyed country life, bought a donkey and called it Figaro. He kept it in the grounds and was happy to let the local children ride it. The twins were only able to enjoy their newly acquired country retreat for a few short weeks before they were arrested on 8 May 1968. After their arrest, the police searched the house and dug up some of the grounds, looking for bodies.

The Brooks was put up for sale in July 2022 with a price tag of £2.25 million.[252]

Tom Mangold, the journalist who had interviewed the twins on television following their acquittal from the charge of demanding money with menaces in April 1965, continued a professional association with the twins. Ronnie asked him to be present and witness the corrupt policeman accepting money in *The Bakers Arms*, and name the bent copper on the BBC. Tom Mangold declined, but continued to be summoned to meet the twins from time to time.

Eventually, word reached him that Ron and Reg believed he knew too much about their involvement with Frank Mitchell's disappearance and were planning to kill him. Tom Mangold took the threat seriously and made arrangements to go to Vietnam and cover the war for BBC television news. Not wishing to give the impression that he was running away, he bravely agreed to meet Reggie in *The Carpenters Arms*. When Reggie discovered the journalist was going to Vietnam, he asked if he could go with him as part of the crew. Tom Mangold told

---

252 rightmove.co.uk: The Brooks, Bildeston.

Reggie that he would discuss it with his bosses – and then made a hasty exit. [253]

Reggie – who was clearly aware that time was running out – discussed with John Pearson the possibility of joining the French Foreign Legion or enlisting in the American Army and going to fight in Vietnam. But this, of course, was just wistful pondering; Reggie could never abandon his troubled twin and he knew it.

By this point in their relationship, John Pearson too was beginning to worry that his life, or at least his good health, was in danger. The twins began to suspect that he was working for MI5 or the police, and signs of their mistrust were becoming apparent. John Pearson gradually began to distance himself from the deadly duo, and it must have been with some relief when he later heard, in May 1968, that the twins had been arrested.

Tom Mangold too must have breathed a sigh of relief; he had been in Saigon for just a few days when a telex arrived informing him of the Kray twins' arrest.

In early November 1964, Ronnie had flown to New York on a tourist visa to meet Angelo Bruno and other top Mafiosi, but he was refused entry by US immigration officials and put on the next flight back to London. On 3 April 1968, Ronnie once again took a transatlantic flight, and this time he passed through immigration control at New York's *John F. Kennedy Airport* without a problem. Alan Bruce Cooper – with the help of the American Secret Service, for whom he was working – obtained Ronnie's visa and told him it had been made possible by his Mafia connections. Mafia connections were the purpose of the

---

253 Mangold, Tom. *Splashed! A Life from Print to Panorama*. Hull: Biteback Publishing, 2016.

trip, and the intention was for Ronnie to meet some leading members of the American Cosa Nostra.

Originally, the plan had been for both twins to take the trip, but Reggie didn't fully trust Cooper and decided not to go. Dickie Morgan took Reggie's place. So, Ronnie, Dickie, and Cooper travelled first to Paris where they collected the visas from a supposed office of the American Consulate and then to New York, flying from Paris *Orly Airport*. They were met in the Big Apple by Joey Kaufman, who had made reservations for them at the *Warwick* hotel in central Manhattan. Mafia-connected go-between Joey Kaufman was already known to Ronnie through his involvement with stolen bearer bonds and Mafia-run gambling clubs in London.

Quite what was hoped to be gained by allowing Ronnie to travel to New York is uncertain, but it was likely a test of the strength of the Kray/Mafia relationship and to see who, on the American side, was involved. Ronnie did not meet any top Mafia people; they knew the FBI would be watching and decided to stay well away. Colombo crime family capo *Crazy Joe Gallo* and his bodyguard Frank Illiano put in a brief appearance, but – along with some other characters Ronnie met – they may well have been actors arranged by Cooper to play the part of New York mobsters.

New York

In early April 1968, Ronnie, Dickie Morgan, and Alan Bruce Cooper flew to New York for a short visit. While there, they stayed at the *Warwick* hotel, in central Manhattan at 65 West 54th Street. Ronnie was introduced to a few characters who were supposedly members of the American Mafia, but some – if not all – were likely actors arranged by Alan Bruce Cooper to play the part of

'*Noo Yoik*' wiseguys. Ronnie did, however, meet some of his American boxing heroes at *Gallaghers Steakhouse*, including the legendary world middleweight champion Rocco Barbella – better known as Rocky Graziano.

The *Warwick* hotel – which has played host to Elvis Presley, James Dean, Elizabeth Taylor, the Beatles, and of course Ronnie Kray – was built in 1926 and remains one of New York's most famous and prestigious hotels.

Gallaghers Steakhouse – still in business today, at 228 West 52nd Street – has, since its opening in 1927, attracted a glamorous mix of actors, socialites, politicians and, in particular, sports stars. *Gallaghers* is where the first 'New York Strip' steak was served.

Back in early December 1967, during his enquiries into the Krays' activities, Nipper Read had approached and talked to Leslie Payne in the hope of gaining information. He was in luck; Payne, who knew that Jack McVitie had been sent by the twins to kill him, decided to help the police. This was the breakthrough Nipper had been hoping for, and when he told Payne that, in return for his cooperation, he would do all he could to keep him from prosecution, Payne began spilling the beans. Nipper learned the details of long firm frauds, dealings in stolen bearer bonds, protection rackets, and numerous violent assaults – but with Payne, a criminal himself, as the only witness, it was not enough to guarantee that the twins would be remanded in custody long enough to execute the next phase of his plan.

Nipper knew that George Cornell had been murdered by Ronnie Kray, and strongly suspected that Frank Mitchell and Jack McVitie had met the same fate, but the only way he would stand a chance of getting witnesses to talk was to get the twins and their cohorts off the streets and safely locked up with no prospect of being released on bail. He needed more substantial charges. Eventually, in April 1968, Read struck lucky and uncovered a plot by the twins to kill a man called George Caruana. Conspiracy to murder is a very serious charge.

Ron and Reg were friendly with Bernie Silver who, along with Maltese gangster Big Frank Mifsud, ran most of the prostitution, pornography, clip joints, and strip clubs in Soho's sleazy square mile. Bernie Silver was paying money to corrupt police officers and had most of the Met's Vice Squad and at least one very senior policeman in his pocket. Nurturing a good relationship with Silver was beneficial to the twins, as they too were able to take advantage of his established police information service.

Following a fallout with a Maltese club owner called George Caruana, Silver approached the twins and asked them to teach Caruana a lesson – but rather than just a beating, as requested, the twins decided to kill Caruana. Realising he'd made a mistake, Silver tried to call the twins off, but it was too late. Ron and Reg saw an opportunity to gain a hold over Silver, which would enable them to move in and help themselves to a big slice – if not all – of his very lucrative business. Prostitution and allied trades was an area of business traditionally avoided by home-grown gangsters, but the huge profits on offer were reason enough for the twins to put moralistic judgements and traditions to one side.

Following the complete failure of a bizarre scheme cooked up by Cooper to relieve some Congolese gentlemen of a large amount of cash, Cooper was losing the trust of the twins – especially Reggie. The plan had been to take the cash as a down payment for a promised but bogus mission by the Krays' men to rescue the Congolese leader Moise Tshombe from imprisonment in Algeria. No money was forthcoming – in fact, none of Cooper's promises, plans, and schemes had so far become a reality, and his continued well-being was looking far from assured. As far as the Krays were concerned, it was the last chance saloon for Cooper, who was given the job of killing George Caruana.

Cooper was under instructions to involve the Krays in conspiracies to commit serious crimes that would ultimately fail, so this was, at least, another opportunity for Cooper – with the help of Paul Elvey – to please his handlers and keep himself out of jail.

Following a meeting that took place just after Ronnie returned from America, Elvey bought a lethal crossbow, paid for by the twins, and practised for a while – but this proved to be unsatisfactory. It was decided that gelignite taped to the underside of Caruana's car – which would detonate when the ignition key was turned – would do a better job. So, Cooper sent Elvey on a trip to Scotland to collect the gelignite.

By means of Home Office-authorised telephone wiretaps, Nipper Read and his team had, for some time, been listening in on the telephone conversations of leading members of the Kray organisation. When Nipper learned of Elvey's trip to Scotland to collect some *dodgy gear,* he immediately contacted an associate in Glasgow City Police. Consequently, Elvey was caught red-handed with the gelignite in his possession and arrested. Nipper and Sergeant Algie Hemmingway flew to Glasgow to interview Elvey who, after a period of interrogation, told all. Nipper heard details of the plot ordered by the twins and devised by Cooper to kill George Caruana, as well as details of the failed attempt, a year earlier, to kill a man with the cyanide briefcase. Nipper telephoned his right-hand man DI Frank Cater in London, and the cyanide briefcase was found in Elvey's garage – and a crossbow in the boot of his car. Nipper sent out an *all-points bulletin* for Cooper's arrest and, on his return to London, Cooper was brought to him at *Tintagel House.*

The Police Crime Museum

New Scotland Yard, Victoria Embankment, London SW1A 2JL

Located in the basement of *New Scotland Yard* is a private museum containing criminal memorabilia dating back to the late 19th century. Among the items held there are the gun used by Reggie Kray when he tried to kill Jack 'The Hat' McVitie, and the cyanide briefcase that was designed to kill Jimmy Evans on the orders of the Kray twins.

Unfortunately, the museum is closed to the public and the exhibits are only accessible to serving police officers. Occasionally, items are loaned to other museums for temporary exhibitions. In 2016, the Museum of London held an exhibition called *The Crime Museum Uncovered* in which the gun and the cyanide briefcase could be viewed by the public. Hopefully, there will be other opportunities for the public to see some of the private collection in the future.

Cooper stuttered his way through the interview in which he continuously denied any connection with Elvey and claimed he knew nothing about the gelignite. *"In that case,"* said Nipper, *"I'm going to charge you with conspiracy to murder."* Cooper then announced that he was working undercover for John Du Rose and had been doing so for the past two years. This came as a surprise to Nipper and, at first, he refused to believe it – but then, after talking to Du Rose, he discovered that Cooper was telling the truth. Unable to make sense of what he was hearing, Nipper's emotions got the better of him and he became upset and angry. Du Rose played the whole thing down and assured Nipper that he would, of course, have told him immediately if Cooper had passed on anything of significance.

Although perplexed and unhappy, Nipper realised — after he'd calmed down – that he had no choice but to accept the circumstances as they now were and use Cooper to his advantage. Worried that Cooper might do a runner, he knew he needed to keep him secured while at the same time getting him back in the field – before his absence aroused the suspicion of the Krays. So, Cooper was ensconced, under guard, in a safe house in Surrey, and a plan was hatched to gain information and hopefully incriminate the twins. Cooper was known, by all who knew him, to suffer from a stomach ulcer, so Nipper installed him in a private clinic – with the cooperation of the doctors – in Weymouth Street, Marylebone under the pretence that his condition had taken a turn for the worse. Hidden microphones were placed in Cooper's room so that Nipper and DI Frank Cater, hiding in an adjacent room, could listen in and record conversations.[254]

Cooper telephoned the twins, told them of his predicament, and asked them to visit. Ronnie was sympathetic, but explained that they were tired having just returned from Suffolk and, instead, they would send Tom Cowley along with some *nice eggs*. Cowley, perhaps suspecting something, was giving nothing away, and Nipper was about to write the whole thing off as a failure when an unexpected bonus presented itself. Mafia go-between Joey Kaufman entered Cooper's room and greeted him with an exuberant, *"Hi, how ya doin?"* Kaufman told Cooper that a new batch of stolen bearer bonds would be arriving by post at his hotel, *The Mayfair*, in a few days' time.

---

254   Read, Leonard with Morton, James. *Nipper Read: The Man who Nicked the Krays*. London: MacDonald & Co, 1991.

After consulting with his right-hand man, Frank Cater, Nipper decided there could be no more waiting – it was time to act. So, in the early hours of Wednesday 8 May 1968, teams of police officers – some of them armed – from ten regional crime squads assembled at *Tintagel House*, their watches synchronised in readiness for the arrest of the twins, and their Firm, in one simultaneous swoop set to take place at 6am sharp.

Earlier that evening, the twins and friends had gathered in *The Old Horns* for a party to welcome Joey Kaufman back from America. When the pub closed at 11pm, a fleet of cars headed to *The Astor Club*, where the party continued into the early hours. Having been watched by the police for years, the twins and The Firm liked to think they could recognise a plain-clothes copper when they saw one. They were used to being watched and generally unconcerned, but this night there seemed to be more than usual.

After 178 Vallance Road and most other houses in the area were earmarked for demolition, the twins' parents had been given a new council flat in a modern tower block, just over a mile away in Bunhill Row. Violet and Charles had moved into their new flat on the ninth floor of *Braithwaite House* in late 1967 or early 1968 and, as before, the twins continued to use their parents' home as a base. Leaving her old home with all its memories – as for so many others – was heartbreaking for Violet, but a bathroom, central heating, and all mod cons must, at least, have been of some consolation.

As day was breaking across London on 8 May, sleeping gangsters and criminal associates were woken by the sound of doors being hammered on or smashed in. Nipper and Frank Cater reserved the arrest of the twins for themselves and, at 6am, Nipper knocked loudly on the door of the ninth-floor flat. Receiving no response, Sergeant Algie Hemmingway jemmied the door and, as it fell off its hinges, a posse of police officers stormed inside. A young man of 22, who had been sleeping on the sofa, was woken and arrested. Reggie was in bed with a young woman (not his girlfriend Carol Thompson) and Ronnie was in bed with a 16-year-old boy. Fortunately for them, the twins' parents Violet and Charles were in Suffolk, staying at *The Brooks*. Drowsy and hung-over after just a couple of hours' sleep, the twins offered no resistance. Arrested and handcuffed, they were taken to *West End Central Police Station* where they were formally charged with conspiracy to murder.

Braithwaite House

Bunhill Row, London EC1Y 8NE

Nearest TFL station: Old Street underground.

Braithwaite House is a 19-storey residential apartment block, typical of the architectural style of the many high-rise, utilitarian buildings erected in the 1960s to house people displaced by the huge slum clearance programmes in London and other cities.

Following a demolition order placed on their Vallance Road home, Violet and Charles Kray, the twins' parents, moved into flat 43 on the ninth floor in late 1967 or early 1968 – and the twins joined them. David Bailey took what are now well-known photographs of the twins at *Braithwaite House*, holding their pet pythons Read and Gerrard, named after the two detectives who, in 1964, tried but failed to have them convicted of demanding money with menaces.

At 6am on Wednesday 8 May 1968, while Violet and Charles were staying at their sons' newly acquired coun-

---

try mansion in Suffolk, the police stormed into the flat and arrested the twins, effectively ending their time on this earth as free men.

Braithwaite House overlooks *Bunhill Fields Burial Ground*, a public garden and final resting place of many notable people from the 17th, 18th, and 19th centuries, including John Bunyan, Daniel Defoe, and William Blake.

Nipper had previously arranged for sufficient cells to be made available at *West End Central Police Station* and, in total, 20 prisoners were brought there following the dawn swoop – among them Joey Kaufman, who protested loudly and continued to do so until two days later when a package containing $190,000[255] in stolen bearer bonds, addressed to him, was picked up at *The Mayfair Hotel*.

Many of The Firm – including Charlie Kray, Connie Whitehead, Tom Cowley, and Tommy 'The Bear' Brown – were now in custody, but others, including Jack Dickson, Albert Donoghue, Ian Barrie, and Ronnie Hart, were still at large. Chief Inspector Harry Mooney, seconded to Nipper's squad the previous year, led a team of 35 officers who were given the task of rounding up the stragglers who'd escaped the first trawl.

More arrests were made in the following days, and Jack Dickson was arrested a week later in *The Coach and Horses*, Stoke Newington. Donoghue hid out in a caravan at Selsey in Sussex with Ronnie Hart for a week but, worried that they looked suspicious among the families of holidaymakers, Albert returned to London and hid in an East End flat with Dickie Morgan. Both were arrested early one morning in late May

---

255 Ibid.

when the police stormed into the flat. Ian Barrie remained at liberty for some time before eventually being arrested on 29 June in the *British Oak* pub on Lea Bridge Road.[256] Big Pat Connolly avoided the purge altogether, as he was in prison at the time beginning a two-year sentence after being arrested for carrying a gun on a train to Glasgow. Ronnie Hart remained unaccounted for, and it wasn't until 3 September when he handed himself in at *Tintagel House* that Nipper was able to interview him. Hart made a formal statement and, on the strength of what Nipper now knew about McVitie's murder, Ronnie Bender, the Lambrianou brothers, and Freddie Foreman were also arrested.

West End Central Police Station

27 Savile Row, London W1S 2EX

Nearest TFL station: Oxford Circus underground.

Situated at the junction with Boyle Street, *West End Central* was built and opened in 1940. It was, until its closure in 2017, the headquarters of C Division of the Metropolitan Police. Nipper Read served at the police station as a Detective Chief Inspector from March 1966 until he was promoted to Superintendent and transferred to *Scotland Yard* in the summer of 1967.

After their arrests in the early morning of Wednesday 8 May 1968, Ron and Reg were brought to *West End Central* and charged with a number of offences – includ-

---

256 Situated at 130 Lea Bridge Road, Lower Clapton E5 9RB, the *British Oak* closed in 1999 and was demolished in 2002. A modern apartment building now occupies the site.

ing conspiracy to murder.

On January 30 1969, while the twins were on trial at the *Old Bailey*, the Beatles famously played an impromptu concert on the roof of their Apple Corps headquarters at number 3 Savile Row. Officers from *West End Central* were dispatched to investigate following complaints about the noise.

The building was sold in 2021 and currently stands empty, awaiting planning permission for complete redevelopment.

Applications for bail at *Bow Street Magistrates Court* began immediately, and those facing the more serious charges of conspiracy to murder and demanding money with menaces were remanded in custody. Nine of the defendants charged with offences relating to long firm frauds and dealings in stolen bearer bonds were released on bail. Further and repeated bail applications were heard over the next few weeks as more people were arrested and fresh charges read out. Committal proceedings were scheduled to begin in June and, for Nipper and his team, the pressure was on. He needed to work fast to get the evidence he required to bring murder charges and convince witnesses to stand up and be counted. This was no easy task, as it was widely believed that the twins were fireproof and that they would soon walk away, free to wreak vengeance on anyone who had dared speak out against them.

Some of the prisoners, including Ron and Reg, were held in *Brixton Prison* and others in *Wandsworth*. As remand prisoners, the twins were still technically innocent and, as such, enjoyed more privileges than convicted criminals. They were allowed to wear their own clothes; food, alcohol, and cigarettes could be brought in from the outside; and there was no limit on the number of visitors they could receive. Although most of the major players were incarcerated, enough old friends were visiting the jail to ensure that the twins' messages to anyone thinking of talking to the police were circulated.

There was a long-held belief in the East End that due to corrupt, paid-off contacts within the police, the twins would quickly be made aware of anyone talking to them about Kray business. This was not an unfounded concern, and Nipper and his team needed to make great efforts to persuade and assure potential witnesses that, in this case, any information given would remain in the strictest of confidence – with absolutely no possible danger of the twins hearing about it. Nipper and the police used all their power and determination to convince the East End community that they were not their common enemy and that the mythical wall of silence imprisoned rather than protected them.

The first of the major players to break ranks and start talking were Billy Exley, Limehouse Willy, and Dickie Morgan, closely followed by Charlie Mitchell, the twins' associate in the bearer bonds business. Lennie 'Books' Dunn – the man whose flat was used to hide Frank Mitchell – in fear of his life, presented himself at *West Ham Police Station*. Lisa – the hostess from *Winston's* nightclub who kept Frank happy at Lennie Dunn's flat – was traced after some clever detective work and, although terrified, made a statement. Without a doubt, Nipper's most important and credible witness was Frances the barmaid from *The Blind Beggar*, present at the time of George Cornell's murder. Chief Inspector Harry Mooney – a genial Irishman – had managed to gain her confidence, persuading her to make a statement and give evidence in court. Frances, to be known only as Mrs X, was now Nipper's trump card.

Jack Dickson asked to see Nipper and then threw in his lot with the prosecution, and Albert Donoghue – who had been told by the twins to take the rap for Frank Mitchell's murder *or else* – did the same. It was from Donoghue that Nipper finally learned that Frank Mitchell, as he suspected, had indeed been murdered – executed on the orders of the Krays. 'Blonde Carol' Skinner, who at first denied any knowledge of the McVitie murder, eventually caved in and told Nipper all she knew. Harry Hopwood – the Kray family friend and owner of the flat where the twins went straight after McVitie's murder – when told he could be charged as an accessory to murder, broke down and told all. Ronnie Hart, who was arrested in early September, turned Queen's evidence and was given police protection; he was to be used as the chief witness for the prosecution in the McVitie murder case. All crown witnesses were given round-the-clock police protection and, through contacts in the underworld, word was put out that the police would tolerate no intimidation tactics and would come down like a ton of bricks on anyone attempting to do so.

Unlike the majority of people arrested on fraud charges alone Joey Kaufman was not given bail and, while remanded in *Brixton*, his run of bad luck got worse. Reggie smashed him in the face with his trademark left hook and broke his jaw. According to Reggie, it was because Kaufman had made a statement blaming the twins for his involvement in the bonds charges.[257] Kaufman needed surgery and was promptly shipped out of *Brixton*.

On 31 May at *Bow Street Court*, Nipper Read – proudly wearing his Murder Squad motif tie – formally charged the twins with Frank Mitchell's murder. Then, on 25 June, the first day of the committal proceedings, Nipper charged Ronnie with Cornell's murder. Reggie was charged with the murder of Jack McVitie on 19 September.

Committal proceedings began at *Bow Street* on Tuesday 25 June and, throughout the summer of 1968, on weekdays, the

---

257 Kray, Reg. *A Way of Life*. London: Pan Books, 2001.

public were treated to a spectacular extravaganza. Roads were closed to traffic and the prisoners were brought to *Bow Street* from *Brixton* and *Wandsworth* in a convoy of armoured prison vans and police vehicles, flanked by motorcycle outriders racing through the streets at high speed with sirens wailing. Journalists questioned the necessity of such a public spectacle, suggesting – with good reason – that it would create prejudice against the accused. Publicity, however, was something the twins thrived on, and Reggie had, on 17 May, chosen the option to have reporting restrictions lifted. The press had a field day and, when it was later realised that this was not necessarily to their advantage, the twins' lawyers tried, unsuccessfully, to have the restrictions reimposed.

Magistrates considered the charges and the evidence put before them. In some of the fraud cases, evidence to support the involvement of a number of individuals was deemed insufficient, and a few – including Micky Fawcett and Sammy Lederman – were discharged. Most of the charges levelled against the twins were given the green light for trial at the High Court, but the charges of conspiracy to murder were dropped. Evidence given by Cooper and Elvey relating to the cyanide briefcase and the gelignite bomb was, the magistrate decided, "*too confusing to be put before a jury.*" During the hearings of the somewhat bizarre conspiracy cases, the press reported an outburst by Reggie: *"Excuse me, sir, is James Bond going to be called as a witness? This is getting ridiculous."*[258]

The committal proceedings at *Bow Street Court* ended in October 1968 and a date was set for the trial at the *Old Bailey* to begin. Nipper Read and the prosecuting council for the crown decided that the lesser charges of fraud, demanding money with menaces, and GBH would be held back in reserve and

---

258 *Daily Mirror*, Thursday 18th July 1968.

dealt with at a later date. Only the charges relating to the three murders would be heard at the main *Old Bailey* trial, and the murders of Cornell and McVitie would be joined in one indictment. A completely separate trial would be held for the murder of Frank Mitchell.

Bow Street Magistrates Court

28 Bow Street, Covent Garden, London WC2E 7AW

There has been a court on Bow Street since 1740. In 1749, in response to rising crime and disorder in the Covent Garden area associated with gin consumption, the magistrate brought together a team of six constables who came to be known as the *Bow Street Runners*. By 1800 there were 68 Bow Street Runners forming the country's first professional, state-sponsored, police force. This pioneering force was disbanded in 1839 and its members were incorporated into Robert Peel's newly-formed Metropolitan Police.

Work on the existing building began in 1878 and was completed in 1881. The date 1879 set in the stonework above the entrance is the date that the work was originally scheduled to be finished. *Bow Street Magistrates Court* was, until its closure in 2006, probably the most famous magistrates court in England.

Following their arrests in 1968, the Kray twins and many of their associates appeared in Court Number One at *Bow Street* for bail and preliminary hearings before being sent for trial by jury at the *Old Bailey*.

Situated directly opposite the *Royal Opera House*, the Victorian court building is now a 91-room luxury hotel called *NoMad,* which opened in May 2021. Around the back of the building in *Martlett Court* is the entrance to the former *Bow Street Police Station* – now *Bow Street Police Museum*, which presents the history of policing in the area from the 18th century until 1992, when the police station closed. The cells in which the Krays and The Firm were held awaiting their appearance in the court now form the museum's galleries.

Due to the unusually large numbers appearing before the magistrates at *Bow Street* in the Kray case, the existing dock – which only seated five at a squeeze – was clearly inadequate. In order to increase capacity and accommodate all the defendants appearing together, a specially built, temporary super-dock was installed. The original *Bow Street* dock is now on display in the *National Justice Museum*, Nottingham. (High Pavement, Nottingham NG1 1HN.)

On Wednesday 8 January 1969, the public gallery in Court Number One at the *Old Bailey* was packed with spectators waiting for what was to be one of the longest and most expensive trials in British History to begin. Presiding over the trial was Judge Sir Aubrey Melford Stevenson, a strict no-nonsense character not known for his tolerance or leniency. Melford Stevenson lived in Winchelsea, East Sussex in a house appropriately named *Truncheons*.[259] Leading the team of prosecuting barristers for the crown was Kenneth Jones, QC. John Platts-Mills, QC represented Ronnie, and Reggie was represented by Paul Wrightson, QC.

Ron and Reg, looking immaculate in sharp suits, freshly pressed white shirts, and neat ties, appeared relaxed and confi-

---

259 *Truncheons* is a 1930s-built, five-bedroom detached private residence at Rectory Lane, Winchelsea, Rother, TN36 4AB.

dent. On entering the court they smiled at friends and family in the public gallery, gave a half-bow to the judge, and respectfully nodded towards the phalanx of assembled barristers. Joining them in the dock were the equally well-turned-out Ian Barrie, Charlie Kray, Freddie Foreman, Chris and Tony Lambrianou, Ronnie Bender, Connie Whitehead, and Tony Barry, part-owner of *The Regency Club* who had delivered the gun to Ronnie on the night of Jack McVitie's murder.

Ronnie Kray and Ian Barrie pleaded not guilty to the murder of George Cornell, and Reg Kray pleaded not guilty to being an accessory after the fact. Ron, Reg, the Lambrianou brothers, Ronnie Bender, and Tony Barry pleaded not guilty to Jack McVitie's murder, and Charlie Kray, Freddie Foreman, and Connie Whitehead pleaded not guilty to being accessories.

Proceedings began with arguments from the defence that the Cornell and McVitie murder cases should be dealt with separately, but Melford Stevenson was having none of it and ruled that there would be no changes. The next day, due to the large number of defendants in the dock, the judge ordered that they wear numbered placards with pink ribbons around their necks for identification. This didn't go down well. The first to object was Freddie Foreman, who tore up the placard and threw the pieces on the floor. With the exception of Tony Barry, all the others followed suit. Melford Stevenson ordered that the prisoners return to the cells and remain there until they complied. Eventually, after much argument by the defence barristers, a compromise was reached and the identification numbers were placed on the front of the dock.

On Friday 10 January the first of the prosecution's witnesses in the case of the George Cornell murder was called; Frances, the barmaid who had seen Ronnie shoot Cornell in *The Blind Beggar*. Despite penetrating questions from the defence, she bravely held her composure and calmly, with eloquence, told the court what she had seen, pointing her finger at Ronnie Kray.

The demure yet courageous little woman in the witness box was totally convincing and it was apparent to all present that the trial was all but ended almost as soon as it had begun. The result was a foregone conclusion and everyone knew it.

Early in the trial, Firm member Jack Dickson pleaded guilty to harbouring Frank Mitchell and was given a nine-month sentence. Having already spent four months on remand, this effectively meant his almost immediate release. Dickson was called as a crown witness and gave evidence against Ronnie in the Cornell murder case. All three Teale brothers – Alfie, Bobby, and David – gave evidence for the prosecution in the Cornell murder case, and so too did Billy Exley, suffering from a heart condition and brought into court in a wheelchair. Ronnie Hart gave damning evidence against the twins in the McVitie case and was backed up by evidence given by 'Blonde Carol' Skinner and old Kray family friend Harry Hopwood.

Ronnie's barrister, John Platts-Mills, refused to be clear and confirm whether it was or was not his client's intention to go into the witness box and give evidence. Taking the stand would of course allow Ronnie to speak in his defence, but it was not necessarily the right choice as he would be subjected to vigorous cross-examination by the prosecution.

On Thursday 30 January, as the court was about to adjourn, Ronnie made his choice and shouted from the dock, "*I'm going into the box!*" Ronnie claimed that he was completely innocent of all the charges; the whole thing was a frame-up and he was the victim of a vendetta by the press and the police. Ronnie spoke of his association with peers of the realm and famous people in the world of entertainment. *"If I wasn't here now I would be having tea with Judy Garland,"* said Ronnie. Under cross-examination from prosecuting barrister Kenneth Jones, Ronnie did himself no favours by responding to questions with aggression and disdain. When asked about the fact that he was referred to in some circles as *The Colonel*, Ronnie retorted by telling the barrister that he was known as *Taffy Jones* and that he would do more good as a coal miner than a prosecutor. Judge Melford Stevenson spoke sharply to Ronnie, telling him he would do no good for himself by being impertinent.[260]

Reggie too demonstrated a propensity for angry, aggressive outbursts for everyone to see; just the kind of behaviour that the misunderstood, victimised, charitably-minded twin businessmen were attempting to deny. On Thursday 6 February, Kenneth Jones asked a female defence witness for Ronnie Bender (Bubbles Shea) about her relationship with Kray's late wife. Reggie jumped up, gripped the edge of the dock, and shouted at Mr Jones, *"You fat slob – what has it got to do with the case?"*

Melford Stevenson ordered, *"Take him down,"* and Reggie pointed a finger at the judge and said, *"You're biased; I've had enough of your comments."*

Then came a torrent of words directed at the police and various people in the court – *"dirty pigs, stinking pigs, bastards, animals, fat slobs."*[261]

On Tuesday March 4 1969, all the defendants – with the exception of Tony Barry – were found guilty. Tony Barry, co-owner of *The Regency Club* who was instructed to take a gun to the flat where McVitie was murdered, insisted he acted under duress and believed that his life would have been in danger had he refused. Barry, who had been kept in *Maidstone Prison* during the trial for his own safety, was found not guilty of murder and discharged.

The following day, Wednesday 5 March, the defendants were brought back to court for sentencing and Melford Stevenson, addressing Ronnie first, gave his now famous sen-

---

260   Morton, James. *Krays: The Final Word*. London: Mirror Books, 2019.

261   *Newcastle Journal*, Friday 7 February 1969.

tencing remarks:

"I'm not going to waste words on you. In my view, society has earned a rest from your activities and I recommend that you be detained for thirty years."

Reggie too was sentenced to life with a minimum tariff of 30 years. Ian Barrie and Ronnie Bender were given life sentences with a minimum of 20 years. Chris and Tony Lambrianou were given life with a 15-year minimum. Charlie Kray and Freddie Foreman, who were both found guilty of being accessories to murder, were each given ten years, and Connie Whitehead was sentenced to eight.

Six weeks later, on 15 April, the Frank Mitchell murder trial began in Court Number Two of the *Old Bailey*, this time presided over by Mr Justice Lawton. Reggie, Ronnie, Charlie Kray, and Freddie Foreman were each charged with Mitchell's murder. Connie Whitehead, Pat Connolly, Tom Cowley, and Wally Garelick all faced charges relating to the escape and harbouring of Frank Mitchell. Absent from court were the three men believed to have accompanied Freddie Foreman in the van in which Mitchell was murdered. Alfie Gerrard, Jerry Callaghan, and Ronnie Oliffe had all disappeared and could not be found; Teddy Smith was also missing. The chief witness for the prosecution was Firm member Albert Donoghue. Other witnesses included Billy Exley, Jack Dickson, Lisa the hostess, and Lennie 'Books' Dunn.

This trial too was not without its dramas. Reggie protested loudly that he was being provoked by one of the attendant police officers and exclaimed, *"If he continues to provoke me, I can't be responsible for my actions. If he likes to come round the back with me or down the cells…"*[262]

Charlie Kray broke down in the witness box under cross-ex-

---

[262] *The Birmingham Post*, Tuesday 29th April 1969.

amination and his wife Dolly collapsed and had to be helped out of court. While Charlie was being questioned, Ronnie took his turn to call prosecuting barrister Kenneth Jones a *"fat slob"*[263] – he was probably getting used to it by now.

Proving the defendants guilty beyond reasonable doubt was more difficult in this trial. Firstly there was no body, and secondly, the defence barristers were able to argue that the case for the prosecution relied almost completely on the testimony of criminals giving evidence to save their own skins. On Friday 16 May after deliberating for seven hours, the jury returned not guilty verdicts on all those accused of murder. Reggie was found guilty of conspiring to effect Mitchell's escape from *Dartmoor* and given five years, to run concurrently with his existing sentence. Pat Connolly was cleared of conspiring to help Mitchell escape. Connie Whitehead and Tom Cowley pleaded guilty to harbouring Mitchell and were each given nine months. The unfortunate Wally Garelick, who had pleaded guilty to conspiring to help Mitchell escape at the beginning of the trial, was given 18 months. A charge of murder against Albert Donoghue was dropped when he agreed to turn Queen's evidence and become a witness for the prosecution. Albert pleaded guilty to the lesser charge of harbouring Mitchell and received 18 months. Having already spent several months on remand, Albert was released shortly afterwards.

---

263   Ibid.

The Central Criminal Court

Old Bailey, London EC4M 7EH

Nearest TFL station: St Paul's underground.

Built and opened in 1907 on the site of the old *Newgate Prison* (which was demolished in 1904), the *Central Criminal Court* known as the *Old Bailey* is named after the street in which it stands. On Wednesday 8 January 1969, in Court Number One, the trial began in which Ron and Reg Kray were charged with the murders of George Cornell and Jack 'The Hat' McVitie. Following the trial, which lasted for 39 days, the twins were found guilty and sentenced to life imprisonment with a minimum of 30 years. Several of the twins' associates were also given harsh sentences ranging from eight years to life imprisonment. Charlie Kray was found guilty of being an accessory to murder and sentenced to ten years. Six weeks later, Ron, Reg, Charlie Kray, and Freddie Foreman appeared in Court Number Two charged with the murder of Frank Mitchell. On Friday 16 May 1969, all were acquitted of murder but Reggie was given five years for conspiring to help Mitchell escape from *Dartmoor Prison*.

On the dome above the court building stands the iconic bronze statue of Lady Justice, holding a sword in her right hand and the scales of justice in her left. In 1972, a new block was added to the old building to increase the number of courts from 4 to 19. Unfortunately, the main entrance to the court and the ornately decorated lobby area under the dome are no longer open to the public – but it is, however, possible to visit the *Old*

Bailey and sit in the public galleries to watch trials taking place. The entrance to the public galleries of the older courts – including the famous, wood-panelled Court Number 1 where the first Kray trial took place – is in Newgate Street. The public galleries of the courts occupying the more modern part of the building are accessed from Warwick Passage, off Old Bailey Street. There is no charge to watch a trial, as the court is a public building, but there are some fairly stringent security measures in place. It is advisable to check the details and requirements before visiting. (Visiting the *Old Bailey*. old-bailey.com)

There has been speculation over the years that the government wanted the Krays put away and were instrumental in making sure it happened. After half a century, there is still uncertainty about the involvement of higher powers in the Krays' demise – including many unanswered questions. Certainly, the twins' association with – and possible hold over – leading members of the establishment who had things to hide was of concern. Boothby and Driberg we know about, but could there have been others? Undoubtedly, the twins held a certain amount of power and influence in the East End, but did the government think they were more powerful than they actually were? The Krays were known to be linked with the American Mafia and although the association was, in reality, tenuous, perhaps it was believed that it was, or could become, stronger? Were the twins considered a threat to the established order, intent on building a Mafia-style criminal empire with invasive tentacles penetrating all levels of traditionally structured society? Or was it simply a case of the public school-educated *powers that be* deciding they'd had enough of the two uneducated East End thugs who were clearly getting a bit too big for their boots? Could it be that Judge Melford Stevenson was a government hatchet man, drafted in whenever a particular verdict needed to be ensured? In the 2000 documentary *The Krays: The Final Word*, Ronnie's defence barrister John Platts-Mills alludes to the fact that he was.

On the subject of joining the Cornell and McVitie murders in one indictment:

"It was quite obvious they should have been tried separately. Not only did I move the court, move Melford, but I got him to stop the trial so I could take the case to the Court of Appeal. They likewise refused. Backroom talk with the Court of Appeal's judges' clerks – WITH THE GOVERNMENT BEHIND THIS, the Court of Appeal weren't going to interfere."

And on the subject of the judge's lack of impartiality:

"Oh yes, he tried to undermine our points and to underscore the points made for the prosecution, there's no doubt about that, but that's within the scope of a wayward judge anyway."[264]

Nemone Lethbridge, the barrister who had defended the twins back in 1961, hadn't seen them for eight years and was watching the trial from the public gallery:

"The thing that struck me most at the time, which was quite odd, was the class aspect. I found something deeply unpleasant about it. It was much more than just a murder trial; it was as though the upper classes had rounded on these two upstarts and thought they'd teach them a jolly good lesson – which they did."[265]

There is some speculation that, had the twins not been ar-

---

264 Reggie Kray: *The Final Word*. Blue Post Production, Mission Television, Murder My Darlings, Warner Vision International, 2001.

265 Ibid.

rested and jailed when they were, they themselves could have been murdered. Serious violence inflicted on so many over the years left the twins with no shortage of enemies, and who knows how many were contemplating revenge? Buller Ward, slashed by Reggie in *The Regency Club*, certainly was. After a failed attempt to shoot the twins from the railway viaduct at Vallance Road, Buller Ward was biding his time and waiting for an opportunity to fulfil his vow to kill them both.[266]

After distancing himself from the Krays and teaming-up with other criminals, former associate Micky Fawcett foresaw conflict and planned to strike first, killing Reggie.[267]

One evening in early 1968, Micky had received a phone call telling him that Reggie was leaving *The Regency Club* with a girl. She lived in a block of flats in Stratford called *Albert Bigg Point*. Micky was driven by a fellow conspirator to the flats and then waited for Reggie to arrive. The plan was to shoot Reggie, cut his throat, and leave him outside the lift. Fortunately for all concerned, Reggie never showed up, but the plan to kill remained in place. Even members of The Firm were toying with the idea of killing the twins whom they referred to, behind their backs, as *Gert and Daisy*. Towards the end of their reign, the twins had lost the respect of Firm members and the organisation was held together by fear – fear that the increasingly unstable twins could turn on any member of their own team at any time, and fear of the consequences if any one of them were to walk away. Leaving The Firm was not a realistic option, but killing the twins – although the final decision was never made – certainly was.

Perhaps the most serious threat to the twins' lives was a

---

266   Ward, Henry and Weeks, David. *Bullets, Blood, and Broken Bodies.* London: New Breed Publishing, 2008.

267   Fawcett, Micky. *Krayzy Days.* Brighton: Pen Press, 2013.

plan to kill them revealed by Freddie Foreman in the 2015 documentary *The Krays: Kill Order.* Freddie Foreman and other leading members of the London underworld were concerned that the Krays had become dangerously unbalanced and that their reckless and wanton violence would bring trouble for them all. During a meeting of the senior directors of London crime at *Simpson's* restaurant in the Strand,[268] it was decided that the twins must be '*ironed out.*' According to Freddie, the twins were to be shot, and if they hadn't been arrested when they were, that's what would have happened.[269]

Albert Bigg Point

1 Abbey Lane, Stratford, London E15 2SF

Nearest TFL station: Stratford underground/ overground.

Albert Bigg Point is a 21-storey apartment building built and opened in early 1968. Shortly before the twins' arrest in May of that year, former Kray associate Micky Fawcett and an accomplice lay in wait for Reggie Kray with the intention of shooting and killing him. Reggie, they had been informed, was on his way to the flats af-

---

268 Originally opening as a club in the early 1820s and becoming a restaurant in 1848, *Simpson's* – next to *The Savoy* hotel – was, until recently, one of London's most iconic restaurants, renowned for roast beef and traditional fare. Tragically, *Simpson's* never reopened after lockdown and it looks as though it may never do so again; in July 2023, the furniture and silverware were sold at auction.

269 *The Krays: Kill Order,* Revelation Films, 2015.

ter a night out with a girl who lived there. Reggie failed to show up that night and, in so doing, literally dodged a bullet.

Lennie 'Books' Dunn, the man whose flat was used to harbour Frank Mitchell, left his Barking Road flat shortly after Frank was murdered and moved into an apartment on the 17th floor of *Albert Bigg Point*. Lennie was worried that, as a witness to the murder, he would be killed by the twins. His concerns were not unjustified; there was indeed talk of getting him drunk enough to *accidentally fall* from his balcony.

Perhaps the giant multi-storey, 1960s-built concrete edifice in Stratford is not the most interesting of destinations associated with the Kray story, but it is situated close to the former Olympic stadium – which, for those who haven't seen it before, is certainly worthy of a *butchers*.

Following the trial, Reggie was sent to *HMP Parkhurst* on the Isle of Wight, Ronnie was sent to *HMP Durham*, and Charlie was sent to *HMP Chelmsford*. Violet, the twins' mother, could see that Ronnie, separated from his twin, was suffering, and began a campaign for Ronnie to be moved to *Parkhurst*. The broken-hearted mum wrote to the Home Office, her MP, the press, and anyone she thought might be able to help. Ronnie was eventually moved to *Parkhurst* in 1971. By 1979, however, Ronnie's mental health had deteriorated significantly and he was sent to *Broadmoor Hospital*, where he would remain for the rest of his life. In January 1981, Reg was moved to *HMP Long Lartin* in Worcestershire and, in the spring of 1982, he was transferred back to *Parkhurst*.

Violet died of cancer on 4 August 1982, aged 72, and the twins – handcuffed to the tallest prison officers that could be found – were allowed to attend the funeral at *All Saints Church*, Chingford, though they were not allowed to attend the grave-side service. The twins' father Charles died on 8 March 1983. Ron and Reg did not request to attend his funeral.

Reggie remained in *Parkhurst* until January 1987, when he was transferred to *HMP Gartree* in Leicestershire. In 1989 Reg was moved to *HMP Lewes* and then back to *Gartree* the following year. In February 1992, Reg was sent to *HMP Blundeston*, where he remained until March 1994 when he was sent to *HMP Maidstone*. Throughout his sentence, Reggie was occasionally – at very short notice – sent (ghosted) to other prisons including *Nottingham*, *Leicester*, and *Wandsworth* for shorter periods.

While in *Broadmoor*, Ronnie married and was divorced twice – first to Elaine Mildener from February 1985 until June 1989. After the novelty of visits to *Broadmoor* and running errands for Britain's most high-profile criminal had worn off, Elaine suggested divorce and Ronnie offered no objections. Then, in November 1989, Ronnie married former kissogram girl Kate Howard. Following the publication of Kate's book, *Murder, Madness and Marriage*, Ronnie alleged adultery and breach of confidence and the couple divorced in May 1994. Kate went on to become a bestselling true crime author and, in 2001, she presented the hit TV series *Hard Bastards,* which profiled several of Britain's most notorious fighting men.

Ronnie died of a heart attack, aged 61, on 17 March 1995, and Reggie – obviously devastated – threw himself into organising the most magnificent funeral the East End had ever seen. On 29 March, Reg was driven in a police car from *Maidstone Prison* to attend the funeral. He was handcuffed to a prison officer for the journey and would remain so throughout the day. The funeral cortège left *W. English & Son* funeral directors and made its way through the streets of Bethnal Green, thronged with thousands of spectators, to *St Matthew's Church*. Ronnie's coffin was carried in a glass-sided hearse drawn by six plumed black horses. After the service at *St Matthew's*, the horse-drawn hearse and a procession of 25 limousines travelled the eight-mile journey through East London to *Chingford Mount Cemetery*, where Ronnie was buried in the family plot alongside his parents and Reggie's wife, Frances.

W. English & Son, Funeral Directors

464a Bethnal Green Road, London E2 OEA

Nearest TFL station: Bethnal Green underground.

Established in 1880, *W. English & Son* have been conducting funerals for over 140 years and have occupied the premises on Bethnal Green Road since the 1930s. Labelled the *undertakers to the underworld*, *W. English & Son* arranged the funerals of all three Kray brothers: Ronnie in March 1995, Charlie in April 2000, and Reggie in October 2000.

Situated just a short walk from Bethnal Green underground station, *W. English & Son* is in the heart of Kray territory, opposite *Pundersons Gardens* and very close to *The Shakespeare* (a pub visited occasionally by the Krays in the 1960s) and the old *Bethnal Green Police Station*.

Reggie met English graduate and businesswoman Roberta Jones, 26 years his junior, in early 1996 and they married the following year in *Maidstone Prison*. Reggie was moved to *HMP Wayland* in Norfolk in August 1997. Roberta gave up her former life, moved to Norfolk, and dedicated herself completely to campaigning for her husband's release.

Charlie Kray was released from *Chelmsford Prison* in 1975 after serving seven years of a ten-year sentence for his part in helping to dispose of Jack McVitie's body. Charlie remained free until 31 July 1997 when he was arrested, convicted, and sentenced to 12 years for conspiracy to smuggle £39 million worth of cocaine into the country. Charlie had lost his son Gary, aged 44, to cancer two years previously. Many people believe that Charlie Kray was targeted and fitted-up on false charges.

Charlie died aged 72 from a heart condition in *Parkhurst Prison* on 4 April 2000. Reggie, once again, arranged a spectacular send-off for his elder brother and, on 18 April, thousands of spectators lined the streets of Bethnal Green. Reggie, who was very ill at this time and looking frail, attended the funeral hand-cuffed to a female prison officer. The service was once again held at *St Matthew's Church* and Charlie was buried in the family plot at *Chingford Mount Cemetery*.

St Matthew's Church

St Matthew's Row, Bethnal Green, London E2 6DT

Nearest TFL station: Bethnal Green overground.

Built and dedicated in 1746, *St Matthew's* served the local community until 1940, when it was bombed and reduced to a roofless shell during the London Blitz. The church was rebuilt between 1958 and 1961 and reopened with a redesigned modern post-war interior.

Funeral services were held at *St Matthew's* for all three Kray Brothers: Ronnie in 1995, and Charlie and Reggie in 2000.

St Matthew's is situated close to the site of the twins' former Vallance Road home and within a short walk-

> ing distance of several other places of interest – including *Wood Close School*, *Repton Boxing Club*, and *The Carpenters Arms*.

During the early years of his sentence, Reggie, understandably, found it difficult to come to terms with the prospect of spending at least 30 years buried alive in something akin to a concrete box. In 1982, he lost hope and, suffering from depression, attempted to take his own life by cutting his wrists. Somehow, Reggie managed to find the strength he needed – and enough positives – to carry on and survive his otherwise hopeless existence. Reggie became a born-again Christian and filled his time by writing books and involving himself in various money-making business ventures. He formed close relationships with several young prisoners and kept himself physically fit and strong by adhering to a strict daily exercise routine.

Around 1998, Reggie began complaining of stomach pains. He was told by the prison doctors that it was nothing serious and to take Milk of Magnesia. After collapsing in his cell at *Wayland Prison* in August 2000, Reggie was rushed to the *Norfolk and Norwich Hospital*[270] where a large tumour was removed from his bowel. Reggie was terminally ill and, after 31 years of incarceration, on 25 August 2000, the Home Secretary, Jack Straw, sanctioned his release on compassionate grounds. Reggie left hospital a month later on 22 September 2000 and – with a life expectancy of just a few weeks at best – he moved into the honeymoon suite of *The Town House Hotel* in Norwich. Friends came to visit for what would probably be

---

270   The hospital – on St Stephen's Road, Norwich – closed in 2003 and its services were transferred to the new Norfolk and Norwich University Hospital.

the last time, and members of the press and media hung around in the hotel bar. Surrounded by friends Wilf Pine, Johnny Nash, Joey Pyle, and Freddie Foreman – and with his wife Roberta and close friend from prison, Bradley Allardyce, at his bedside – Reggie, aged 66, died on Sunday 1 October 2000.

The Town House Hotel

18-22 Yarmouth Road, Thorpe St Andrew, Norwich NR70EF

In September 2000, Reggie Kray, terminally ill with cancer, left the hospital in Norwich and moved into the honeymoon suite at the hotel. Reggie had been granted his freedom in August but was too ill to leave his bed. He could, at least, enjoy the view of the River Yare and *Whitlingham Country Park* from his window. Less than two weeks after moving into the hotel, surrounded by friends and with his wife Roberta at his bedside, Reggie passed away on 1 October 2000.

Three days before leaving the *Norfolk and Norwich Hospital* and moving into *The Town House Hotel*, Reggie gave a final interview from his bed, which was filmed for the TV documentary *Reggie Kray: The Final Word*. The documentary was first screened on BBC1 on Thursday 29 March 2001 and is currently available to watch on YouTube or can be purchased on DVD.

Reggie's widow Roberta took charge of the funeral arrangements and, in keeping with family traditions, on the morning of Tuesday 10 October 2000, the funeral cortège left *W. English &Son* – the funeral directors on Bethnal Green Road

– and made its way to *St Matthew's Church* for the service. In contrast with Violet's, Ronnie's, and Charlie's funerals, where tens of thousands of spectators lined the streets, Reggie's was a comparatively modest affair, with less than 3,000 turning out to watch. Reggie was, of course, the last to die and therefore there were no living members of the Kray family to look at. Reggie's coffin made the mile or so journey from the undertakers to the church in a Victorian-style glass-sided hearse bedecked with floral wreathes spelling out the words *FREE AT LAST* and *RESPECT,* pulled by six plumed black horses. Roberta wanted the funeral to reflect and celebrate her husband's latter years as a changed man – rather than his criminal past.

Old friends expecting to carry Reggie's coffin were not asked; instead, Roberta chose friends of the reformed Reggie as pallbearers, including East 17 singer Tony Mortimer and former prison friend Bradley Allardyce. Apart from Frankie Fraser, who put in an appearance, many of the old faces were conspicuous by their absence. After the service, with the tones of Frank Sinatra's *My Way* playing through the church speakers, Reggie's coffin was placed in a limousine. Following Ronnie's funeral service at *St Matthew's* five years earlier, the horse-drawn hearse had made the full eight-mile journey to *Chingford Mount Cemetery* and, on arrival, the poor animals had been completely exhausted. This time, in order to spare the horses, the coffin was taken to the cemetery by car. Reggie was buried in the family plot alongside his wife, his parents, his nephew, and his two brothers.

Chingford Mount Cemetery

121 Old Church Road, Chingford, London E4 6ST

Nearest TFL station: Walthamstow Central underground. From Walthamstow bus station, take the 215 or 97 bus to Chingford Old Church (Stop X).

Opened in May 1884 on land previously owned by Caroline Mount, *Chingford Mount Cemetery* is the final resting place of three generations of the Kray family. First to be buried in the family plot was Reggie's wife Frances in 1967. In 1982, the twins' mother Violet was laid to rest, followed by their father Charles in 1983, Ronnie in 1995, Charlie's son Gary in 1996, Charlie in

April 2000, and finally Reggie in October 2000.

Enter the cemetery by the smaller left-hand entrance, opposite *All Saints Church*, and follow the path straight ahead. After a brisk five-minute walk, Memorial Way meets Remembrance Walk at plots B8 and B9, forming what has come to be known as *Kray Corner*, the site of the graves of the Kray family.

Two major feature films have been made about the life and times of the Kray twins. Neither could be described as an accurate account of their lives (there are plenty of documentaries that do that), but both are hugely entertaining and ensure that the story of the Kray twins will continue to live on in the minds of the British public for a long time to come.

In the late 1980s, Roger Daltrey – The Who's front-man – acquired the film rights to John Pearson's book, *The Profession of Violence,* and then, in 1989, sold them on to Jim Beach, the manager of the band Queen. Ron and Reg decided that Roger Daltrey owed them some money but none was forthcoming, and Roger Daltrey, for a while, was the focus of some Kray displeasure.

As convicted criminals are not allowed to profit from their crimes, the film company Parkfield Films paid Charlie Kray £250,000 and the money was split three ways. The twins' share was paid to a lawyer who *in theory* was to hold on to the money until such a time that they could legally collect. During the film's production, Charlie was paid £500 a day to act as technical adviser and took a lump-sum payment of £10,000 to forgo any share of future profits from the film.

The Krays – directed by Peter Medak and starring Gary and Martin Kemp as the twins, Billie Whitelaw as Violet, Tom Bell as Jack McVitie, Steven Berkoff as George Cornell, and Kate Hardie as Frances – opened in April 1990 and was a great success in terms of both critical acclaim and box office revenue.

Ron and Reg were not happy. Firstly because they hated the film, particularly the portrayal of their mother and her use of bad language – something that Violet never did – and secondly because of Charlie's decision to accept a payment of £10,000 without consulting them and, in so doing, throwing away their rights to a share of the profits. *The Krays* went on to gross millions in the UK and the USA but the twins never saw another penny.

September 2015 – 15 years after Reggie Kray's death – saw the release of the second major Krays movie, *Legend,* once again based on John Pearson's book, *The Profession of Violence.*[271] Written and directed by Brian Helgeland, *Legend* achieved great success and introduced the Krays' story to a new generation of film fans. Presented from the perspective of Reggie's wife Frances, played by Emily Browning, *Legend* stars Tom Hardy who gives a remarkable performance playing both twins. According to Kray family friend Maureen Flanagan, who knew the twins better than anyone left alive, Tom Hardy's Ronnie is excellent but his Reggie is nothing short of amazing.

To end this tour of the Kray twins' world, there are two more places in London's East End that may be of interest to Kray enthusiasts and film fans alike. Both are pubs, open and trading, and both have been used as locations in the Kray films.

---

271   John Pearson sadly passed away in 2021, aged 91.

The Royal Oak

73 Columbia Road, London E2 7RG

Nearest TFL station: Hoxton overground.

Built in 1923 for *Truman's Brewery* on the site of an earlier pub and situated on the northwest fringes of Bethnal Green, *The Royal Oak* has long had a close association with *Columbia Road Flower Market*, opening at 9am on Sundays to cater for market traders and customers.

The Royal Oak was used in the 1990 film *The Krays* as the location where Ron and Reg fictitiously shot-up and trashed the Maltese gang's pub. *Legend* includes scenes shot in some genuine Kray locations including *Cedra Court* and *Pellicci*'s cafe, but the shooting of George Cornell in *The Blind Beggar* was filmed in *The Royal Oak*.

The Royal Oak was also used as a location in Guy Ritchie's 1998 film, *Lock, Stock and Two Smoking Barrels,* and from 1993 to 1999, *The Royal Oak* was Nicholas Lyndhurst's local pub and time portal in the BBC TV sitcom *Goodnight Sweetheart.*

Although not known to be a *Krays pub*, the fact that it stands in the heart of their manor, and on the edge of their home turf of Bethnal Green, means there is a strong possibility that the twins could have crossed the pub's threshold a time or two.

Turner's Old Star

14 Watts Street, London E1W2QG

Nearest TFL station: Wapping overground.

Turner's Old Star is one of a declining number of traditional local pubs left in the East End of London, and it has an interesting history. In 1833, JMW Turner – one of Britain's greatest-ever artists – inherited two cottages in Wapping, converted them into a tavern, which he named *The Old Star,* and installed his mistress, the widowed Mrs Booth, as proprietor. In 1987, the property was extensively refurbished and renamed *Turner's Old Star.*

The interior and exterior of the pub was used as the location for the fight scene in *Legend* in which Ronnie and Reggie, both played by Tom Hardy, take on and vanquish a gang of men supposedly sent by Charlie Richardson to 'knock the granny' out of them.

In reality, this never happened, but the scene was likely inspired by an incident that took place around 1950 in *The Coach and Horses* pub at Mile End, where the twins used vaguely similar tactics to defeat a nine-strong gang.

Did the Kray twins ever visit the pub for real? There is no record of them doing so and it is perhaps unlikely, but Wapping is part of the East End and only just over two miles from Bethnal Green… so you never know.

SELECTED BIBLIOGRAPHY

All the books consulted are referenced in the footnotes of this book. Listed below are those that the author believes are of particular importance and are recommended for further reading.

Bennett, John. *Krayology*. London: Mango Books, 2016.

Dickson, John. *Murder Without Conviction*. London: Sidgwick and Jackson, 1986.

Donoghue, Albert and Short, Martin. *The Krays' Lieutenant*. London: Smith Gryphon, 1995.

Fawcett, Mickey. *Krayzy Days*. Brighton: Pen Press, 2013.

Flanagan, Maureen with Hyams, Jacky. *One of the Family: 40 Years with the Krays*. London: Century, 2015.

Foreman, Freddie. *Respect*. London: Arrow Books, 1997.

Fry, Colin and Kray, Charlie. *Doing The Business*. London: John Blake, 1993.

Hyams, Jacky. *Frances: The Tragic Bride*. London: John Blake, 2014.

Kray, Charlie with McGibbon, Robin. *Me And My Brothers*. London: Grafton, 1988.

Kray, Reggie. *A Way of Life*. London: Sidgwick and Jackson, 2000.

Kray, Reggie. *Born Fighter*. London: Century, 1990.

Kray, Reg. *Villains We Have Known*. London: Arrow Books, 1996.

Kray, Reg and Ron with Dinenage, Fred. *Our Story*. London: Sidgwick and Jackson, 1988.

Kray, Reg and Gerrard, Peter. *Reggie Kray's East End Stories*. London: Sphere, 2010.

Lambrianou, Chris and McGibbon, Robin. *Escape From The Kray Madness*. London: Sidgwick and Jackson, 1995.

Lambrianou, Tony with Clerk, Carol. *Inside the Firm*. London: Smith Gryphon, 1991.

Lee, Joe, Smith, Rita and Gerrard, Peter. *Inside the Kray Family*. London: Carlton Books, 2008.

Lucas, Norman. *Britain's Gangland*. London: Pan Books, 1969.

McConnell, Brian. *The Rise and Fall of the Brothers Kray*. London: David Bruce and Watson Ltd, 1969.

Morton, James. *Krays: The Final Word*. London: Mirror Books, 2019.

O'Leary, Laurie. *Ronnie Kray: A Man Among Men*. London: Headline, 2001.

Payne, Leslie. *The Brotherhood*. London: Michael Joseph, 1973.

Pearson, John. *Notorious*. London: Century, 2010.

Pearson, John. *The Cult Of Violence*. London: Orion Books, 2001.

Pearson, John. *The Profession of Violence*. London: Weidenfeld and Nicolson, 1972.

Read, Leonard with Morton, James. *Nipper Read: The Man who Nicked the Krays*. London: MacDonald & Co, 1991.

Teale, Bobby with Campbell, Clare. *Bringing Down The Krays*. London: Ebury Publishing, 2012.

Teale, David. *Surviving the Krays*. London: Ebury Press, 2021.

Webb, Billy. *Running with the Krays*. Edinburgh: Mainstream Publishing, 1993.

Printed in Dunstable, United Kingdom

67858785R10278